Love as Law—Obedience and Identity Formation

Love as Law—Obedience and Identity Formation

A Comparative Study of Romans 13:8–14 and Matthew 22:34–40

ENDALE SEBSEBE MEKONNEN

PICKWICK *Publications* • Eugene, Oregon

LOVE AS LAW—OBEDIENCE AND IDENTITY FORMATION
A Comparative Study of Romans 13:8–14 and Matthew 22:34–40

Pickwick Publications
An Imprint of Wipf and Stock Publishers
199 W. 8th Ave., Suite 3
Eugene, OR 97401

www.wipfandstock.com

PAPERBACK ISBN: 979-8-3852-5900-7
HARDCOVER ISBN: 979-8-3852-5901-4
EBOOK ISBN: 979-8-3852-5902-1

Cataloguing-in-Publication data:

Names: Mekonnen, Endale Sebsebe, author.

Title: Love as law—obedience as identity formation : a comparative study of Romans 13:8–14 and Matthew 22:34–40 / Endale Sebsebe Mekonnen.

Description: Eugene, OR: Pickwick Publications, 2026. | Includes bibliographical references.

Identifiers: ISBN 979-8-3852-5900-7 (paperback). | ISBN 979-8-3852-5901-4 (hardcover). | ISBN 979-8-3852-5902-1 (ebook).

Subjects: LCSH: Bible. NT—Criticism, interpretation, etc. | Bible. Romans XIII:8–14—Criticism, interpretation, etc. | Bible. Matthew XXII:34–40—Criticism, interpretation, etc. | Love—Biblical teaching. | Law (Theology)—Biblical teaching.

Classification: BS2417 M45 2026 (print). | BS2417 (ebook).

VERSION NUMBER 03/02/26

Scripture quotations in both Greek and English are taken from Nestle-Aland, *The Greek-English New Testament*, 8th rev. ed. Stuttgart : Deutsche Bibelgesellschaft, 1994.

Contents

List of Tables

List of Tables

Acknowledgments

I OWE MY DEEPEST gratitude to my supervisors Prof. Jeremy Punt and Prof. Marius Nel. Without their continued optimism concerning this work, insightful comments, gentle critique, encouragement, guidance, and support this study would hardly have been completed. I would also like to thank both my supervisors for providing me ample room to express my own voice. Therefore, for all the shortcomings in this study, I take full responsibility.

I owe a great debt of gratitude to Shiloh Bible College Ethiopia and Fire Over Africa for granting me study leave and covering all my tuition, transportation, living expenses and one-year accommodation. I would like to thank Dr. Gary Munson, the president of Shiloh Bible College Ethiopia, who supported me in his prayers throughout the years of my study, for his encouragement and advice and for raising the funds for my studies.

I am also deeply grateful to George Whitefield College and Evangelical Research Fellowship in South Africa for granting me a bursary for accommodation, auspicious study facilities, and a convenient environment where I could combine both rigorous academic work and a Christian walk.

I am indebted to many of my colleagues who prayed, encouraged me, and extended their warm fellowship to dispel my loneliness created by the many days of isolation from my family.

Lastly, not least, my special gratitude goes to Meskerm Asefa, my wife, for lifting all family burdens from me and carrying all the responsibility of caring for our children, and for being patient with me while I was away, and for prayer and encouragement without ceasing in all the different seasons of my studies. I would also like to express my deepest appreciation to my children, Abiah, Amanuel, Elsa, Samuel, and Selam for their prayers and understanding.

List of Abbreviations

BCE	Before Common Era
CBQ	*Catholic Biblical Quarterly*
CD	Cairo Damascus Document
CE	Common Era
JSNT	*Journal for the Study of the New Testament*
JSNTSup	Journal for the Study of the New Testament Supplement Series
KJV	King James Version
LN	Louw and Nida, *Greek–English Lexicon of the New Testament: Based on Semantic Domains* (in Bibleworks)
LXX	Septuagint (Ancient Greek Translation of the Old Testament)
MT	Masoretic Text
NAB	New American Bible
NAS	New American Standard
NIV	New International Version
NovT	*Novum Testamentum*
NovTSup	Novum Testament Supplements
NPP	New Perspective on Paul
NTL	New Testament Library
NT	New Testament
NTS	*New Testament Studies*

OT	Old Testament
RNPP	Radical New Perspective on Paul
RSV	Revised Standard Version
SBLDS	Society of Biblical Literature Dissertation Series
SM	The Sermon on the Mount
SNTSMS	Society for New Testament Studies Monograph Series
TGL	Thayer's Greek Lexcon
WUNT	Wissenschaftliche Untersuchungen zum Neuen Testament
YLT	Robert Young, *Young's Literal Translation of the Holy Bible* (1889)

1

Introduction

BACKGROUND

For centuries, the role of the Law in the New Testament has been negatively perceived or devalued, and sometimes even dismissed. A number of reasons can be given for such unwarranted perceptions; however, only three are relevant here: (1) an *a priori* theologically-fueled interpretive lens; (2) a taxonomist interpretive model, and (3) a corollary of the two previous interpretations.

Since the time of Augustine the assumption of the distinction between grace and the Law has erected a strong fence between these two inextricably intertwined theological concepts.[1] Particularly during the Reformation, the gap between grace and the Law continually increased until it extenuated the role of the Law from its important place in the New Testament. Suffice it to mention Tomson's summary of this particular assumption on Pauline studies: "(1) the centre of his [Paul's] thought is a polemic against the Law; (2) the Law for him no longer had a practical meaning; and (3) ancient Jewish literature is no source for explaining his letters."[2]

1. Zetterholm, *Approaches to Paul*, 58.
2. Tomson, *Paul and the Jewish Law*, 1.

Of particular significance is Weber's conclusion regarding Judaism as a legalistic religion as opposed to Law free Christianity, which became a paradigm for the next generation of scholars for interpreting the New Testament, not least the relationship of grace and the Law.[3]Despite the protest of C. C Montefiore, George Foot Moore and Krister Stendahl, against the negative perception of Judaism, Bousset, Bultman, Käsemann, and Bornkamm, among others, ossified the perception of Judaism as a legalistic religion.[4] Consequently, their studies established a negative interpretive lens as to the role of the Law in the New Testament because the Law is the hallmark of Judaism as legalistic religion. Using the Weber–Bousset–Billerbeck scheme as its bulwark, the *a priori* theological position (which Tomson denounces) has not only created a negative view of the Law but has also precluded perceiving the role of the Law beyond theological concern. For example, Ladd and Hagner insist that the Law must be understood in theological terms.[5] Likewise, Hans Conzelmann argues, "the doctrine of the Law must be understood in specifically theological terms . . . the whole doctrine of the Law is simply a theological interpretation."[6] By this, he means that the role of the Law is just a disclosure of where human beings stand in relation to God. Hence, its role is to function as a disclosure of sin, and an instrument of condemnation, wrath and death.

It cannot be objected that the Law plays such roles; however, it is only one part of the story. The theological reading, while it lays a heavy emphasis on scrutinizing the vertical role of the Law with respect to God–human relationship, downplays its horizontal role in person–to–person relationships. However, the God–human relationship cannot be seen separately from the person–to–person relationship. In fact, the role of the Law, as regulating conduct, addresses the relationship of a person–to–person relationship within its theological interpretive lens. The fact of the matter is that the theological interpretive lens sees the role of the Law from an ethical perspective, how contemporary Christians ought to act towards a fellow person. It does not question as to whether the Law had a role in constructing the first–century Jesus followers'[7] ethos and

3. Sanders, *Paul and Palestinian Judaism*, 2.

4. Sanders, *Paul and Palestinian Judaism*, 3–6; Zetterholm, *Approaches to Paul*, 69–94.

5. Ladd and Hagner, *A Theology of the New Testament*, 539.

6. Conzelmann, *An Outline of the Theology of the New Testament*, 221, 228.

7. The term "Jesus-followers" is preferred over the term "Christians" in this

identity against the 'other' within their contemporary social world. In so doing, a *priori* theologically infused interpretation not only impairs one's understanding of the role of the Law in its fuller sense but also severs the text from its contemporary context. It is worth noting Dunn's caveat: there is "the danger of setting 'social' and 'theological' interpretations in antithesis, a danger to which several succumb."[8]

The second perception is based on a taxonomist interpretive model. While the first interpretive assumption is based on an *a priori* theological position, influenced primarily by the interpretation of Pauline letters, the second interpretive model, a taxonomist model is influenced mainly by the interpretation of the synoptic Gospels. A taxonomist interpretive model has to do with the categorization of the synoptic Gospels into different smaller local communities as a point of departure for studying each Gospel. The inception of this model was within the redaction critical method. Redaction critics assume that the text is a direct impression of the social context and interpreters "can engage in one-to-one mapping between a body of textual details and a community profile, and that the situation of the intended readers can be read off directly from the nature of the text itself."[9] Judith M. Lieu has, however, argued that such an assumption rests on a shaky foundation.[10] Others have also pointed out that "not all redaction critics were especially concerned with the evangelists' community."[11]

The problem with the taxonomist model is not its insistence on the existence of a specific community for which each Gospel is written. Rather, what is problematic is that the taxonomist model works with the redaction criticism method, focusing on the author's theology or understanding of the Law based on an isolated text at the expense of the wider context of the text and its role in the life of first-century Jesus followers in their social as well as religious context. For whatever reason the author understands and defines the Law, in such studies the role of the Law receives hardly any attention in regard to its definition, nature and

---

dissertation since the term "Christian" is an anachronist concept in regard to the NT; for the sake of consistency, the term is used throughout the dissertation and thus also in my discussion of the Pauline letters (Romans and others) even though it is not the common term used for the communities of Paul.

8. Dunn, *The New Perspective*, 29.

9. Donaldson, "The Law That Hangs (Matthew 22:40)," 11.

10. Lieu, *Christian Identity*, 13.

11. Bauckham, *Gospels for All Christians*, 17.

theology. Barth, Banks, and Loader are the quintessential instances of such works on the topic of the Law in the Synoptic Gospels.[12] Secondly, since the taxonomist model assumes virtually a homogeneous community, it downplays the place of the minority group in the community and emphasizes the positions of the majority.

In the case of Matthew, it is a scholarly consensus, with minor differences, that Matthew is written for a largely Jewish-Christian community;[13] which was therefore, a Law-observant community. As a result of this, the place of the Law is defined in terms of dominant members of the community. The opposite assumption functions in a similar manner: if the majority of the members are Gentiles, then it is a Law-free community. Nonetheless, such reconstructed communities are hypothetical, "many of which piled guess upon guess about specific matters for which no data remain."[14] It is argued that Gentiles are the minority in the Gospel of Matthew whereas in Romans the makeup of the community is debated ("mostly Jewish-Christian, mostly Gentile-Christian, or a balance of the two."[15] Despite uncertainty regarding the dominant members in Romans, the scholarly consensus goes that the Law has an important role in the Matthean community while it has a diminished role in the letter to the Romans.

The third reason is the corollary of the above two assumptions—the importation of words such as 'ethics' and 'paraenesis' to describe the conduct praxis of the Law under either of these two terms. Philip F. Esler, in his study of Rom 12–15, has shown the source of these terms and the problems they pose.[16] Esler argues that the word 'ethics' is problematic because "in the modern world 'ethics' largely refers to the systematic formulation of rules for good conduct by individuals."[17] Since ethics is philosophically approached, such terminology does not help to deal with biblical texts mainly because the New Testament is neither a systematic reflection of the good nor a detailed description of conduct.[18]

12. Barth, *The Epistle to the Romans*, 63; Banks, *Jesus and the Law*; Loader, *Jesus' Attitude Towards the Law*.

13. Harrington, *The Gospel of Matthew*, 20.

14. Keener, *The Gospel of Matthew*, 45.

15. Witherington and Hyatt, *Paul's Letter to the Romans*, 7.

16. Esler, *Conflict and Identity*, 2003.

17. Esler, *Conflict and Identity*, 52.

18. Esler, *Conflict and Identity*, 53.

Esler argues that the Greek word 'paraenesis' does not appear in the New Testament.[19] He finds that 'paraenesis' is used only once in the Septuagint in Wisdom 8:9. According to Esler, Martin Dibelius introduced its usage to the New Testament studies. 'Paraenesis' refers to "texts which string together admonitions of general ethical content."[20] Dibelius applied this term to Pauline letters with an assumption that sections like Rom 12–15 are not directly relevant to Paul's theology. Other terms used by scholars instead of paraenesis are 'indicatives' and 'imperatives.' The use of such terminology (paraenesis, indicatives and imperatives) reveal the *a priori* theological commitment to avoid using terms related to 'the Law.' In the Pauline letters, one finds terms that best describe the demands in the so-called exhortation sections. For instance, ἐντολῶν θεοῦ (the commandments of God) (1 Cor 7:19) or πλήπωμα νόμου (fulfillment or fullness of the Law) (Rom 13:8–10) can serve the purpose of expressing the Law's practical roles. Importing or creating other terms which do not convey the intrinsic nature, the demands Paul lays upon the day–to–day life of the Jesus followers, however, is the result of the underpinning theological assumption that the Law has no role in the New Testament. Yet, the terms do not faithfully convey in either Romans, or Matthew, the role they ascribe to the Law as it is interpreted in their respective traditions.

However, recent research has demonstrated the fallacy of such assumptions—Judaism is an antithesis of the faith of Jesus' followers and grace displaces the Law. Suffice it to mention a few influential works at points germane to the present study,[21] following his predecessors (Montefiore, Moore, and Krister Stendahl), has brought a new perspective on Judaism.[22] He has successfully shown that Judaism is not a legalistic religion, though it is different from the Pauline religion. Indeed, Sanders is often criticized for setting Judaism and Paul apart. Nonetheless, he made a great contribution to the understanding of the religion of Judaism and its relationship to the New Testament. Sanders concluded that Judaism includes the principle of covenantal *nomism* (covenant plus the Law). Getting into the covenant is through grace (election which is initiated by God) whereas 'staying in' the covenant is by obedience to the Law. It might be argued that the corollary of his conclusion is that there is no

19. Esler, *Conflict and Identity*, 53.

20. Esler, *Conflict and Identity*, 53.

21. Sanders, *Paul and Palestinian Judaism*, 1977.

22. Dunn, *The New Perspective on Paul*, 5.

antithetical relationship but only functional differences between grace (election) and the Law.

Dunn, taking his point of departure from Sanders' conclusion, focuses his studies on the phrase "works of the Law" and argues that the phrase refers to Jewish national identity markers such as circumcision, Sabbath observance and food laws.[23] For Dunn, the Law continues to have multiple roles in Pauline theology that run as sub–themes: the Law serves "as a measure of sin, defines sin, makes sinners conscious of their sin, [and] provides a yardstick by which sin will be judged."[24] Dunn rejects the claim that Paul has broken with the Law and insists that it still has an important role in the New Testament.

Morna Hooker, *pace* Sanders, finds similarity between the pattern of religion of Judaism and the pattern of religion of Paul.[25] For Hooker, Paul still functions within a covenantal *nomism* scheme: first he anticipates judgment in the future, therefore deeds have implication. Secondly, although righteousness is apart from the law, Paul still maintains obedience of faith as a prerequisite for membership of the Jesus movement; and thirdly, since judgment lies in the future, their way of life must be appropriate to the people of God.[26] Hooker maintains that the Law is dethroned by the death and resurrection of the Messiah because it is inadequate to justify the sinner. Thus, what is unclear with Hooker's analysis is: what part of *nomism* is contained in Paul. For Sanders, *nomism* is the Law, but Hooker does not explicitly state which part of *nomism* is contained in the Law, as she holds that the Law is dethroned from its function yet insists that Paul has not broken with the Law. Hooker's argument that a pattern of covenantal *nomism* still exists in the Pauline scheme is an important contribution but is however not defined clearly enough.

Peter J. Tomson also acknowledges Sanders' sublime achievements on there interpretation of Judaism, but he criticized him for studying Paul apart from Judaism.[27] Tomson accentuates the practical aspect of the Law and argues, "the Law retained a practical function, as *halakah* taught by Jesus."[28] In his analysis, he observed that "for Paul 'faith' and 'commandments' are so to say on a different level and that the emphasis

23. Dunn, *The New Perspective on Paul*, 2008.
24. Dunn, *The New Perspective on Paul*, 53.
25. Hooker, *From Adam to Christ*, 1990.
26. Hooker, *From Adam to Christ*, 163.
27. Tomson, *Paul and the Jewish Law*, 16.
28. Tomson, *Paul and the Jewish Law*, 18.

on faith need not exclude the observance of commandments."[29] Tomson contends that justification by faith does not negate the existence of the practical aspect of the Law and therefore the "traditional assumptions on Paul and the Law are inadequate. The Law does have practical significance for Paul . . ."[30]

Scholars who are stoutly defending the traditional position and interpretation de-emphasize, even deny, the continuity and the role of the Law in Pauline theology. Examples of scholars who take this stance Andrew Das,[31] Simon J. Gathercole,[32] and Stephen Westerholm,[33] amongst others. However, Frank S. Thielman, who is among the defenders of the traditional position, is of the opinion that while Paul denies the validity of circumcision, food laws, and Sabbath, he does not deny the continuity of the Law.[34] However, Thielman argues it is impossible to keep the Law without the help of the Spirit and therefore only those who are in Christ and have the Spirit can fulfil it.[35]

From the discussion above, the following negative and positive conclusions can be drawn. The negative conclusion: earlier studies' assumptions, *a priori* theologically fueled interpretations, are based on the view of an antithetical relationship between grace and the Law. This assumption not only eschewed the matter but also confined the study of the role of the Law to a theological concern. Likewise, the categorist approach confines the understanding of the text to the theological interest of the authors within the dominant members of the author's audience. Consequently, the role of the Law is perceived in terms of the dominant members of the community: the majority vs. the minority of Jews or Gentiles. This perception assumes that the Law has a role insofar as there are dominant members of Jews in a given community of Jesus followers who are Jews.

The positive conclusion: current research has established: 1) that the Law and grace are not antithetical,[36] and 2) that the Law has continu-

29. Tomson, *Paul and the Jewish Law*, 66.
30. Tomson, *Paul and the Jewish Law*, 220.
31. Das, *Paul, the Law, and the Covenant*, 2001.
32. Gathercole, *Where Is Boasting*, 2002.
33. Westerholm, *Perspectives Old and New on Paul*, 2004.
34. Thielman, *From Plight to Solution*, 2008.
35. Thielman, *Paul & the Law*, 53.
36. Sanders, *Paul and Palestinian Judaism*, 1977.

ity and a practical role in the New Testament,[37] Tomson,[38] Hooker,[39] and Thielman.[40] The logical conclusion is, thus, that the role of the Law predicates on neither the majority nor the minority ethnic group within the community of Jesus followers; rather, its role is dependent on its function within the community.

THE RESEARCH QUESTION AND DELIMITATION

Granting the above conclusions that the Law is not abrogated entirely, the general question is whether the Law has any specific role in the Jesus follower's faith life. What kind of approach would better explain its role? It is difficult to undertake such broad questions particularly within the purview of the present study unless the focus is on a specific question. Since the New Testament contains diverse literatures that seem to be impossible to interpret into a singular theological position, in some cases, it is appropriate to study the texts that seem to oppose each other. In this case, the Gospel of Matthew and Paul's letter to the Romans are appropriate candidates for comparison. This is so, particularly because in Romans Paul painstakingly discusses and argues about the role of the Law in the plan of salvation, and Matthew devotes a considerable portion of his narration to it. Yet, comparing the role of the Law in both texts in their entirety would still be a broad and unattainable undertaking in a study like this one, since the material is too vast.

However, both Paul in Rom 13:8–14 and Matt in 22:34–40[41] concisely state the Law despite their different contexts and formulations. In addition to this, the compositions of their immediate readers are most probably both Jesus followers of various origins, namely: Jews who are Christians and Gentiles who are Christians.[42] For these mixed readers

37. Dunn, *The New Perspective on Paul*, 2008.

38. Tomson, *Paul and the Jewish Law*, 220.

39. Hooker, *From Adam to Christ*, 163.

40. Thielman, *Paul & the Law*, 53.

41. The reference to Rom 13:8–14 and Matt 22:34–40 without abbreviation (i.e. Romans and Matthew respectively) will be maintained throughout the work to indicate that this is the researcher's core investigation. The abbreviated forms (Romans or Matthew) will not be repeated in the discussion where the whole chapter deals with the same book, but it will be included when it appears at the beginning of a sentence, introduces a subtopic or whenever a comparison is made either in the whole chapter (e.g., Chapter 6) or in a given discussion.

42.Gundry, *Matthew*, 1994; Moo, *Romans*, 1996; Tomson, *Paul and the Jewish Law*,

of Matthew and Romans the issue of the Law was a common concern so that the summary of the Law must have had an important purpose and role: both authors' interpretation of the Law hinges on it having both theological and practical functions. The question is thus what role the summary of the Law played in the first-century Jesus followers' expression of faith.

Since the identity of the Jews and Gentiles is one of the major concerns within Matthew's Gospel and the letter to the Romans, regarding their relationship to the Law, the summary of the Law in both books must have contributed to their relationship to the Law and their identity construction. Studying these relationships has not always gathered much interest in research, especially not in as far as the use of the summaries of the Law are concerned. Hence, the fundamental question of the present research is *what is the role of the summary of the Law in the Gospel of Matt 22:34–40 and in Paul's letters to the Rom 13:8–14 in the identity construction of their respective communities of Jesus followers?* Thus, the concern of the study is to investigate the role of the summary of the Law in the identity construction of Jesus followers of various origins in Matt 22:34–40 and in Rom 13:8–14 in a Greek-infused Roman imperial world. Before this can be done, some important studies on the summary of the Law will be reviewed.

STUDIES ON THE SUMMARY OF THE LAW

This section deals with publications that have contributed to the study of the summary of the Law. First, studies on Rom 13:8–14 and then studies on Matt 22:34–40 will be reviewed. However, since the published material on these texts is numerous for varying perspectives, only those studies that specifically focus on these two pericopae will be reviewed. With the risk of oversimplification, studies that have relatively similar stances are subsumed and will be studied together.

Romans 13:8–14–The Summary of the Law

The summary of the Law in Rom 13:8–14 has been interpreted from different perspectives but can be grouped into four major positions.

1990.

Accentuating the Centrality of Love and the Continuity of the Law

Pauline scholars like Murray,[43] Cranfield,[44] Käsemann,[45] Dunn,[46] and Thielman[47] unanimously agree on the centrality of love in Rom 13:8–10 with a different emphasis depending on their theological predilections. Murray represents the view that the summary of the Law underscores the centrality of the love commandment within the Law even if it does not replace it.[48] Murray argues, "Paul does not say that law is love but that love fulfils the law, and the law has not in the least degree been depreciated or deprived of its sanction." His reasoning predicates on four features of the Decalogue: (1) it is permanent and has relevance; (2) it is correlative with love because it is an example of how love can fulfil the Law; (3) it is compatible with love; (4) its commandments are norms within which love operates.[49] Love, therefore, is an intrinsic part of the Decalogue. Regarding the summary, for Murray "sum up" could mean repeated (recapitulated), condensed or reduced.[50] Nevertheless, he concludes, "all the commandments receive their fulfilment and so they can all be reduced to this demand [the summary of the Law]."[51] Although Murray makes the commandment of love compatible within the Decalogue, he reduces the whole commandment of the Decalogue into one commandment. Yet, his major stance is that love does not wholly replace the Law, but it has primacy over the other commandments and exists within the Decalogue.

Following Murray, other scholars are also of the opinion that the summary of the Law holds love as the center within the Law. Cranfield and Sanday perceive the Gospel and the Law as one and refuse the notion of calling the summary of the Law as a "principle of love" insisting that love is the sum total of what the Law requires.[52] Therefore, all the particular commandments are intact and needed. They postulate that the role of the summary of the Law is to save the believer from handling the

43. Murray, *Romans*, 160.
44. Cranfield, *Romans*, 262.
45. Käsemann, *Romans*, 361.
46. Dunn, *Romans 9–16*.
47. Thielman, *Paul & the Law*, 53.
48. Murray, *Romans*, 160.
49. Murray, *Romans*, 160.
50. Murray, *Romans*, 160.
51. Murray, *Romans*, 160.
52. Cranfield, *Romans*, 862.

commandments legalistically.[53] Käsemann also espouses the view that the summary of the Law maintains the continuity of the Law but only "the ethical portion of the Torah."[54] He thinks that a tradition was emerging "which regards only the moral law of the Old Testament (OT) as binding in the community."[55] Thus, Paul adopted this tradition to exhort his community. Unlike Cranfield, Käsemann, while asserting the continuity of the Law in the summary of the Law, qualifies his assertion limiting the continuity of the Law only in its moral elements. For Cranfield, love is the sum total of the requirement of the Law. Whether this means all the cultic and ritual particularities of the Law, is unclear. While Cranfield tends to presume the role of the summary is to protect Jesus followers from being legalistic, Käsemann ascribes a minimal role to it despite underscoring the continuity of the Law.

Dunn also contends that all commandments are "covered by the summary of the Law."[56] For Dunn, while the summary plays the role of assuring the fact that "Paul's Gospel was not antinomian, it asserts the continuity of the Law."[57] What Paul is doing, in the summary of the Law, according to Dunn, is that he is delivering the Law from its ethnic particularity. While Dunn is in line with Murray regarding the centrality of love in the summary of the Law, he does not reduce all the commandments to a single demand. For him, rather, the summary of the Law transforms and transposes the commandments and serves as a guiding principle for moral practices.[58]Dunn's concern is to demonstrate that Paul is not against the Law. However, Dunn employs the unqualified term "covered" which is too blurred to perceive in what sense the summary of the Law included all commandments of the Law.

Thielman, quoting Rom 13:8–10 in full, contends that Paul continues to use the Mosaic Law in his ethical admonitions. "In some sense, therefore, the Mosaic law continues to function for the believers as the boundary marker between conduct that pleases God (compare Rom 8:7–8) and sin (compare Rom 3:20; 7:7). It contains God's will; the believer should fulfil it . . . and therefore it cannot simply be discarded."[59] These

53. Cranfield, *Romans*, 678–79.

54. Käsemann, *Romans*, 361.

55. Käsemann, *Romans*, 361–62.

56. Dunn, *Romans 9–16*, 782.

57. Dunn, *Romans 9–16*, 782.

58. Dunn, *Romans 9–16*, 782.

59. Thielman, *Paul & the Law*, 53.

boundary markers are defined as "the law of faith."[60] Similarly, Beker and Dunn view the summary of the Law as the law of faith, the law of the Spirit or the law of Christ.[61] Thielman must be commended for taking a step further in the discussion, because while other scholars focus on the love and the continuity of the Law, he is able to see that the Mosaic Law, in the form of the summary of the Law and as the will of God, continues to serve as a boundary marker. Thielman's brief comments insinuate that the summary of the Law has a social dimension as well as an identity construction role. Unfortunately, he does not develop the concept.

Replacing the Mosaic Law

This reading is espoused by scholars like Douglas Moo,[62]and Ben and Hyatt.[63] Douglas Moo realizes that love does not make all commandments irrelevant; therefore, to love others is not the only commandment relevant to Jesus followers. Nonetheless, he insists that Jesus followers are not under the old Mosaic Law but under the "new law" which is the law of Christ. Love is the center of this new law. Moo offers two interpretive choices about the summary of the Law: "the love command *replaces* these [Lev 19:18; Deut 6] commandments or . . . it simply *focuses* them by setting forth a demand that is integral to each one of them (italics his)."[64] He chooses the former and denies the intrinsic existence of love in the Mosaic Law; hence, love is the central character of the new law, that is, a Jesus follower who loves fulfils the requirements of the Law. The problem with the phrase "new law" is that it is undefined. What the "Law of Christ" means in terms of "new law" is thus unclear. The characteristic which makes the Law of Christ new is also not explained.

Employing the socio-rhetorical method to interpret Romans, Witherington and Hyatt postulate that an "other law" has replaced the Mosaic Law. They understand the "other law" (Rom 13:9) as the Law of Christ, insisting that the other law, the Law of Christ, "contains the sum and substance or heart of the Mosaic Law."[65] When one fulfils Christ's Law, one

60. Thielman, *Paul & the Law*, 211, 213.

61. Beker, *Paul the Apostle*; Dunn, *Romans 9–16*.

62. Moo, *Romans*, 816.

63. Ben and Hyatt, *Romans*.

64. Moo, *Romans*, 816.

65. Witherington and Hyatt, *Romans*.

has accomplished the intent or aim of the previous law. One therefore, "need not go on to keep the Mosaic Law as well," because Christ is the end of the Law.[66] Witherington and Hyatt conclude, "that 'another Law' has replaced and fulfils the heart of the old Mosaic Law."[67] Like Moo, Witherington and Hyatt are aware of the existence of other commandments and that the summary of the Law is "not a substitute for law," but love in itself is a law which goes beyond not harming the other.[68] However, love is not the Mosaic Law; it is rather the new Law. The problem with Moo, Witherington and Hyatt is that they assume the Mosaic Law functions outside of the realm of love and it is just a form of dry legalism. Thus, what makes the 'new law' new is also difficult to understand from their argument and, above all, they base their contention on dubious phrases such as 'another law'; and that Christ is the end of the Law.

Radically Reducing but Never Abrogating the Law

Scholars who hold this position are, for example, Räisänen,[69] Hübner,[70] and Watson.[71] Räisänen has argued for the thesis that Paul has an inconsistent and oscillating view of the law. However, he contends, "the law has indeed been superseded in Christ. Yet, it would be one-sided to conclude that Paul is a 'consistent antinomist' who rejects the law altogether."[72] Though Räisänen is convinced of the fact that "there remains a 'kernel' law'" which Jesus followers must obey, he rejects the opinion that the essence of the law is defined in terms of love. Instead, for Räisänen, love is defined in terms of the Law.[73] The focus in Rom 13:8–10 is the significance of love as defined by the Law,[74] and the summary of the Law is, hence, a reduced form of the Law.[75] Likewise, Francis Watson reckons the summary of the Law is a "reduced law" that is "a law without circumcision, dietary restrictions, cults, or sacred days—that remains operative

66. Witherington and Hyatt, *Romans*, 316.
67. Witherington and Hyatt, *Romans*, 316.
68. Witherington and Hyatt, *Romans*, 317.
69. Räisänen, *Paul and the Law*.
70. Hübner, *Law in Paul's Thought*, 85.
71. Watson, *Paul, Judaism, and the Gentiles*.
72. Räisänen, *Paul and the Law*, 62.
73. Räisänen, *Paul and the Law*, 63.
74. Räisänen, *Paul and the Law*, 63.
75. Räisänen, *Paul and the Law*, 27, 67–68.

within the Christian community."[76] For Räisänen, the summary of the Law has two functions—one is to define love, and the other is to reduce the Law into one commandment.

However, for Watson, a reduced law means the law without its cultic rituals and sacred observance. Watson argues that the Mosaic Law and the summary of the Law do not differ in their content but in their context.[77] In the same line, Hans Hübner maintains the summary as a reduction within the Law.[78] However, he further qualifies his position stating that in Rom 14 there is abrogation of the Law. Reduction and abrogation are complementary in that, while the abrogation deals with the cultic part of the Law, the reduction maintains the moral dimension thereof for the sake of those who think they are bound to keep the cultic law. Hübner perceives the summary not as a "*concentration* of the entire Torah but in fact its *reduction* (italics his)."[79] Concurring with the view that love is the sum of the Law, Hübner contends that love demands legal stipulations which are abrogated. Paradoxically, however, the abrogated legal stipulation must be kept in individual cases for the sake of the neighbor (love in action). Hübner's paradoxical approach does not do justice to the contexts of the summary of the Law and its significance as he limits its role in individual cases as well as in issues related to cultic laws. Hübner is probably right in connecting Rom 13:8–10 to 14. Nonetheless, his exegesis is questionable because he assumes that Paul summarized the law for the sake of those who think they are obliged to keep the cultic law but were offended by its abrogation. Paul did not say that the summary of the Law is to appease those who are offended by the abrogation of the cultic Law.

Supplementing Paraenesis with Information

Thurén, being dissatisfied with the new and old approaches to Pauline studies and attempting to merge them, contends that Rom 13:8–10 refers "not only to moral rules or the Decalogue, but to any ordinance in the law."[80] He claims that fulfilment means fulfilling its intention, purpose, or 'demand.' Therefore, for Thurén, the love command is the "greater

76. Watson, *Paul, Judaism, and the Gentiles*, 214.
77. Francis Watson, *Paul, Judaism, and the Gentiles*, 288.
78. Hübner, *Law in Paul's Thought*, 85.
79. Hübner, *Law in Paul's Thought*, 85.
80. Lauri Thurén, *Derhetorizing Paul*, 25.

principle behind, even beyond the particular commands" and that it is "a recurrent theme in the OT."[81] Paul is not reducing the law to a moral code, but he is using Jewish rhetoric whereby the "whole law" may be expressed "with a single commandment."[82]

In considering this position it must be kept in mind that the role of the summary of the Law is just to provide supplementary support to Paul's moral principles. Therefore, its use as supplementary "validates neither the whole law nor its [Decalogue] kernel," consequently, it does not possess a continuing relevance for Christians except for on certain occasions, as resource material for moral issues.[83] For Thurén, the difference between the Law and paraenesis comes from "the dichotomy of man, the distinction between flesh and spirit."[84] While the Law evokes sin, the paranaesis does not because it addresses people driven by the Spirit. While Thurén argues against the view that the summary reduces the Law, he reduces its role by relegating it to the role of a moral guide and to a useful treasure chest of information.

Conclusion

It is noticeable in the previous section that each scholar has made important contributions to explain the issue entailed in understanding Paul's intension in summarizing the Law. As the studies have shown, two conclusions have been reached so far: one, Rom 13:8–10 summarizes the law, and two, it has a significant role with respect to the relationship of Jesus followers with the whole Law. However, no consensus exists among scholars as to its role, i.e. whether it replaces the Law, articulates the central intension of the Law, or reduces the Law to moral principles. Although the theological and the practical are inseparably intertwined, the above studies place a heavy theological emphasis on Rom 13:8–10 whereas the text is formulated to address the day-to-day relationship and activities of the community. Apparently, the influence of the debate over grace versus Law has precluded studies from seeing the role of the summary of the Law within its social, political and religious context. It is evident that the summary of the Law's role as identity constructor is totally unexplored.

81. Thurén, *Derhetorizing Paul*, 75.

82. Thurén, *Derhetorizing Paul*, 108.

83. Thurén, *Derhetorizing Paul*, 133–34.

84. Thurén, *Derhetorizing Paul*, 137.

Matthew 22:34–40–The Summary of the Law

The interpretations of Matt 22:34–40 can be grouped together in one major position.

The Essence and Interpretive Principle of the Law

There is a consensus among Matthean scholars that the summary of the Law is the essence of the Law. Gunther Bornkamm serves as a prime example of scholars who claimed that the summary of the Law is the essence of the Law.[85] However, his student, Gerhard Barth, employing a redaction-criticism analysis, offered five conclusions about it:

(1) It is the essence of the Law;

(2) it validates and confirms the continuity of the Law;

(3) it serves as an interpretive principle to understand the Law;

(4) it keeps the whole Law; and

(5) there is a possibility of deducing the whole Law from it.[86]

The summary as the essence of the Law is the foundational concept from which the other four roles emanate. Therefore, Barth's conclusion has become the foundation for studies on the summary of the Law in the Gospel of Matthew. Whether the text is studied in a broader context, or on its own, Barth's conclusions are adopted by several scholars.

Following Bornkamm and Barth, Robert Banks also regards the summary as the essence of the Law.[87] After undertaking a comprehensive study of Jesus' attitude towards the Law, Banks accedes to Barth's conclusion that the summary is the essence of the Law while rejecting his conclusion that the whole Law can be deduced from it. His sole reason for rejecting Barth's fifth conclusion is that Jesus did not put his own demand on it.[88] The prominence of the summary is its being "the essence of the teaching of the law and the prophets" and no more than that. While Banks grants a prominent place to the summary, he, on the other hand, denies its importance. He argues that one should not give "too prominent

85. Bornkamm, "End-Expectation and Church," 15–38.

86. Barth, "Matthew's Understanding of the Law," 77–78, 85.

87. Banks, *Jesus and the Law*, 1975; Furnish, *The Love Command*, 1972.

88. Banks, *Jesus and the Law*, 234–44.

a position . . . to the love-commandment in the teaching of Jesus."[89] Banks is probably right in rejecting the view of subsuming the whole Law and the prophets to the love commandments, but he is inconsistent as to the role of the summary of the Law within the teaching of Jesus.

Unlike Banks, Furnish maintains most of the conclusions of Barth on the summary of the Law in Matt 22:30–40. He confirms "all the other statutes of the law can be deduced [from the summary]" that "these two contain all the others" and "constitute it [the Law], or better, provide the decisive word about its meaning and thus enable its correct interpretation."[90] Furnish holds at least three conclusions of Barth, namely that the summary of the Law is: (1) the essence of the law, (2) other commandments can be deduced from it, and (3) it plays a decisive role for the correct interpretation of the Law. Furnish's uncritical acceptance of Barth's conclusion must be rejected (particularly his assumption that other commandments can be deduced from it). Furnish's studies are also not on the summary of the Law as such, as his approach is so comprehensive that it does not undertake a detailed study of the topic. His goal is instead to offer a broad theological base for ethical practices.

Like Banks, Loader's studies on the Law are comprehensive. His discussion on the summary of the Law is extremely brief. He simply accentuates the interpretive role of the summary of the Law.[91] It is unclear whether Loader reckons the summary of the Law is the essence of the Law or not. However, it is obvious that his position resonates with that of Barth on the interpretive role of the summary. Gerhardsson, who devoted an article to the hermeneutical role of the summary of the Law, argues that Matt 22:37–40 is the hermeneutic program by which Matthew interprets the Holy Scripture and Jesus, the Messiah.[92] The article briefly analyzes the text to demonstrate how Matthew employed his hermeneutical program regarding the Old Testament. He concludes that the summary of the Law is an interpretive lens and a continuator of the validity of the Old Testament books.[93]His work is a reaffirmation of Barth's conclusion of the role of the summary of the Law as an interpretive principle.

89. Banks, *Jesus and the Law*, 234–44.

90. Furnish, *The Love Command*, 33–34.

91. Loader, *Jesus' Attitude Towards the Law*, 225–37.

92. Gerhardsson, "The Hermeneutic Program in Matthew 22:37–40," 129–50.

93. Gerhardsson, "The Hermeneutic Program in Matthew 22:37–40," 139–40.

Other works, such as Luise Schottroff,[94] and John Piper[95] are specifically concerned with love for the enemy. The summary of the Law is studied in the light of it; therefore, there is no direct discussion of it. Pheme Perkins'[96] approach to the love command is mainly dependent on the works of her predecessors, particularly Piper. Perkins' concern is ethical, and her approach is broad. She briefly comments that Jesus summarized the Law to "answer the challenges about the intent of the law."[97] In the introduction of her book, she claims to show the role of the love commandments in identity formation as she states that: "Later, we will see the role that love commandments played in shaping the identity of the developing Christian community."[98] Yet, no clear attempt is made in the book to show the role of the love command in identity formation. Her concern is to provide ethical guidelines and not with identity formation.

Unlike the above-mentioned scholars, Terence L. Donaldson introduces a different methodological approach to the topic. He applied sociology of knowledge and cognitive dissonance theory to Matt 20:40, to examine its contribution to the understanding of Matthew's Gospel.[99] Donaldson recognizes the weakness of traditional redaction criticism and proposes a "textured form of redaction criticism" to apply a social scientific method to the text.[100] He finds that Matt 20:40 falls "into one of the main categories of dissonance-reducing strategies, that of explanatory or hermeneutical programs providing a framework of interpretation within which the tension between dissonant cognitions can be released, or at least deflected."[101] For Donaldson, therefore, the summary of the Law mediates or lessens the tension within the community by playing an interpretive role. Donaldson's contribution encourages the study to take a new route to find the significance of the summary of the Law. In the end his study is however just a reinforcement of the conclusions of Barth through a new approach, especially the interpretive role of the summary of the Law.

94. Schottroff, *Essays on the Love Commandment*, 1978.

95. Piper, *"Love Your Enemies,"* 1979.

96. Perkins, *Love Commands*, 1982.

97. Perkins, *Love Commands*, 25.

98. Perkins, *Love Commands*, 15.

99. Donaldson, "The Law That Hangs."

100. Donaldson, "The Law That Hangs," 12.

101. Donaldson, "The Law That Hangs," 708.

Warren Carter, however, makes an opprobrious remark about Matthean studies for assuming the Gospel is only a religious text and for taking a myopic approach to it.[102] Carter undertakes a metonymic approach to Matt 22:34–40. He convincingly argues that the text in question is a counter–imperial practice against the so–called religious leaders. The commands in Matt 22:34–40, according to Carter, are dangerous because "they are socially transformative."[103] In doing so, Carter attempts to rescue the text from a confined and a short–sighted interpretation of the text by exposing it to the wider context within the Gospel itself, as well as to the matrix of the world within which it was produced and read. Carter's contribution must be commended for placing the texts in their social, political, economic, and religious contexts of its day.

Conclusion

The studies on Matt 22:34–40 are limited to their interpretive role and their role as accentuating the essence of love within the Law (except Carter's work). However, these studies' contributions should not be minimized. Scholars who studied the texts have confirmed that the summary of the Law has an important role in interpreting Matthew's understanding of the Law and a transformative vision for its social vision. However, its role as identity constructor for Jesus followers within its context has not been studied at all.

Paul and Matthew on the Law: Comrades or Foes?

It can be stated that an important difference between Matthew and Paul is their understanding of the Law. Studies on Paul's and Matthew's understanding of the Law support this fact.[104] How the differences are interpreted, however, depends on one's interpretive lens. Most of the studies on Paul's and Matthew's understanding of the Law and their relationship are based on comparing the theological angles of Matthew and Paul. Yet, no consensus has been achieved in such studies.

102. Carter, "Love Your Enemies."

103. Carter, "Love Your Enemies," 44.

104. E.g. Brandon, *The Fall of Jerusalem and the Christian Church*, 1957; Sim, "Matthew's Anti-Paulinism," 2002; Davies, *The Sermon on the Mount*, 1966; Goulder, *Midrash and Lection in Matthew*, 1974; Mohrlang, *Matthew and Paul*, 1984; France, *Matthew*, 1987; and Luz, *The Theology of the Gospel of Matthew*, 1995.

Since David Sim has given a review of the studies on the topic, there is no need to belabor the point. Sim and others summarized the major positions: (1) Matthew is an anti-Pauline text.[105] Brandon first conceived this position with which Sim agrees. (2) Matthew and Paul are theologically close to each other. Scholars who consent with this position, despite differences in their arguments, are Davies.[106] (3) Matthew and Paul were different, but complementary.[107]

Recently, Sim has vehemently contended that Matthew is anti-Paul.[108] In doing so he admits that his proposal is a renaissance of Brandon's thesis. Considering that it is David Sim who has resurrected and extended the thesis of Brandon, this section will focus on his articles. His articles have contributed to placing the issues in the limelight of scholarly discussion. In his articles, Sim strongly argued that Matthew is anti-Pauline with regard to their respective perspectives on the Law.

Sim claims that Matthew was propagating a Law–observant mission to both the Jews and the Gentiles, while Paul, on the other hand, was promoting a Law–free mission among the Gentiles.[109] He writes, "Matthew was engaged in a bitter and sustained polemic against Paul himself."[110] His arguments hinge on three texts from the Gospel of Matthew: Matt 5:17–19; 7:13–23; and 16:17, and on his reconstruction of the history and social setting of the Matthean community. For Matthew, according to Sim, every part of the Law is valid and therefore must be obeyed and taught until the parousia whereas, for Paul, the Law is functional until the resurrection of Jesus Christ.[111] Consequently, Matthew and Paul are theologically antagonistic, particularly in light of Matt 7:13–23, which for Sim, demonstrates Matthew's anti-Pauline stance. Coupling Matt 7:24–23 with 16:17, Sim advances his cases by ascribing the rock to Peter (Matt 16:17). The two

105. David C. Sim, "Matthew's Anti-Paulinism, 767–83; Brandon, *The Fall of Jerusalem and the Christian Church*, 1957.

106. Davies, *The Sermon on the Mount*, 1966; Goulder, *Midrash and Lection in Matthew*, 1994; Meier, *A Marginal Jew*, 2009.

107. Sim, "Matthew's Anti-Paulinism," 772–74; Mohrlang, *Matthew and Paul*, 1984; France, *Matthew* 1987; Luz, *The Theology of the Gospel of Matthew*, 1995.

108. Sim, *The Gospel of Matthew and Christian Judaism*, 188–211; Sim, "Matthew 7.21–23, 325–43; Sim, "Matthew, Paul and the Origin and Nature of the Gentile Mission, 377–92; Sim, "Matthew's Anti-Paulinism," 774–81.

109. Sim, "Matthew, Paul and the Origin and Nature of the Gentile Mission," 390.

110. Sim, "Matthew's Anti-Paulinism," 777.

111. Sim, "Matthew's Anti-Paulinism," 779.

houses in Matt 7:24–23 refer to the two traditions.[112] That is, the house built upon the rock represents the Petrine tradition or the law–observant community whereas the house which is built on the sand represents the Pauline tradition or law–free community. He arrives at the conclusion that "the evangelist [Matthew] sought to challenge or deny Paul's claim that he was divinely commissioned to conduct a mission independently of the Jerusalem church. Matthew portrays Peter instead as the recipient of a divine revelation and as the foundation of Jesus' church with the authority to match. The result is that Paul's later claim to have had a similar experience to that of Peter looks hollow, implausible and derivative."[113]

Although Sim's conclusion might be conceivable, his arguments are not convincing. At least four reasons can be noted for Sim's unconvincing arguments. First, Sim does not define his understanding of the term *Torah*. Since he argues that Matthew is a sect,[114] he should have explained how Matthew understands the *Torah* differently from other sects. If the Matthean community is one of the sects that differs from and avoids those of "formative Judaism," and stands against Paul, then what is the *Torah* in the light of Matthew's Gospel? If the Matthean community conceded to the validity of the *Torah*, why would Mathew's community reject the coalition in "formative Judaism"? In fact, Sim has pointed out that "the Matthean community follows the interpretation of Jesus who came to fulfil the Law and not to abolish it (5.17) . . . and messianic exegesis of Jesus is guided by the principle of love of God and neighbor (22.34–40; cf. 7.12)."[115] Yet, he does not discuss the implication of this statement and its difference from the Pauline definition of *Torah* in his arguments in his later articles. Sanders writes, "this [Matt 7.12] is meant to epitomize the whole law, though in terms of content it summarizes only the second table."[116] If this is so, what was Matthew's concept of *Torah*? Sim's argument that Matthew demands "the observance of the Mosaic Law in full"[117] is also questionable, because no empirical evidence is given to demonstrate the claim and no convincing explanation concerning the meaning of observing the law in full is offered.

112. Sim, "Matthew's Anti-Paulinism," 779.
113. Sim, "Matthew and the Pauline Corpus," 418.
114. Sim, "The Gospel of Matthew and the Gentiles," 36.
115. Sim, "The Gospel of Matthew and the Gentiles," 37.
116. Sanders, *Judaism*, 257.
117. Sim, "Matthew, Paul and the Origin and Nature of the Gentile Mission," 388.

The second problem is methodology. Sim's approach to the issue is to focus on selective texts that seem obviously to be contradicting some of Pauline teachings. He also did not demonstrate how the whole teachings of Matthew's Gospel are organized against Pauline teachings. He did not discuss the texts he selected in terms of Matthew's interpretation of *Torah*. Instead, he compared and contrasted texts that seem to be contradicting Pauline texts. As a result, in his arguments the agreement between Matthean texts and Pauline texts is ignored.

Third, Sim interprets the relationship of Matthew and Paul through the window of first century conflicts, contentions, and arguments. He does not seem to be open to the possibility of concession being made between first–century communities of Jesus followers. Other scriptural narrations demonstrate that concessions were made (e.g., in Acts 15). Paul, for example, also affirms that what he preached and what other Apostles preached is the same Gospel (1 Cor 15:11). In Galatians 2, Paul argues that an agreement had already been reached between him and the Jerusalem church and that he had received confirmation from the pillars of the church about his teaching. Paul further rebuked Peter for his hypocritical actions and not for the kind of Gospel he preached. Paul opposed their apparent hypocrisy because it damages their credibility (Gal 2:13). Therefore, Sim does not give adequate weight to the possibility of an agreement among Matthew and Paul's followers or interpreters.

Fourth, Sim did not discuss the genres and the mega theme of each book and their effects on interpretation. There is no explicit evidence that substantiates the idea that the central issue for Matthew in his Gospel is Paul's teaching of the Law, as Matthew predominantly focuses on the person and the work of Jesus, the Messiah. From Sim's argument, it however seems that Paul's theology is at the center of Matthew's Gospel. Therefore, all the above drawbacks in the discussion of the articles call for a deeper study on the interpretation and understanding of the Law on the part of both Matthew and Paul.

It is understood that the debate above is the result of the major interpretive assumption started by Augustine and standardized by Bultman, Käsemann, and Bornkamm. Notwithstanding the different conclusions arrived at by each scholar, the underpinning assumption is that grace and the Law are in an antithetical relationship. Particularly in the works of Sim this assumption is clear. For Sim, Matthew proclaimed a Law–observant mission whereas Paul proclaimed a Law–free Gospel. This is tantamount to saying that the antithesis of grace is the Law. This *a priori* theologically guided interpretation is so ingrained in scholarly discussion of the Law that it has obfuscated the role of the Law particularly in identity construction in the Gospel of Matthew and Paul.

Section Conclusion

Studies on Rom 13:8–14 and Matt 22:34–40 have explored the texts to examine the nature of the summary of the Law within the theological framework of Paul and Matthew. Although such studies are legitimate, they are confined to one aspect of the issue. However, the studies are important in showing the significance of the summary of the Law. They, however, fail when exploring its role in constructing the identity of Jesus followers. The studies, particularly conducted on the comparison of Paul's and Matthew's understanding of the Law and their relationship so far, have offered divergent conclusions. The problem remains unresolved. It, therefore, demands further study with a different question that approaches the problem from a new angle. This research will attempt to propose such a new approach by focusing on the role of the summary of the Law in the letter to the Romans and in Matthew's Gospel in constructing the identity of their respective communities in their context, in an attempt to offer some direction in tackling the problem of Paul's and Matthew's understanding of the Law.

TERMINOLOGY

Defining some important terms is mandatory for the sake of clarity and consistency. The following three groups of words will be defined below: 1) *Torah*/*Nomos*/Law; 2) Identity and Boundaries; and 3) Moral, Ethics and Ethos.

Torah (νόμος) Law

According to John Meier, the root of the problem of correctly understanding the meaning of *Torah* can be traced back to etymology.[118] Meaning derived through etymological study is rejected because it is not "a

118. Meier, *A Marginal Jew*, 4:27.

sure guide to later usage and meaning."[119] For instance, the etymological study of the word "Torah" is dependent on the Hebrew word *yrh* meaning to "throw," to "cast," or "toss" therefore the meaning is assumed to be a symbol of casting a lot to know God's will, or to throw a figure or a hand to show a direction. It is understood as an oracle in the sense of the prophets of Israel who claim that what they announce is the word of God.[120]Torah is sometimes understood as "divine instruction" or "divine directive" that is, every single teaching or direction that came through the priests and prophets (Lev 6:2; Exod 18:16). This concept of Torah perceives Torah as "a huge written corpus."[121] Therefore, Torah is the teaching, instruction, and direction given by God to his people through his prophets, and priests in written form particularly in the form of the revelation given to Moses at Mount Sinai.

The Greek word *nomos* has a wider range of meanings in ancient Greek. The standard English word "law," therefore, does not appropriately represent the scope of its meaning, since in ancient Greek the word "*nomos* was used in various and often overlapping contexts that included religion, civil society and law, philosophy, cosmology, and royal ideology."[122] The Gospels, however, used the word in a number of different senses: "the nomos contains laws that command (e.g., Matt 22:36–40), narratives that recount the origins of Israel (e.g., with "Moses" as a surrogate for "the Law," John 3:14; 6:31–32), and prophecies that point forward to Jesus (Matt 11:13)."[123]

Both in Paul and Matthew, *nomos* refers to the Law of Moses. In this research, *nomos* and Torah will be understood as referring to the Law of Moses in the sense of teaching or instruction (and therefore not first and foremost as legalistic concept) serving as "covenant obligation" as it is understood by James Dunn.[124] To identify it clearly, the English word 'Law' will be employed, and the first letter will be consistently capitalized in order to differentiate it from other sense.

119. Meier, *A Marginal Jew*, 4:27.

120. Meier, *A Marginal Jew*, 4:27.

121. Meier, *A Marginal Jew*, 4:28.

122. Meier, *A Marginal Jew*, 4:38.

123. Meier, *A Marginal Jew*, 4:38.

124. Dunn, *The Theology of Paul the Apostle*, 131–33.

Identity and Boundaries

Fundamentally, "identity involves people's explicit or implicit response to the question of: 'who are you?' It is self definition of individual, small group, larger social group . . . [It] comprises 'How you act as being' interpersonal and intergroup interaction and the social recognition or otherwise that these actions receive from other individual or group."[125] Tolmie also defines identity in a similar fashion, "Identity refers to the way in which the members of a community view themselves and why they do so."[126]According to Judith M. Lieu, identity entails "the idea of boundedness, of sameness and difference, of continuity, perhaps of degree of homogeneity, and recognition by self and by others."[127] Lieu adds, "the description of the self–demands the description of the other; 'us' implies 'them'; the positive invites or presupposes the negative."[128] In this research, identity refers to the self–definition, and self–understanding of Jesus followers, and the Jesus followers defining others and they being seen or defined by others in light of the summary of the Law.

There are two major perspectives on the concept of identity: identity theory and social identity theory. The former is a micro–sociological theory that aims at explaining individuals based on role–related behaviors. It therefore focuses on role identity, identity salience and commitment while the latter is a socio–psychological theory which attempts to explain group process and intergroup relationships.[129] Their difference lies in their disciplinary root: identity theory is sociological while social identity theory is a psychological concept. Social science scholars are currently arguing that their difference is a matter of emphasis and discipline root; therefore, both theories can possibly be used.

There is no intention at this stage of the research to present a detailed discussion on the complexity of both theories. A brief description of both will be sufficient for the present purpose. For identity theory, "self reflects the wider social structure insofar as self is a collection of identities from the role position occupied by the person."[130]Social identity

125. Vignoles, Schwartz, and Luyckx, "Introduction: Toward an Integrative View of Identity," 2011.

126. Tolmie, "Liberty-Love-the Spirit," 242.

127. Lieu, *Christian Identity*, 12.

128. Lieu, *Christian Identity*, 13.

129. Hogg, Terry, and White, "A Tale of Two Theories," 225, 258.

130. Hogg, Terry, and White, "A Tale of Two Theories," 259.

theory predicates its theory on a two-foundation socio-cognitive process: self-categorization and self-enhancement. While self-categorization "sharpens intergroup boundaries by producing group-distinctive stereotypical and normative perception and actions, and assigns people, including self, to the contextually relevant category," self-enhancement "guides the social categorization process such that in-group norms and stereotypes largely favour the in-group."[131] Self-enhancement is achieved in groups by comparing relevant out-groups in a way that favors the in-group. This evaluative perception against the other creates positive self-concept within the in-group. In this study, social identity theory is followed insofar as it almost always includes both the personal as well as the group role in studying identity construction. Not least, its focus on the group identity is germane to the present study.

Boundaries are an integral part of the idea of identity, because "it is boundaries that both enclose those who share what is common and exclude those who belong outside, that both ensure continuity and coherence, and safeguard against contamination or invasion."[132] In Judaism, the boundary markers are circumcision, food laws, and the Sabbath, which are mainly national boundaries. *Boundary and boundary markers* in this research refer to particular traits of Jesus followers that are shared among insiders and are used to exclude outsiders based on the summary of the Law in Romans and the Gospel of Matthew.

Morals, Ethics and Ethos

One of the ways in which identity is constructed is through moral commitments. Meeks states, "Making morals and making community are essentially one, indistinguishable process."[133] Etymologically, *ethics and morality* have the same meaning. Ethics comes from the Greek word *ethos* meaning "custom" whereas morality comes from the Latin word *mos* or *moris* meaning "custom."[134]However, philosophically, ethics as a theoretical science gives principles or a basis of right or wrong actions whereas morality actualizes the theory. According to Tolmie, ethics "refers to an underlying theological substructure in particular, the *principle*

131. Hogg, Terry, and White, "A Tale of Two Theories," 260.

132. Lieu, *Christian Identity*, 98.

133. Horrell, *Solidarity and Difference*, 29.

134. Babor, *Ethics*, 2.

or *ethical pointers* which serve as guidelines as to how one should act" and *ethos* "refers to the things that humankind do, actions that could be viewed as morally right or wrong. It is a lifestyle (italics his)."[135] *Ethos* emphasizes the way of life, the ways in which morality is actually practiced. This research retains the etymological similarity between ethics and morality with a simple distinction between ethics and ethos made by Tolmie. It focuses primarily on ethics (morality) as a fixed set of morals. However, both ethics and ethos will be discussed as a means of identity construction of the community but in the sense of lifestyle or a way of life as understood by Warren Carter.[136]

PRESUPPOSITION OF THE RESEARCH

A number of presuppositions of this study need to be addressed briefly. Hence, the following presuppositions form the contextual framework for this research:

1. There was networking and communication among first century churches despite their different ethnic identity and geographical locations.[137]
2. A community must be grounded in the past.[138] The Law is one of the past traditions; therefore, it is a necessary ground for the construction of identity.
3. Identity is dynamic and negotiable[139] since Matthew and Paul had ethnically and culturally mixed groups of Jesus followers. Through their texts, they are reconstructing the identity of Jesus followers in their respective communities; in such milieux identity negotiation plays an important role.
4. Texts and interpretation are used to construct identity.[140] Reinterpretation of scripture and its appropriation are how Paul and Matthew had constructed their new communities. Their texts provide continuity with the past, clarify boundaries, and create a world for

135. Tolmie, "Liberty-Love-the Spirit," 242.

136. Carter, *Matthew and the Margins*, 7–11.

137. Bauckham, *Gospels for All Christians*, 1998.

138. Meeks, *The Origins of Christian Morality*, 213–19.

139. Lieu, *Christian Identity*, 97; Punt, "Enscripturalised Identity," 8.

140. Lieu, *Christian Identity*, 19–55.

the community that can be envisioned as reality and through which cohesion can be maintained. All the above serve as underpinning presuppositions of this research.

HYPOTHESIS

The Bible contains numerous identity–shaping and defining texts in the form of stories, Law, wisdom, teachings, and prophetic messages. According to Meeks,[141] a moral community must be grounded in the past. The Law is embedded in the story of Israel as identity–shaping text. In the New Testament, the past is however, imported in different ways: redefined, re-interpreted, re-told, and modelled, particularly in the life, teaching, and ministry of Jesus. The Law is one of these sources and functions as a community–forming text for the New Testament authors. Based on this understanding, this research aims to test the following hypothesis:

1. Paul and Matthew formulated the summary of the Law (as a text used for identity construction) in order to format the identity of their respective communities. This summary directed and defined the ethos (as a way of life) of their respective communities. "Religious belief and worldviews play an important role in shaping one's identity—especially in relation to values, commitments, and conviction."[142] The Law informs the conviction and values of the community. A Law-informed cluster of convictions "helps to define certain boundaries" which in turn defines the identity of the community by stipulating "what may be incorporated as beneficial and what will be excluded as harmful" for the community.[143] Boundaries are "typically indicated by a set of rules of a written or unwritten moral code which all those who are included [in the community] should adhere to."[144] Therefore, the Law, as interpreted and understood by Rom 13:8–14 and Matt 22:34–40, continued to play the role of constructing the identity of Jesus followers.
2. In the Epistle to the Romans and in the Gospel of Matthew, the Law played the role of identifying sin, defining values and virtues,

141. Meeks, *The Origins of Christian Morality*, 213–19.

142. Conradie, *Christian Identity*, 17.

143. Conradie, *Christian Identity*, 17.

144. Conradie, *Christian Identity*, 17.

stipulating criteria for remaining in the community and in setting the boundaries that serve as social and religious boundaries to form their identity as well as to direct the ethos of Jesus followers.

3. Therefore, this research hypothesizes that neither Matthew nor Paul claims the nullification or the irrelevance of the Law for Jesus followers, but they interpreted it anew in light of the summary of the Law in order to construct the identity of Jesus followers as a holy community. This research thus attempts to investigate the role of the Law, as summarized and interpreted in Matt 22:34–40 and in Rom 13:8–14, in the identity construction of Jesus followers in the Gospel of Matthew and in the letter to the Romans in the Roman imperial world.

METHODOLOGY AND APPROACH

The primary research methodology of the research is socio-rhetorical criticism. Vernon K. Robbins defines socio-rhetorical criticism as an "approach to literature that focuses on values, convictions, and belief in the text we read and in the world in which we live."[145] Socio-rhetorical criticism is an integrated and a multidisciplinary approach that brings various approaches to the "intricate, detail exegesis of texts."[146] In fact, its challenge is to bring a number of different practices of interpretation together. To address this challenge, it provides five methods to view a text from different angles and to employ a multifaceted approach: inner texture, intertexture, social and cultural texture, ideological texture, and sacred texture.[147] In this study, only inner texture and intertexture[148] will be used because using all possible approaches for analyzing two whole NT texts is beyond the limits of this research.

145. Robbins, *Exploring the Texture of Texts*, 1.

146. Robbins, *Exploring the Texture of Texts*, 1.

147. Robbins, *Exploring the Texture of Texts*, 3.

148. The researcher is aware of the benefit of using the rest of the textures available through socio-rhetorical criticism, and in particular, social and cultural texture and ideological texture. But due to the size of the books investigated here, the researcher will focus on two textures for the sake of being able to study them in depth. However, the analysis is made with an awareness of the social, cultural and ideological textures of the texts. Furthermore, socio-rhetorical criticism does not expect the interpreter to apply all the textures of texts in one interpretation project (so Robbins, *Exploring the Texture of the Texts*, 5).

First, the study begins with an inner texture analysis which is on detail exegesis of the text by focusing on repetitive texture, topical progression and argumentative texture. It focuses on words, word patterns, voices, structures, and devices which are the context for meaning and meaning effect.[149] This approach corresponds to traditional approaches such as structural analysis, syntactical analysis, lexical analysis, and thematic analysis of the text. However, the inner texture method offers wider and more flexible approaches with which to reach the goal of analyzing a text: repetition, progression in the text, narration structure, opening–middle–closing of the text, argumentative dimension, and the sensory aesthetic phenomena. While focusing on the repetition, progression, narration structures and argumentative dimension for both texts under question, all inner texture analysis methods might be employed as needed.

Then, the intertexture that deals with the world outside the text will follow. Robbins explains intertexture of a text as "the interaction of the language in the text with outside material and physical 'objects,' historical events, texts, customs, values, roles, institutions, and systems."[150] One of the subcategories of intertexture is oral–scribal texture that investigates what other text has used of a given text outside of itself. Hence, the study focuses on oral–scribal texture to analyze the historical context of Rom 13:8–14 and Matt 22:34–40 such as Jewish sources: Josephus, Philo, the Dead Sea Scrolls, a number of Apocrypha books, Pseudepigrapha, and Hellenistic literatures.

PURPOSE AND CONTRIBUTION

The possible value or impact of the research is to fill the knowledge gap regarding the role of the summary of the Law in the Gospel of Matthew and in the Epistle to the Romans especially its use to construct identity. As there is no specific study undertaken so far on the topic, it will make a significant contribution filling this lacuna in the area of both Matthean and Pauline scholarship. In addition to this, the outcome of the comparison of Paul's understanding of the Law as seen in the summary of the Law in Romans and Matthew's understanding of the Law in his Gospel, will contribute to a better understanding of the study of Paul and

149. Robbins, *Exploring the Texture of Texts*, 7.

150. Robbins, *Exploring the Texture of Texts*, 40.

Matthew's relationship. The findings of this research will also inform current Christian identity construction in multi-ethnic, multicultural, multilingual nations.

RESEARCH DESIGN

The research is divided into eight chapters.

Chapter One deals with introductory issues: Background, problem and delimitation of the research, review of previous studies, terminology, presupposition of the research, hypothesis of the research, methodology and approach, purpose and contribution and the design of the research.

Chapter Two is concerned with inner texture analysis of Rom 13:8–14. The chapter specifically studies and examines the inner texture of the text in order to understand the context within the text and to draw out the meaning thereof. Here, repetitive texture and topical progression of *νόμος* and *ἀγαπη* are investigated.

Chapter Three is a sequel on inner texture analysis of Rom 13:8–14 focusing on Rom 13:8–14's argumentative texture.

Chapter Four undertakes the inner texture analysis of Matt 22:34–40, investigating the repetitive texture, topical progressive texture, narrational texture and pattern and argumentative texture of *νόμος* and *ἀγαπη*.

Chapter Five is a sequel to the inner texture analysis of Matt 22:34–40, investigating narrational texture, opening–middle–closing, and argumentative texture.

Chapter Six comprises two investigations. First, it investigates the intertexture of Rom 13:8–14 and Matt 22:34–40 and then compares Rom 13:8–14 and Matt 22:34–40 based on the results of the previous chapters' findings. It investigates the intertexture of Rom 13:8–14 and Matt 22:34–40 in Pentateuch, Philo, the Dead Sea Scrolls, a number of Apocrypha books, Pseudepigrapha, Greco-Roman literatures, the synoptic Gospels and Pauline literatures. Finally, it applies the findings from the previous chapters to compare Rom 13:8–14 and Matt 22:34–40.

Chapter Seven deals with the role of Rom 13:8–14 and Matt 22:34–40 as identity-shaping text for the community of Jesus followers.

Chapter Eight concludes the study and presents the research findings.

2

Romans 13:8–10

Inner Texture Analysis

8 Owe no one anything, except to love one another; for he who loves his neighbor has fulfilled the law.	8 Μηδενι μδὲν ὀφείλετε εἰ τὸ ἀλληλους ἀγαπᾶν.Ὁ γὰρ ἀγαπῶν τὸν ἕτερον νόμον πεπελήρωκεν.
9 The commandments, "You shall not commit adultery, You shall not kill, You shall not steal, You shall not covet," and any other commandment, are summed up in this sentence, "You shall love your neighbor as yourself."	9 τὸ γὰρ οὐ μοιχεύσεις, οὐ φονεύσεις, οὐ κλέψεις, οὐκ ἐπιθυμήσιεσς, καὶ τις ἐτέρα ἐντολή, ἐν τῷ λόγῳ τούτῳ ἀνακεφαλαιοῦται ἐν τῷ ἀγαπήσεις τὸν πλησίον σου ὡς σεαυτόν.
10 Love does no wrong to a neighbor; therefore love is the fulfilling of the law. (Nestle–Aland Greek–English New Testament)	10 ἡ ἀγάπη τῶ πλησίον κακὸν οὐκ ἐργαζεται .πλήρωμα οὖν νόμου ἡ ἀγάπη.

INTRODUCTION

Different approaches have been employed to analyze the literary genre and structure of the letter. For example, the rhetorical approach classifies the letter in various formats: epideictic,[1] protreptic, and diatribic.[2] Despite these differences in approach there is a consensus that

1. Kennedy, *New Testament Interpretation*, 152–56.
2. Stowers, *A Rereading of Romans*, 326.

Rom 12—15:13 is one single unit and it is treated as rhetorically. Hence, the analysis focuses on only the repetitive and topical progressive texture of Rom 13:8–14. Due to the vastness of the data two topical progressions (*ἀγάπη* and *νόμος*) will be analyzed. The repetitive texture will be analyzed, followed by the topical progression.

ROMANS 13:8–10: REPETITIVE TEXTURE ANALYSIS

According to Robbin, repetitive texture appears whenever "words and phrases occur more than once in a unit."[3] Not only words, but also grammatical, syntactical, verbal, and topical repetitions in a unit are a repetitive texture. But repetitive texture does not reveal 'the inner meaning," rather it introduces the overall picture of the unit and gives access for a closer scrutiny of the text.[4] Progression texture, which is an extension of the repetitive texture of the unit, allows for examining the occurrence of the word and topics in the entire work of the discourse. Although the investigation includes Rom 13:11–14 for the sake of focus and the need for detailed analysis of the topical progressions in the entire letter, only the repetitive words appearing in Rom 13:8–10 will be analyzed.

Μηδενὶ μηδὲν	ἀγαπᾶν ἀγαπῶν	γὰρ	ἕτερον	Νόμον	πεπλήρωκεν			
	ἀγαπήσεις	γὰρ	ἑτέρα	ἐντολή?		οὐ οὐ οὐ οὐκ	_εις _εις _εις _εις _εις σου σεαυτόν	Πλησίον
	ἀγάπη ἀγάπη			Νόμου	πλήρωμα	οὐκ		Πλησίον

Table 1: Repetitive Texture of Romans 13:8–10

The repetitive texture of Rom 13:8–10 raises several questions that deserve deeper analysis. The analysis of repetitive texture "introduces interpreters to the overall forest" and the data "gives initial insight into the overall picture of the discourse . . . [and] invites the interpreter to

3. Robbins, *Exploring the Texture of Texts*, 8.

4. Robbins, *Exploring the Texture of Texts*, 10.

move yet closer to the details of the text."[5] Therefore, the following initial observations can be made from the data of the repetitive texture:

1. The second person singular "you" is repeated seven times along with its variant forms within the citation. It raises the question of identity of the audience.
2. It also reveals that ἀγάπη is one of the key themes that develops from v. 8a as an obligation to a reason (v. 8b) to evidence (v. 9b), then to a claim (v. 10a) and finally to a conclusion (v. 10b). It occurs in each of the verses as a key term and concept in connecting the whole argument of the rhetorical unit (13:8–10). It also serves as an *inclusio* by framing the beginning and the ending of the textual unit.
3. The data exhibits that νόμος is a key theme and concept that is equally important for the progression of the unit under analysis, though numerically, it occurs only three times including ἐντολή. It raises a question of whether νόμος in vv. 8b and 10 is to be understood as Roman law, Jewish law, or as a principle. A further complication surfaces with the question of whether ἕτερος should be taken as an adjective of νόμον or an object of ἀγαπῶν; ἕτερος in v. 9 also raised additional questions when it modified ἐντολή, i.e. whether it refers to the rest of the Ten Commandments or to any other commandments within and outside the scripture.
4. πεπλήρωκεν and πλήρωμα (their noun form: πληρόω) are the two important words related to love and Law. The former carries the verbal while the latter the noun forms. They carry the key claims of the rhetorical unit of 13:8–10. Yet, it is difficult to decide their meaning with precision in reference to both love and the Law.
5. Another important repeated word is πλησίον which significantly connects the rhetorical unit along with love and the Law. The question is whether the identity of the neighbor is inclusive or exclusive.
6. γάρ indicates a logical and rational movement of the rhetorical unit connecting the first imperative statement to the conclusion. However, at its first appearance whether it should be understood as explanatory or causal must be decided, as it makes significant meaning differences in terms of motivation.

5. Robbins, *Exploring the Texture of the Texts*, 8.

As the aim of this section is to analyze the repetitive inner texture of the rhetorical unit, it does not deal with deeper issues and meaning. It also leaves out other important concepts and key words that are important for the understanding of the unit because they are not repeatedly used within the unit (13:8–10) such as ὀφείλω, ἀλλήλων, κακός, ἀνακεφαλαιοῦται and ἐργάζομαι. Other concepts that play secondary roles are also not analyzed; these are Οὐ μιοξεύσεις, Οὐ φονεύσεις, Οὐ κλέφις, and Οὐκ ἐπιθυμήσεις, but these will be analyzed along with the major concepts and topics. However, the overall rhetorical movement and the major themes of the unit have been revealed through the key terms repeated within the unit: love, the Law, neighbor, and fulfillment. These major themes will be unpacked in the ensuing section of this chapter.

ROMANS 13:8–10: TOPICAL PROGRESSION ANALYSIS

The analysis above has shown different repeated words and topics within the rhetorical unit of Rom 13:8–10. In the next section, the topics and concepts repeated in the rhetorical units under question will be investigated—first the topical progression of ἀγάπη and then the topical progression of νόμος.

Topical Progression of ἀγάπη in Romans

The analysis of the repetitive texture has revealed that ἀγάπη is one of the key repetitive words and concepts in the rhetorical unit of Rom 13:8–10. However, it is virtually impossible to do justice to the interpretation of the concept without analyzing its progression in the entire letter. The word and the concept of ἀγάπη appear in Rom 5:5, 8; 8:28, 35, 37, 39; 12:9; 14:15; and 15:30. In the ensuing section, these verses will be investigated to disclose the topical progression of ἀγάπη in the entire letter.

Romans 5:5 and 8

The topical progression of ἀγάπη begins at 5:5. John Murray has correctly observed that Rom 5:5 is the "most condensed statement in the epistle."[6] However, the phrase ἡ ἀγάπη τοῦ θεοῦ has been rendered with two

6. Murray, *Romans*, 164.

different meanings. It can be understood either as subjective genitive, meaning God's love for the believers,[7] or as objective genitive, meaning believers' love for God (our love for God poured out into our heart through the Holy Spirit.[8]

The subjective genitive position reasons that it fits the context of the chapter and that Rom 5:8 speaks of assurance of hope based on the love of God to believers and that it controls their hearts to endure affliction.[9] Therefore, if it is speaking of believers' love towards God, the assurance and security of believers is jeopardized.[10] However, those who argue for the objective genitive, think that God is the source of love according to the phrase, ἐκκέξυται ἐν ταῖς καρδίαις ἡμῶν. The love of God pours out into the heart; therefore, it is possessed. Fitzmyer contends, "love, after all, can only be accepted if it is given in return."[11]

Against the general agreement among scholars that Rom 5:5 is about God's love towards us, not our love towards God,[12] Dunn questions whether it excludes "love for God."[13] For Dunn, the genitive form yields no indication as to what kind of genitive, therefore, it is the context that determines its function. The immediate context of Rom 5:5 lists both the positive benefits and experiences such as justification, access to grace, peace (5:1–2), love and indwelling Spirit (5:5) and the negative experience here and now—suffering (3–4) with a positive end which is the glory of God. It also states two agents of the benefits—justification through Jesus Christ and love through the Holy Spirit. Jewett argues that the text speaks of the current experience of Jesus followers, not least overcoming shame, and he complains that commentators' interpretation of the text is preoccupied with doctrine of eternal security.[14] As a result, the two sides of the context—the positive and the negative—are not given a due balance.

Romans 5:1–5 succinctly provides two important features of love: 1) the context of love is suffering and 2) the source of love is God whereas the locus of love is the heart of the Jesus followers. Jewett thinks that the text is about "overcoming shame and transforming the shape of boasting"

7. Cranfield, *Romans*, 1:262; Murray, *Romans*, 164;

8. Wright and Sampley, *The New Interpreter's Bible*, 517.

9. Cranfield, *Romans*, 1:262.

10. Murray, *Romans*, 164.

11. Fitzmyer, *Romans*, 42.

12. Dunn, *Romans 1–8*, 252.

13. Dunn, *The Theology of Paul the Apostle*, 380.

14. Jewett, *Romans*, 356.

of the Jesus followers in the society where honor has to be maintained in the midst of adversary, but he did not bring the centrality of suffering to the fore.[15] Paul discusses love in the context of suffering both in 5:1–5 and in 8:28. In particular, God's love for the community in 5:8 is demonstrated in light of suffering. The death of Jesus Christ for the ungodly is the quintessential demonstration of God's love. It appears that Paul is insinuating that the love that poured out in the hearts of the Jesus followers expresses itself in the context of suffering which is akin to the love of God demonstrated in giving up his son for the ungodly.

The source and destination of the love of God is also revealing. Paul asserts that the community has already been given the Holy Spirit (πνεύματος ἁγίου τοῦ δοθέντος ἡμῖν) and the abiding Spirit of God is the agent for the pouring of love in the hearts of the believers. Paul is portraying an abiding love that seems to be already in the heart of the individuals before they experience suffering. Jewett postulates that this love is imparted in the heart at the time of conversion or baptism.[16] However, it is hardly possible to pin down the timing with certainty although it is generally discernable that the arrival of the Spirit in the heart of the believers cannot be separated from the infilling of love in the heart.

The purpose of pouring out the love of God must have an experiential dimension in a sense that it should be practically applied not abstractly intellectualized. The context of experiencing love is suffering and challenges, as is the similar concept of endurance and suffering reflected in Rom 12:9–21. Granted, love has an emotive dimension, but it comes to the fore during challenges and suffering. The ambiguity of the genitive, though it cannot be said to be deliberate with certainty, serves both sides—God's love to the believers and the believers' love to God. God's love, poured out into the heart of the believers, binds the relationship between the believer and God during the time of suffering so that the believers interpret the adversities positively and respond accordingly.

Romans 8:28, 35, 37, and 39

The next occurrence of love is in Rom 8:18–39 at four specific locations: vv. 28, 35, 37, and 39. Beginning from Romans 6, Paul begins to relate the effects of righteousness of God by faith in the life of Jesus followers.

15. Jewett, *Romans*, 357.

16. Jewett, *Romans*, 356.

Romans 8:18–39 takes up the idea of suffering and glory which is reminiscent of Romans 5:1–11. Jewett has discerned seven parallels between 5:1–11 and 8:33–39.[17] In 5:1–5, Paul succinctly renders the effect as well as the challenges of being the followers of Jesus and its glorious destiny. A similar theme resonates and develops in 8:18–39. While 8:17 introduces suffering and glory, 8:18–39 elaborates on suffering, glory, Spirit, hope, love and victory over adversaries. Likewise, in 5:1–5, Paul speaks of suffering, the Spirit, hope, glory, and love. Hence, in both places the context of love is suffering, hope, and glory.

Romans 8:28 describes the ideal characters who might as well be those who experienced suffering and challenges and are bewildered about their condition to the point that they do not know what to pray. Paul qualifies these groups as those who love God. Gundry is probably correct in regarding them as those who fulfill the righteous requirement of the law.[18] The characters, in the context of Rom 8:17–39, are described within the context of the suffering and the glory that Jesus followers will share with Jesus.

Yet, a textual variation of πάντα συνεργεῖ εἰς ἀγαθόν has created difficulty in translation as well as in interpretation. Cranfield has enumerated eight possible readings of πάντα συνεργεῖ; however, there is no need to belabor the point here.[19] For the topic under question, suffice it to concentrate on πάντα. What Paul said before and after 8:28 elucidates that πάντα here refers to "the suffering of the present time" (8:18). Futility and decay of creation (vv. 20 and 21), groaning of creation (v. 22), the inward groaning and weakness of Jesus followers (vv. 23 and 26), tribulation, distress, persecution, famine, nakedness, peril, and sword (v. 35) are the major trials that Paul lists. In particular, in v. 37, Paul repeats ἐν τούτοις πᾶσιν which appears to be the explanation of πάντα in 8:28, although, it is rather distant from it. Considering the immediate context, πάντα must be referring to the suffering of the present time (*pace* Moo, who thinks it refers to our daily life including sin)[20] which Jesus followers experience. The connection between 8:1–17 and 8:19–30 is mainly by repetition of Spirit (vv. 23, 27), sonship (vv. 14, 15, 16, 19, 21), glory (v. 18) and hope (v. 24), but the next section (that is vv. 31–39) seems to be

17. Jewett, *Romans*, 535.

18. Gundry, *Commentary on the New Testament*, 601.

19. Cranfield, *Romans*, 1:425.

20. Moo, *Romans*, 529.

a conclusion for the whole discussions on suffering, love and hope that started at Romans five.

Romans 8:31–39 can be treated as a separate section of Romans 8, but it cannot be separated thematically. Not least Τί οὖν ἐροῦμεν πρὸς ταῦτα v. 31 refers back to the immediate context of 8:1 and possibly to the larger context of 5:1–8:30 insofar as it elaborates and develops the themes raised in Rom 5:1–11. According to Jewett, Paul raises ten *erotesis*[21] rhetorical questions arranged in three sections (8:31–32, 33–34, 35–37).[22] Two themes continue emphatically in the section; namely, love and suffering. The love of God towards the community of Jesus followers demonstrated through the act of God giving up his Son for the sake of the community or the elect and the Son died, was raised, is now sitting on the right-hand side of God and is interceding for the community (8:31–34).

Although vv. 31–34 do not explicitly say anything about the suffering of the community, it seems that there is an accusation against the community as Paul rhetorically questions, "Who is against us?" "Who shall bring charge against God's elect?" Jewett speculates that Paul might be defending his own experience of suffering and that of the Jewish Jesus followers who were evicted from Rome against triumphalist believers who think that true discipleship does not entail suffering and suffering disqualifies and divorces one from Christ.[23]Although there might be such an attitude towards those who are suffering in Rome, it is not evident either in the wider 8:1–39 or the immediate 8:18–39 context of vv. 31–39. For instance, Paul uses children (vv. 14, 16), sons (also daughters) (vv. 15, 19, 23), those who love God (v. 28), God's elect (v. 33) and if one follows the RSV translation, the inclusive first-person plural pronoun occurs 21 times within 8:18–39. It is hard to imagine that Paul is defending a particular group within the Roman congregation. Instead, he is portraying what it means to share the suffering of Christ in order to share his glory as the followers of Jesus.

If this analysis is granted, v. 35 explicitly connects love and suffering: "Who shall separate us from the love of Christ?" (τίς ἡμᾶς χωρίσει ἀπὸ τῆς ἀγάπης τοῦ Χριστοῦ). Commentators have noted that ἡμᾶς is grammatically in an emphatic position and indicates that Paul is referring

21. *Erotesis* is "(an interrogation with animated questions) in affirmative negation, in which the questions are put in the affirmative, but the answers must be supplied by the audience in the emphatic negative" (Jewett, *Romans*, 533).

22. Jewett, *Romans*, 533.

23. Jewett, *Romans*, 548.

to what he experienced.[24] With respect to the phrase, τῆς ἀγάπης τοῦ Χριστοῦ, the majority of commentators read it as subjective genitive, that is the love of Jesus for the Jesus followers.[25]

However, this reading is not convincing at all. First, the context of 3:8–39 evinces that suffering and glory are intertwined as typified in the death of Christ and his resurrection. Within this context, love is one of the elements Paul repeatedly discusses. Rom 8:28 evinces that the love of Jesus followers is demonstrated in the endurance in different sufferings and challenges they experienced as Jesus followers. Particularly, πάντα primarily refers to the suffering, challenges and troubles that the Jesus followers experience because of being part of the community of Jesus, or as it is stated in 8:18, that they share the suffering of Christ. As argued earlier, the text refers to both directions backwards, referring to the general as well as the specific suffering of the children of God and to the forward reference to the benefit and the suffering that Jesus followers will experience. The positive end implies that what the community passes through is negative, which works to the positive end.

Second, reading vv. 29–34 reveals that God's purpose and actions are a demonstration of God's love. God's purpose is expounded from vv. 29–30 while God's action is claimed in vv. 31–34. In the latter section both God and Christ are involved in justifying the Jesus followers: God gave his Son (aorist tense) and justifies (present participle), whereas Christ died, was raised, and intercedes (present tense). Both sections imply the love of God, but the second part in particular, speaks volumes about the love of God who justifies the ungodly and Christ who died for the ungodly and repeats the theme of 5:1–11 in a graphic manner.

If this is so, the next section vv. 35–39 deals with the suffering, picking on three words mentioned in the first section of vv. 29–34: ὑπὲρ ἡμῶν/ against us/ (v. 31), ἐγκαλέσει /bring charge/ (v. 33) and κατακρινῶν / condemn/ (v. 34). The words might refer to outsiders who are opposing the community of Jesus followers. In the next verses Paul appears to be providing examples of what those oppositions, accusations or condemnations look like. He might as well be referring to ontological accusations such as the wrath of God in the last days if Rom 5:9, 10 is kept in view, especially as 8:18 compares the present time with the coming of

24. Dunn, *The Theology of Paul the Apostle*, 504; Cranfield, *Romans*, 1:439; Jewett, *Romans*, 543

25. Jewett, *Romans*, 543–48; Cranfield, *Romans*; Dunn, *Romans 1–8*; Hultgren, *Romans*; Murray, *Romans*, 330.

the revelation of the glory. Nonetheless, the immediate context related to suffering makes more sense than the former.

Third, Paul's catalogue of suffering and citation of the Old Testament in v. 36 substantiates that the community of Jesus followers is suffering for God's and Jesus' sake. Jewett have observed that "for your sake" refers to the cause of the suffering of the community.[26] He argues "for your sake" is in the emphatic position and reveals that the suffering of the community is for Christ's sake and the list of suffering is not a rhetorical ploy but a list of genuine issues.[27] Cranfield commented that Paul himself experienced all the suffering he listed except the last one, which is the sword.[28] The suffering listed in v. 35, according to Dunn, is "evidence of union with the crucified one, not a cause for doubting his love."[29] If this is granted, then it is logical to conclude that Paul and the community of Jesus followers encounter suffering for the sake of God and his Christ.

In light of the above analysis, there is neither thematically nor linguistically compelling reason to interpret τῆς ἀγάπης τοῦ Χριστοῦ in v. 35 as subjective genitive. First, Paul moves from discussing the love of Jesus followers towards God (v. 28) to the Love of God towards Jesus followers (vv. 32–34) then to the love of Jesus followers towards Jesus (vv. 34–36) and finally to the love of God towards Jesus followers (vv. 37–39). Second, the love of Jesus followers towards God, as argued above, discussed within the context of suffering and πάντα in v. 28 refers to suffering, therefore v. 35 enumerates specific kinds of suffering that the community of Jesus followers may encounter. The community has actually faced such challenges *for the sake of God and his Christ*; therefore, the logical conclusion would be that the list of this suffering is the experiences of the community which demonstrates their love to God and Christ. Hence v.35 must be interpreted as an objective genitive as "who separates us from our love towards Christ?"

If the subjective genitive is taken in v. 35 the meaning is confusing and the interpretation is forced because τίς (v. 35), translated as "who" does not fit in the listing of suffering; Jewett has proposed that "what" must be added.[30] If this is so, the lists are regarded as answers to what might possibly separate the Jesus followers from the love of Christ. The

26. Jewett, *Romans*, 548.

27. Jewett, *Romans*, 548.

28. Cranfield, *Romans*, 1:440.

29. Dunn, *Romans 1–8*, 504.

30. Jewett, *Romans*, 543.

objects of the suffering are the followers of Jesus who are negatively affected and challenged by them, not Jesus being affected by the suffering. Therefore, it is not the love of Jesus expressing itself in the suffering. One might argue that the text is speaking of the love of Jesus expressing itself in caring for the suffering ones. This reasoning has five fallacies.

Firstly, the text does not promise the evading of sufferings but encourages facing them steadfastly as has noticed.[31] Secondly, this reading portrays Jesus followers as passive and forced followers of Jesus not as respondents of love for what they have received in vv. 29–34. Thirdly, it contradicts the interpretation of v. 36. Jewett, Dunn, Cranfield, and others have interpreted this verse as the suffering of Jesus followers for the sake of God and his Christ.[32] What does it mean "for the sake of him" in v. 36, unless it means "because they love him"? Fourthly, if the subjective genitive is taken as love of Jesus to the Jesus followers, it implies that those suffering affect Jesus' love for his community. That is, they are capable of separating Jesus' love from the community as if the love that Jesus has for the community will be endangered because of the suffering the people experience. Jewett interpreted χωρίσει as "severance of personal relationships, as in divorce."[33] Why would Paul rhetorically question the faithfulness of Jesus' love after he argued that God loves even the ungodly (5:8)? Yet, Paul's understanding of the love of Christ does not depend on any condition as he died for the ungodly (5:8). Fifthly, the subjective reading is based on theological assumptions and predilections.

All the assumptions that wholly ascribe this love to Jesus come from a deeply entrenched persuasion that human beings are nothing and can do nothing because they are wretched, and whatever a person does in terms of relationship to God, is work. Therefore, "who separates us from the love of Christ?" in 8:35 is completely ascribed to Jesus loving the sufferer. But it is hard to imagine that those who are suffering are suffering not because of their love for Christ.

One example of evidence that seems to be strongly supporting the subjective reading of τῆς ἀγάπης τοῦ Χριστοῦ in v. 35 is διὰ τοῦ ἀγαπήσαντος ἡμᾶς /through him who loved us/ v. 37. Verse 37 is about the means or agency of victory. Jewett wrongly reads the verse as "the particular victory Paul has in mind is won through love rather than

31. Cranfield, *Romans*, 1:441.

32. Jewett, *Romans*, 543; Dunn, *Romans 1–8*, 504; Cranfield, *Romans*, 1:262.

33. Jewett, *Romans*, 543.

competition."[34] The text does not say it is through love that they win the suffering, but through a person—Jesus Christ. The participle ἀγαπήσαντος identifies ἡμᾶς /him/ through his character and ἀγαπήσαντος is an aorist participle and refers to a single act of love in the past. Therefore, this verse does not convey continuous action but refers to the cross, especially 5:8 and 8:32–34. God's love is manifested on the cross therefore the love that defines Christ is the love demonstrated one time on the cross. Therefore, τοῦ ἀγαπήσαντος ἡμᾶς does not specifically refer to v. 35 but rather it refers to the entire work of Jesus. Similarly, v. 39 refers to the love of God revealed through the sacrificial death of Jesus (8:32–34).

Love in Chapter 8 is not one-sided. It is not only God loving the believers but the believers loving God and expressing this love by enduring suffering for the sake of Christ and God (8:36). The role of the Spirit is prominent. The Jesus followers are in the realm of the Spirit and freed from condemnation and bondage (8:1–7), filled with the love by the Spirit (5:5), in the hope of future glorification with Christ. At present, they share the suffering of Christ (8:17) not because they are forced to, but because they love him through the love they received from the Spirit.

The love Paul is ascribing to the Jesus followers in 8:28 has to do with their response *in obedience to God despite the adverse situation* they are experiencing. Perceiving love in terms of relationship, Mounce contends, "a vital ongoing love is a necessary prerequisite for his [God's] intervention in the affairs of our life."[35] For Mounce, love is a two-sided phenomenon: God calls and man responds.[36] Scholars such as Cranfield, Dunn, and Jewett have also shown that loving God as a response in one's entire being to God's revealed love has a rich background both in the Old Testament and in the Jews' background.[37] Therefore, given the context of 8:28, *love is maintaining the relationship with God despite adverse situations and challenges that hinder Jesus followers from walking in the Spirit, in order that the just requirement of the Law might be fulfilled* (8:4, 5, 12, 13, and 14). *Love therefore is an active obedience of faith (1:5) to the teaching of the Gospel (6:17) or it is walking in the Spirit in order to please God (8:8) even in the midst of suffering and challenges.*

34. Jewett, *Romans*, 549.

35. Mounce, *Romans*, 188.

36. Mounce, *Romans*, 188.

37. Cranfield, *Romans*, 1:425; Dunn, *Romans 1–8*, 481; Jewett, *Romans*, 526.

Romans 12:9

Romans 12:1—15:13 is usually taken as one of the major blocks of the letter dealing directly with obedience to a righteous life. Romans 12 particularly calls for committing oneself to the service of God. It can be divided into three sections: 12:1–2, 3–8 and 9–21. Rom 12:1–2 sets out the main theme for the whole chapter and even probably for 13, 14, and 15. The word *παρίστημι* reconnects to the theme of Romans 6 where the word is used five times in connection to obedience and Romans 12 develops it further. Romans 12:3–8 describes the ideal Jesus followers' community corporately as well as individually as one body and individual members having a particular function within the body. Romans 12:9–21 attends to specific injunctions on the matter of relationship. Walter T. Wilson who studied the gnomic feature of 12:1–21 contends that 12:9–12 is not only dealing with the relationship of Jesus followers among themselves but also their relationship with people outside their community, even with respect to their enemies.[38] Cranfield also argues that 12:9–13 is concerned with Jesus followers' relationship among themselves, whereas 12:14–21 deals with their relationship with outsiders.[39] Granting this, then 12:9–21 prescribes a righteous life within and outside the community of Jesus followers.

However, although the significant place of 12:9 is recognized, its internal structure is debated. Cranfield rejects the possible connection of v. 9a to 9b and 9c, insisting that it is unnatural to separate the two participle clauses from the other participles, therefore, they are loosely connected.[40] However, Wilson has shown that Ἡ *ἀγάπη ἀνυπόκριτος* serves as a thesis and the verses that follow can be incorporated under it.[41] Wilson also contends that the imperative participles are not true participles and should not be read as real imperatives, reasoning that Paul employed a mixed style: Semitic or Jewish tradition of imperative participle and his own rhetorical representation organizing them under three major themes: vv. 9b–13, 16a–b, and 17–19a.[42] Organizing participles in such a manner intensifies the interconnectedness of the sayings and the

38. Wilson, *Love Without Pretense*, 131.

39. Cranfield and Sanday, *Romans*, 2:629.

40. Cranfield and Sanday, *Romans*, 2:631.

41. Wilson, *Love Without Pretense*, 150. See also Mounce, *Romans;* Dunn, *Romans 9–16;* Jewett, *Romans*; Nygren, *Romans.*

42. Wilson, *Love without Pretense*, 161–62.

dependence of the imperatival participle to other participles in the section.[43] If Wilson's argument that Ἡ ἀγάπη ἀνυπόκριτος (12:9) is a thesis statement for the 12:9–21 then the verses that follow describe the features of Ἡ ἀγάπη ἀνυπόκριτος.

According to Wilson, Ἡ ἀγάπη ἀνυπόκριτος is a definition of love.[44] Jewett proposes adding a copula between the noun and the adjective.[45] If the copula is added then the adjective is a predicative adjective and asserts the quality or the feature of the noun—love is without pretension. Alternatively, it could also be possible to bring the adjective to the attributive position—unpretentious love. In both cases, the adjective clearly states that love can be pretended. If this is so, then the nature of ἀγάπη is subjective and can be counterfeited. The term ἀνυπόκριτος is derived from υπόκριτης which means "actor." Jewett believes that it contains an implicit warning against pretension.[46] Luther had already pointed out the danger. He writes, "For just as nothing ought to be more free of dissimulation than love, so nothing can be more polluted by dissimulation than love. Nothing so shrinks from dissimulation as love, and nothing suffers so much from dissimulation as love."[47]

Thus, ἀνυπόκριτος raises a serious question about the nature of love. In fact, as Cranfield has observed, up until 12:9 divine love is used.[48] However, this does not necessarily mean that 12:9 is devoid of divine love. In 5:5, Paul already informed the audience that divine love had been poured into the hearts of the Jesus followers. The statement "let love be without pretense" implies the existence of love in the community.[49] In the previous section, Paul discussed love in the context of suffering and love to God and God's love to his people. Here it is love to other fellow members within the community of Jesus followers and to outsiders. Paul's concern is not lack of love but pretentious love. Love's true motive can only be known by the person who is either pretending or genuinely practicing it. Therefore, *so long as love is subjective, it is not a dependable character when practiced by fellow believers unless its true nature is defined*

43. Wilson, *Love without Pretense*, 162.
44. Wilson, *Love without Pretense*, 151.
45. Jewett, *Romans*, 756.
46. Jewett, *Romans*, 759.
47. Martin Luther, *Luther's Works*, 451.
48. Cranfield and Sanday, *Romans*, 2:631.
49. Wilson, *Love Without Pretense*, 155.

with restrictive contents. If this is granted, in 12:9b–21 Paul is restricting and giving content to real love.

In 12:1 Paul picks up the theme of παρίστημι which he left off in Romans 6:13, 15, and 19. Paul urges the followers of Jesus to present their bodies within the image of a sacrifice which harks back to 3:25 and 5:8–10. The sacrifice of Christ Jesus, the demonstration of God's love, is related to solving the problem created by sin and sin itself. So also, the call for the community of faith to present their bodies as a sacrifice is related to overcoming the world of sin (12:1–2) and serving the community of Jesus followers (12:3–8) and loving both insiders and outsiders (12:9–21). Hence, ἀγάπη is the community presenting its body as a holy sacrifice to God.

But such a sacrifice must be accompanied by a transformed mind which is able to discern the will of God. Wilson argues that ἀγάπη is "not a mere given but must be discerned with the correct understanding."[50] Thus, ἀγάπη must be discerned whether it is pretentious or based on its restrictive content. The contents are enumerated in 12:9b–21. The list includes abhorring evil, clinging to good, respecting one another, being zealous for God, serving God, enduring tribulation, continuously praying (e.g., 15:30), blessing the opponents, sharing others' joy and suffering, relating to one another in humility, avoiding revenge, thinking what is noble, living peacefully with others, overcoming evil with good (12:9–21), and abrogating one's right for the sake of another (14:15). If Wilson's argument that 12:9 is a "thematic statement and protreptic maxim" stands, the list reveals that ἀγάπη *is an intelligible, conscious and deliberately chosen act of Jesus followers in accordance with the revealed will of God towards fellow believers and enemies.*

Thus, love in 12:9 is the love of Jesus followers towards their fellow believers and outsiders. It is one of the means of presenting the body as a holy and living sacrifice to God. However, it is subjective and can be pretended unless otherwise directed by restrictive content enumerated by Paul. The content evinces that love towards fellow believers and outsiders is a deliberate and intellectual choice and an act of obedience to the instruction of God.

50. *Wilson, Love Without Pretense,* 155.

Section Summary and Conclusion

The topical progression of ἀγάπη *reveals that love is an act of obedience through a deliberate* and *intellectual choice based on the understanding of the content of the Gospel and the specific commandments of God.* In Rom 5:5 God is the source of love through the Holy Spirit indwelling in the hearts of the Jesus followers being modelled by the obedient sacrifices of God's Son (5:8). God's love for the Jesus followers and Jesus followers' love for God cannot be separated because through the mediation of the Spirit the love that dwells in the hearts of the believers responds to God's love to them by maintaining the relationship in adverse and life-threatening situations (8:28–31). Similarly, love for fellow believers and outsiders is also an extension of love for God and it expresses itself despite all negative conditions. For Paul, love is subjective and could be pretended unless it is restricted with content. The content is the sacrificial act of God towards the sinners expressing itself in the obedience of Jesus Christ to the point of death, and the specific commandments Paul has enumerated in 12:9–21.

Topical Progression of νόμος in Romans

The term νόμος occurs seventy-four times in four forms and ἁμαρτία occurs forty-eight times in seven forms in the letter to the Romans. Such prolific occurrence of the words indicates that the Law and sin are the two most important topics in Romans. In most cases, both words occur together and are discussed with respect to one another particularly in 5:12–21, 6:14–15 and 7:1–25. But managing such vast data demands choosing a suitable approach and establishing points that create a convenient platform for the interpretation of the data.

Klyne Snodgrass submits that interpreting the Law in terms of sphere of influence solves the problem of Paul's treatment of the Law.[51] Different conclusions on the place of the Law in Pauline theology are symptomatic of lack of a governing theory. Of course, no single theory can be a panacea for solving the difficulty posed by Paul's treatment of the subject. But "a holistic view of Paul's theology of participation in Christ" seems to be promising. Snodgrass argues that forensic and participatory theories are not mutually exclusive. Rather, the forensic terms are better understood "in the participationist language" as that "one is justified

51. Porter, *Pauline Writings*, 154–74.

only *in* Christ."[52] For Paul, salvation is a transfer from "one sphere of Lordship to another" which basically assumes "'spheres of influence' or 'power fields.'"[53] Such theoretical framework deemed to be promising to yield a positive result. It is therefore adopted to analyze the data under investigation.

In addition to the need for a particular approach, other important points must be established: clear points about the Law, Paul's style of treating topics in Romans, and point of departure for analyzing the data. Snodgrass provides eight points but only three are relevant for the data under question: (1) Paul never undermined obedience to the will of God, (2) for Paul the center of gravity is Christ, (3) Paul's letters are situational and therefore do not systematically discuss the Law; they are coherently presented. The third point is relevant to Paul's style of treating the topic of the Law.[54]

In Romans, Paul gives a snippet of introduction on a theme either with a brief treatment or with a rhetorical question. He returns to treat that specific point at length at a later stage of the letter. Such style is discernable such as 3:1–9 is detailed in 9–11, and 3:31 is detailed in 7–8, and 5:3–5 is detailed in 8:18–39, and 5:20 is detailed in 7:7–13, and 6:12–13 is detailed in 12:1–21. Paul's discussion on the topic of the Law follows a similar trend; thus, analysis of the data in question commences with its short introduction and follows through to its fuller discussion.

Νόμος, except its concept, is introduced for the first time in 2:12–13. In this section alone, it occurs five times as ἀνόμως (twice), ἐν νόμῳ, διὰ νόμου, οὐ οἱ ἀκροαταὶ νόμου, and οἱ ποιηταὶ νόμου introducing the topic of the Law with opposing polarities: ἀνόμως vs. ἐν νόμῳ and οὐ οἱ ἀκροαταὶ νόμου vs. οἱ ποιηταὶ νόμου. Dunn has also observed that Paul did not use these contrastive forms as an *ad hoc* introduction.[55] Unfolding discussions on the topics are discernible at the subsequent stages of the letter.

For instance, Romans 1:18—2:11 describe and analyze mainly those who have sinned without the Law (ἀνόμως) and will perish or die[56] without the Law and 5:12–14 partially continues describing a similar concept. If ἀνόμως (2:12) is parallel to 2:14 "who do not have the Law"

52. Porter, *Pauline Writings*, 161.

53. Porter, *Pauline Writings*, 161.

54. Porter, *Pauline Writings*, 158–61.

55. Dunn, *Romans 1–8*, 1:95.

56. Jewett, *Romans*, 210.

(τὰ μὴ νόμον ἔχοντα)[57] then its meaning in the first part of 2:12a (all who have sinned without the Law . . .) should be "without the *possession* of the Law." Nonetheless, the latter part of the sentence 2:12b (. . . will also perish without the Law) conveys a slightly different meaning, that is, judgment will take place without *using* the Law. Granting this, then Paul develops the topic of both meanings in the letter with other expressions such as χωρὶς νόμου (3:21), χωρὶς ἔργων νόμου (3:28), χωρὶς ἔργων (4:6), οὐκ ἔστιν νόμος (4:15), ἄχρι νόμου (5:13), μὴ ὄντος νόμου (5:13), χωρὶς νόμου (7:8), and χωρὶς νόμου (7:9).

On the other hand, ἐν νόμῳ means within the law[58] or "under the Law" (RSV) and refers to those who have the Law. If the RSV translation is granted, then Paul employs the same as well as a slightly different phrase in his ensuing discussion: ἐν τῷ νόμῳ (2:20), ἐν νόμῳ (2:23), ἐν τῷ νόμῳ (3:19), and ὑπὸ νόμον (6:14 and 15). However, the phrase is sporadic in the sense that the discussion is not concentrated and completed in one section of the letter appearing in 2:17–24; 3:1–9; 4; 7:1–25; and 10:1–13.

Next, οὐ οἱ ἀκροαταὶ νόμου (not the hearers of the Law) contrasted with οἱ ποιηταὶ νόμου (the doers of the Law) (2:13) also introduces another group. The former most probably refers to the Jews who hear the Law but do not obey it. Insofar as the statement is generic, it may not refer to the Jews in their entirety, who have the Law but particularly to those who hear it but do not practice it. The latter is inclusive, the Jews and the Gentiles who observe the Law, for the statement is also generic and 2:14 claims that those without the Law observe it. The discussion of οὐοἱ ἀκροαταὶ νόμου in the ensuing section of the letter overlaps with the discussion of ἐν νόμῳ; οἱ ποιηταὶ νόμου gets attention at 2:14–15; 2:25–28; 3:27–31; 8:1–11 and 13:8–10.

John Gager rightly said one's choice of departure determines the result or "the end depends on the beginning."[59] For instance, a study might start with Rom 3:31 or Rom 10:4 depending on one's predilection. However, the *topical progression approach* forces the study to give equal attention to the appearance of the concept without being eclectic and such are the ways in which the progression of νόμος will be analyzed in this chapter, starting the discussion from where Paul explicitly starts discussing it. Hence, in light of the above discussion, 2:12–13 introduces

57. Dunn, *Romans 1–8*, 95.

58. Dunn, *Romans 1–8*, 95–96.

59. Gager, *The Origins of Anti-Semitism*, 204–5.

and roughly outlines the topic of νόμος embedding the meaning that is waiting to be unpacked in the ensuing body of the letter. Therefore, these verses serve as a point of departure and outline for the analysis of the data on the Law *without attempting to harmonize* them. The investigation and analysis will be processed as the data lends itself to the meaning in context: first, ἀνόμως and χωρὶς νόμου (without the Law), then ἐν νόμῳ and ὑπὸ νόμον (under the Law), and finally οἱ ποιηταὶ νόμου (doers of the Law) will be analyzed from the standpoint of sphere of influence as conceptual interpretive framework.

ἀνόμως and χωρὶς νόμου—without the Law

Rom 2:12a ὅσοι γὰρ ἀνόμως ἥμαρτον, ἀνόμως καὶ ἀπολοῦνται

Rom 3:21a Νυνὶ δὲ χωρὶς νόμου δικαιοσύνη θεοῦ πεφανέρωται

Rom 3:28b λογιζόμεθα γὰρ δικαιοῦσθαι πίστει ἄνθρωπον χωρὶς ἔργων νόμου

Rom 4:15b ὁ γὰρ νόμος ὀργὴν κατεργάζεται: οὗ δὲ οὐκ ἔστιν νόμος, οὐδὲ παράβασις

Rom 5:13a ἄχρι γὰρ νόμου ἁμαρτία ἦν ἐν κόσμῳ

Rom 5:13b ἁμαρτία δὲ οὐκ ἐλλογεῖται μὴ ὄντος νόμου:

Rom 7:8b χωρὶς γὰρ νόμου ἁμαρτία νεκρά.

Rom 7:9a ἐγὼ δὲ ἔζων χωρὶς νόμου ποτέ

The data is complex, for a number of reasons. Firstly, the texts appear in different places as part of a sentence. It is hardly possible to analyze them without their specific context. Doing a detailed analysis of each *section is not the purpose here* but the *aim is to get cumulative evidence* for the analysis of Rom 13:8–14. Secondly, the data uses different words which might connote different meanings depending on the context: χωρὶς, οὐκ, ἄχρι, and μὴ. But each context will be given careful attention in the course of the analysis. Notwithstanding the complexity and vastness of the data, an attempt will be made to extrapolate the result by treating the texts *without attempting to harmonize them.*

Thirdly, the texts in the data occur at different stages of Paul's argument. Yet, structuring the argument of the letter has never produced a 'one does it all' structure. Nonetheless, most scholars agree that the letter can be divided into seven sections: 1:1–17; 1:18–3:20; 3:21–4:25; 5:1–8:39; 9:1–11:36; 12:1–15:13; 15:14–16:23 and 16:25–27. The data in question occurs in three blocks 1:18–3:20; 3:21–4:25; 5:1–8:39. Each block assumed to have an overarching topic that it undertakes, but this does not mean that Paul has offered a systematic presentation of his theology. Rather, he introduces an idea and comes back later to unfold it. Hence, the analysis of the data under consideration mainly follows topical as well as conceptual connections and development within the wider and immediate context of the texts rather than a literary structure of the letter.

Romans 2:12a: The Existence of Sin and Death

Νόμος occurs nineteen times as a central theme of 2:12–29. In 2:12a, it occurs as *ἀνόμως*. The word *ἀνόμως* has different meanings depending on the context—1 Cor 9:12; Mark 15:28; Luke 22:37; Acts 2:23, 1 Tim 1:9; 2 Thess 2:8; and 2 Pet 2:8. Whereas Thayer defines it (2:12a) as "without knowledge of the Law" or ignorance of the Law,[60] LN (33.57) defines it (2:12a) as "without the Law" that is "pertaining to being without the Law (specifically the first five books of the OT)." LN considers the context of the word in 1 Cor 9:21 and defines it as "not being under the obligation of the law or not being bound by the Law." LN notes that the phrase in Rom 2:12 must not be interpreted as "lawless" or "heedless of the law"; rather it refers to "those who are ignorant of the law and thus not bound by it."

Stowers defines *ἀνόμως* as "lawless," although he admits that Isocrates' *Paneguricus* 39 uses it in the sense of without the Law or lack of possession of the Law.[61] For him, it means living in a lawless manner. But Stowers's interpretation is rejected. First, Jewett observes that *ἀνόμως* is closely related to "Jewish definition of non-Jewish" and used only once in LXX 2 Macc 8:17 in reference to lawless.[62] Second, Rom 2:12 compares two groups of people based on their relationship to the Mosaic Law.[63] Basing his analysis on *ἐν νόμῳ*, Michael Winger consents that *ἀνόμως* refers to the Mosaic Law, although he is hesitant whether *νόμος* refers to Judaism or not.[64] Contextually, *ἀνόμως* must refer to the

60. Thayer, *A Greek-English Lexicon of the New Testament*, 48.

61. Stowers, *A Rereading of Romans*, 134–420.

62. Jewett, *Romans*, 210.

63. Dunn, *Romans 1–8*, 96; Schreiner, *Romans*, 118; Jewett, *Romans*, 210; Das, *Paul, the Law, and the Covenant*, 178; Moo, *Romans*, 145.

64. Winger, *By What Law?* 9–80.

Mosaic Law particularly because the second half of 2:12 contrasts the standard with which the judgment will be carried out—*διὰ νόμου*—for those who sinned under the Law. Further, 2:14 explicitly states that the Gentiles *μὴ νόμον ἔχοντα* (do not have the Law).

Yet, Sandy and Headlam argue that the anarthrous *νόμος* refers to a general Law.[65] It is Paul's custom to use an article before *νόμος* when referring to the Mosaic Law hence the absence of an article is an indication of reference to a general Law. It is further argued that when the article is missing, it is referring to "qualitative" *νόμος*.[66] Burton thinks when Paul uses *νόμος* without an article, he is thinking not as Old Testament system but as the character of the Law.[67] Winger rejects this reading not least because Greek has no fixed rule on usage of its article because they are omitted after prepositions and of 47 occurrences of *νόμος* in Pauline literature, 35 occurrences lack the article.[68] Therefore, one cannot agree more with Cranfield, "It is safe to assume that in Paul's epistle *νόμος* refers to the OT law unless the context clearly shows this to be impossible."[69]

Does "without the Law" mainly refer to ignorance of the Law or lack of possession of the Law? Thayer's definition emphasizes the knowledge of the law whereas LN's emphasizes the lack of the possession of the Law (see above). Paul seems to be emphasizing the possession of the Law though he is also in view of knowledge of the Law (Rom 2:17–24). Obedience to the Law does not necessarily depend on the possession of the Law (Rom 2:14–15). Nor does possession of the Law necessarily presuppose obedience to the Law (Rom 2:17–24). For Paul, possession of the law is neither a necessary nor a sufficient condition for obedience and judgment. If this is granted, then Paul is using "without the Law" primarily to refer to lack of the possession of the Law whereas knowledge of the Law is a subsidiary agenda though it is hard to separate one from the other.

Rom 2:12–13 concludes what is proceeding and introduces what is ensuing. Schreiner argues that 2:14–16 explains 2:12 because v. 12 is not complete and does not explain why the Gentile will perish.[70] Possibly vv. 14–16 explains v. 12, but 2:12–13 serves as a conclusive explanation to the impartial judgment of God argued in 1:18—2:11 and introduces the

65. Sanday and Headlam, *Romans*, 58.

66. Winger, *By What Law?* 45.

67. Burton, *Galatians*, 455.

68. Winger, *By What Law?* 45.

69. Cranfield, *Romans*, 1:0.

70. Schreiner, *Romans*, 119.

topic of the Law and sin.[71] First, Paul's statement at 2:12–13 is explicit in that those who are sinning *without the Mosaic Law* are *not sinning within the Mosaic Law*. Whether 2:14–16 is about sinning against conscience as pagan Gentile or as Gentile Jesus followers who have the Law written in their hearts does not change the meaning. The issue at the core is whether one is sinning outside or within the Mosaic Law and whether the judgment is in accordance with the Mosaic Law or not. Second, 2:14–16 does not explain 2:12–13 for it does not answer the question as to the state of the Law with respect to sin and death. Third, the judgment in vv. 14–16 is not according to the Mosaic Law, but God judges according to the Gospel of Paul through Jesus Christ (2:16). Although 2:14–16 is an immediate context for 2:12–13, it does not explain it. Therefore, it connects what is preceding and what is following.

According to 2:12a, two things can take place "without the Law": sin and death; ἁμαρτία appears here for the first time along with νόμος. The aorist tense (ἥμαρτον) used in terms of looking back from final judgment or as a reason for judgment. In the words of Dunn, "in the final judgment the whole life can be summed up as a single past event."[72]In a Greek infused Roman and Jewish environment the connotation of ἁμαρτία is to miss the mark, failure to meet the standard or it means to transgress.[73] If this definition can be sustained, then ἀνόμως ἥμαρτον means missing the standard without the Mosaic Law. Put differently, sinning without the Law is not missing the standard of the Mosaic Law. Likewise, ἀνόμως ἀπολοῦνται could mean perish without the standard of the Mosaic Law. Then, it follows that sin and death actively exist and function outside of missing the standard of the Law. Although the definition is attractive, it does not square with the evidence in Romans and therefore should be rejected.

What precisely does ἀνόμως ἥμαρτον mean? LN (283) provide three alternatives in their definition of ἁμαρτία: "sin," "being evil" and "guilt" applying to different contexts. Commentators used the word "sin" without giving adequate explanation. It needs to be explained as it is not connected to breaking any explicitly stated commandment in 2:12a. The meaning, therefore, must be decided based on Paul's usage of the word in Romans. In 3:9, Paul used πάντας ὑφ' ἁμαρτίαν for the first time in

71. Cranfield, *Romans*, 1:153.

72. Dunn, *Romans 1–8*, 96.

73. Jewett, *Romans*, 210; Dunn, *Romans 1–8*, 96

the entire NT. "Under sin" is interpreted as to be under the power of sin or under the control of sin.[74]It is not only power, but it is also individual human action as the catena of sin enumerated in 3:10–17.[75]

Further, Paul speaks of sin as reigning (5:21), enslaving (6:6, 17, 20) or ruling (6:12) by exercising Lordship (6:14). Sinners (ἁμαρτωλός) (5:8) are described as ἀσθενῶν (ἀσθενής) (5:6) that is morally weak LN (88.117) and parallels with ungodly (ἀσεβής) (5:6) and sinners (5:8). Yet, Paul describes the sin of Adam as τῆς παραβάσεως Ἀδάμ (5:14) but does not relate this transgression to the Law of Moses. If Paul understands sin as power that controls all humanity, then the traditional definition of sin as transgression of the Law of Moses or not meeting its standard cannot be sustained. The concept ἀνόμως ἥμαρτον does not mean to sin out of ignorance of the Law.[76] Nor does it derive from not having the Law. Rather it is an evil disposition that exists and functions outside of Mosaic Law and controls human's disposition. Therefore, 2:12a asserts that sin and death (judgment) occur outside of the Law and there is neither cause and effect nor intrinsic relationship between sin and the Law of Moses.

ROMANS 3:21, 28: RIGHTEOUSNESS WITHOUT THE LAW

In this section, two texts will be examined: 3:21 manifestation of God's righteousness without the Law and 3:28 without works of the Law.

χωρὶς νόμου δικαιοσύνη θεοῦ (3:21)

Romans 3:21–26 is taken as one of the key sections of the letter of Romans next to 1:16–17. A detailed discussion is beyond the purview of this analysis but only χωρὶς νόμου δικαιοσύνη θεοῦ will be discussed in light of its topical progression. The section starts with Νυνί and its function is understood to be either temporal,[77] a logical contrast with the preceding argument,[78] or both logical and temporal shift.[79] It is erroneous to exclude

74. Jewett, *Romans*, 258; Käsemann, *Romans*, 86

75. Dunn, *Romans 1–8*, 149.

76. Cranfield, *Romans*, 1:153–54.

77. Fitzmyer, *Romans*; Schreiner, *Romans*; Cranfield and Sanday, *Romans;* Moo, *Romans;* Cranfield, *Romans*, 1:201; Dunn, *Romans 1–8*, 164

78. Jewett, *Romans*, 272.

79. Barrett, *Romans*.

the logical connection insofar as Paul is developing his argument that justification is without works of the Law. He is contrasting justification by works of the Law against righteousness apart from the Law. Although it is not impossible that Paul is thinking in temporal terms, the emphasis and priority is on the works of the Law.

Scholars are divided over whether χωρὶς νόμου modifies πεφανέρωται[80]or if it modifies δικαιοσύνη θεοῦ.[81] The former reading is plausible because Paul is not declaring a new righteousness insofar as the Law and the prophets already witnessed about God's righteousness (3:21b). Instead, Paul is expounding the ways in which the righteousness of God is made public apart from the ways and manner of God's righteousness revealed in the Law.

The meaning of the righteousness of God, in fact, matters here: 1) the status or gift of righteousness;[82] 2) justifying activity of God that is God's intervening activity to deliver humanity;[83] 3) God's righteous attribute or his uprightness;[84] and 4) both his activity of righteousness and his righteous character.[85] It should be noted that Paul did not say the righteousness of God is dispensed or bestowed but it is manifested. Nonetheless, this does not necessarily mean the righteousness of God was hidden or unknown in the past.[86]But it means that now the manifestation of the righteousness of God is without the Law.

If the righteousness of God is the saving activity of God, and if it had been witnessed by the Law and the Prophets (3:21b) then there had been manifestation of God's saving activity through the Law among the Jews while they were under the Law. If this is the case, then what does manifestation of God's righteousness (χωρὶς νόμου) precisely mean? Moo correctly pointed out, "Paul's purpose is to announce the way in which God's righteousness has been manifest rather than to contrast two kinds of righteousness."[87] Yet, Moo has not stated what this means precisely.

Pointedly, χωρὶς νόμου means God himself acting outside of the realm of the stipulation of the Law, not man receiving the status of

80. Moo, *Romans*, 222. Jewett, *Romans*, 272. Cranfield, *Romans*, 1:201.

81. Murray, *Romans*; Mounce, *Romans*.

82. Schreiner, *Romans*. Murray, *Romans*, 1959; Dunn, *Romans 1–8*.

83. Moo, *The Epistle to the Romans*.

84. Fitzmyer, *Romans*, 1993.

85. Moo, *The Epistle to the Romans*. Barrett, *Romans*.

86. Meyer, *Romans*, 1:163.

87. Moo, *Romans*, 222.

righteousness by faith. There are key terms and concepts that are important to unfold, what Paul means without the Law: such as redemption in Christ Jesus (διὰ τῆς ἀπολυτρώσεως τῆς ἐν Χριστῷ Ἰησοῦ) (3:24), propitiation (ἱλαστήριον) (3:25), and in his blood (ἐν τῷ αὐτοῦ αἵματι) (3:25). *Redemption, propitiation and blood are the language of the Law and are the ways in which God revealed his righteousness* (his saving activities) under the Law and served as witness to the righteousness of God. Similarly, the prophets witnessed the coming of the Messiah (1:1–2). Yet Paul focuses on the sacrificial aspect of the Law, in the immediate context, in his explanation of the manifestation of the righteousness of the Law, rather than the promise. No explicit statement is stated in the Law (probably except the prophets, namely Isaiah 53) that God would send God's son in the likeness of sinful flesh and offer him as a sacrifice to manifest his righteousness. *The Law is against human sacrifice* (Lev 18:21; Deut 12:31; 2 Kgs 16:3; 2 Kgs 17:17). If this is granted, χωρὶς νόμου is not about how one gets status of righteousness before God without doing or fulfilling the requirements of the Law as Moo claims.[88] Nor does it mean that God abrogated the Law; rather it means that he did not use OT prescriptions for *redemption, propitiation and blood* for his salvific activity *from his side.*

χωρὶς ἔργων νόμου (3:28)

This concept (χωρὶς ἔργων νόμου) occurs only in 3:28 but it occurs as ἐξ ἔργων νόμου in 3:20, and the singular form τὸ ἔργον τοῦ νόμου in 2:15. The phrase appears only in these places of Romans where Paul extensively discusses God's impartial judgment and the sinfulness of both the Jews and the Gentiles. Romans 3:20a begins with the word διότι which links it with v. 19 introducing reason,[89] but γὰρ in 3:20b explains v. 20a. The Bultmann school believed that ἔργων νόμου refers to doing the Law and the very intent and attempt to do the Law is sin.[90] Those closer to Bultmann's position contend that ἔργων νόμου refers to doing good work to achieve salvation.[91] Other scholars, although rejecting Bultmann's thesis

88. Moo, "Israel and Paul in Romans 7:7–12," 222.

89. Jewett, *Romans*, 265.

90. Bultmann, *Theology of the New Testament*, 264; Hübner, *Law in Paul's Thought*, 113–24; Fuller, "Paul and the Works of the Law," 28–42; Käsemann, *Romans*, 89, 102–3.

91. ; Sanday and Headlam, *Romans*, 76, 94; Cranfield, *Romans*, 1:197–98; Nygren, *Romans*, 142–43, 162–65; Barrett, *Romans*, 70–71, 82–83; Leenhardt, *Romans*, 96–97, 108–11; Murray, *Romans*, 107, 122–23; Morris, *Romans*, 171, 185–87.

that the very attempt of doing good is evil, affirm that ἔργων νόμου refers to doing the requirements of the commandments of the Law but no one can keep them.[92] Still others think that ἔργων νόμου denotes keeping the rituals part of the Law.[93]

While Dunn, proponent of the NPP, affirms that χωρὶς ἔργων νόμου refers to the conduct prescribed by the Law, he insists that it also refers to a social and ethnic identity and formulates the definition of ἔργων νόμου as "privileged status *attested* and *maintained* by obedience to the Law"[94] (italics his) arguing that ἔργων νόμου is addressed to the Jews not to the Gentiles.[95] Dunn contends that 2:17–21 is not relevant to ἔργων νόμου because ἔργων νόμου is not related to breach of the Law[96]insofar as it refers to performing what the Law requires;[97] the role of the Law is not to produce justification but to create awareness of sin (3:20),[98] and ἔργων νόμου is associated with boasting in 3:27 because they think that God is only the God of the Jews,[99] and 4 QFlor. 1.1–7 deeds of the law refers to what distinguishes Qumran community from others.[100]Dunn concludes that Paul is against the Jews' assumption that status within the covenant ensures final acquittal and that disobedience to the commandments of God will not deter one from entering to the age to come because sacrificial cult dissolves the problem of sin.[101] Therefore, Paul's indictment is both disobedience to the Law and a boasting attitude towards the others.[102]

The RNPP–representatives such as Lloyd Gaston proposes an experiment approach and John Gager, reading νόμου as subjective genitive, argue that ἔργων νόμου is synonymous to the curse the Law brings to the non-Jews. It does not refer to commandments of the Law to be obeyed by someone. Rather it refers to what the Law produces (wrath and evil

92. Westerholm, *Israel's Law and the Church's Faith*, 120–21; Thielman, *From Plight to Solution*, 61–65; Moo, "'Law', 'Works of the Law', and Legalism in Paul," 208.

93. Wiles, *The Divine Apostle*, 67–69.

94. Dunn, *The New Perspective on Paul*, 23–25; Dunn, "Yet Once More—'The Works of the Law,'" 111.

95. Dunn, *The New Perspective on Paul*, 44;Dunn, "Yet Once More—'The Works of the Law,'"' 105

96. Dunn, *The New Perspective on Paul*, 45.

97. Dunn, "Yet Once More—'the Works of the Law,'" 109.

98. Dunn, *The New Perspective on Paul*, 47.

99. Dunn, "Yet Once More—'The Works of the Law,'" 110–11.

100. Dunn, "Yet Once More—'The Works of the Law,'"103.

101. Dunn, "Yet Once More—'The Works of the Law,'" 108.

102. Dunn, "Yet Once More—'The Works of the Law,'" 108.

things such as inciting sin in 7:10–11) when it encounters those who are outside of the covenant of the Jews and hence, Paul added Jesus for a means of salvation for them.[103]Gaston maintains that the judgment in Rom 2:17–19 refers only to a specific group of Judaizers who insist that Gentiles must convert to Judaism and keep the Law not to the Jews as a whole,[104] but the Law continues to be a means of salvation for the Jews. A number of scholars have shown the weakness of Gaston and Gager's interpretation, such as Thielman[105]hence no need of rehearsing. Nonetheless, Gaston–Gager's interpretation contributes to the fact that in no place in Romans has Paul urged the Jews to abandon the Law. Daniel Boyarin, on the other hand, while affirming the NPP position by arguing that *ἔργων νόμου* refers to the identity markers such as circumcision, kashruth, the observance of the Sabbath and the holidays, he contends that Paul is a Jewish cultural critic, a culture which is in tension between "ethnocenterism and universalist monotheism."[106] Boyarin divides the Law or *ἔργων νόμου* into literal and allegorical. But he argues for the allegorical approach that hermeneutically "Paul understood "works" as the material signifier of "faith," that is, his essentially allegorical appropriation of Scripture . . ."[107] However, there is hardly any convincing evidence that Paul is thinking the Law allegorically in Romans. Nanos understands *ἔργων νόμου* as referring to Jews' status (such as circumcision) which created Jews' ethnocentric exclusivism that "denied equal access to God's mercy for non-Jews . . ."[108] Basically, Nanos agrees with the NPP on the meaning of the *ἔργων νόμου*.

The major perpetuating problem with the traditional interpretation is imposing Christian soteriology upon first century Jewish understating of salvation. Paul is not castigating the Jews because they thought that they are sinners and wanted to be accepted before God by fulfilling the requirements of the Law. This does not emerge from Romans. Instead, what emerges from Romans particularly in 2:17 is that *a typical Jew thinks* that (1)'Ἰουδαῖος ἐπονομάζῃ (he is a Jew), (2) ἐπαναπαύῃ νόμῳ (he is resting in the Law) and (3) καυχᾶσαι ἐν θεῷ (he boasts in God). A typical Jew does not think of himself/herself as outside of God's people and hence

103. Gaston, *Paul and the Torah*, 100–107.

104. Gaston, *Paul and the Torah*, 138–39.

105. Thielman, *From Plight to Solution*, 1989, 123–24.

106. Boyarin, *A Radical Jew*, 36–37.

107. Boyarin, *A Radical Jew*, 36–37.

108. Nanos, *The Mystery of Romans*, 9, 11.

does not strive to be accepted before God as his people by keeping the commandments. On the contrary, a typical Jew boasts of his knowledge of God, discerns the truth, possesses the Law, claims the promise given to the fathers, and the glory (3:1; 9:4–5; 11:10). For a typical Jew, circumcision has advantage (3:1) because it is the seal or the sign of righteousness (4:11). A typical Jew believes in the God of Abraham with the same faith as Abraham, which is believing in one God (3:29–30). Paul is not claiming that Abraham believed in Jesus Christ and got righteousness, but that Abraham believed in one God and the promise God gave him is reckoned to him as righteousness (4:16–24). Jewish people share this faith and do not believe less. Therefore, Paul is not accusing the Jews of not having faith in God. But *Paul is arguing that the Jews did not believe in the Messiah like the Jesus followers do* (3:24–25) and did not accept Paul's argument that all have sinned and short of the glory of God (3:23). What emerges from Romans about the Jews is not that they are striving to please God so that they might be accepted and be saved, but they are confident that they are already accepted by God and need no other means of salvation.

Further, within the community of Jesus followers, it seems that the strong and the weak are judging one another (14–15). Paul did not ask the weak to leave their practices even though he sides with the strong, he warns the strong not to be obstacles to their brothers. Nor did he accuse them of trying to secure their salvation by keeping dietary law but affirms and encourages them to do it in the realm of faith in Christ. In light of this overall portrayal of the Jews in the letter, the proponents of the traditional reading downplay the historical and focus on the theological. It is hardly convincing to read ἔργων νόμου as a Jew striving to get acceptance before God.

Nor is it correct to think that Paul is contending that it is impossible to keep the Law. Neither is he limiting works of the Law to national identity. On the contrary, Paul argues that the commandments of *the Law must be obeyed because disobeying it dishonors God.* Keeping the commandment is related to honoring God among the Gentiles (2:24) not related to salvation or *just* keeping boundaries because the commandments of God are entrusted to the people of God who have already been recognized as God's people before the giving of the Law. Enduring in doing good works and seeking glory, honor and immortality rewards the Jews and Gentiles with glory, honor, peace, and eternal life (2:7, 10). The *content* of the good works is the commandments of the Law. All these dynamics of Paul's concept on work must be kept in view while interpreting ἔργων νόμου. Neither is the Law evil *per se* nor *does* evil, rather the Law is *good, holy* and *spiritual* (7:13–14). Therefore, ἔργων νόμου is an inclusive expression both obedience to the commandments and as an identity marker.

So χωρὶς ἔργων νόμου in 3:28 and ἐξ ἔργων νόμου should be interpreted as modified understanding of the new perspective that is as a reference to both the sociological exclusivism of ἔργων νόμου as well as obedience to the requirements of the Law. Entering salvation through Jesus Christ is not by ἐξ ἔργων νόμου yet staying in Christ in faith requires obedience. This concept will be developed later under the topical analysis of "The doers of the Law."

ROMANS 4:15B: NO LAW, NO TRANSGRESSION

Romans 4 is part of the second larger block of the letter—3:21–4:25. Its connection to Romans 3 is debated. Richard Hays argues that Paul seeks to demonstrate through the story of Abraham what it means to "uphold the Law," that is "righteousness through faith is prefigured in the Law."[109]Therefore, Paul shifts from "reading the Law as *commandment* to a reading of the Law as *narrative of promise.*"[110] (italics his). For Hays, the Law in Romans 4 is understood as a scripture. Although Paul uses the story of Abraham as hermeneutical center, he made a distinction between the Law and the promise (4:13–15). Paul does not attempt to discuss establishing the Law as Hays claims, not least because he still negatively speaks about the Law (4:13–15). Instead, he develops the argument that God is the God of the Jews and the Gentiles (3:30). And Abraham is the father of both the circumcised and the uncircumcised, and salvation is by faith. Note that Abraham's story and the promise are before the Law (without the Law). Paul makes it clear later in the letter that when he speaks of the Law, he *is speaking from the time of Moses onwards* (5:14). Therefore, Romans 4 is about the situation of the absence of the Law among the Jewish nation, not the upholding of the Law.

Paul uses an important phrase οἱ ἐκ νόμου (4:14) to describe the Jews. Different translations of the phrase are proposed but the literal

109. Dunn, *Paul and the Mosaic Law*, 160.

110. Dunn, *Paul and the Mosaic Law*, 160.

translation is much better, "those of the law."[111] The phrase should be understood in light of the context. Paul describes two nations: the circumcised (the Jews) and the uncircumcised (the Gentiles) (4:9). Another way of describing the Jews is οἱ ἐκ νόμου (those of the Law). Those translations that add a verb to the phrase do not do justice to the expression because the added verb would be theologically loaded. Paul is arguing that the promise is not only to those who are under the Law or in the sphere of the Law. But it is for both, for those outside of the Law and for those under the Law. Hence, the phrase οἱ ἐκ νόμου designates the Jews as those under the Law and does not describe their attitude or action towards the Law.

Paul argues that *the promise given to Abraham is outside of the realm of the Law*. The fulfilment of the promise does not require one to be among those who have the Law. However, Paul provides a difficult reason for his claim γὰρ νόμος ὀργὴν κατεργάζεται (4:15). It should be noted that Paul already identified to whom the Law belongs using the phrase οἱ ἐκ νόμου, that is, to the Jews who are under the Law. According to Godet and Chambers, and Dunn, the Law refers to the Law of Moses specifically to the circumcised not to the Gentiles.[112] In light of Paul's preceding argument, the Jews (2:17–24; 3:19) broke the Law and are under the wrath of God just as Gentiles are under the wrath of God (1:18–32). Paul argues that those who are of the Law are not better off than those who are without the Law because they are both under the wrath of God. *This implies that neither the wrath of God depends on the Law, nor the promise given to Abraham.*

Nonetheless, Paul asserts that the Law produces (κατεργάζεται) wrath which nullifies both faith and the promise if it qualifies the entitlement of the promise. The wrath is not against the Gentiles but against the Jews because the statement refers to the Jews. Paul is responding to the question, 'who is eligible to inherit the promise?' Against Moo, it is not the Law *per se* that produces wrath. Neither does it provoke God's wrath (*pace* Schreiner) for God's wrath exists before or outside of the Law (1:18–32; 5:12–14).[113] Paul's statement must be understood in light of 4:15b: where there is no Law there is no transgression (οὗ δὲ οὐκ ἔστιν νόμος, οὐδὲ παράβασις).

The clause "Where there is no Law. . ." refers to the absence of the Law in *the time of Abraham or to the state of Jews without the Law*. Jewett's arrangement of the enthymeme is much better than the solution proposed

111. Jewett, *Romans*, 326.

112. Godet and Chambers, *Romans*, 177; Dunn, *Romans 1–8*, 215.

113. Moo, *The Epistle to the Romans*, 276; Schreiner, *Romans*, 230.

by Murray and Moo as their arrangement simply focuses on the function of the Law rather than the question of who inherits the promise, which is the immediate concern of Paul.[114] Jewett suggests this arrangement: "first comes the law, then the transgression, then the response of divine wrath."[115] Granting this arrangement, first, the coming of the Law and the coming of the promise are separated. Second, it can be inferred that there was a time that the law does not exist (where there is no Law). Third, if the relative *ou–* is locative (where) as most translators hold, then it refers to the absence of the Law among the Jews. Although this reading could be accused of forced reading, the implication is not impossible. Fourth, the converse might also be true "where there is Law, there is transgression." Hence, transgression (παράβασις) implies the presence of the law, albeit not sufficient condition for God's wrath for the wrath of God happens without the Law.

Paul uses the word παράβασις (2:23, 4:15; 5:14) closely with the Law except in one place 5:14. LN (4794.36.28) defines παράβασις "to act contrary to the established custom or law, with the implication of intent." Cited examples are Matt 15:2; Luke 11:42; Acts 23:3; Rom 2:23. Romans 2:23 and 5:14 use the genitive form παράβασις. The derivative of παράβασις which is παραβάτης, is used in 2:25 and 27 referring to a person who breaks the Law. Specifically, the context of 2:23, 25, 27 and 4:15 is the Law. It might safely be said that παράβασις in this particular context is a violation of the Mosaic Law. However, in 5:14 "the transgression of Adam" (τῆς παραβάσεως Ἀδάμ) does not explicitly relate to any law unless Gen 2:16–17 is assumed behind it. Except for 5:14, it might be concluded that παράβασις refers to a violation of the Mosaic Law in the letter to the Romans.

However, there is one closely related word that needs to be addressed, namely: παράπτωμα. It occurs nine times in the letter and LN (4859: 88.297) defines it as "what a person has done in transgressing the will and law of God by some false step or failure." It is briefly defined as "sin." The word appears in 4:25; 5:15, 16, 17, 18, 19, 20; and 11:11, 12. Among these occurrences, only 5:20 is directly related to the Law. Contrary to Barrett, Cranfield contends that παράπτωμα and παράβασις cannot be synonyms in Chapter 5; rather παράπτωμα is equivalent to sin

114. Jewett, *Romans*, 327; Käsemann, *Romans*, 121; Murray, *Romans*, 143; Moo, *Romans*, 276–77.

115. Jewett, *Romans*, 327.

because Paul's focus is not on Adam's violation of a specific commandment.[116] Dunn also consents that παράπτωμα conveys a broader concept of sinning than παράπτωμα which specifically means a "deliberate breach of the law."[117] Jewett admits the comprehensive application of the word παράπτωμα stating that it addresses the violation of both Jewish and Greek infused Roman norms described in 1:18–3:25 as well as Adam's transgression (5:15–20).[118] Daniel Napier puts it this way: "all transgression is sin but not all sins are transgression."[119]

It can be concluded that both refer to sin but while παράπτωμα refers to a wider sinning within or outside of the Law, παράβασις conveys *mainly* sin committed against specific and explicit commandments. Particularly in Romans, 99% use of the word παράβασις is employed to convey the idea of violating the Mosaic Law. If this conclusion is correct, then οὗ δὲ οὐκ ἔστιν νόμος, οὐδὲ παράβασις does not refer to sins committed outside of the Law. Nor does it mean the absence of the Law is absence of God's wrath against sin, for God's anger has already been revealed against all inequity (1:18). Neither does it mean there is no sin if there is no Law. But it means that in the absence of the Law no penalty of sin incurred based on stipulation of the Mosaic Law, for no specific commandment is broken.

Romans 5:13a–14: The Reign of Sin and Death

Paul in 5:13a continues to argue that sin and death exist outside the Law. However, the place of 5:12–21 in the overall structure of the letter is debated and a full discussion of them is beyond the purview of this study. For some, it refers to 1:17–5:11 or concludes 1:18–5:21 (Sanday and Headlam, Stuhlmacher, Johnson, and Cranfield).[120]Others see it as the center of the entire letter.[121]Still others consider it as a digression.[122]Moo, however, argues for a both-side-connection.[123] He claims a specific con-

116. Barrett, *Romans*, 106. Cranfield, *Romans*, 1:284.

117. Dunn, *Romans 1–8*, 279.

118. Jewett, *Romans*, 343.

119. Napier, "Paul's Analysis of Sin and Torah in Romans 7:7–25," 20.

120. Sanday and Headlam, *Romans*, 131; Dunn, *Romans 1–8*, 271; Stuhlmacher, *Romans*, 83;Longenecker, *New Dimensions*, 301; Cranfield, *Romans*, 1:271.

121. Nygren, *Romans*, 207.

122. Klassen and Snyder, *Current Issues in New Testament Interpretation*, 153.

123. Moo, *Romans*, 315.

nection between 5:18–19 which is the condemnation of Adam and the central theme 1:18–4:25. The section also introduces concepts such as grace, the reign of death and sin as the power and the effect of the Law.

It appears that Paul is moving from the particular to general then to the particular; 5:12–21 might possibly be seen as a summative of the particulars discussed in the preceding section of the letter specifically from 1:18–5:11, albeit a closer connection is discernible between 5:1–11 and 2:12–21. Then, as Moo has suggested, it further introduces and develops the concept of sin and death (among others) as a sphere of power that dominates the life of humanity and the Jews' relationship to the Law. Undertaking a thorough analysis of the structure of 5:12–21, Hofius finds connection between 5:12–21 and the preceding discussion.[124] He has shown that ἀσεβής (5:6) and ἁμαρτωλῶν (5:8) are connected to πάντες ἥμαρτον (5:12) indicated in 3:23 and have already been expounded in 1:18—3:20. Therefore 5:12–21 "supplements and deepens what was said in 1:18—3:20."[125] Unrighteousness, wickedness, judgment of God, sin, death, the Law, faith, righteousness, and grace are introduced before 2:12—5:11. However, concepts such as sin, death and the Law introduced at 2:12–13 are not explained as to when sin started, why death incurred, when and why the Law is added and their relationship to humanity as a whole before 5:12–21. Hence, 5:12–21 picks up 2:12b and elaborates on them. In the next section of the study, data 5:13a (in light of what is preceding and following) shall be explored and analyzed.

It is worth noting that 5:12 asserts the entrance of sin and death into the world: ἡ ἁμαρτία είς κόσμον εἰσῆλθεν [δι' ἑνὸς ἀνθροωπου] and ὁ θάνατος [εἰῆλθεν] διὰ τῆσ ἁμαρτίας. No significant differences exist among scholars regarding the meaning of τὸν κόσμον. It is the world of humankind or human life[126] or the world of human existence and experience or to all the descendants of Adam.[127] Paul portrays sin as coming from another world and entering into the world of humankind through an agent—δι' ἑνὸς ἀνθρώπου. Many scholars identified "one man" as Adam of Gen. 3:1–24, albeit that there are differences of opinion on whether Adam should be understood as an historical or hypothetical figure.

Furthermore, 5:12a has only one verb εἰσῆλθεν and it means "to move into a space either two dimensional or three dimensional—"to

124. Dunn, *Paul and the Mosaic Law*, 178–79.

125. Dunn, *Romans 1–8*, 179.

126. Cranfield, *Romans*, 1:274.

127. Jewett, *Romans*, 374.

move into, to come into, to go into, to enter'" (LN15.93). It is used to describe a supernatural being entering an object in Mark 5:12. LN suggests that this use can be understood as grab, control, and command (LN 15.93). However, its meaning in Rom 5:12 is defined as "to happen, with the focus upon the initial aspect" (LN 13.110). In Paul's description, sin is personified but it does not necessarily mean he is using εἰσῆλθεν metaphorically, because first Paul separates sin temporally and experientially from Adam. The verb implies that Adam was living without experiencing sin sometime in the past. Second, from 5:21–7:25 onwards Paul describes sin as a real power that dominates human disposition therefore it appears as an entity. Third, the separation between the agent, Adam, and sin continued in Paul's description (5:21–7:25). Hence, the word εἰσῆλθεν does not speak of the beginning of sin. Nor does it speak of its coming to existence. But it speaks of its entrance as an entity into the life and nature of humankind. Although LN's definition of the term as initial or beginning might be possible but still it does not reflect the existence of sin before Adam experienced it. Paul might be thinking that sin had already existed in some kind of form in another sphere if he is thinking of the story of Genesis 3. Paul was most probably thinking of the word εἰσῆλθεν as Mark 5:12, that is, sin as an alien disposition infused into humankind affecting the fabrics of their character.

Likewise, θάνατος (death) became part of human experience through the entrance of sin. Death should not be confined to physical death.[128] But it is both spiritual and physical death incurred upon Adam and his pedigrees as judgment for sin. It is not sin *per se* that brought death but death is God's response to sin. That is, God alienated humankind from God as judgment, punishment, or condemnation, or reward for conjoining with sin (5:16, 18; 6:23; 7:9, 11).

In 5:12b Paul claims that death spread (ὁ θάνατος διῆλθεν) to all men. But the meaning of ἐφ' ᾧ πάντες ἥμαρτον is debated particularly the meaning of ἐφ' ᾧ is still under discussion, albeit Dunn's assertion of its settlement.[129] Johnson discusses five positions on the issue.[130] They can be subsumed under two major categories: (1) attributing antecedent to ᾧ a) νόμος[131] but rejected because νόμος is not mentioned prior to ἐφ' ᾧ;

128. Sanday and Headlam, *Romans*, 132–33; Murray, *Romans*, 1959, 181–82; Ziesler, *Romans*, 145.

129. Dunn, *Romans 1–8*, 273.

130. Longenecker, *New Dimensions*, 303.

131. Danker, "Romans v. 12," 424–39.

b) θάνατος,[132] it is rejected because it is redundant[133] and the phrase ἐφ' ᾧ is idiom elsewhere.[134] c) ἑνὸς ἀνθρώπου and ἐφ' understood as "in whom" (Augustinian reading) but in Pauline usage ἐφ' ᾧ could mean because (2 Cor 5:4), for which (Phil 3:12) or indeed (Phil 4:10) but not "in whom" and it is remote.[135]

(2) Explaining the function of ἐφ' ᾧ: (a) causal "because all sinned"[136] but different readings are assigned: "in that,"[137] or "in so far as."[138] A causal reading suggests two readings of the text: corporate sin verses individual sin. Corporate understanding is espoused by Luther.[139] But it is refuted because the verb ἥμαρτον refers to a voluntary action which individuals commit (2:12; 3:23).[140] Cranfield reads it as an individual sin because of corrupted nature,[141] but he is criticized for interpreting ἥμαρτον as corruption.[142] (b) Locative: ἐφ' ᾧ refers to the world in which humans commit sin.[143] Human beings are responsible for the spread of sin throughout the world.

(c) Consecutive: consecutive reading translates the phrase as "with the result that all sinned"[144] but not convincing because the example provided to substantiate this reading can also be translated as "upon the basis of which [death]."[145] Schreiner has proposed a logical consecutive connection to the idea of death, not a specific connection to death itself. In this reading, "all sinned" refers to individual sinning because all human beings born after Adam enter into the world alienated from God or spiritually dead humankind, therefore, all human beings sin. The

132. Stauffer, *New Testament Theology*, 270.

133. Longenecker, *New Dimensions*, 273.

134. Schreiner, *Romans*, 273.

135. Longenecker, *New Dimensions*, 304–5.

136. Moule, *An Idiom Book*, 50. Dunn, *Romans 1–8*, 273; Longenecker, *New Dimensions*; Moo, *Romans*, 333–41.

137. Wedderburn, "The Theological Structure of Romans v. 12," 350.

138. Englezakis, "Romans 5:12–15," 232.

139. Murray, *Romans*, 183; Ridderbos, *Paul*, 96–97; Longenecker, *New Dimensions*, 304–7.

140. Käsemann, *Romans*, 148–49; Fitzmyer, *Romans*, 417; Wedderburn, "The Theological Structure of Romans v. 12," 351.

141. Cranfield, *Romans*, 1:274.

142. Longenecker, *New Dimensions*, 311.

143. Jewett, *Romans*, 376.

144. Fitzmyer, *Romans* ; Mounce, *Romans*, 27:274.

145. Schreiner, *Romans*, 274.

objection that might be lodged against this position is that sin is the cause of death, not death the cause of sin.[146] However, it is counter argued that "the result of spiritual death is a lifestyle of sin."[147]

All the above readings have significant contributions to the understanding of the text, but not all are satisfying. Searching for possible antecedents did not tease out the problem, instead it yields significantly different meanings. Causal reading, although it arrayed the guild of scholars on its side, it does not adequately solve the question of why people individually sinning without the Law. It also minimizes the power of the result of sin. Paul has already claimed, "death reigned from Adam to Moses, even over those whose sins were not like the transgression of Adam . . ." (5:14) and "many died through one man's transgression . . ." (5:15). Here it is not sin that is emphasized, but death.[148] A locative reading cannot be sustained because what is spread is not sin, but death. While the consecutive reading is attractive, the logical consecutive reading proposed by Schreiner best explains the relationship of sin, death, and the Law. Paul argued that sin and death entered through one man (5:12ab). Sin produced alienation from God. Death spread to all persons through one person's action because of which they continue sinning not in the likeness of Adam (5:14) but of their individual volition.

Death as a ramification of the entrance of sin is assumed as power or king (ἐβασίλευσεν ὁ θάνατος) (5:14, 17). Portraying death as a king is uniquely Pauline because no parallel is found in Greek and biblical literature.[149]Jewett observes that in the Roman imperial context the word implies "irresistible coercive power."[150] Jewett notes that Paul is not speaking of death as an individual penalty but as a power determining one's destiny. The inevitability of death as a penalty to all humankind makes it powerful because death (both as spiritual and physical) as judgment has already been passed on Adam and his descendants (5:17). The irresistible power of sin has meaning only because it results in death and then dominates in the sphere of death. Sin without death (alienation from God) as penalty is powerless for it does not produce anything.

146. Byrne, *Romans*, 83.

147. Schreiner, *Romans*, 276.

148. Klassen and Snyder, *Current Issues*, 152; Dunn, *Romans 1–8*, 273; Garlington, *Faith, Obedience, and Perseverance's* 86; Byrne, *Romans*, 176

149. Jewett, *Romans*, 377.

150. Jewett, *Romans*, 377, 150.

Sin reigns in death (ἐβασίλευσεν ἡ ἁμαρτία ἐν τῷ θανάτῳ) (5:21). It is hard to decide the function of the preposition ἐν: spherical (sin reigns in the sphere of death), causal (death causes the reign of sin) or instrumental (sin used death to reign) or association (sin reigns along with death). Although spherical and causal reading presupposes the existence of death before sin, in view of the preceding analysis they make sense. True, sin must come first for death to happen because death is the result of the end of sin (6:21). However, sin and death are not described as king or dominant powers before they enter into the world. It is after the entrance of sin into the world that it resulted in death and then sin has become powerful. Death (as alienation from God) is God's judicial response to the act of sin which resulted in being a conducive sphere in which sin reigns and exerts its irresistible coercive power.

It can be concluded, then, that sin and death existed without the Mosaic Law. None of them were described as king or dominant coercive force before entering into the world of humankind. Nonetheless, the entrance of sin into the world through one person resulted in death (as alienation from God) which created a sphere where sin controls and dominates humankind. If this conclusion is granted, then 5:13a and 5:14a state that sin had been reigning and ruling humankind in the sphere of death (alienation from God) (5:15b) before the Law was given. Likewise, death had also been reigning in the sense of prevailing sphere where sin actively works (5:14a). Therefore, *sin and death function independently of the Law.*

Romans 5:13b: No Law, No Reckoning of Sin

Romans 5:13b is part of 5:12–14 and particularly closely tied to 5:13a but needs a closer analysis on its own right in connection with v. 13a. Some scholars contend that Paul is contradicting himself because on the one hand he says sin is not reckoned without the Law and, on other, he claims that people died because of sin without the Law.[151] However, v.13a must be read based on Paul's preceding argument in 2:12; 4:15; and 5:12. The conclusions of the analyzes of these verses have evinced the following relationship among sin, death and the Law: 1) sin and death exist, function and reign over all humankind independently of the Law. 2) The

151. Klassen and Snyder, *Current Issues*, 153–54; Hübner, *Law in Paul's Thought*, 81; Sanders, *Paul, the Law, and the Jewish People*, 35–36;Räisänen, *Paul and the Law*, 145–47; Ziesler, *Romans*, 131.

Law was given at a certain point in time to a specific people in a sphere where sin and death had already been reigning. 3) Transgression does not exist apart from commandment, breaking the specific commandments of the Law is considered as transgression.

Although no attempt will be made to harmonize the texts, Paul is virtually repeating 4:15 here in 5:13b.[152] First, his contention is that sin and death had already been in the world, and they were reigning with their power before the Law was given (5:12–14) *therefore the Mosaic Law has nothing to do with them*. Second, if the Law has nothing to do with sin and death, what is the role of the Law? It is to this question that Paul briefly comments in v. 13b. Third, the Law is given to specific people, not to all. *The name Moses excludes Gentiles by default*. Therefore, the *Jews before Moses, the promise and the Gentiles are outside of the Law*, albeit the reign of sin and death. Therefore, 5:13b must be read in light of these variables.

Dunn explains v. 13b as that Paul has in mind sin as individual accountable responsibility and sin as "given human character and social environment."[153] Both are included in ἁμαρτία as a comprehensive term and can be committed without and within the Law. Yet this reading does not account for the role of the Law in relation to sin and death. Räisänen's contention that the coming of the Law does not make any difference because people still die, must be taken seriously.[154] Räisänen, however, v. 13a does not state the condition of the coming of the Law, rather the condition of the absence of the Law. Nor does Paul argue that the Law has come to all human beings. Neither does he claim *that reckoning sin is a necessary condition for judgment*. Rather, he is contending that *there is no reckoning of sin based on the Mosaic Law before the presence of the Law*.

The interpretation of the verb ἐλλογεῖται varies from exegete to exegete. However there appears to be a consensus that it means "impute." Barth interpreted 5:13b as sin not noted, registered or charged to the account.[155] Others hold the meaning that transgression is not imputed to the sinner before the Law was given in the heavenly book–keeping (which is Jewish tradition).[156]Some others maintain that prior to giv-

152. Räisänen, *Paul and the Law*, 147.

153. Dunn, *Romans 1–8*, 275.

154. Räisänen, *Paul and the Law*, 1983, 146n49.

155. Barth, *Christ and Adam*, 98.

156. Jewett, *Romans*, 376; Dunn, *Paul and the Mosaic Law*, 194.

ing of the Law sin was not a matter of transgression.[157] However, Hofius makes a compelling case that the verb ἐλλογεῖται does not denote an activity in heaven even though the verb is passive and God is the subject.[158] Instead, it denotes the act directed toward the debtor. He insists that the verb conveys the idea of making known the debtor lucidly what he or she is owed. In other words, for Hofius, the account of sin is "presented to the sinner in and with the Torah."[159]For Hofius, the role of the Law is to inform the sinner about his or her sin and therefore before the Law such knowledge does not exist.

Hofius' assertion of presenting "the sinner in and with the Torah" faults at two counts. First, he assumes that the Law presents the account of sin to all humankind through Moses. However, Paul is explicit that the Law is given to Moses or to the Jews. Second, he downplays the role of the Law in the process of judging sin. Paul's statement must be understood in light of the previous two statements he made about the absence of the Law and sin: 2:12 and 4:15. In 2:12, he already insisted that there are people without the Law even after the giving of the Law; therefore, they will be judged without it. In 4:15, he claims that there is no transgression without the Law. As argued earlier that there is no breaking of a specific commandment of the Law and so no corresponding penalty based on the stipulation of the Law. If this is granted, a similar concept is reflected in 5:13a. Without the specific commandment of the Law, sin does not get a specific corresponding penalty as stipulated by the Law.

Contrary to Hofius' claims, the context of 5:12–14 is about judgment. With the entrance of sin, death (alienation from God or judgment) spread to humankind. Whether it is informing the debtor or God himself recording sin is in view here, the purpose is one and the same—to penalize sin. The Law penalizes the transgressor based on the corresponding penalty stipulated in the Law therefore reckoning only exists if the Law exists. In that sense, reckoning sin is incurring penalty for breaking the Law in accordance with the corresponding penalty stipulated in the Law. Nonetheless, Paul argues that sin is being penalized without being reckoned according to the Law because death reigned from Adam to Moses (from Adam to the giving of the Law). It should also be kept in mind that the Law is given through Moses to the Jews therefore the reckoning of the Law

157. Schreiner, *Romans*; Sanday and Headlam, *Romans*; Cranfield, *Romans*; Murray, *Romans*; Moo, *Romans*; Dunn, *Romans 1–8*.

158. Dunn, *Paul and the Mosaic Law*, 194–95.

159. Dunn, *Paul and the Mosaic Law*, 194–95.

works only with respect to the Jews based on the assertion of Paul in 2:12. Paul might be responding to the Jews who might be thinking reckoning of sin and its judgment is based on the law (an undeliberate or a deliberate transgression). Thus, ἁμαρτία δὲ οὐκ ἐλλογεῖται μὴ ὄντος νόμου means no judgment based on the stipulation of the Law in the absence of the Law.

Romans 7:8b–9a: A Dead ΑΜΑΡΤΙΑ and a Living ΕΓΩ

Romans 7 is found within 5:1—8:39 where Paul intensively expounds sin, death, and the Law. The chapter normally taken as an expansion of 5:20 which is also extended in 6:14–15 as it is dealing with the relationship of sin, death and the Law.[160]However, Rom 7 fits to the topical progression of ἐν τῷ νόμῳ or ὑπὸ νόμον because it speaks of experience under the Law.[161] But since Paul reflects on experience without the Law 7:8a–9a, it is appropriate to discuss this particular text as a part of the topical progression of without the Law. The chapter is normally divided into two: 7:1–6 and 7:7–25 but 7:7–25 again can be divided into two 7:7–12 and 7:13–25. The analysis of 7:8b–9a will focus on 7:7–12 though a broader context is still in view. Before delving into the analysis an interpretive decision must be taken with regard to the identity of ἐγὼ and νόμος. First the Law, then the identity of ἐγὼ and finally the verses will be analyzed.

The kind of Law envisioned at different places in the chapter, particularly in 7:1–6, and 21–25 is debated by scholars. Scholars such as Sanday and Headlam contend that the Law in 7:1–6 is a general Law whereas[162] reads it as the Roman Law.[163] Against general or Roman law, several scholars maintain that the Law in 7:1–6 is the Law of Moses.[164] It is reasoned that the subject of discussion is the Mosaic Law in 7:2–5 especially the immediate context 5:20 and 6:14–15 confirm this. The marriage law mentioned here is Jewish, not Roman because the Roman wife has the right to divorce her husband. Further, Paul cites the tenth commandment of the Decalogue (7:7, 12). Hence, there is no adequate reason to imagine either a Roman or a general law here insofar as the wider and immediate contexts of Rom 7 deal with the Mosaic Law.

160. Gieniusz, "Rom 7,1–6: Lack of Imagination?," 395.

161. Das, *Paul, the Law, and the Covenant*, 222.

162. Käsemann, *Romans*, 70.

163. Sanday and Headlam, *Romans*, 172.

164. Calvin, *Romans and Thessalonians*, 137; Fitzmyer, *Romans*, 455–56.

No consensus exists among scholars either regarding the meaning of νόμος in 7:21–25: εὑρίσκω ἄρ τὸν νομον (7:21), τῷ νόμῳ τοῦ θωοῦ (7:22, 25), ἕτερον νόμον, τῷ νόμῳ τοῦ νοός μου (7:23), and τῷ νόμῳ τῆς ἁμαρτίας (7:23, 25). It is argued that εὑρίσκω ἄρα τὸν νόμον (7:21), ἕτερον νόμον in v. 23 and τῷ νόμῳ τῆς ἁμαρτίας (7:23, 25) refer to the power of sin as order, principle and rule. Whereas τῷ νόμῳ τοῦ θεοῦ (7:22, 25) and τῷ νόμῳ τοῦ νοός μου (7:23) refer to the Mosaic Law.[165] It is argued that first εὑρίσκω ἄρα τὸν νόμον is a direct object of the verb and is the normal reading. Second, "other law" is contrasted against "the law of my mind" therefore both cannot be referring to the same law. Third, the law of sin is metaphorical and refers to sin exerting its power on ἐγώ. Jewett, while consenting that εὑρίσκω τὸν νόμον refers to the Mosaic Law, equates ἕτερον νόμον and τῷ νόμῳ τῆς ἁμαρτίας interpreting them as an alien force and as antithesis of τῷ νόμῳ τοῦ νοός μου.[166] Particularly, he argues that "the other law" and "the law of sin" are the same which twist "the performance of the Law into a means of status acquisition."[167]

Contrary to the above position, several scholars argue νόμος in 7:21–25 refers only to the Mosaic Law.[168] This position reasons that εὑρίσκω τὸν νόμον can be translated as "I found with reference to the Law" because νόμον is accusative of reference.[169] Furthermore, ἕτερον νόμον and τῷ νόμῳ τῆς ἁμαρτίας in vv. 23 and 25 also refer to Mosaic Law in the sphere of sin.[170]Paul is not switching to different concepts of the Law, but he is diagnosing how sin relates to the Law against those who attempt to obey it in the sphere of sin and death. In this analysis, νόμος is taken as the Mosaic Law in all its occurrences in Romans 7 and 8.

The identity of ἐγώ (7:7–25) is also controversial. It is understood as

165. Cranfield, *Romans*, 1:361–62; Käsemann, *Romans*, 205; Ziesler, *Romans*, 197–98; Moo, *Romans*, 487–88, 490–92; Seifrid, "The Subject of Rom 7:14–25," 240; Räisänen, *Jesus, Paul and Torah*, 48–94; Lambrecht, *The Wretched "I" & Its Liberation*, 53–54; Fitzmyer, *Romans*, 475–76. Thielman, *Paul & the Law*, 200; Byrne, *Romans*, 228, 232.

166. Jewett, *Romans*, 469–70.

167. Jewett, *Romans*, 470.

168. Morrison and Woodhouse, "The Coherence of Romans 7:1—8:8," 10–12; Porter, *Pauline Writings*, 169–73; Dunn, *Romans 1–8*, 392–95; Martin, *Christ and the Law in Paul*, 27–28; Fortna, and Gaventa, *The Conversation Continues*, 78–79; Longenecker, *Eschatology and the Covenant*, 240–41.

169. Schreiner, *Romans*, 366.

170. Porter, *Pauline Writings*, 172.

1. referring to Adam's experience with God's commandment in the garden of Eden because in 7:9 Paul says I was living formerly apart from the Law, and according to 5:12 the Mosaic Law did not exist before Moses.[171] The example of the sin mentioned is coveting which relates to what Eve had for the fruit (7:9–10). In this reading life and death is taken in theological sense.[172] Moo rejected this reading because Paul is referring to the Decalogue and the era of the Law is distinguished from the time of Adam (5:13–14).[173] Nonetheless, such objection is deflated in that the Jewish tradition believe that Adam had possessed the Law in the Garden of Eden.[174]

2. It refers to Israel's transgression and subsequent death, which explains vv. 8–10 or to the experience of Israel at Mount Sinai.[175] Paul distinguishes between general sin and transgression in 4:15; 5:13; and 5:20 and already argued that sin exists apart from the Law (5:12–14). Therefore, it is the increase of sin that Paul is addressing in Rom 7 not the entrance of the sin. However, this reading is challenged because of 7:9 "I was alive formerly" and Israel was dead in Adam before Sinai (5:12–14). Moo responds to the challenge arguing that life does not necessarily refer to spiritual life in Paul and death is understood as condemnation because of disobedience.[176] In the same line Napier claims that the "I" in 7:12–14 is the personification of Israel recapitulating the fall of Adam.[177] Napier's argument hinges on 5:13–14 that the death reigned upon humanity who did not transgress in the likeness of Adam. After the coming of the Law, sin came in the likeness of Adam's transgression. Therefore, for Napier 7:7–25 is speaking of transgression which is re-enacted in Israel.

171. Longenecker, *Paul, Apostle of Liberty*, 92–96; Ziesler, *Romans*, 45; Dunn, *Romans 1–8*, 378–84; Garlington, "Romans 7:14–25," 237–39; Seifrid, *Justification by Faith*, 149; Stuhlmacher, *Romans*, 106–7; Käsemann, *Romans*, 196; Longenecker, *Eschatology and the Covenant*, 237–39.

172. Schreiner, *Romans*, 362.

173. Moo, *The Epistle to the Romans*, 124.

174. Stuhlmacher, *Romans*, 107.

175. Stauffer, *TDNT* 2:358–62; Schrenk, *TDNT* 2:550–55; Moo, "Israel and Paul in Romans 7"; Karlberg, "Israel's History Personified," 65–74; Trudinger, "An Autobiographical Digression?" 173–74; Russell, "Insights from Postmodernism's Emphasis," 523; Byrne, *Romans*, 218.

176. Moo, "Israel and Paul in Romans 7," 125, 128.

177. Napier, "Paul's Analysis of Sin and Torah in Romans 7," 20.

3. It refers to Gentiles who attempted to be Judaized but were unsuccessful.[178] This reading is dismissed because it did not take 5:12–14 into account and did not show the difference between transgression and sin.

4. It refers to the autobiography of Paul's experience based on vv. 14–25.[179] This reading contends that Paul's personal experience is paradigmatic showing the fate of all those under the Law.[180] In so doing, Paul is including both Adam and Israel in his experience as recapitulation of both. The objection lodged against this reading is that there was no time Paul was without the Law, nowhere has Paul indicated that his pre-faith in Christ's life had such experience; particularly Phil 3:4–6 attests the opposite.[181]

The identity of ἐγώ must address both rhetorical as well as historical levels. Paul is a historical figure and cannot separate himself from historical reality, especially because he used the first-person plural "we" right before he started using first person singular. Paul is probably presenting himself heuristically and paradigmatically without denying its historical reality—standing in solidarity with Israel's struggle in keeping the Law. Further, he is reflecting his spiritual life before faith in Christ against specific commandments based on his new life in Christ. Napier's thesis of Israel recapitulating Adam's fall (which is transgression of a commandment) makes a plausible explanatory alternative for the conundrum of the identity of ἐγώ. This will be expounded further below.

With no doubt, 7:8a–9a appear to be contradicting the conclusion that sin existed before the Law and all died because of sin 5:12–14. Paul claims that sin is dead without the Law (7:8a) and I was alive without the Law (7:9a). Paul formulates a rhetorical question, "Is the Law sin?" to clarify his notorious claim in 7:5 (τὰ παθήματα τῶν ἁμαρτοῶν τὰ διὰ τοῦ νόμου ἐνηργεῖτο ἐν τοῖς μέλεσιν ἡμῶν εἰς τὸ καρποφορῆσαι τῷ θανάτῳ). Yet his answer to the question creates more problems than it solves.

To understand what Paul said here, it is better to start with what is more clear: (1) the Law is holy, the commandment is holy, just and good,

178. Stowers, *A Rereading of Romans*, 273–84.

179. Gundry, "The Moral Frustration of Paul," 229; Dunn, "Rom 7,14–25 in the Theology of Paul," 260; Cranfield, *Romans*, 1:345; Segal, *Paul the Convert*, 225; Milne, "Romans 7:7–12," 12.

180. Schreiner, *Romans*, 365.

181. Fung, "The Impotence of the Law," 34.

and spiritual (vv. 12, 13, 16). 2) "I am carnal, sold to sin (v. 14), and I know that nothing good dwells within me" (v. 16). At least these are clear and particularly no. 2 agrees with "while we were in the flesh . . ." (v. 5). Based on these two clear claims, it could be argued that whatever Paul says about the relationship of the Law, sin and death must be because of these two different states of being: the Law being holy, just, good and spiritual while Paul is carnal and a slave of sin and nothing good dwells within him. Paul already argued that sin and death had already been in the world before the Law was given. However, it seems that 7:8a and 9a are contradicting insofar as they claim that sin is dead without the Law. Nonetheless, it should be noted that Paul's conclusion is, "I am carnal and slave to sin" which clearly means he could not stop sinning. This seems to be contradicting his claims that "I was once alive apart from the Law" (v. 9) and "the wage of sin is death" (6:23).

Which time is Paul referring to in 7:8b and 9a? "Apart from the law sin lies dead. I was once alive apart from the Law"? *It must be the time between Abraham and Moses.* Two things must be clear. Paul already said there *is no Law before Moses* (5:13a) but *sin existed before the giving of the Law.* Second, the Law Paul is discussing in Rom 7 is the Mosaic Law. As argued above, Paul is identifying himself with the Jews as a Jew under the Law. For Paul, four persons are important in the letter: Adam (5:12–21), Abraham (4:1–25; 9–11), Moses (5:13–14; 9–11) and Jesus (1:1–5; 5:15–18). Between the time of Adam and Moses, there is Abraham. Paul argued that the promise did not come through the Law (4:13–15). In other words, *there was no law between Abraham and Moses*; therefore, there was no transgression; consequently, there was no wrath based on the Law. *If death is alienation from God, to be alive is to have a relationship with God.* Without the Law (before the giving of the Law through Moses), following the example of the faith of Abraham the Jews were alive. Paul must be describing this span of time and *Israel's relationship with God before the Law when he claims,* "I was once alive apart from the Law."

Yet, it is still hard to understand "Apart from the law sin lies dead" (7:8a) in light of what Paul said in 1:18–32 and people sin without the Law (2:12). The death of sin should be understood in relation to what the Law does. Paul says the Law speaks and makes sin known to him (7:7). Before the giving of the Law, there was no outright ban on sin, although sin was there active and alive. However, after the declaration of the Law, sin is known as an enemy and rose for war against God's Law and fought those of the Law (4:14). Paul portrays sin as a warrior fighting against the positive desire of the one whose desire is to keep the Law (7:23). *Sin is dead in a sense that there was no intense war based on the knowledge of the Law that sin wielded against Jews before Moses.* This is confirmed by the words 'seizing opportunity', which is an opportunity to fight against all righteousness (7:8a). Paul used the same language of war in 6:13. Sin is portrayed as a fighter and wars are waged using the members of human beings. Sin defeated the Jews (2:17–24; 3:19, 23) despite their knowledge about its evilness and the Law condemned them as being the same as other nations. They need the Messiah for their deliverance from the power of sin.

Hence, Paul's statement of "apart from the Law sin lies dead" does not mean sin was inactive before the Law came to the Jews *but Paul is referring to the time of the Jews' relationship with God before the coming of the Law as the time that no transgression or condemnation is reckoned against the Jews based on the Law.* Before the coming of the Law, there was no conscious war between sin and the Jews based on the knowledge received through the Law. In those days, they were alive, and sin was not fighting and condemning them. *Such a time can only be traced from the time of Abraham to the time of Moses when membership as people of God was only by prerogative and no definite requirement was stated to maintain the membership.*

Section summary and conclusion

The topical progression of ἀνόμως and χωρὶς νόμου has shown several important concepts of the Law and its relationship with sin and death. First, sin and death are not the result of the Law because sin entered into the world and reigned in the sphere of death prior to the introduction of the Law therefore there is no intrinsic relationship between the Mosaic Law and sin, and sin is not primarily breaking Mosaic Law. Second, there is no transgression of the Law in the absence of the Law. Nor is there the reckoning of sin in the absence of the Law, therefore, there was no conscious war against sin in the mind of typical Jews and no penalty of sin based on the Law between the time of Abraham and Moses (before the Mosaic Law). Thus, Jews were alive (or were not punished) based on their faith and the promise given to Abraham.

ΕΝ ΝΟΜΩ AND ΥΠΟ ΝΟΜΟΝ—UNDER THE LAW

Rom 2:12 ὅσοι ἐν νόμῳ ἥμαρτον, διὰ νόμου κριθήσονται

Rom 2:20b ἔχοντα τὴν μόρφωσιν τῆς γνώσεως καὶ τῆς ἀληθείας ἐν τῷ νόμῳ

Rom 2:23 ὃς ἐν νόμῳ καυχᾶσαι, διὰ τῆς παραβάσεως τοῦ νόμου τὸν θεὸν ἀτιμάζεις

Rom 3:19 ὅτι ὅσα ὁ νόμος λέγει τοῖς ἐν τῷ νόμῳ λαλεῖ

Rom 6:14 οὐ γάρ ἐστε ὑπὸ νόμον ἀλλὰ ὑπὸ χάριν

Rom 6:15 ἁμαρτήσωμεν ὅτι οὐκ ἐσμὲν ὑπὸ νόμον ἀλλὰ ὑπὸ χάριν;

Similar concepts will be analyzed in groups.

SIN AND DEATH UNDER THE LAW (ROMANS 2:12; 5:20; 7:14–15)

ἐν νόμῳ ἥμαρτον (2:12) describes Jews who commit sin under the Law. A similar expression is repeated in ἐν τῷ νόμῳ | (3:19). "under the Law" in 3:19 is understood with different nuances by commentators such as referring to living in subjection to the Law,[182] the Jews who know the scripture,[183] the authority of the Law speaking to both the Jews and the Gentiles[184]or being directed by the Law. Rom 2:12 explicitly distinguishes two groups of people based on possession of the Law. In 3:2, Jews are entrusted with τὰ λόγια τοῦ θεοῦ. Therefore, ἐν τῷ νόμῳ in 2:12 and 3:19 ἐν τῷ νόμῳ refer to the Jews who live under the stipulation of the Law.

Paul insists that although the Jews possess the Law and boast in the Law, like the Gentiles, they are under sin (ὑφ' ἁμαρτίαν) (3:9). The Law speaks to those who are under the Law (3:19). The Law witnesses against the sin of the Jews, that they are ὑφ' ἁμαρτίαν (3:9). The expression ὑφ' ἁμαρτίαν means "under the control of' sin (LN) or under the power of sin,[185] or "dominion of sin."[186] Kaye, however, opposes the idea of sin as power arguing that sin throughout Romans is a sinful act.[187] But

182. Schreiner, *Romans*; Barrett, *Romans*; Moo, *Romans*.

183. Cranfield, *Romans*.

184. Fitzmyer, *Romans*.

185. Jewett, *Romans*, 259.

186. Barrett, *Romans*.

187. Kaye, *Thought Structure of Romans*, 137.

his contention is dismissed particularly because Paul's understanding of sin goes beyond Jewish traditional understanding of transgression of commandments.[188] Paul's insistence that sin exists apart from the Law (2:12; 5:13–14) and his description of it with terms conveying dominion and subjugation such as reigning and enslavement (5:21; 6:6; 6:12, 14; 7:14) evidence that ὑφ' ἁμαρτίαν is sin as dominion of "irresistible coercive power."[189]

Insofar as Jews are ὑφ' ἁμαρτίαν, Paul argues in 5:20 that the giving of the Law to the Jews did not break the power of sin, rather it aggravated transgression because the Jews' disobedience to the commandments is not out of ignorance (2:17). The word παρεισέρχομαι (slipped in, encroached) (5:20) has a negative connotation. Jewett contends that the derogatory sense of the word must not be softened.[190] Contrary to Jewett, many understood the word to mean "alongside" or "in addition to."[191] So also, the interpretation varies: it is the Law's parenthetic dispensation,[192] it does not represent the whole purpose of the Law,[193] and it relativizes the importance of the Law in salvation history.[194]Disturbingly, Paul aggravates the negative connotation claiming that the Law came in to increase trespasses. But it is not the increase of legalism, against Leenhardt.[195] Nor is it subjective consciousness of sin, *pace* Morris,[196] but it is the concrete increase of breaking specific commandments of God in Israel.

Paul elaborates on 5:20 through a detailed analysis of the relationship of sin and the Law in 7:5 and 7:7–25. The Law is neither sin nor the cause of death (7:1, 13). But Paul argues that sin took the opportunity of the presence of the Law in Israel. In 7:8, the place of the phrase διὰ τῆς ἐντολῆς is debated. Some take it with κατειργάσατο[197] whereas others take it with ἀφορμὴν δὲ λαβοῦσα. [198] The latter seems to be more

188. Jewett, *Romans*, 259.

189. Jewett, *Romans*, 377.

190. Jewett, *Romans*, 387.

191. Meyer, *Romans*, 1:276; Cranfield, *Romans*, 1:292; Dunn, *Romans 1–8*, 286.

192. Sanday and Headlam, *Romans*.

193. Murray, *Romans*, 1959.

194. Moo, *Romans*; Schreiner, *Romans*, 295.

195. Leenhardt, *Romans*, 150.

196. Morris, *Romans*, 241.

197. Cranfield, *Romans*, 1:350; Dunn, *Romans 1–8*, 1:380. Lambrecht, *The Wretched "I" & Its Liberation*, 45–46.

198. Theissen, *Psychological Aspects of Pauline Theology*, 225; Moo, *Romans 1–8*,

plausible, not least because 7:10 states that the purpose of the Law is to produce life, but it produced the opposite. And γάρ in 7:11 introduces the explicit reason: sin took the opportunity through the commandment.

One of the key words that unlock Paul's analysis of the role of the Law in increasing transgression, is ἀφορμή. The word refers to "the "base of operation," or "bridgehead," required for successful military operations."[199] LN (22.46) defines it as "a set of favorable circumstances for a particular activity or endeavor." The term was first used in "Greek orators in the context of trade, agriculture, and war."[200] Paul also used it in other places 2 Cor 5:12; 11:12; Gal 5:13. The opportunity is not bad *per se*, but Paul contends that the coming of the Law created a favorable bridgehead for sin to war against those who are under the Law.

What precisely is this favorable operation base for sin? Sin probably takes advantage of two favorable conditions: *the nature of the Law and the condition of those under the Law*. Räisänen asks whether 7:14 is a consequence or a reason for the experience described in 7:7–1.[201] He opts for the latter particularly because γὰρ forcefully gives reason for the experience described in 7:7–11. Paul compares those who are under the Law with the nature of the Law in 7:14 and concludes that *the realm where the Jews attempt to obey the Law and the realm of the Law are different*. The Jews are in the realm of the flesh and are under sin while the Law is spiritual, holy and righteous. Sin dwells in Jews, and enslaved them, and nothing good dwells in them and they are of the flesh (7:17–18). Knowledge of the Law (2:17–24) created *a positive desire* for the good and hatred for the evil (7:15, 18, 19) and revealed the consequence of doing good and breaking the Law. On top of this, the Law is diametrically opposite to the character of sin. It is holy, good, just, and spiritual. Any intent and action that does not comply with its character ignites wrath (4:15) or judgment or death (alienation from God). Contrary to the Law, sin has the power of deception (7:13) with its sinful desires and works in the members (7:5). Such *opposing states* created the opportunity for sin to ignite the wrath of God against the Jews by warring against the good will and delight they have for the Law and defeating them through deception. The Law was powerless to deliver and to give life because of the state of the Jews (7:5; 8:3).

460; Schreiner, *Romans*, 367; Jewett, *Romans*, 449.

199. Moo, *The Epistle to the Romans*, 435.

200. Jewett, *Romans*, 449.

201. Räisänen, *Paul and the Law*, 1983, 143.

For instance, the main thrust of 2:17–23 reveals that disobedience to the Law dishonors God (2:23), and by implication obedience to the Law honors God. Rom 2:17–24 is not about the judgment of the Jews and the denial of their privilege as people of God.[202] Nor does it argue that the Jews used the Law as a way to salvation. Wright thinks that Paul is castigating the Jews for using the Law as a covenant badge by which they exclude others.[203] Although Wright is correct if the broader picture of salvation history reading is kept in mind, this text does not say anything about excluding other Gentiles. Rather it contends that although the Jews depend on the Law, they broke it and as a result, the name of God is dishonored among the Gentiles. Therefore, living under the Law produced more transgression (conscious violation of specific Law) (5:20) which resulted in dishonoring God's name. This was the case because the Jews received the Law while they were in the realm of the reign of sin.

ROMANS 2:17–24: THE LAW EMBODYING KNOWLEDGE AND TRUTH

In 2:17–24, commentaries and monographs lay emphasis on the identity and privilege of the Jews described in the text whereas less attention is rendered to the feature and function of the Law. Paul not only describes the Jews who depend on the Law, teach the Law and boast for possessing the Law but also describes the function of the Law. The Law: (1) provides knowledge of God's will (v. 18), (2) provides the ability to discern what is good, (3) guides the blind by being light to those in darkness, (4) corrects foolishness, (5) embodies knowledge and truth and (6) specifies sins such as stealing, committing adultery, and worshipping idols.

The concept γινώσκεις τὸ θέλημα (2:18)—you know the will—is translated by RSV as "you know his will"; "his" is inferred from the context. Dunn points out that the absolute use of the "the will" is equivalent to "God's will" and it reflects Jewish usage.[204] So also Moo consents that it is a Jewish expression of God's will in 1QS 8:6; 9:23.[205] However, Jewett complains that he did not find any exact expression of the absolute form the way Paul used it, although he finds similarity in Bar 4:4 and

202. Das, *Paul, the Law, and the Covenant*, 184.

203. Dunn, *Paul and the Mosaic Law*, 139–41.

204. Dunn, *Romans 1–8*, 111.

205. Moo, *Romans*, 160.

Wis 15:2–3. Hence, Jewett assumes that Paul's formulation is somewhat different from Jewish tradition and carries "elements of presumption that would have been immediately apparent to the Roman audience that expects a continuation of the ironic diatribe."[206] However, a word for word expression is not a necessary condition to import a similar idea as long as the expression employed sufficiently shows the same concept, in this case, the absolute expression "the will" most probably be understood in a positive manner as "the will of God" not carrying any attitude of presumption. Paul is not negatively criticizing the function of the Law as source for knowledge of the will of God, but he simply agrees that a Jewish teacher has such knowledge.

The Law "provides insight into God's will"[207] but more than that it contains the will of God.[208] The Law not only detects what a Jew must do in a certain daily activity or relationship but it also contains the comprehensive purpose, promises and specific commandments (1:2; 3:2, 21) of God although Paul seems to be challenging the Jewish teacher in a specific practical aspect of the law (2:21–24). Paul himself wants to know the will of God (Rom 1:10; 15:32) and urges the Jesus followers in Rome to approve what is the will of God. He describes the will of God as what is good, well-pleasing and perfect (εἰς τὸ δοκιμάζειν ὑμᾶς τί τὸ θέλημα τοῦ θεοῦ, τὸ ἀγαθὸν καὶ εὐάρεστον καὶ τέλειον) (12:2).

Not only θέλημα is reused for Jesus followers in 12:2 but δοκιμάζω is also used, which means "to test, to examine, to try to determine the genuineness of, testing" (LN 27:45). However, before Paul employs it to the Jesus followers, he positively used it in the latter part of 2:18 (δοκιμάζεις τὰ διαφέροντα). The word δοκιμάζω first appeared in 1:28 and was used in relation to knowledge. The people described in 1:28 tested and examined and deliberately rejected the knowledge of God as the necessary part of their lives.[209] Inversely, the Jewish teacher is able and willing to test and approve what is important and excellent (τὰ διαφέροντα) because he is instructed from the Law.

The Law is the embodiment of knowledge and truth (2:20). The word μόρφωσις must not be understood in light of 2 Tim 3:5 where it is used negatively to describe those who have outward religious practices but do not have inner reality. Dunn declares that "There is now

206. Jewett, *Romans*, 223.

207. Schreiner, *Romans*, 130.

208. Schnabel, *Law and Wisdom from Ben Sira to Paul*, 232–33.

209. Dunn, *Romans 1–8*, 66.

general agreement that μόρφωσις must mean "embodiment, complete expression."[210] Knowledge and truth is revealed and contained in the Law in a much clearer and detailed form than knowledge and truth revealed in 1:18–19, 25, 28, and 35.

However, Paul emphasizes the will of God, knowledge of discernment, guidance, correction, truth, and particular commandments. He must have maintained these features of the Law as the core of the Law; otherwise, he would not have mentioned them to charge the Jews for not exercising them. Breaking the Law dishonors God. Paul also did not say that these things are so difficult to keep them; rather he appears to be expecting the Jews to obey the commandments so that God's name would be honored among the nation which is also his goal in taking the Gospel to the Gentiles (1:5).

Christ the τέλος of the Law

The most debated text in the letter of Romans, is 10:4, for two reasons. Firstly, Paul's claim has Christological and soteriological significance with respect to the Law. Secondly, the ambiguous meaning of τέλος produced varied understanding on the Christ–Law relationship. Currently, the main alternative meanings are "goal" (teleological), "end" (temporal–termination) or "both." Many scholars espouse the meaning "goal."[211] Several other scholars have opted for "end."[212] Yet other scholars find both meanings intended.[213]

Entering the finer points of the debate would be superficial and unfair within the purview of this analysis. Yet adumbrating the major argument of all positions is in order. Reading τέλος as "goal" insists that the Law pointed or directed to Christ in the sense of purpose. Nevertheless,

210. Dunn, *Romans 1–8*, 113.

211. Howard, "Christ the End of the Law," 333; Cranfield and Sanday, *Romans*, 2:519–20; Campbell, "Christ the End of the Law," 74–77; Fuller, *Gospel and Law*, 84–85; Rhyne, *Faith Establishes the Law*, 103–4. Gaston, *Paul and the Torah*, 130; Ziesler, *Romans*, 257–58; Davies, *Faith and Obedience in Romans*, 187–89; Fitzmyer, *Romans*, 584; Thielman, *Paul & the Law*, 207; Bechtler, "Christ, the Telos of the Law: 288–308; Stowers, *A Rereading of Romans*, 304; Byrne, *Romans*, 312, 315; Jewett, *Romans*, 619.

212. Sanday and Headlam, *Romans*, 283–84; Nygren, *Romans*, 379–80

213. Barrett, *Romans*, 184; Leenhardt, *Romans*, 266; ; Bandstra, *The Law and the Elements of the World*, 105–6; Ellison, *The Mystery of Israel*, 60–61; Seifrid, "Paul's Approach to the Old Testament in Rom 10:6–8," 7–8; Schnabel, *Law and Wisdom*, 91; Das, *Paul, the Law, and the Covenant*, 249–51.

the sense of purpose is understood with different nuances.[214] (1) Christ as fulfillment of the Law which is mainly espoused by church fathers. (2) Christ as true content, substance, and inner meaning of the Law and Jews would have found it within the Law. (3) Christ as aim, or goal of the Law and Jews could have recognized Christ because the Law was pointing to him. Adduced arguments include historically accepted by the church and lexically demanded.[215] Contextually, the "goal" harks back to racing imagery in 9:30–32 because 10:1–3 is closely related to 9:30–33 and to 10:4 as it supports 10:2–3, hence, Christ is the goal of the race, but Jews stumbled over him while Gentiles attained it.[216] Further, the disruption of the parallel in 19:30–32 introduced two roles of the law: its demand and its witness to the righteousness and faith; hence, the latter points to the "goal" in 10:4.[217] There is no negative critique of the relationship between the Law and relationship, instead Israel is blamed for not arriving where it should be through the Law (11:7).[218] Such reading understands Paul is presenting Christ the true goal of the Law that Israel sought but did not attain and Christ the true inner meaning of the Law.

Arguments for τέλος as "end" are also adduced. 1) Lexical data strongly support the translation "end." 2) γὰρ in 10:4 logically connects 10:4 to 10:3. 3) The immediate context contrasts between righteousness from the Law and righteousness from faith in vv. 5 and 6. 4) Paul is against Jewish ignorance and mistake in striving to establish their own righteousness.[219] The meaning of "end" of the Law hence means termination of the Law with the coming of Christ. Nonetheless, the precise nuances vary. Some hold that the Law has ceased with the inauguration of the Messianic ear.[220] Others maintain that the Law has ceased to be a way of salvation or establishing one's righteousness.[221] Still others believe that it is about the end of the exclusive prerogative of the nation of Israel.[222]

214. Moo, *Romans*, 639n39.

215. Badenas, *Christ the End of the Law*, 7–37, 38–80.

216. Badenas, *Christ the End of the Law*, 114–15. Gaston, *Paul and the Torah*, 130; Campbell, "Christ the End of the Law," 76

217. Das, *Paul, the Law, and the Covenant*, 244, 250.

218. Rhyne, *Faith Establishes the Law*, 103.

219. Räisänen, *Paul and the Law*, 54; Schreiner, *Romans*, 547.

220. Schweitzer, *The Mysticism of Paul the Apostle*, 191–92; Schoeps, *Paul*, 171–75.

221. Longenecker, *Paul, Apostle of Liberty*, 152–53; Murray, *The Epistle to the Romans*, 49–50; Nygren, *Romans*, 389.

222. Dunn, *Romans 9–16*, 598; Watson, *Paul, Judaism, and the Gentiles*, 165.

Barrett argues for both meanings: Christ "puts an end to the law, not by destroying all that the law stood for but by realizing it."[223] In this reading both the race imagery and the immediate context of 10:4 are held together arguing that "end" means reaching the goal.[224] In the words of Moo, "Paul is implying that Christ is the 'end' of the law (he brings its era to a close) and its 'goal' (he is what the law anticipated and pointed toward)."[225]

It is hard to choose between the two positions: "goal" or "end." Räisänen also admits the difficulty of choosing between these two readings given the ambiguity of the word and evidence pointing to both directions.[226]Taking Dunn's caveat avoiding an extreme either/or position, Paul is possibly deliberately ambiguous to maintain both senses.[227] Paul is not arguing that the coming of Jesus Christ put an end to the Law as he has already argued that the Gospel establishes the Law (3:31). Paul also perceives that the Law does not only prescribe but witnesses to the righteousness of God acted through Jesus Christ. The context of the discussion of the Law is explicitly about the status of the Jews before God. Therefore, their status as righteous and elected people through the Law have ended because of the coming of Christ.

Section Summary and Conclusion

The phrases ἐν νόμῳ and ὑπὸ νόμον are mainly about the Jews living under the stipulation of the Law beginning from the time of Moses. The Jews, like many other nations, were under the power of sin prior to the giving of the Law, yet they had special privilege due to the promise and covenant of Abraham. The giving of the Law did not produce life because they were dominated and governed by sin, which produced death or judgment in Israel. They were once alive owing to the promise and faith in one God but with the coming of the explicit knowledge of the will of God through the Law, explicit accountability and due punishment to its transgression also incurred. Therefore, the Law increased transgression among the Jews through the breaking of specific commandments, and it ceased to

223. Barrett, *The Epistle to the Romans*, 197.

224. Moo, *Romans 1–8*, 641.

225. Moo, *Romans 1–8*, 641.

226. Räisänen, *Paul and the Law*, 1983, 53.

227. Dunn, *Romans 9–16*, 589.

be the basis of status and identity in the sight of God. Nonetheless, the Law serves as a source of knowledge, an expression of God's will, and a direction of life which brings glory to the name of God.

ΟΙ ΠΟΙΗΤΑΙ ΝΟΜΟΥ—DOERS OF THE LAW

2:13b οἱ ποιηταὶ νόμου δικαιωθήσονται

2:14a ὅταν γὰρ ἔθνη τὰ μὴ νόμον ἔχοντα φύσει τὰ τοῦ νόμου ποιῶσιν

2:25a περιτομὴ μὲν γὰρ ὠφελεῖ ἐὰν νόμον πράσσῃς

3:31 νόμον οὖν καταργοῦμεν διὰ τῆς πίστεως; μὴ γένοιτο, ἀλλὰ νόμον ἱστάνομεν

8:4 τὸ δικαίωμα τοῦ νόμου πληρωθῇ ἐν ἡμῖν τοῖς μὴ κατὰ σάρκα περιπατοῦσιν ἀλλὰ κατὰ πνεῦμα

In this section verses that deal with "doing the Law" will be analyzed (2:12–15; 2:25–28; 3:27–31; 8:1–11 and 13:8–10). Since 13:8–14 is the core investigation of this study, its analysis is deferred but the result of the analysis will be used to investigate its meaning.

ROMANS 2:12–16: THE LAW IN THE HEART OF BELIEVING GENTILES

It is in this section that Paul, for the first time in the letter, explicitly mentions the Law. But it is notoriously difficult to reach consensus as to the meaning of the pericope, thus it is taken by some scholars as an anomaly. Sanders and Raisanen have concluded that it contradicts what is said about the Law in the letter, therefore Paul's understanding of the Law is inconsistent.[228] Different avenues have been taken to resolve the issue, yet no consensus has been reached so far.

Generally, 2:1–29 is understood as part of the bigger section of 1:18—3:20 where Paul argues that both the Jews and the Gentiles are under the impartial judgment of God as no one is righteous before the sight of God. Within this major block, 2:12–29 is discerned as a pericope of its own and normally divided into three sections: 2:12–16, 2:17–24 and 2:25–29. Nineteen occurrences of the word νόμος in this pericope alone

228. Sanders, *Paul, the Law, and the Jewish People*, 125; Räisänen, *Paul and the Law*, 1983, 123.

evinces that its major theme is the Law. It also discusses two groups of people, namely: Jews (circumcised) and Gentiles (uncircumcised).

However, the exegesis of 2:12–29 puzzled many interpreters. Not least vv. 13b–15 has created interpretation difficulties on two questions: (1) Is Paul saying that the law continues to have a justifying role in v. 13b? (2) Who are the Gentiles that do the law in vv. 14–15? There are three major proposals: non-believing Gentiles, believing Gentiles, and Gentiles from before the Jesus followers righteous Gentiles and unrighteous Jews. A majority of scholars interpret the identity of Gentiles in vv. 13b–15 as non-believing Gentiles. But a number of scholars espouse the position that the doers of the Law in vv. 14–15 are Gentile Jesus followers.[229] The interest here is to present only two prominent views: those of the non-believing Gentiles and believing Gentile readings. It is hardly possible to present detailed arguments on both sides, but an attempt will be made to present the summary of their arguments.

1. A non-believing Gentile interpretation argues as follows: it is just to contrast Jews and non-believing Gentiles as they are not contrasted in other places; while 2:7 and 2:10 speak of godly Gentiles, 2:12 speaks of Gentiles to be condemned; believing Gentiles know the OT and therefore, they cannot be described as having no Law; τὸ ἔργον τοῦ νόμου γραπτὸν ἐν ταῖς καρδίαις does not speak of the new covenant in Jeremiah 31 as Jeremiah did not use the phrase "work of the Law"; Gentiles do not observe all the Law as in 2:14 ὅταν ("whenever") implies a conditional phrase; and here Gentiles are used hypothetically.[230] Rom 2:13b parallels to v. 12b not to v.14 and the word φύσις (2:14) does not occur at the end of a phrase therefore it must be understood adverbially modifying the verb ποιῶσιν (2:14) not adjectivally with τὰ μὴ νόμον ἔχοντα.[231] Furthermore, Paul is referring to natural law because he refers to the conscience of the Gentile that reflects the general knowledge of good and evil. The context of 2:12–16 is 1:18—3:30 and the general thrust of the immediate context of the text is that of impartial judgment and while

229. Gathercole, "A Conversion of Augustine," 327–58; Gathercole, "A Law unto Themselves," 29–30. Barth, *Christ and Adam*, 98; Cranfield, *Romans*, 1:274; Dunn, *Paul and the Mosaic Law*, 131–50; Jewett, *Romans*, 213; Kömig, "Gentiles or Gentile Christians?," 53–60.

230. Thielman, *Paul & the Law*, 174.

231. Dunn, *Romans 1–8*; Fitzmyer, *Romans*, 1993.

the larger context is one of humanity under sin, therefore Paul is speaking of non-believing Gentiles.

2. The interpretation of Gentile Jesus followers is that: Paul makes quite a variety of contrasts within Rom 2, such as in 2:7–8 (contrast between those who do good and evil) and in 2:13 (a contrast between Jews who do the Law and Jews who hear but do not do the Law); in 2:25–29 (a contrast between disobedient Jews and obedient Gentiles; in 9:30 and 11:11–14 (a contrast between unbelieving Jews and believing Gentiles).[232] Therefore, it is unconvincing to argue contrasting Jews and non-believing Gentiles. However, there is a stark contrast between Gentiles described in 1:18–32 and those described in 2:14–15.[233] The heart of the Gentiles in 1:18–32, especially in v. 21, is contrasted against the heart of those in 2:14–15. However, there are parallels and similarities between 2:14–15 and 2:25–29 where a true Jew is described. Hence, the contrast must not be limited between 2:12 and 2:7, 10. "The things of the Law" (v. 14) refers to not some of the Law but it is an expression of a comprehensive and inclusive sense of the Law,[234] and doing the things of the Law refers to fundamental knowledge of the Law. Paul is acquainted with the Old Testament and is alluding to LXX Jeremiah 38:33 where an internalization of the Law is promised which can only be done by God. Paul's use of "work of the Law" in 2:12–16 is not a sufficient condition to assume that Paul did not have Jer 31:33 in mind while writing about the Law written in the hearts. Paul uses terms interchangeably when he speaks of obeying the Law as well as its features.[235] Furthermore, work of the conscience is not connected with doing the law but it testifies that God's judgment in the final days is impartial. The term φύσις refers to identity, it has no connection with conscience in the text. It "characterizes some groups" and identity.[236] Therefore, it refers to identity rather than behavior (Gal 2:15 4:8; Eph 2:3–4; Rom 2:27; 11:21, 24).[237]

232. Fitzmyer, *Romans*, 1993;Cranfield, *Romans*, 1:156.

233. Gathercole, "A Law unto Themselves," 39.

234. Gathercole, "A Law unto Themselves," 34.

235. Davies, *Faith and Obedience in Romans*, 65.

236. Achtemeier, *Romans*, 45.

237. Gathercole, "A Law unto Themselves," 36.

Structurally, there is a connection between 2:13 and 2:14, that is, between the doer of the Law in v. 13 and a comprehensive doing of the Law in v. 14. In v. 14 γάρ explains v. 13, hence, the principle of "the doer of the law will be justified" is immediately applied.[238] There is logical, syntactical, and verbal similarity between" doing of the Law" (v. 13) and "the things of the Law" (v. 14). It is evident that φύσις belongs to the first clause in 2:14 and does not modify the "doing of the law" because it is best understood as an adjective, as it normally describes character in Pauline usage, except in 1 Corinthians. *Pace* Dunn and Fitzmyer, φύσις occurs at the end of a phrase.[239] For example, Wis 13:1a; Ignatius, *Eph.* 1.1; Josephus, *Ant.* 8.152 and Greek is free in placing words in a sentence.

As argued earlier in this work, Paul is in the habit of suggesting themes which he intends to develop later in the letter, for example 3:1–9 is dealt with in detail in Romans 9. Jewett argues that from a rhetorical point of view Gentile Jesus followers make sense: wrath on Gentiles (1:18–31), Jews are not exempted from judgment (2:1–13) and 2:14–16 strategically describe Gentile Jesus followers to provoke the Jews by praising Gentiles.[240] The reading on the believing Gentile fits into the rhetorical context of the letter.

The third position contends that Rom 2:12–29 is about the righteous Gentiles and unrighteous Jews.[241] The righteous Gentiles hold the pre-Christian Gentile faith and by inferencing it, it includes Gentile Jesus followers.[242] This interpretation reasons that 2:13 is timeless and that God's principle of impartiality is also timeless.[243] Romans 2:14 does not describe Gentile Jesus followers because they cannot be described as those who do not have the Law in the same way as Gentile Jesus followers who do know the Old Testament. The Gospel is yet to be expounded in 3:21–26 and if it is interpreted as Gentile Jesus followers, it intrudes in Paul's logical argument.

No conclusive evidence is yet provided from all readings. However, weighing the evidence submitted by the readings on believing Gentiles and non-believing Gentiles, interpretive decisions must be made to arrive at a plausible understanding of the text for the purpose set in this

238. Gathercole, "A Law unto Themselves," 33.

239. Dunn, *Romans 9–16*, 589; Gathercole, "A Law unto Themselves," 36.

240. Jewett, *Romans*, 213.

241. Davies, *Faith and Obedience in Romans*, 59.

242. Davies, *Faith and Obedience in Romans*, 65.

243. Davies, *Faith and Obedience in Romans*, 60–67.

research. The interpretation of the non-believing Gentile attempts to alleviate the difficulty of the interpretation by maintaining the traditional assumption that Rom 1:18—3:20 *is a linear discussion* on the theme of universal dominion of sin over humanity and the judgment of God.

The non-believing Gentile reading has several pitfalls in the interpretation of 2:12–16, in addition to counterarguments provided by the Gentile Jesus followers' reading. Many scholars have shown that the Law that Paul is discussing in Rom 2 is the Law of Moses, not natural law. First, if the non-believing Gentiles can uphold the Law (whether it is natural or the Mosaic Law) and are thereby justified, then it runs against the whole theme of Paul's argument in 3:9, 20, and 23.

Second, if God does the writing of the work of the Law in a person's heart, then the impartiality of God argued for in the section is endangered because the non-believing Gentile position assumes that *some* non-believing Gentiles have the law being written in their hearts and not all Gentiles. The corollary of this assumption would be that God *is selective and arbitrary* insofar as the majorities who are described in 1:18–32 are judged because their *hearts are darkened* and they *desire evil* and *do evil.* In 1:18–32, there is no indication of the writing of the work of the Law in the hearts of the Gentiles and there is also no indication that those described in the section are doing evil all the time. Instead, it simply says that God's hidden behavior, that is, his power, is revealed to them through creation (1:18). If this is so, then it implies that there is partiality in God in providing the work of the Law in the hearts of only some non-believing Gentiles. This cannot be the case, because it runs against the very thing that Paul is defending, namely that all human beings are sinners.

Third, this reading makes qualitative distinctions between the non-believing Gentiles described in 1:18–32 and non-believing Gentiles described in 2:14–15 insofar as the interpretive position in question assumes that they are in the same category.

Fourth, if those non-believing Gentiles uphold the Law occasionally and are justified before God, then the Jews also occasionally obey the Law, therefore, they can also be righteous before God since Paul did not say that the Jews break the Law all the time. This mitigates Paul's argument that "none is righteous, no, none" (3:10).

Fifth, the conscience Paul describes is not a guiding principle of day-to-day practice of the Law; rather it is about being witness (συμμαρτυρούσης) on the day of judgment (v. 16). Schreiner's argument that the law written in their heart does not lead to salvation does not account for Gentiles doing what the Law requires (2:14) and "the doers of the law who will be justified" (2:13b).[244]

Strictly, Paul's concern and argument is that Gentiles, even though they do not have the Law, they do the things of the Law (2:14), whether it is understood occasionally or as a way of life. Then it follows that from v. 13b they will be justified and the future tense (δικαιωθήσονται) (2:13) attests to the fact that observing the Law is a requirement for future justification on the last day of judgment. Therefore, neither is natural law the source of knowledge for obeying God in daily practical matters; nor is the conscience a means to observe the Law. Rather it is the work of the Law that is written in the heart that functions as the source of knowledge. The law scripted in the heart is what makes the difference. Paul does not tell who scripted this law in the heart until the reader comes to 2:29 and gets a hint. The reading of non-believing Gentiles has exegetical, logical and theological pitfalls. It is unsatisfactory in its explanation and therefore cannot be a plausible alternative.

Although the identity of the Gentiles in question is not explicitly stated, it is plausible to assume that Paul is introducing Gentile Jesus followers in a general way as it is his habit to introduce a concept or a theme that appears in the later part of the letter. For example, 3:1–9 is detailed in v. 9, 5:3–5 is detailed in 8:18–39, and 6:12–13 is detailed in 12:1–21. Similarly, Paul is providing small sections of information on the Gentile Jesus followers, which he later develops in Rom 8:1–4 and 13:8–10. Stowers observes that the text "creates an opening for the claim that Gentiles can fulfil the just requirement of the law [8:4] through the spirit of Christ" or "Gentile in Christ can do the Law."[245]

In support of the reading on Gentile Jesus followers, this work further argues that Paul conflates his Gospel and the Mosaic Law in 2:12–16:

1. There is continuity between 2:1–11 and 2:12–16. Many scholars have discerned that 2:1–16 is about the impartial judgment of God. In 2:12, Paul appears to be providing an explanation for how God executes his impartial judgment. This reading becomes evident if γὰρ is maintained as a continuation and explanation of 12:11 regarding the basis of the impartial judgment of God. Paul then expounds the Law as a standard for judgment, particularly in 12:13b, where he

244. Schreiner, *The Law and Its Fulfillment*," 195.

245. Stowers, *A Rereading of Romans*, 141.

emphasizes that the "doers of the Law" are the ones who will be righteous before God. "The doers of the Law" are inclusive—both Jews and Gentiles. If the continuation of 2:1–11 and 12 is maintained, then the "observers of the Law" in 12:13b are those who seek glory, honor, and immortality by doing good deeds through patience (2:7 and 10), from the Jews as well as from the Gentiles. Therefore, in 2:12–29 Paul develops the idea of doing good in terms of the relationship of the Jews and Gentiles to the Law. He begins with the Gentiles in vv. 14–15 and then goes on discussing Jews in vv. 17–24. He finally comes to the discussion and conflation of both (Gentiles but Jesus followers and Jews but Jesus followers) identities in one as ὁ ἐν τῷκρυπτῷ'Ιουδαῖος (2:25–29) whose praise is from God.

2. Both the Law and the Gospel work within the internal aspect of the Gentiles in question. That is, the work of the *Law is written in their heart* (v. 15) and the judgment according to the Gospel of Paul is the *revelation of what is in the secret or heart* of men by Jesus. It should be noted that the Gospel that Paul is referring to is "my Gospel" which is the Gospel for Gentiles (1:5) that produces obedience of faith. While the work of the Law written in the heart stipulates what must be obeyed or done (although this is not a condition for salvation), the Gospel offers the ways in which the last day of judgment will take place (2:16). The justification of which 2:12–16 speaks is based on the totality of life.[246] Therefore, action is informed and guided by the Law, but judgment is in the light of the Gospel of Paul through Jesus Christ. In so doing, Paul is able to conflate the role of the Law and the Gospel within the impartial judgment of God and salvation.

Romans 2:25–29: Obeying the Law as a Mark of Authenticity

In this section of the pericope, Paul continues to expound the importance of obedience to the Law. As Dunn observed, the argument narrows down from "doing good" in 2:7 and 10 to the more specific "upholding the Law" (2:12–16) and now to one commandment—circumcision.[247] It

246. Wright, and Sampley, *The New Interpreter's Bible*, 144.

247. Dunn, *Romans 1–8*, 119.

is argued above that Paul is conflating the role of the Law and his Gospel in 2:12–16: *the Law informing the heart and action, with the Gospel assuming the authority of judging in the end.* In this section, Paul contends that a circumcised heart and obedience to the Law are the two marks of hidden Jews who are composed of Gentiles and Jews.

In 2:14–16 Paul ascribes the authority of judgment to Jesus Christ according to the Gospel of Paul. Yet, in 2:25–29, Paul insists that an uncircumcised person (Gentile) who fulfils the Law (τὸν νόμον τελοῦσα) or observes the righteous requirements of the Law (τὰ δικαιώματα τοῦ νόμου φυλάσσῃ; Rom 2:26) judges the circumcised person who transgresses the Law. In fact, this does not mean that the Gentile who fulfils the Law takes the place of Jesus. Rather, the Gentile who obeyed the Law will be evidence during the prosecution of the last day.[248]

In 2:25–29, Paul argues that Jewishness is an inward feature and a result of obedience to the Law. Outward circumcision (which is given before the giving of the Mosaic Law) can only have value when it is accompanied by obedience to the Law. Outward Jewishness and outward circumcision are synonymous (2:28). Jewishness and circumcision, for Paul, is κρυπτός and καρδία respectively. In other words, both Jewishness and circumcision are transferred into the inward quality of the person in question. Such an inward experience is open for both the circumcised and the uncircumcised because circumcision with a corresponding obedience to the Law is also profiting. On the other hand, circumcision without obedience to the Law is reckoned as uncircumcision which is a reversal of status. Schreiner pointed out that to be reckoned as uncircumcised means to become a Gentile and unsaved before God's sight.[249] Therefore, obedience (2:27) to the Law is a mark of a real Jewishness or membership in the community of God.

The word τελέω (2:27) can be translated as, "keep" (RSV), "fulfil" or "satisfy,"[250] or it "may be rendered simply as 'to do what the Law says one must do'" (LN 36:20). It conveys fulfilling the law qualitatively or in a deeper sense than quantitative performance of detailed ritual requirements.[251] The difference between the circumcised disobedient person and the uncircumcised obedient person is the locus and the kind of circumcision. For Paul what counts is circumcision of heart, and such circumcision is

248. Cranfield, *Romans*, 1:174.

249. Schreiner, *Romans*, 137–45.

250. Jewett, *Romans*, 234.

251. Dunn, *Romans 1–8*, 122.

the work of the Spirit. Cranfield rejects reading ἐν πνεύματι as the human spirit as the inwardness and the unseen part of the person in question is adequately expressed by καρδία.[252] The idea of circumcision of heart by the Spirit probably harks back to the promise given in Ezek 11:19–20 and 36:26–27 where the Spirit will be sent into the hearts of the people of God. According to the promise, obedience to the Law is the result of the work of the Spirit in the heart of the people of God.

The debate over the identity of the Gentiles here is still under discussion. No need of belaboring the point here as it is already discussed above in 2:12–16. Following a number of scholars,[253] the position taken here is a reference to Gentile Jesus followers. Suffice it to submit the following evidence: first, Paul uses words and language that he used in another place, that carry the same concept and subject. The language of 2:29 contrasts spirit and flesh which Paul uses to distinguish between Jesus followers and non-believing others, for instance, Rom 7:6; 2 Cor 3:6; and Phil 3:3. This language and concept in 2:25–29 evoke the subject of covenant renewal which is in the biblical and extra-biblical Jewish texts where the spirit and the flesh are contrasted (Ezek 36:24–28; 11:19). Paul used the word "reckoned" which is a language of justification and change of status (3:28; 4:3, 4, 5, 6, 8, 9, 10, 11, 22, 23, 24; 9:8; 2 Cor 5:19; Gal 3:6).

Second, structurally, the word γὰρ in 2:28 gives reason how Gentiles obey the law without being physically circumcised (2:28–29). The reason that Gentiles can observe the Law is because God is involved in transforming their hearts, which is metaphorically expressed as a circumcised heart by the Spirit. Particularly, the antithetical polarity between the Spirit and the letter is Paul's expression of distinguishing the believer and unbeliever (7:6; 2 Cor 3:6).

Third, Paul is arguing in other places of the letter that the Jesus followers can keep the Law (3:27; 8:4; 13:8–10). In 3.27, Paul's Gospel establishes the Law. The law here is νόμος, not principle and Paul explains it later in the letter but hints at it here. According to Rom 8:4–9 the mind of the flesh cannot submit to God's Law; by implication the mind of the spirit can and does the things of God.[254] Rom 10:4–11 quoted Deut 30,

252. Cranfield, *Romans*, 1:175.

253. Cranfield, 1:173; Dunn, *Romans 1–8*, 122; Dunn, *Paul and the Mosaic Law*, 132–39; Gathercole, "A Law unto Themselves"; Schreiner, *The Law and Its Fulfillment*, 196–204; Das, *Paul, the Law, and the Covenant*, 185–86.

254. Dunn, *Paul and the Mosaic Law*, 137.

the new covenant passage, when someone believes Christ, he is keeping the Law.[255]

Evidently, Paul is contrasting the Jews who are boasting because of the status and possession of the Law and the Gentiles who neither possess the Law nor are proselyted, but the Law is engraved in their hearts through the Spirit. Hence, the pericope must be speaking of the Law being obeyed in the transformed lifestyle of the Jesus followers to bring honor to the name of God and authenticates the true believer.

ROMANS 3:31: UPHOLDING THE LAW

In this section, Paul declares that νόμου πίστεως excludes boasting (3:27) and that πίστις upholds the Law. But differing meanings have been ascribed to the word νόμος in this text. One interpretation offers a metaphorical meaning as "principle," "order" or "rule," or "norm,"[256] or "religious system."[257] Another view maintains a literal meaning—the Mosaic Law.[258]

Räisänen, a proponent of the metaphorical reading, contends that νόμος in 3:27 cannot be the Mosaic Law adducing: (1) that νόμος has various meanings, for instance in 7:21–8:2; (2) that the Mosaic Law does not exclude boasting, rather it is Christ's events, which is God's activity 3:21–26 that does it.[259]

Räisänen's thesis must be rejected for the following reasons: (1) it is weak as there are compelling cases that νόμος in 7:21–8:2 is the Mosaic Law. (2) It is mitigated by the nature of the question itself: Paul related the question to the Law, and boasting is already related to the Law, as 2:17 and 23 adduce. (3) The Law has a positive role in witnessing to the righteousness of God 3:21; hence, the Law "characterized by faith"[260]has an opposing role against boasting. Moo also argues for the metaphorical reading, contending that the question of Paul only makes sense if the

255. Dunn, *Paul and the Mosaic Law*, 137.

256. Westerholm, *Israel's Law and the Church's Faith*, 122–26; Murray, *Romans*, 122–23; Sanders, *Paul, the Law, and the Jewish People*, 33; Watson, *Paul, Judaism, and the Gentiles*, 132; Ziesler, *Romans*, 118; Räisänen, *Paul and the Law*, 116.

257. Barrett, *Romans*, 79.

258. Cranfield, *Romans*. Dunn, *Romans 1–8*; Rhyne, *Faith Establishes the Law*, 67–70; Hübner, *Law in Paul's Thought*, 138–39. Porter, *Pauline Writings*, 167.

259. Porter, *Pauline Writings*, 164.

260. Porter, *Pauline Writings*, 165.

negative function of the Mosaic Law and the law of faith are different.[261] Das trivializes this contention arguing that Paul responded positively about the Law in v. 31.[262] Further, Paul uses "we" referring to those of faith including himself (1:12), that is, the family of faith establishes the Law (v. 31) through faith.

The responses to Räisänen and Moo's arguments serve as compelling evidence for the support of reading νόμος as the Mosaic Law. But additional evidence can be adduced: (1) the context demands that it be read as Mosaic Law. Consistently, Paul uses the word νόμος in Rom 3 as the Mosaic Law, therefore there is no compelling reason for him to switch it to another meaning. (2) It is not the Law that is excluded but boasting about having the Law. (3) Rom 3:29 confirms that Paul is thinking of the Mosaic Law as the source of division between the Jews and the Gentiles.[263] (4) Reading it as the Mosaic Law unifies the content of 3:21–22 with the discussion of the Law in 3:21–22. The weight of the evidence adduced for the literal meaning reading plausibly concludes that νόμος in 3:27–31 is the Mosaic Law.

Granting that Paul is referring to the Mosaic Law in 3:27–31, the concern is 3:31. Paul formulates a rhetorical question, "Do we then overthrow the Law by this faith? By no means! On the contrary, we uphold the Law" (3:31). In 3:30, Paul already claims to the *Shema* of the Mosaic Law which is the reflection of the first commandment of the Decalogue and fundamental part of the Mosaic Law (Exod 20:3 and Deut 6:4). Paul argues that there is only one God and that this is what the Law declares. This declaration of the Law stands against excluding Gentiles from faith in one God for God is not only the God of the Jews. For Paul, *faith is believing what the Law declares already (i.e. there is only one God—the Shema)*. Therefore, acceptance of the uncircumcised based on faith (there is only one God) is obeying the Law. However, Paul in 3:30 mentions only one commandment of the Law. The interlocutor's question seems to be whether Paul is overthrowing the rest of the Law on the assumption that believing in monotheism does it all. Paul rejects this conclusion: 'No, we uphold the Law.'

Two questions surface from Paul's response to the question: who are the "we" who uphold the Law? And what does upholding or establishing

261. Moo, *The Epistle to the Romans*, 248–49.

262. Das, *Paul, the Law, and the Covenant*, 197.

263. Das, *Paul, the Law, and the Covenant*, 196.

the Law mean? Although Paul begins his letter describing what marks him off from the recipient of the letter (1:1), he ties himself with others under the lordship of Jesus Christ (1:4). However, whether the pronoun ἡμῶν refers to the people who received grace and apostleship (1:5) or the recipient of the letter as a whole, is not immediately clear. If it is referring to v. 5 then it is referring to himself and other fellow apostles only. Yet, v. 6 seems to be including the audience in the ἡμῶν of v. 4 because Paul uses ἡμῶν in v. 7 too which is a direct address to the audience. The word "called" verses (1, 4, 6, and 7b) bind together closely and claims the lordship of Jesus Christ upon the audience as well. If the three verses are read together then ἡμῶν refers to three categories of people: Paul himself, Paul's fellow apostles and the audiences.

However, ἡμῶν does not occur between 1:7 and 3:4. In other words, Paul does not include himself in the discourse, but he uses the second person plural. Since the pronouns here are highly imaginative and rhetorical only a few comments will be rendered. For instance, in 3:5 ἡμῶν is used within the diatribe section which starts in 2:1. But the dialogue with the interlocutor in the first section (2:1–16) is an undefined imaginary interlocutor whereas beginning from 2:17, it is with a Jewish teacher. However, there is no agreement among scholars to whom ἡμῶν in 3:5 refers in the dialogue. The majority of the scholars such as Kruse[264] ascribe the question to Paul himself whereas scholars, like Stowers,[265] ascribe it to the interlocutor. The former take ἡμῶν as referring to all humanity whereas the latter takes it as referring to some of the Jews who did not carry out their responsibility within the Gentiles and became a cause for the blaspheme of God's name. However, in light of the context that begins in 2:17–24, ἡμῶν must refer to the Jews, not least the teachers of the Law among the Gentiles.

Nonetheless, Paul separates himself and those who are under the lordship of Jesus from the other group in the dialogue by employing the first-person plural as a subject in 3:8 "why not do evil so that good may come? As some people slanderously charged us with saying." The word τινες/some/ refers to those who misrepresented Paul's message and the Jesus followers. Not only have they misrepresented the message, but they also slandered them. Paul did not say "I am slandered" but "we are slandered." Paul is probably including other apostles who received grace

264. Kruse, *Romans*, 157–58.

265. Stowers, *A Rereading of Romans*, 170–71.

and apostleship (1:5; 16:21) as well as the audiences. It must also be noted that τινες seems to be referring either to the Jewish teacher of the Law who is in dialogue with Paul or some other group of opponents of Paul and Jesus followers, most probably the ones mentioned in Rom 16:17–18.

The question of the interlocutor in 3:9 states: "What then? Do we have advantage?" The verb here is inflected containing the subject "we,ĠG and it must be related to the interlocutor's question in 3:1. And the response is of Paul. However, Dunn rejects this interpretation because 3:1 has narrower reference (to the Jews) whereas 3:9 has a broader reference and brings the whole discussion of the diatribe into conclusion. Therefore, according to Dunn, it must be read as ". . . we humans . . ."[266] However, the dialogue between the interlocutor and Paul controls the questions and answers in the context of the status of the Jews. Jewett interprets the connotation of προαιτιάομαι as "previously allege; establish."[267] Likewise, Stowers has shown that the "we" as "a dialogical we" and reads it as "I, Paul, and you, the interlocutor, in our discussion have already concluded."[268] If the diatribe is kept in view, the "we" in the response to the question refers to Paul while the "we" in the question comes from the interlocutor.

Similarly, the οἴδαμεν (we know) in 3:19 also refers to Paul, the interlocutor, the audience because it is about "the common knowledge."[269] However, the "we" in 3:28 λογιζόμεθα ("For we hold that a person is justified by faith apart from works of law") must be referring to Paul and the Jesus followers' common belief. Stowers argues that the "we" here is also "a dialogical we."[270] His argument assumes consensus between Paul and the interlocutor. However, the ensuing discussion makes it clear that further justification is needed to corroborate Paul's thesis of justification by faith. Up until 3:28, there is no indication of the interlocutor buying into the claims of a law-free justification. Therefore, "we" in 3:28 must be referring to Paul and his fellow believers of the claim.

Likewise, the "we" in the response in 3:31 refers to Paul and the Jesus followers in Rome. If "we" simply refers to the interlocutor and Paul himself as Stowers[271]claims, it does not make sense in terms of argument because Paul is defending his position and interpretation of Scripture in

266. Dunn, *Romans 1–8*, 147.

267. Jewett, *Romans*, 258.

268. Stowers, *A Rereading of Romans*, 180.

269. Jewett, *Romans*, 264.

270. Stowers, *A Rereading of Romans*, 236.

271. Stowers, *A Rereading of Romans*, 236.

the face of an opposing Jewish interlocutor. The question of nullifying the law must be in the mind of the interlocutor but the answer is provided and related to 3:28 where Paul states his stance and that of the Jesus followers. Paul's response is that the teaching of the community surely upholds the law. Therefore, Paul used "we" representing himself and the community.

What does Paul mean by "we uphold or establish the Law"? Since it is already argued that νόμος is Mosaic Law, contrary to Jewett,[272] there is no need to enter into the debate whether the Law here is a general law or not. Yet, there are varied interpretations of what Paul means by upholding the Law: (1) establishing its convicting and condemning role;[273] (2) establishing its testifying role to faith;[274] (3) establishing it by not dividing Jews and Gentiles;[275] and (4) establishing its prescription by obeying its commandments.[276]

The first interpretation is unconvincing as Paul is not dealing with the conviction of sin here. The second reading is contextually correct but faults at connecting the function of v. 31 and v. 27 because establishing the Law and the role of the Law as witness to the righteousness of God by faith is not apposite.[277] Paul includes prophets also in the role of witness to the righteousness of God. It is the whole scripture (the Law and prophets) that bear testimony about the righteousness of God. Such reading is confirmed by 4:3 where Paul uses "the Scripture." Rom 4 also does not elaborate 3:31 because it does not start with "because" rather with "therefore." This is unconvincing in light of Rom 2:1–29; 8:2–4; 12; 13:8–10. The third interpretation is probably correct, but it falls short by not accounting for obedience to the commandments of the Law. The fourth reading is more plausible because it accounts for the texts that speak of obeying the commandments of the Law. However, a variant view which assumes that believing in Christ (which is faith) per se, not keeping its

272. Jewett, *Romans*, 303.

273. Watson, *Paul, Judaism, and the Gentiles*, 1986, 134–35.

274. Käsemann, *Romans*, 105; Rhyne, *Faith Establishes the Law*, 71–93; Hübner, *Law in Paul's Thought*, 142–44; Westerholm, *Israel's Law and the Church's Faith*, 122; Ziesler, *Paul's Letter to the Romans*, 120; Longenecker, *Eschatology and the Covenant*, 207; Byrne, *Romans*, 138.

275. Dunn, *Romans 1–8*.

276. Schreiner, *Romans*.

277. Schreiner, *Romans*, 207.

commandment, is upholding the Law[278] must be dismissed as it does not account for the context that demands obedience to the commandments. Instead, Paul is insisting that *Jesus followers continue obeying* the Law although he did not specify which commandments are to be obeyed in the community.

Thus, the Law of faith is characterized by faith or the Law fused with the message of the Gospel and obtains its fulfilment in the community of Jesus followers; and thus the message of the Gospel establishes the Law.

ROMANS 8:4: FULFILLING THE REQUIREMENT OF THE LAW

Rom 8:1–4 is usually connected to the previous discussion in Rom 7 particularly to 7:6 where Paul declares freedom from the Law. Verbal and thematic connection is discerned between these two sections.[279] Before engaging with 8:1–4, it is important to address 7:6 first. Paul declares that Jesus followers are discharged and dead to that which held them in bondage so that they might serve in the Spirit and not in the letter. The focus of the discussion here is on the question of 7:4, "you have died to the Law through the body of Christ" which relates to "dead to that which held us captive."

Who is the person that died? The general explanation is that death changes the position of a person with respect to the law.[280] Some interpret the wife as a believer but the husband as the Law.[281] Others argue that the wife is a true self whereas the husband is the old person (therefore, the Law condemned the old self).[282] The role of the Law is not negatively expressed in 7:1–2 rather it is respected. It administers marriage to avoid adultery. It also continues with the risen Christ or another man who is contrary to the old person. The law of marriage, that is, faithfulness to the new person is intact in the life of the Spirit.

The person who died should be the old person. The concept of death in Christ as a separation introduced in 6:2–4 particularly 6:6 speaks of

278. Moo, *Romans*, 257.

279. Schreiner, *Romans*, 398.

280. Schreiner, *Romans*, 349; Murray, *Romans*, 1959, 241–43; Cranfield, *Romans*, 1:335; Käsemann, *Romans*, 187; Dunn, *Romans 1–8*, 361; Fitzmyer, *Romans*, 187; Nygren, *Romans*, 270.

281. Bruce, *Romans*, 137.

282. Sanday and Headlam, *Romans*, 172; Hafemann, *Paul, Moses, and the History of Israel*, 177; Longenecker, *Eschatology and the Covenant*, 232

the death of the old person through the death of Christ. Death and sin lost their dominion because the old person was crucified with Christ. This immediate context evinces that Paul must have a similar image when he uses death of the followers of Christ in 7:4. It is the death of the old self (the husband) through the death of Christ, not through the church, that brought freedom from the Law. If this is granted, and death is a due reward of sin according to the standard of the Law, therefore it appears that the Law executed the old person which is sin, in the flesh (7:5) and freed the wife from condemnation (8:1). In the words of Hafeman "The Law as 'letter', the fixed declaration of God's will, when it encounters the life in the flesh of those who are apart from Christ, condemns and kills as God's declared punishment for sin."[283]

Romans 8:1 declares that Jesus followers are free from condemnation because they are freed from the dominion of sin.[284] Rom 8:2–4 begins with γὰρ offering reasons for 8:1—the Law of the Spirit of life freed them from the Law of sin and death. But the meaning of νόμος continues to be debated. The metaphorical reading (the principle of the power of sin or simply power) rejects the literal reading (the Mosaic Law).[285] It argues that nowhere in the letter is the Law rendered freedom from sin, and it contradicts what Paul said in Rom 7.

Snodgrass rejects the metaphorical reading for its unwarranted move from 8:2, the Law as power of sin, to a different meaning in 8:3.[286] Instead the Law of sin and the Law of death refer to the Old Testament Law as "commandeered by sin to effect death"[287] so also Schreiner.[288] Rom 8:6 confirms that the Spirit produces life. In 8:2 ὁ γὰρ νόμος τοῦ πνεύματος τῆς ἐν Χριστῷ Ιησοῦ announces the Law is in the realm of the Spirit that gives life. This is probably parallel to 7:14 and the Law of sin and death might as well be parallel to 7:5 and 7:13 respectively. Snodgrass argues that the genitive must receive the emphasis, and the Law is still playing

283. Hafemann, *Paul, Moses, and the History of Israel*, 179.

284. Murray, *Romans*, 1959, 274–75; Gundry, "Grace, Works, and Staying Saved," 31–32.

285. Meyer, *Romans*, 1:41; Sanday and Headlam, *Romans*, 190; Murray, *Romans*, 276; Cranfield, *Romans*, 1:375–76; Ziesler, *Paul's Letter to the Romans*, 202; Moo, *Romans 1–8*, 505–7; Fitzmyer, *Romans*, 483; Fee, *God's Empowering Presence*, 522; Thielman, *Paul & the Law*, 201; Byrne, *Romans*, 242.

286. Porter, *Pauline Writings*, 172.

287. Porter, *Pauline Writings*, 172.

288. Schreiner, *Romans*, 400.

the role.[289] Verse 3 also starts with γάρ and seems to be briefly summarizing the relationship of the Law and sin discussed in chapter 7. Paul claims that the Law could not produce righteousness due to the flesh (8:3) (this parallels to 7:10). Rom 8:3 implies that the Law was expected to produce life and righteousness, but God accomplished what the Law was expected to do. Hence, it seems that now in Christ the Law has taken its rightful location to produce freedom and life in the life of Jesus followers (8:2).

Rom 8:4 begins with ἵνα, introducing the purpose of God's saving action and freedom through the Law of the Spirit for the fulfilment of the requirement of the Law. The forensic reading argues that the believers' obedience to the Law is not in view here.[290] The adduced argument for the view is that πληρωθῇ is passive and it is God who fulfills in Christ's believers not the believers fulfilling the Law. Further, ἐν ἡμῖν evinces God's act of saving on the cross of Christ forensically fulfilling the just demand of the Law, that is, Christ's vicarious death satisfied the Law's demand of condemnation of the sinner therefore sinners are now accepted before God, free of guilt.

Granted that God is the one who is working, it can also be argued that 8:4 is about Jesus followers' obedience to the requirement of the Law. Paul uses the present participle περιπατοῦσιν describing the kind of people that fulfill the Law; namely those who are walking according to the Spirit. Paul does not simply state it but describes it by negation "not according to the flesh." Paul does not say that the requirement of the Law will be fulfilled in those who believe in Christ but in those "who do not walk according to the flesh." The negative alternative must be emphasized because there is a possibility of walking according to the flesh and avoiding it is the responsibility of those who believe in Christ. Those who walk according to the flesh are the enemies of God because they do not subject themselves to the Law of God (8:7). Hostility to God, in other words, not to be able to subject oneself to God's Law, conversely, by implication obedience to the Law, is pleasing God (8:8). Walking according to the Spirit therefore is believers' obedience to the Law.

The phrase τὸ δικαίωμα τοῦ νόμου (8:4) is singular and the plural is used in 2:26. The singular is understood differently: the law of love based on 13:8–10, all other Laws except circumcision, Sabbath, food laws,[291] all

289. Porter, *Pauline Writings*, 173.

290. Calvin, *Romans and Thessalonians*, 160; Käsemann, *Romans*, 218; Moo, *Romans 1–8*, 514–17; Fitzmyer, *Romans*, 487–88.

291. Sanders, *Paul, the Law, and the Jewish People*, 100, 102.

the moral Laws,[292]and prohibition of coveting.[293] There is no significant difference among these positions. But the phrase refers to all righteous acts that the Law puts as a demand. This can be adduced by Paul's use of the terms δικαιόω (3:4) and ἀδικία in several places in the letter: 1:18, 20; 2:8; 3:5; 6:13; and 9:14. δικαιόω refers to something morally right or to be right (LN 88:16) and ἀδικία is living against God's truth. Of significance, is that 1:18 reveals that it is breaking the first commandment of the Decalogue (1:19–23) which results in all wickedness (1:20) and it is against τὸ δικαίωμα τοῦ θεοῦ (1:32). Disobeying the truth (2:8) is obeying wickedness. But the truth is in the Law (2:20) and Jewish disobedience to it is called unrighteousness (wickedness) in 3:5. Jesus followers are called not to present their body to ἀδικία (6:13) and to avoid all ἀκαθαρσία and ἀνομία (uncleanness and lawlessness). In the face of all this evidence, τὸ δικαίωμα τοῦ νόμου must be taken as Jesus followers obeying the Law's demand, not least because both the Law and the believers are in the realm of the Spirit.

SECTION SUMMARY AND CONCLUSION

In Rom 2:12–16, it is argued that Gentile Jesus followers can keep the Law because it is written in their hearts but in 2:25–29 Paul argues that both believing Jews and Gentiles can keep the Law because their hearts are transformed by the works of the Spirit and it is the mark of authentic relationship with God. In 3:27 and 31, Paul argues that the Law is in the category of faith as it demands to believe in monotheism, therefore the believing community established the Law through faith in Jesus. Further, those who walk according to the Spirit fulfil the righteous requirement of the Law. Hence, the topical analysis under the Law reveals that believing community can obey the Law. The Law and the Gospel are not antithesis but synthesis, if not synergetic. The Law and the Gospel are conflated under the realm of the Spirit in a sin–freed community of faith. Disobedience to the Law dishonors God but obedience to the Law pleases and honors God, therefore it is the characteristic of those who walk in the Spirit.

292. Cranfield, *Romans*, 1:384.

293. Ziesler, *Romans*, 78–79.

CHAPTER CONCLUSION AND IMPLICATION FOR THE INTERPRETATION OF 13:8–14

The following conclusions can be drawn from the analysis of topical progression:

Ἀγάπη is a conscious, intellectual, and deliberate act of choice towards God and fellow believers or the "Other" in accordance with the content delineated in the Pauline Gospel, it is to act accordingly despite opposing and adverse conditions. Although the source and example of ἀγάπη for the community is God through the Spirit and his acts through the obedience of Christ, it could be pretended, therefore *it must be guided and restricted with content that describes its nature.* This has a tremendous implication for the interpretation of Rom 13:8–14 because ἀγάπη is directly connected to the commandments of the Law.

The phrases ἀνόμως and χωρὶς νόμου are discussed with respect to sin and death. Sin and death exist, function, and dominate without the Law. *There is no cause-and-effect relationship between "the Law" and "sin and death."* Once, Israelites, as children of Abraham, lived under the promise without the Law or before the giving of the Law of Moses. In such conditions, although Israelites were dominated by sin, like other nations, they were free from the wrath of God or punishment as their relationship with God was based on the promise given to Abraham. The revelation of the righteousness of God without the Law refers to God's own act of salvation towards sinners without being bound by the Mosaic Law not sinners being given status before God. This has an important relevance to the interpretation of Rom 13:8–14, because the law is not the cause for sinning, rather it is against sin and all unrighteousness which opposes the will of God.

The phrases ἐν νόμῳ and ὑπὸ νόμον refer to the condition of Jews since the time of Moses, which was life under the stipulation of the Law. The Law did not produce righteousness because the Jews were under the power of sin and therefore the Law increased transgression as they knowingly transgressed the Law which is different from the time of Abraham to Moses (living under the promise without the Law). The Law therefore functions as revealing the true nature of sin, truth, and knowledge of God by offering divine knowledge, wisdom, and the will of God that brings honor to God. But it also became a standard with which God punishes the sin of the Jews. Yet, due to death and sin reigning over the life of the Jews, they could not obey the Law therefore they were under punishment like any other nations. Nonetheless, *the Law is still good, spiritual, and a treasure of knowledge, wisdom, and will of God.* The implication of this concept of the Law is important insofar as Paul prescribes the summary of the Law (13:8–14) *to those who are freed from the dominion of sin, and as the commandments enumerate what are acceptable and unacceptable in the sight of God.*

The topical progression of οἱ ποιηταὶ νόμου has shown that it is indeed possible to keep the Law. There is a community of people who can keep the Law and honor God. The community of Jesus followers establishes the Law through faith in Christ by walking according to the Spirit. *The Law and the Gospel synthesized or conflated within the realm of the Spirit* and *acted out in the life of those who walk according to the Spirit.* Such people please God. Therefore, the Law has obtained it's just sphere and match, namely: the hearts of those who are freed from the old person and from condemnation and indwelled by the Spirit and walking according to the Spirit. This has bearing particularly on the interpretation of the summary of the Law (13:8–14), because Paul already developed a positive concept of the Law and its relevance to the believing community throughout the letter and has insisted that obeying the *Law is pleasing God and honoring his name* among the Gentiles which is also one of the key role of the Gospel of Paul.

3

Romans 13:8–14

Analysis of Argumentative Texture

INTRODUCTION

THE TOPICAL PROGRESSION ANALYSIS of *ἀγάπη* and *νόμος* in Chapter 2 has revealed that the wider rhetorical context of Romans has important bearings on the interpretation of Rom 13:8–14. The current chapter undertakes argumentative texture analysis of Rom 13:8–14 in order to investigate Paul's argument regarding the relationship of *ἀγάπη* and *νόμος* and their role in the identity formation of the Christ-believing community. The first step is to establish the structure, context and the inner logical movement of Rom 13:8–10. But Rom 13:11–14's structure will not be discussed in detail except its connection to 13:8–10 as the focus is on the summary of the Law. Then, discussion on the issues of translation of terms within the unit and a detailed analysis of argumentative texture will ensue. Finally, a comparative analysis of *ἀγάπη* and *νόμος* as the key concepts of 13:8–10 will follow.

ESTABLISHING THE RHETORICAL UNIT: STRUCTURE, CONTEXT, AND INNER LOGICAL MOVEMENT OF 13:8–14

Different methods have been used to structure Rom 13:8–14 such as structural exegesis, discourse analysis, and rhetorical criticism. Nonetheless, no one method claims a definitive approach. A number of scholars have also attempted to connect 13:8–10 to the preceding chapters and paragraphs according to the following themes: justice,[1]obligation[2] and love.[3]Others have observed verbal connections between 13:8–10 and 13:1–7: πᾶσιν (13:7) corresponds to μηδὲν (13:8a), and ὀφειλάς (13:7) corresponds to ὀφείλετε (13:8a),[4] and Μηδενὶ μηδὲν repeats the positive injunction of 13:7.[5] Yet, none of them makes a significant connection among the three chapters; namely 12:1—15:13.

After critiquing three methodologies (structural exegesis, discourse analysis and rhetorical criticism) in structuring Rom 12:1—15:13, Kuo-Wei Peng proposes an eclectic approach with a two-dimensional reading strategy.[6] Beginning his analysis with 12:9–21 followed by 13:1–7 as a basis for the constituting subsection of 12:9–13:10, he went on to analyses 12:1–8 and 13:11–14, followed by 14:1—15:13. Finally, he proposed a structure in the following format: (1) 12:1–8 as a prerequisite for the discernment of the will of God; (2) 12:9–13:10 the will of God to be discerned as genuine love; and (3) 14:1—15:13 the will of God as to be discerned in the community.[7] According to Peng, the overarching theme is discerning the will of God, which is love without pretense (12:9a) which is also defined as holding fast to the good and hating evil.

For a number of reasons, Peng's structure and a two-dimensional reading of the text are generally adopted in this study. First, his eclectic approach is flexible and allows the use of the strength of different structuring methods. Second, his structuring closely ties the three chapters through internal analysis and thematic connection that work in a similar fashion with the progressive texture analysis done in the previous chapter of this study. Third, his two-dimensional arrangements: "good" and "evil" (primary dimension), on the one hand, and "in-group" and "out-group" (secondary dimension), on the other, allow to hold the structure, the rhetorical and social context, and the logical movement of the rhetorical unit in view.

1. Godet and Chambers, *Romans*, 303–4.
2. Beet, *Romans*, 345; Jewett, *Romans*, 804.
3. Stuhlmacher, *Romans*, 208.
4. Leenhardt, *Romans*, 338; Käsemann, *Romans*, 360; Dunn, *Romans 1–8*, 775.
5. Cranfield, *Romans*, 1:674.
6. Peng, *Hate the Evil, Hold Fast to the Good.*
7. Peng, *Hate the Evil, Hold Fast to the Good*, 197–98.

Peng insists that "let love be genuine" (12:9a) is a theme for the unit being followed by two subtitles: "hate what is evil" (12:9b) and "hold fast to what is good" (12:9c); 12:10–16a deals with "what is good," and 12:16b–21 deals with "what is evil."[8] The admonition has two directions: in relation to insider (12:10–13 and 15–16a, holding good; 12:16b-c, hating evil), and in relation to outsider (12:14—holding good and 12:17–21 hating evil).[9] Hence, the 12:9–21 is a "'two-dimensional' arrangement . . . the primary dimension . . . [is] 'good and evil' and the secondary dimension . . . [is] in-group' and 'out-group.'"[10]

A similar technique (a two-dimensional view, the first dimension: doing good and hating evil) is also applied to analyzes the structure of 13:1–7 and 13:8–10. However, 13:1–7 is about the Christ-believing community's relationship to the society and holding fast to what is good, such as a positive attitude towards government authority, paying tax, and giving honor. In 13:8–10, the root ἀγαπ occurs five times therefore it connects to the heading 12:9a (let love be genuine). The two dimensions: insider and outsider as well as the dimension of "good" and "evil" can also be discerned. The positive injunction in 13:7 is expressed in the negative 13:8a which continues the theme of relation to outsider in μηδενὶ which can also be equated to πάντων ἀνθρώπων in 12:17–18. The concept ἀλλήλους (13:8b) speaks about the relationship among insiders connecting to 12:10–16. The negative prohibition in 13:8a (not to be in debt to another) and the positive injunction in 13:8b (loving one another) continue the dimension of "evil" and "good." Therefore, 13:8a–b provides a succinct summary of 12:10–13:7.[11] The dimension of evil to be avoided and good to be followed continues in 13:8c, 9–10 by the citation of the Law. The relationship between the insider and outsider is expressed by all embracing (outsider and insider) terms such as ἕτερον (13:8c), and πλησίον (13:9–10) which connect to πάντων ἀνθρώπων in 12:17–18. Therefore, 13:8–10 concludes 12:9–13:7 and reflects a two-dimensional reading of the text. Peng proposes the following arrangement of the structure of 13:8–10: v. 8a negative injunction (out-group relation); v. 8b positive injunction (in-group life); v. 8c supporting reason/explanation (all-embracing statement); v. 9a negative commands (which

8. Peng, *Hate the Evil, Hold Fast to the Good*, 109.

9. Peng, *Hate the Evil, Hold Fast to the Good*, 63–65.

10. Peng, *Hate the Evil, Hold Fast to the Good*, 65.

11. Peng, *Hate the Evil, Hold Fast to the Good*, 110.

is the expansion of v. 8c); v.9b positive injunction; and v. 10 summary for the negative commands in vv. 9a and 10b.

Despite distinct features of 13:11–14 due to its eschatological emphasis, metaphorical language and contrast,[12] the connection which is detected between 13:8–14 and 13:11–14 is based on Καὶ τοῦτο (13:11a).[13] Alford reads it as "let us do this" referring to love in 13:11–14 and others think it summarizes all that precedes practically 13:8–10 enforcing love by eschatological motivation.[14] Still others connect it to 12:1—13:10 in the sense of Paul enforcing the exhortation by imminence of the end; particularly 12:1–2 is echoed in 13:12b and 14.[15] Structurally, it can generally be divided into 13:11a–12a referring to the nearness of the end and 12b–14 laying aside the works of darkness. In light of the above discussion, it seems that Paul thematically connected the injunction from 12:1—13:14. Hence, 13:8–10 and 13:11–14, although considered as separate units on their own, will be discussed together as the nearest context of the summary of the Law in the ensuing analysis.

TRANSLATION ISSUES: ΟΦΕΙΛΕΤΕ (13:8A), ΕΙ ΜΗ (13:8B), ΕΤΕΡΟΝ (13:8C), AND Η ΑΓΑΠΗ (13:10)

Meyer, Murray, Hodge and Alford argue that ὀφείλετε (13:8a) must be translated imperatively.[16] Particularly Hodges rejects that the indicative, for it requires Οὐδενὶ οὐδὲν, not Μηδενὶ μηδὲν. Sandy and Headlam also read Μηδενὶ μηδὲν as imperative because it is negative and transitionally summarizes the preceding 13:7.[17] No compelling evidence is adduced to interpret ὀφείλετε in the indicative mood. For instance, John rejects the imperative because it is harsh.[18] Nonetheless, the imperative mood keeps the injunction Paul has begun at 13:7 (ἀπόδοτε πᾶσιν τὰς ὀφειλάς)

12. Peng, *Hate the Evil, Hold Fast to the Good*, 134.

13. Alford, *Alford's Greek Testament*, 448–49.

14. Denney, "Romans," 689; Hendriksen, *Romans*, 349; Murray, *Romans*, 164; Käsemann, *Romans*, 680;

15. Barrett, *Romans*, 232; Cranfield and Sanday, *Romans*, 2:680; Stuhlmacher, *Romans*, 212; Moo, *Romans*, 820; Schreiner, *Romans*, 697; Peng, *Hate the Evil, Hold Fast to the Good*, 142.

16. Meyer, *Romans*, 1:285; Murray, *Romans*, 158; Hodge, *Romans*), 407; Alford, *Alford's Greek Testament*, 44.

17. Sanday and Headlam, *Romans*, 373.

18. John Brown, *Romans*, 494.

therefore there is no reason to shift the mood and tone down the force of the injunction.

No consistent translation of εἰ μὴ (13:8b) has been rendered as it is translated either antithetically or inclusively.[19] For example, KJV translates it as "but" whereas NAB, NAS, RSV, and NIV render "except." An antithetical translation reads, "but you ought to love one another,"[20] whereas an inclusive translation reads, "except to love one another." Cranfield is right in contending that an antithetical translation forces the supply of the verb used in the first half of the sentence.[21] The problem is not supplying the verb *per se* but the change it introduces in the text which does not exist in the Greek. The antithetical translation changes not only the sense but also the mood.[22] The term ὀφείλετε, which is imperative, loses its force of command when changed into indicative. The mood and the sense can only be intact if the natural reading εἰ μὴ as "except" is maintained. In so doing, the second half of the sentence remains under the influence of the imperative mood. Supplying "but you ought" emphasizes the obligation and deflates the command. Therefore, to maintain the imperative mood and its sense of command εἰ μὴ should be translated as "except" as the natural reading of the sentence.

A few scholars argue that ἕτερον (13:8c) is an adjective and modifies νόμον; therefore, ἕτερον νόμον must be translated as "the other law," and understands the "other law" referring to the Mosaic Law as opposed to Roman law or the law of Christ (the double commandment).[23] But Paul mentions neither the Roman law nor the law of Christ here. Instead, the citation from the Decalogue asserts that only the Mosaic Law is mentioned. Other scholars understand it as the object of ἀγαπῶν hence interpreted it as "the other."[24] Ἀγαπῶν needs an object in order to be a full sentence and therefore ἕτερον (13:8c) must be translated as "the other."

A translation question regarding ἡ ἀγάπη (13:10) is whether to retain the article in the English translation or not. Deleting the article in

19. Jewett, *Romans*, 806.

20. Barrett, *Romans*, 229–30; Murray, *Romans*, 159; Käsemann, *Romans*; Luther, *Romans*, 185.

21. Cranfield and Sanday, *Romans*, 2:674.

22. Cranfield and Sanday, Romans, 2:674.

23. Bruce, *Romans*, 226; Leenhardt, *Romans*, 337.

24. Meyer, *Romans*, 285; Godet and Chambers, *Romans*, 315; Parry, Romans, 252; Parry, *Romans*, 170; Cranfield, *Romans*, 1:675; Murray, *Romans*, 160; Dunn, *Romans 9–16*, 776; Jewett, *Romans*, 807.

the English translation imposes abstractedness in the noun and loses its particularity as Jewett argues.[25] Jewett's intention for insisting that the articular form must be retained in the translation is because he understands ἡ ἀγάπη as the agape meal.[26] Whether this reading is legitimate or not must go under scrutiny because first the general aspect cannot be obliterated if v. 8a is considered as a command to love one another, which is accompanied with a rational proposition in v. 8b "a person who loves the other . . ." Particularly, ὁ γὰρ ἀγαπῶν τὸν ἕτερον as a singular personal pronoun insinuates a general statement although the "ὁ" might refer back to the subject of the imperative ὀφείλετε. Secondly, if the article ἡ ἀγάπη is maintained it must refer to the sentence that precedes it. In this case, "You shall love your neighbor as yourself." The love Paul is referring to is the love of one's neighbor not agape meal. Therefore, in this study ὀφείλετε is imperative, εἰ μὴ means "except," ἕτερον is the "other," and ἡ ἀγάπη is love referring to love for one's neighbor.

ANALYZING THE ARGUMENT OF THE UNIT (13:8–10)

Robbins defines the study of argumentative texture as investigating "multiple kinds of inner reasoning in the discourse."[27] The assertion is supported by logical reasoning "which provides the basis or proof which supports the text's thesis."[28] The rationale provides "reasons that the thesis is true to be believed. . .[and it] often begins with 'for' or 'because.'"[29] Logical argumentation is mostly characterized by "the function of unstated premises," and "identifying and articulating these premises reveals aspects of the argumentative texture in its social and cultural [the author] may never state."[30] The concern of this section is to study Paul's logical argument in 13:8–10. The section begins by identifying the identity of ἀλλήλους, τὸν ἕτερον and πλησίον, then analyzes the claim, stated reasons and unstated reasons of the unit followed by the study on what constitutes Paul's argument regarding ἀγάπη and νόμος.

25. Jewett, *Romans*, 813–14.

26. Jewett, *Romans*, 814.

27. Robbins, "Dictionary of Socio-Rhetorical Terms," 21.

28. Robbins, "Dictionary of Socio-Rhetorical Terms."

29. Robbins, "Dictionary of Socio-Rhetorical Terms."

30. Robbins, *The Tapestry of Early Christian Discourse*, 59.

Identifying the Identity: ἀλλήλους, τὸν ἕτερον and πλησίον

In his reasoning, Paul states three indefinite objects of love one after the other in the progression of his arguments. If the line of argument is closely followed, it may be seen that they occur in the following order: *one another*, *the other*, and *the neighbor*. However, the indefinite reciprocal pronoun ἀλλήλους, the adjective τὸν ἕτερον, and the adverb πλησίον as objects of ἀγάπη raise the question of the identity of the addressees of the injunction. Scholarly debate over the identity of the addresses of the letter to the Romans has never ended. Diverse and opposing proposals have been submitted since Ferdinand Christian Baur first proposed an entirely Jewish audience. No matter how unconvincing Baur's conclusion may be, his evidence for the existence of Jewish audience has continued their influence in the next generation of scholars. Scholars such as J. H. Ropes, W. Manson, T. Fahy, and S. Mason, for instance, modified Baur's position and argued for mainly Jewish audiences. Core evidence adduced to this position entails: Paul's concern for the spiritual life of his kinsmen (1:16; 10:1–3; and 11:13–36), calling Abraham our father (4:1), those who know the Law (7:1), Jewish themes such as the Law, righteousness, redemption, and election of Israel, the remnants, and application of Jewish rhetoric.[31]

Unlike an audience made up entirely or of a majority of Jews, a few scholars argued for an exclusively Gentile audience.[32]Among others, Andrew Das has made extensive and sustained argument for exclusively Gentile audiences; therefore, his point of view will be discussed at length followed by a critique of his position.

Das contends that it is possible to discover the purpose and situation of the letter from encoded readers of the letter defining the encoded audience "as reconstructed from the letter itself and as conceptually distinguished from the *actual* original hearers" (italics his).[33] By "encoded readers," he means that whether the Jews physically existed in the congregation of Jesus followers in Rome or not, Paul is addressing exclusively Gentile Jesus followers. Das' reconstruction of the audience of the letter of Romans is predicated on the following assumptions: (1) There were many God–fearing Gentiles in Rome and they were attending the Synagogue

31. Longenecker, *Introducing Romans*, 76.

32. Munck, *Paul and the Salvation of Mankind* ; Stowers, *A Rereading of Romans*; Gaston, "Reading the Text and Digging the Past," 35–42;

33. Das, "The Gentile-Encoded Audience of Romans," 29.

along with the Jews. (2) Later, they accepted the Gospel along with Jews. (3) But Claudius' edict evicted the Jewish Jesus followers, which resulted in the complete separation of the Gentile God-fearing believers form the synagogue. (4) Thereafter, new Gentiles, who were not God-fearers, were added to the community of Jesus followers. (5) They created problems for the Gentile God-fearers in terms of their keeping Jewish law. (6) Therefore, Paul is writing his letter to bring peace and build bridges between them through his letter. The entire assumption raises the question of plausibility as an argument from God-fearers, which has created a hypothetical subgroup to validate his claim. The evidence that adduces the assumption does not satisfy a sufficient condition to put the Jewish Jesus followers' audiences out of the equation.

Das' exegetical argument impinges upon five key texts: (1) Greeting in 1:1–7 is about obedience of all the Gentiles not among all nations, because the preposition ἐν is partitive, the parenthetical structure of the phrase attracts the attention of the audience, and no grammatical break exists between vv. 5 and 7. Therefore, "all the Gentiles" in v. 4 is equated with "all God's beloved" in v. 7.[34] (2) "Thanksgiving" in 1:8–15 refers to the rest of the Gentiles in relation to the Roman reader particularly in 1:13, and in 1:15 "to you also who are in Rome" is also used to designate non-Jews (2:14, 24; 3:29; 9:24, 30; 11:11–13, 25; 15:9–12, 16). More especially, Paul directly identifies his readers in 11:13 and "impurity" and "iniquity" in 6:17–19 do not fit the Jews as they mean "law-less" and unclean respectively for describing Jews with such terminology is an insult.[35] Similarly, Rom 13:11–14 does not speak of the Jews, because they are lists of vices reminiscent of 1:18–32. However, Das concurs that the vices in 1:18–32 and 13:11–14 could also include the Jews. Paul identifies the "weak" in 15:15–16 as Gentiles who are sympathetic towards Judaism based on Josephus and Horace's documents.[36] For Das, the names listed in Rom 16 do not necessarily show a Jewish audience because they are in second person plural asking the recipient of the letter to pass the greeting on behalf of them. Finally, Das contends that there is a break between Jews in the synagogue and the Gentile Jesus followers after the edict of Claudius in 49 CE.

There is no question that Paul emphasized Gentiles in his greetings; however, there is not sufficient reason to conclude that he is addressing

34. Das, *Solving the Romans Debate*, 54–56.

35. Das, *Solving the Romans Debate*, 60–64.

36. Das, "The Gentile-Encoded Audience of Romans," 64–66, 69–70.

exclusively Gentiles because an equally tenable argument for "all nations" can also be maintained in 1:5. Nor is 1:5 hard evidence for an exclusively Gentile audience, because it focuses on the purpose of the gift of apostleship, not on the identity of the addressees. Paul insists that apostleship, including other apostles, is "to bring about the obedience of faith among all the nations" (RSV). The extract, ". . . including yourselves who are called to belong to Jesus Christ" (v. 6) is also primarily connected to the purpose than to the nations. The purpose of the apostolic mission is to bring the obedience of faith from the unbelieving nation, whether Jews or Gentiles, and from the believing community in Rome for the sake of God's name. Further, πᾶσιν in vv. 5 and 7 cannot be the same insofar as the former is general and the latter refers to a specific location—"in Rome." The term Πᾶσιν in v. 7 also betrays Das' argument of an exclusively Gentile audience as Paul uses more inclusive terms, such as "all God's beloved in Rome, who are called to be saints." If Das accommodates the possibility of the physical presence of the Jews among the believing Gentiles in Rome, then Paul is including them as well in his greetings, πᾶσιν τοῖς οὖσιν ἐν Ῥώμῃ. However, since this text mitigates Das' arguments, he totally evades it from his discussion.

Knowledge of Scriptures content (which is Baur's contention for a Jewish audience), discussion of the Law (in Rom 2, 3, 7, and 13), circumcision (in chapter 4), faithfulness of God to Israel (in Rom 9–11), knowledge of the Law (in Rom 7:1), and Jewish scripture citations are some examples of the concrete evidence in the letter. Das, however, argues that Gentile God-fearers know the Scripture, particularly Rom 7:1, which is not difficult to know with a limited knowledge of the Scripture. However, Das himself thinks that "Ancient readers did not normally have written manuscripts available for study in the same way as the modern reader."[37] He adds, "even if Paul's Gentile readers somehow had access to synagogue manuscripts of the Scriptures, only ten to twenty percent of the people were literate in a world where most people struggled to survive."[38] If this is granted, then it is hardly possible to be sure whether the God-fearing Gentiles ever read the Scripture for themselves. Further, Das' description of the Gentile God-fearers' knowledge of Scripture and the concept of sin in Rom 7 do not fit with Paul's discussion of the relationship between the Law and sin. Das trivializes the importance of the story and context of the

37. Das, *Solving the Romans Debate*, 35.

38. Das, "The Gentile-Encoded Audience of Romans," 35.

Scripture, cited in the letter when he said that understanding of Scripture is not necessary in order to understand Paul's point.[39] Particularly, in light of Rom 4 where Paul's argument hinges on the timing of the circumcision of Abraham, Das' claim fails to recognize how important for Paul even the details of scriptural knowledge are. Furthermore, the discussion on Israel in Rom 9–11 demands a detailed knowledge of the Scripture as Paul is making historical as well as theological arguments based on the Scripture.

Das assumes that Paul already taught about marriage in 1 Cor 7:10–11, 39–40, therefore the Gentile readers in Rome know Rom 7:1–6.[40] This reading demands an assumption that what is taught in 1 Cor 7:10–11, 39–40 must have been taught in Romans. Paul had never been in Rome and nor is there evidence that the letter to the Corinthians was being read by the Roman congregation. Nor does Paul speak about it or is alluded to it. Although there is no explicit mention of the Jews in 7:1, there is no fallacy in including the Jewish readers within the equation insofar as no compelling evidence is adduced to read it otherwise.

The evidence for a Jewish audience also comes from 2:17 where Paul calls "a Jew" and from a listing of Jews who are Jesus followers in 16:1–16. Since Das consents that "Discerning an imaginary interlocutor, as opposed to a very real person, is difficult in actual letters,"[41] his conclusion on this text as speaking of imaginary Jews is not conclusive. The listing of Jews in 16:1–16 particularly Prisca and Aquila, Andronicus, Junia and Herodion (16:11) are also taken as one of the strongest pieces of evidence for a Jewish audience. But Das' transferring the literal "synenes" to metaphorical language in 16:17 is hardly convincing. For one, he did not demonstrate the existence of such a word describing someone in metaphorical kinship language from contemporary letter either Roman or Greek literature.[42] Das himself observes, "Whenever synenes are employed in context with words such as 'brother', 'sister', or 'mother' in ancient Greek literature, the meaning is always 'relative' and "Loyalty and trust in the first century were primarily to one's blood relatives."[43] Then, he assumes this loyalty is transferred to the Christian community and speculatively concludes: "Paul is using 'affectionate language' to build

39. Das, "The Gentile-Encoded Audience of Romans," 36–37.

40. Das, "The Gentile-Encoded Audience of Romans," 35.

41. Das, *Solving the Romans Debate*, 89.

42. Das, *Solving the Romans Debate*, 91.

43. Das, *Solving the Romans Debate*, 93.

'bridges' with the Roman congregation."[44] If "syn" heightens the familial kinship, why did Paul not use the term for all the 24 names so that he could build a better bridge? Why, out of the 24, did only three receive such a designation?

Paul calls for welcoming one another in 15:7–9; this is also used as evidence for a Jewish audience. Das speculates that there were Gentile God-fearers who followed the Jews without adducing hard evidence.[45] Paul, in 15:8–9, points towards serving the circumcised or the Jews mentioning Jesus as a model. The circumcised according to 4:12 must be the Jews; no God-fearing Gentiles are called circumcised in the letter. Jesus glorified the father by serving the circumcised and so the followers are expected to do the same. Welcoming and receiving one another (15:7) addresses both groups: the circumcised and the uncircumcised. It is hardly possible to discount Jewish audience of the letter.

Others take a middle ground claiming that the audiences of the letter are Jews (minority) and Gentile (majority) Jesus followers. The reasoning behind this conclusion is based on historical reasoning (particularly the eviction of Jews from Rome by Claudius in 49 AD) and mirror reading of the text which was first proposed by Sandy and Headlam.[46] The mirror reading mainly depends on the evidence within the text. Romans 1:5–6, 13–15; 11:13; and 15:16 are examples where the audiences are explicitly identified as Gentile readers. In Rom 2 the diatribe form of Hellenistic argumentation reflects Gentile literary culture. "The people of Israel, my brothers and those of my own race (9:3), my own people (11:14)" are expressions that distinguish Paul from the Gentiles.[47] Romans 16 lists both Jews and Gentile Jesus followers whom Paul personally knows.

Paul's discussion on the "weak" and the "strong" in 14:1—15:13 is evidence adduced towards Jews and Gentile audiences. However, no consensus has been reached regarding the identity of the 'weak' and 'strong'. According to Reasoner, the different conclusions about them can be divided into two points of departure: those who read the section through the lens of the situation in Corinth and those who read it through the lens of the situation of Roman society and Jews in the diaspora.[48] Sandy

44. Das, *Solving the Romans Debate*, 93.

45. Das, *Solving the Romans Debate*, 105.

46. Denney, "St. Paul's Epistle to the Romans;" Dunn, *Romans 1–8*, xlv; Jewett, *Romans;* Moo, *Romans.*

47. Longenecker, *Introducing Romans*, 77.

48. Reasoner, *The Strong and the Weak.*

and Headlam and Karris hold the first position.[49] The second position has reached at least three different conclusions in determining the identity of the 'weak': (1) it is impossible to know; (2) they are non-Christian Jews;[50] and (3) they are Christian. However, those who hold a Christian identity arrived at diverse conclusions: (a) the weak Christians are Jews[51] (b) they are both Christian Jews and Gentiles;[52] and (c) they are entirely Gentile Christians.[53] While agnostic reading deprives the text of its historical context, non-Christian Jewish reading denies the existence of believing Jews among the community although it grounds its assumption on Gentile believers and non-believing Jews meeting in the same synagogue. Nanos, a proponent of the latter position, is refuted by Robert Gagnon.[54] The "weak" is said to be whom Christ died for (14:15 which parallels 1 Cor 8:11). Both the "weak" and the "strong" are called upon to build and bear one another mutually (14:19; 15:1, 2 parallels 1 Cor 14:3). The prayer wish in 15:5–6 includes the "weak" as Paul criticized them, along with the "strong." Both the "weak" and the 'strong' should welcome one another (15:7), and the "weak" stands in faith by the Lord (14:4). Therefore, there is a strong indication in the text that both the "weak" and the "strong" are Jesus followers.

Nonetheless, Paul neither mentions their identity nor treats them as separate sects or groups. Instead, he seems to be addressing them within the same community notwithstanding their difference in diet, Sabbath and Calendar. Every extreme position goes into unwarranted speculation. However, it can be safely concluded from two fronts: historically, there is a growing consensus that Jews and God–fearing Gentiles existed in Rome, albeit during Claudius' eviction of the Jews in 49 CE. Exegetically, as majority of the scholars believe, the existence of Christ–believing Jews

49. Sanday and Headlam, *Romans*; Karris, "Romans 14:1—15:13 and the Occasion of Romans," 65–84.

50. Nanos, *The Mystery of Romans*.

51. Godet and Chambers, *Romans*, 467; Cranfield and Sanday, *Romans*, 2:690–97; Käsemann, *Romans*, 368–69; Jewett, "The Law Coexistence of Jews and Gentiles in Romans," 354; Watson, *Paul, Judaism, and the Gentiles*, 94–98; Tomson, *Paul and the Jewish Law;* Fitzmyer, *Romans*; Barclay, "Do We Undermine the Law?" 287–308; Moo, *Romans*; Dunn, *Romans 9–16*.

52. Wedderburn, *The Reasons for Romans*; Ziesler, *Paul's Letter to the Romans*; Reasoner, *The Strong and the Weak*.

53. Stowers, *A Rereading of Romans*.

54. Nanos, *The Mystery of Romans*, 85–165; Gagnon, "Why the 'Weak' at Rome Cannot Be Non-Christian Jews," 64–82.

and Christ-believing Gentiles in Rome is highly probable. The 'weak' most probably are the Jews but could also include God-fearing, believing Gentiles and the "strong" believing Gentiles. Granted this, the audience of the letter could be Jewish Jesus followers, God-fearing Gentile Jesus followers, and Jesus-following Gentiles though the majority seems to be Jesus-following Gentiles.

This conclusion has direct bearing on the discussion of the identity of ἀλλήλους, τὸν ἕτερον and πλησίον. It is argued that since Μηδενὶ μηδὲν (13:8a) is a universal negative and influences the next section of the sentence, ἀλλήλους must refer to a wider application.[55] Although this conclusion might be legitimate, the use of the term in the entire letter must be considered to decide its function in this unit. The term ἀλλήλους occurs mainly within discussions related to intramural topics except in 1:27 where it speaks of disobedient outsiders. It is a reciprocal pronoun stating a reciprocal spiritual benefit (1:12), functional dependency (12:5), unity in thinking (12:10a; 16; 15:5), respect (12:10b), avoiding judgment (14:13), seeking peace and mutual building (14:19), accepting fellow believers (15:7), admonishing (15:14) and greeting (16:16). The word is used mainly in building the community by keeping peace and unity. It refers to the interdependence of each member of the Jesus followers for the construction and existence of the community. Hence, ἀλλήλους ἀγαπᾶν refers to love among or within the Jesus followers (believing Jews, believing God-fearing Gentiles and believing Gentiles).

The phrase τὸν ἕτερον (13:8c), as argued above, is the object of ἀγαπῶν. Yet, most scholars ascribed an indefinite identity to it such as any person brought to the believing community or mutual relationship among men.[56] Paul seems to be using the word for contrasting categorically similar or differing groups or things. In 2:1, Paul castigates a person who judges the other (κρίνεις τὸν ἕτερον). The term ἕτερον here might be in the same or different category in the sense that Gentiles or Jews, for the judge seems to take τὸν ἕτερον different from himself in a given behavioral standard. In 2:21, the Jew teaches another person (ὁ οὖν διδάσκων ἕτερον) who might as well categorically be from the same group (a Jew) or a different group (a God-fearing Gentile). However, the person who is taught

55. Parry, *Romans*, 170; Moule, *Romans*, 358; Murray, *Romans*, 166; Cranfield, *Romans*, 1:675.

56. Parry, *Romans*, 170; Murray, *Romans*, 160; Cranfield, *Romans*, 1:676; Ziesler, *Romans*, 317.

is different from the Jewish teacher in terms of knowledge of God. In 7:3–4, marrying a different person is also understood as ἕτερον which is also a different relationship. The 'other' Law in 7:23 refers to a different Law. In 8:39 any other creature might also be understood as a different creature other than that listed by Paul. 'Any other' commandment (13:9) refers to additional commandments different from what have been listed. In all its occurrences in the letter, ἕτερον *contrasts persons or things* in the same or different category, highlighting their differences.

In case of 13:8c ἕτερον could refer to either categorically different or similar groups insofar as the whole sentence is indefinite. Romans 13:8c portrays a paradigmatic character (see chapter seven of this study) that the community should emulate and hence ἕτερον is not limited categorically. It embraces either a categorically different group or a similar group. Nonetheless, as the use of the word within the letter demonstrates, it contrasts and highlights differences against the one who is the subject of the verb 'love' in 13:8c. Therefore, ἕτερον in 13:8c is the all–embracing 'Other' (i.e. both insider and outsider) emphasizing differences.

The term πλησίον is used only three times in the whole letter (13:9, 10; 15:2). A few scholars think that it refers to all men or any person with whom the community interacts.[57] However, the citation from Lev 19:18 and Paul's use of it in 15:2 seem to indicate that πλησίον refers to the insiders. In the former case, it refers to Israel but is transferred to the Jesus followers and, in the latter case, it refers to the members of the believing community particularly to 'the weak' because Paul uses οἰκοδομήν which is edifying the believing community. Therefore, primarily πλησίον refers to the believing community.

Hence, while ἀλλήλους and πλησίον refer to the insiders, that is, the audiences of the letter namely: the believing Jews, the believing God–fearing Gentiles and believing Gentiles, τὸν ἕτερον embraces categorically different groups: both believing and unbelieving persons. The phrase τὸν ἕτερον underlines differences within the same or different category while ἀλλήλους and πλησίον underscore similarities within a category despite diversity and differences in opinion or practices.

57. Moule, *Romans*, 358; Sanday and Headlam, *Romans*, 373; Lenski, *Romans 8–16*, 800; William, *Romans*, 240; Hendriksen, *Romans*, 2:439; Cranfield, *Romans*, 1:676; Käsemann, *Romans*, 361; Stuhlmacher, *Romans*, 209.

Investigating Claims, Reasons and Unstated Assumptions of 13:8–10

Scholars have attempted to identify enthymemes in Pauline letters. According to Harper's study on Aristotle's enthymemes, an enthymeme is any "argument containing a claim and reasons to support the claim."[58] Enthymeme is "an assertion supported by another statement."[59] While scholars debate over whether enthymeme has unstated premises, Antoine C. Braet, after investigating Aristotle's rhetoric, concluded that one of the defining features of enthymeme in Aristotle's rhetoric is implicit premises.[60] Particularly, he argued, such a feature stands out in an oratorical situation and is "always characterized by the omission of those parts of the argument which are known to the audience and which they can fill in for themselves. . . [therefore] at least one extra premise must be assumed . . .[which] can be reconstructed by means of Aristotelian forms of Argument."[61]

Marc J. Debanne investigated enthymemes in the letter of Paul.[62] He adduced Rom 13:8–10 as one of the pieces of evidence for the existence of enthymemes in the letter of Paul.[63]He identifies the following syllogism:

Major premise: Any principle which prohibits wronging a neighbor fulfils the Law.

Minor premise: The love principle prohibits wronging a neighbor (Rom 13:10a).

Conclusion: The love principle fulfils the Law (13:10b).

Although Debanne's identification of enthymeme in 13:8–10 has contributed to the analysis of the textual unit, it does omit other unstated premises that are working in the argumentation process. Further, any principle' in the major premise seems to go beyond Paul's context of argument, and it cannot be adduced from the letter itself. Instead, Paul formulates his thesis with one rationale and two supporting reasons:

Thesis: Love one another (13:8b)

58. Harper, "An Analytical Description of Aristotle's Enthymeme," 309.

59. Debanne, *Enthymemes in the Letters of Paul*, 29.

60. Braet, "The Enthymeme in Aristotle's Rhetoric," 1999.

61. Braet, "The Enthymeme in Aristotle's Rhetoric,"107–8.

62. Debanne, *Enthymemes in the Letters of Paul.*

63. Debanne, *Enthymemes in the Letters of Paul*, 183.

Rationale: for [any Jesus follower] who loves the other has fulfilled the Law (13:8c)

Reason 1: for "love your neighbor as yourself" summarizes the Law (13:9b)

Reason 2: [for] love does not do wrong to a neighbor (13:10a)

Conclusion: Therefore, love fulfils the Law (13:10b)

The rationale and the two supporting reasons to be true must have unstated assumptions. For instance, Paul reasons, "any Jesus follower who loves the other has fulfilled the Law." But he has never stated the reason for the introduction of the Law in the injunction of love. The diagram on page 123 maps Paul's reasons and probable assumptions and conclusions. The assumptions are crucial to understanding why Paul is insisting on loving one another and its connection to the fulfilment of the Law. Three assumptions are discernible: 1) Jesus followers should fulfil the Law; 2) all the commandments of the Law are about doing right to a neighbor; 3) all the commandments of the Law prohibit doing wrong to a neighbor. Each assumption will be discussed below:

Assumption #1: Jesus followers should fulfil the Law

The verse, "for [any Jesus follower] who loves the other has fulfilled the Law" (13:8c) functions as a ground for the injunction of love. Particularly, γὰρ, according to Robbins introduces the rationale as the basis or proof of a thesis.[64] Cranfield proposes two alternatives for the purpose of γὰρ in 13:8c: either as reason or explanation.[65]But, one can also think of it as "result." However, whether γὰρ introduces a reason, an explanation, or a result, no significant difference exists in terms of its function so long as it is a ground for Paul's claim. Cranfield's reading of γὰρ as explanation of the impossibility of paying the debt of love is entirely unconvincing.[66] Firstly, Paul is not discussing the impossibility of loving the other insofar as he believes that love exists in the heart of believers (5:1–3). Reading love as an unpayable debt is a long–standing conviction since the patristic period, but Murray rejects such reading arguing for its practicability.[67]

64. Robbins, *Exploring the Texture of Texts.*

65. Cranfield, *Romans*, 1:676.

66. Cranfield, *Romans*, 1:676.

67. Murray, *Romans*, 156.

Secondly, the injunction of love presupposes the existence of love within the believing community and Paul warns them not to pretend it (12:9). Thirdly, Cranfield's reason is based on theological commitment that if γὰρ is providing reason, then there will be theological inconstancy for no one can fulfil the Law. Such reading dismisses what Paul has been arguing and developing in the previous section of the letter. Paul already argued for the reason why it was impossible to keep the Law and the solution to the problem in Rom 7 and 8 of the letter. For Paul, it is possible to keep the Law in the realm of the Spirit. Therefore, it is impossible to downplay the importance of the Law because of theological predilection.

If 13:8c is a proof of the thesis, then why does fulfilling the Law become the basis for the thesis? No explicit answer is provided. Nevertheless, there must be a solid ground for Paul to claim that fulfilling the Law to be a reason for carrying out the injunction of love. First, fulfilling the Law is the big question in the letter; therefore, it is connected to the previous discussions of the letter. Particularly, it functions as an answer to Paul's insistence that the believing community upholds the Law (3:31) and fulfils the righteous requirements of the Law (8:4–8). Wright also perceives that 13:8–10 looks back to 2:17–29 just as 12:1–2 looks back to 1:18–32.[68] Paul's goal is to bring the obedience of faith for the sake of his [Jesus] name among all the nations (1:5). Yet, those who do not obey the Law are a cause for the blaspheming of God's name among the Gentiles (2:24). Those who are in the flesh do not submit to God's Law therefore cannot please God (8:7), but the Jesus followers are called to seek what is pleasing God (12:1–2). Such background discussion of the Law elucidates that the Jesus followers are expected to fulfil the requirements of the Law, although Paul did not explicitly state it, he used *fulfilling the Law as a reason for loving one another*. Without the assumption that the Jesus followers should fulfil the requirement of the Law, fulfilling of the Law cannot be a ground for Paul's claim for loving the other.

Assumption #2: All the commandments of the Law are about doing right to a neighbor

Γὰρ again occurs in 13:9a providing a reason for the summation of the second table commandments and the other commandments, which in turn serves as motivation for the rationale. Paul lists only four prohibiting

68. Wright, *Romans*, 724.

commandments: no adultery, no killing, no stealing, no coveting, but he omits the fifth one—no lying. Nygren wrongly concludes that the Law is always characterized by negative quality prohibiting and straining sin.[69] Nonetheless, the fourth and the fifth commandments, "keep the Sabbath" and "honor your parents," are positive commands. Likewise, Paul summarizes the commandments with a positive commandment from Lev 19:18 "love your neighbor as yourself." Fredrikson has shown that the second table of the ten commandments is about justice towards others.[70] Justice is doing right towards others. Similarly, love, though not in the Ten Commandments, is one of the commandments of the Law that apparently speaks of the right relationship towards the other. Paul is not reasoning to supplant the Law with Love. Instead, he is building his case that loving one another will allow the Jesus followers to fulfil the Law. Love is a term that Paul uses to designate the application of Law–recommended actions towards a neighbor. In his summary of the Law, his unstated premise is that all the commandments of the Law are about doing right to a neighbor that can be expressed in the language of love with the Law being its content.

Assumption #3: All the commandments of the Law prohibit doing wrong to a neighbor

Paul's second reason "love does no wrong to a neighbor" is not introduced by γὰρ but it stands as a reason to support the first rationale. However, it is closely connected to "love your neighbor as yourself." It explains what it means to love a neighbor as oneself: it is not doing wrong to a neighbor. If this is granted, then the Law delineates what wrongdoing is. Since loving a neighbor summarizes the Law because loving a neighbor means not doing wrong to a neighbor, then the assumption goes: the Law prohibits doing wrong to a neighbor. Paul does not explicitly state this but assumes that his readers know it from his argument; not least because he lists the specific commandments that prohibit evil.

69. Nygren, *Romans*, 434.

70. Fredriksen, "Romans," 803.

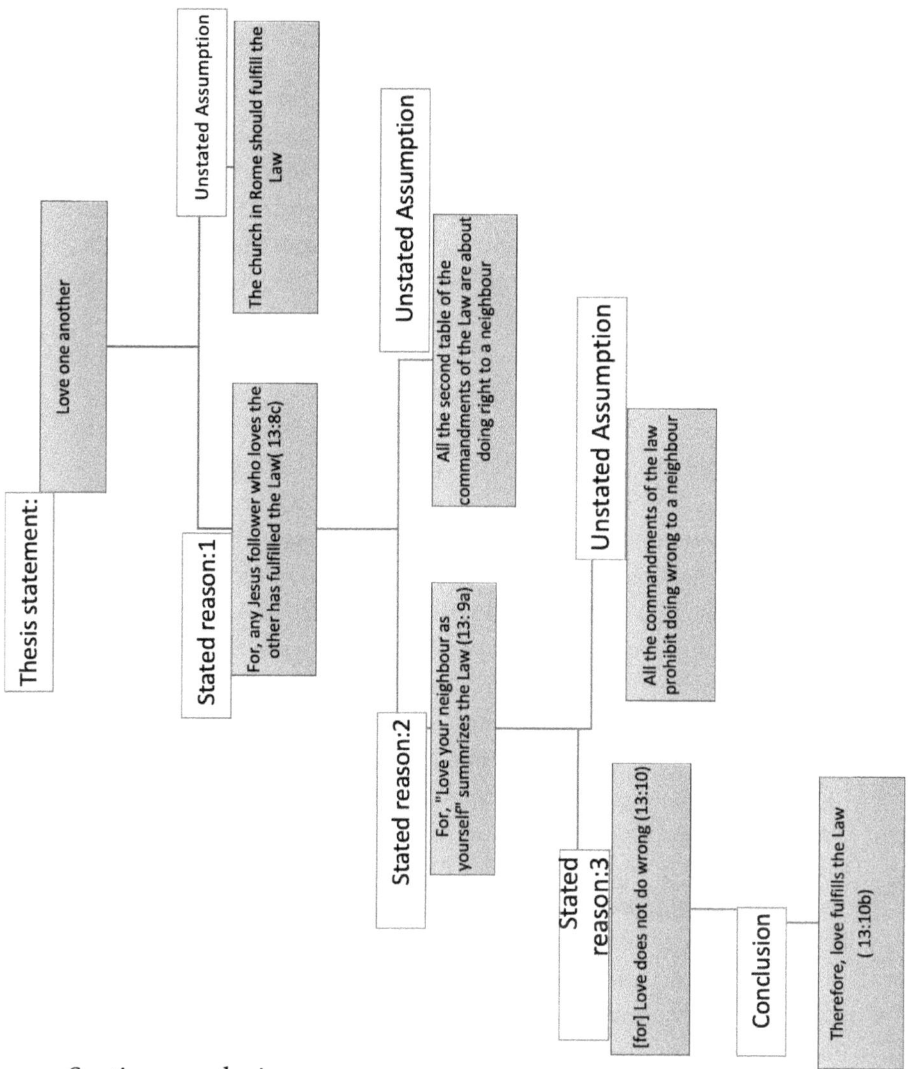

Section conclusion

The injunction of loving one another is fundamentally based on the unstated conviction that any Jesus followers should fulfil the Law, not least the second table of the Law which fundamentally deals with doing right to a neighbor. Paul summarizes the Law in terms of love not because love is qualitatively superior to the Law; nor does it supplant the Law with love. Rather, Paul is *employing love-language* to *represent the Law in a succinct fashion* because the Law *defines and gives content* to love, not the other way round.

COMPARING THE KEY CONCEPTS: ΑΓΑΠΗ AND ΝΟΜΟΣ IN 13:8–14

In Chapter 2 of this study, three conclusions have been reached regarding *ἀγάπη*: (1) *ἀγάπη* could be pretended, hence, it needs to be restricted with content (12:9); (2) the source of *ἀγάπη* is God; and (3) *ἀγάπη* is a conscious and deliberate act choosing to do right towards God and fellow believers despite opposing and adversarial conditions and environment. With regard to *νόμος* it is concluded that Jesus followers establish the Law by walking according to the Spirit, therefore obedience to the Law is now possible for those who live in the sphere of the Spirit. However, Paul did not bring these two concepts into close comparison until 13:8–14. In 13:8–14, he is not only summarising the Law, but he argued his case by comparing *ἀγάπη* and *νόμος* within the rhetorical unit under question. In this section, the two concepts will be compared within the pericope in light of discussions and conclusions made in Chapter two.

Paul has reasoned that *ἀγάπη* summarises *νόμος*, because "*ἀγάπη τῷ πλησίον κακὸν οὐκ ἐργάζεται.*" This statement reveals the key feature of *ἀγάπη* being compared to *νόμος* in the rhetorical unit. According to Hendriksen the statement is a form of litotes, a negative expression implying strong positive affirmation.[71] Beginning from the ancient interpreters such as Chrysostom, Pelagius, Theodoret of Cyr, Theodoret of Mopsuestia, and Augustine, *ἀγάπη* in this context is understood as having two qualities: abstaining from evil and doing good.[72] Others added to this that it is a relational and legal duty in doing good and avoiding evil,[73] performing justice despite being hated or abused by opponents.[74] However, Murray explains *ἀγάπη* as emotive (creates affinity), motive (impels to action) and expulsive (expels what is alien which love seeks to promote).[75] Murray's analysis of love is not evident in the letter to the Romans, however, it seems to be an attractive explanation. Achtemeier right in saying love is not a state of emotion but an action.[76] As Peng's (2006) conclusion ascertained, there is consensus that *ἀγάπη* is holding

71. Hendriksen, *Romans*, 2:439.

72. Bray and Oden, *Romans*, 331–32.

73. Brown, *Romans*, 495; Barth, *Romans*, 496; Moule, *Romans*, 358; Hendriksen, *Romans*, 2:439;

74. Luther, *Romans*, 168.

75. Murray, *Romans*, 161.

76. Achtemeier, *Romans*, 209.

fast to what is good and hating what is evil.[77] Even this is not only attitudinal change towards something good or evil. Rather, it is doing good and abstaining from doing evil.

Granting this conclusion, then what is "good" and what is "evil" are the two hallmarks that distinguish what is an act of love and what is not an act of love. The concept of evil is described in chapter 1:18–32 as the disposition of those who refused to obey or worship the true God. The phrase ἐφευρετὰς κακῶ (devisers of evil) (1:30) is one of the sins they commit.[78] thinks that the phrase signifies the depth of evil and Cranfield[79] interprets it as "ever more hateful methods of hurting and destroying their fellow men." However, in 1:30, it is just one sin among many other sins, albeit that it encompasses all kinds of evilness. Nevertheless, κατεργαζομένου τὸ κακόν (who does evil) (2:9) seem to be representing all kinds of unrighteousness and disobedience to God described in 1:18–2:5. Those who act evilly are those who rebel against their creator by worshipping idols, exchanging the truth for lies (1:22–26a) and practicing all kinds of malicious immorality (1:26b–31). Consequently, they are handed over to their desires, base minds, and improper conduct. In light of this, all evil works are related to the refusal of acknowledging God and his ways.

A similar thought is developed in the following section of the letter. The κακὸν in 7:19, 21 contrasted against ἀγαθόν which was difficult for ἐγώ to perform. The κακός refers to sin or actions that are prohibited by the Law (all kinds of covetousness 7:8) whereas ἀγαθός refers to the things demanded by the Law (7:18, 19, and 21). Particularly 12:21 can be contrasted to 7:23 because Paul insists that one can overcome evil by doing good whereas 7:23 speaks of one who is defeated by evil. Barth thinks that love is "the good work by which evil is overcome"[80] or a genuine love is hating what is evil and holding on to what is good.[81] κακός in 12:9–13:7 entails haughtiness (12:16b), conceit (12:16c), paying evil for evil (12:17), avenging (12:19), breaking civil laws (13:3, 4), and in 14:20 becoming an obstacle to fellow believers and destroying the work of God. Paul finally calls the Jesus followers to avoid κακός and promote ἀγαθός which is the goal of wisdom (16:19). In light of Paul's discussion of κακός in the letter, it is a thought pattern, action and behavioral practice against the revealed

77. Peng, *Hate the Evil, Hold Fast to the Good*, 2006.

78. Schreiner, *Romans*, 98.

79. Cranfield, *Romans*, 1:132.

80. Barth, *Romans*, 496.

81. Peng, *Hate the Evil, Hold Fast to the Good*, 108.

will of God either through nature (1:20–21) or through explicit teaching of the Law (1:32; 2:17–24 and 7:19, 21).

The term ἀγαθός refers mainly to action approved or recommended by the Law, but κακός is what the Law prohibits and disapproves. Paul contrasts the Law against sin and the state of the ἐγὼ in 7:12–13. The Law is ἅγιος (holy), and its commandment is holy, just and good (ἡ ἐντολὴ ἁγία καὶ δικαία καὶ ἀγαθή). The Law by its origin and nature is good, just and holy (7:12–13). In 2:7&10, ἀγαθός describes a different group of paradigmatic characters, to be emulated by the Jesus followers, therefore, they are diametrically opposite in attitude, action, behavior, desire and destiny from the ones that are described in 1:18–2:5. Although no Law is mentioned in this place, it is insinuated in 2:12–15 as it is the closest context for 2:10. On the contrary, no ἀγαθός is used in 13:8–10 but Paul cited in 13:9 the second table of the Decalogue albeit in different order. Nonetheless, no absolute agreement exists on the type of νόμος. For instance, Beet, Sandy and Headlam and Lenski understand νόμος in 13:8–10 as a general principle of right and wrong which was later historically formulated in the Law of Moses.[82] Lenski argues that the quotation cited in 13:9 is just to provide an example of pure law. On the other hand, David Brown, Vaughan, Denney, Alford, Nygren, Murray, Leenhardt, Dunn, Fitzmyer, and Schreiner opine that the Law in 13:8–10 is none other than the Law of Moses.[83] In no other place, in this letter, did Paul use νόμος to refer to apart from the Mosaic Law as argued in Chapter two of this study. There is no compelling reason to think of different laws here. If this is granted, ἀγαθός is also assumed, based on 7:12 in 13:8–10 and the commandments prohibiting κακός such as: killing, stealing, coveting and adultery and any evils not listed here (any other commandments), and the sins committed by those who know the decree of God (2:28–32; 3:9–17 and 7:7–24).

Further, the contrast between light and darkness in 13:11–14 develops the concept of κακός. In particular, κακός is used in 2:9 in relation to not living according to the Law. The people who do not know the Law and do not practice it are blind and live in the darkness, not least those who break the first commandment of the Decalogue by worshiping

82. Beet, *Romans*, 345; Sanday and Headlam, *Romans*, 373; Lenski, *Romans 8–16*, 798.

83. Brown, *Romans*, 134; Vaughan, *Romans*, 232–33; Denney, "St.Paul's Epistle to the Romans," 698; Alford, *Greek Testament*, 448; Nygren, *Romans*, 433; Murray, *Romans*, 162; Leenhardt, *Romans*, 434; Dunn, *Romans 9–16*, 776; Käsemann, *Romans*, 360; Fitzmyer, *Romans*, 678; Schreiner, *Romans*, 692.

images (1:21). On the contrary, those who teach and practice the Law are those who are walking in the light (2:19) because they know the will of God which is the main theme of 12:1–2. The light is the will of God whereas darkness is against it. Peng argues that the will of God is not only having the right relationship with someone, but it is "concerned with a decent individual's moral compatibility with Christian salvation. . ."[84]The list of works of darkness is not exhaustive but they are briefly adding or reminding of the ones listed in 1:29–31; in particular, ἔριδι is one of the sins found in the list. The terms σαρκὸς and ἐπιθυμίας are reminiscent of Paul's discussion of 6:12—7:25. The concept μὴ in 13:13 and 14 negates the evil which closely follows the prohibiting formulation of the commandments of the Law in 13:9. This granted, κακός in 13:11–14 is something that the Law implicitly prohibits. In this case, ἀγαθός is to put on like a cloak, the Lord Jesus Christ in whom the Law of the Spirit of life works to bring freedom from sin and death and empowers the believer to fulfil the requirement of the Law (8:2–4).

In 12:9–13:7, Ἀγαθός is also discernible: honoring one another "in exceptional degree" (LN 78:35) (12:10), serving the Lord (12:11), hope, patience in tribulation, prayer, financial support to the needy saints, hospitality, blessing opponents, identifying with others with their joy and mourning, living in harmony, thinking what is noble, feeding the enemy, good conduct, and paying revenue. Except serving the Lord, hope, and prayer, which signify a relationship with God, the others are related to person-to-person relationships. While supporting the needy saints, feeding the enemy, paying tax, identifying with others in their joy and mourning are specific, thinking noble thoughts, good conduct, living in harmony and blessing one's opponents are general and have no specific commands. No explicit parallel with the Mosaic Law is discernible because Paul is dealing with a specific situation and context of the Jesus followers in Rome.

However, a closer parallel is discernible between 13:9 and 2:21–24. A Jew preaches and teaches against stealing, adultery, and idols. These are practical matters related to what a Jew should practice with respect to God as well as in social relationships. However, in 2:17–20, Paul might be referring to a Jew teaching God-fearing Gentiles who are in darkness and blind to the things of God. The commandments of the Law, at least the Decalogue and specifically the second table of the Decalogue prohibit

84. Peng, *Hate the Evil, Hold Fast to the Good*, 142.

stealing, killing, false witnessing, coveting, and adultery which deal with person-to-person relationships. In other words, not to steal, not to kill, not to witness falsely, not to covet and not to commit adultery are ἀγαθός and they are all compatible with what Paul enumerated as good in 12:9—13:7. Therefore, what is good and what is evil is defined and explicated by the Law. Love is avoiding what is evil and not doing wrong, or positively defined, it means doing good. Therefore, *love is practising what the Law prescribes as good and avoiding what the Law designates as evil.*

However, ἀγάπη and νόμος differ in several ways. First, love does not provide knowledge of ἀγαθός and κακός. Love simply practices ἀγαθός and hates κακός based on a set standard of what is good and what is evil. But νόμος provides knowledge of God's will, approves what is excellent, provides light and guidance, embodies knowledge and truth and serves as a source of instruction (2:17–24; 3:2; 9:4) and it is a permanent expression of God's will.[85] *Therefore, the Law is the source of knowledge and the ground for love's action.*

Second, love is not concretely defined. Paul defines love by what "it does not do" not by "what it is," but "what it does" is assumed. While the Law is explicitly defined as good, just, and holy (7:12–13), love is described as not doing wrong to a neighbor (13:10) which paraphrases its feature as fulfilling the Law.[86] Schreiner rightly said that love is "a plastic word that can be twisted to fit almost anything"[87]and therefore, particular commandments are needed "in which the Law breaks down the obligation to save us from sentimentality and self-deception. . . "[88] Hence, love can only be discerned by "what it does not do," but "what it does"; and what "it does not do" is governed by "what is good" and "what is evil" which in turn is defined by the Law.[89]

Third, love is not synecdoche, a part representing the whole. Nor does it supplant the Law because it is one of the commandments of the Law (13:9). Rather, *it heads and provides the language to express the different commandments of the Law succinctly.* The term ἀνακεφαλαιοῦται (13:9b) is defined as literary or rhetorical summation: to sum up, recapitulate (Rom 13:9; Eph 1:10) or mathematically: total sum up, ledger

85. Leenhardt, *Romans*, 337.

86. Räisänen, *Paul and the Law*, 65.

87. Schreiner, *The Law and Its Fulfillment*, 38.

88. Cranfield, "St. Paul and the Law," 67.

89. Watson, *Paul, Judaism, and the Gentiles*, 288.

entry.[90] Commentators translated it as 'summarily repeats,'[91] summing up the scattered particulars into one,[92] common denominator,[93] and essential points.[94] LN (63.8) defines it as "to bring together" whereas TGL (346) defines 13:9 as: to sum up (again), to repeat summarily, or to condense into a summary (as a substance of speech) but it defines Eph 1:10 as "bringing all things together." The term ἀνακεφαλαιοῦται (Rom 13:9, cf Eph 1:10) in the context of Rom 13:8–10 could mean bringing all things together in one "head" or leading concept, without denying the role of the particulars. Hence, love, being one of the particulars among many commandments in the Law, does not assimilate all the particulars of the commandments of the Law, nor does it contain all the commandments in itself. Rather, love leads the commandments of the Law in the sense that *it comes first to serve as an expression* for the result and meaning of doing what the Law commands.

While scholars noted that 13:8–10 focuses on love, not on the Law,[95] they failed to appreciate the indispensable role of the Law in Paul's reasoning. Fulfilling the Law is the concern within the believing community, which probably created division (Rom14–15). Paul wants cohesion within the community by settling the question of the role of the Law within the believing community. Therefore, he reintroduced the two concepts in such a way that one depends on the other. Love being part of the commandments of the Law, leads any other commandments by *creating the mode and language* within which they should be practiced. In particular, ἐργάζεται is the key word as it emphasises action that carries out a set standard. The Law is the bedrock as foundation and a resource of discernment and guidance for love because it is impossible for love to summarise the knowledge embodied in the Law, but the love command serves as a spear on the forefront, creating the mode, the language, and the attitude for practising the other commandments: doing good and hating evil.

Fourth, it is the Law that love fulfils (13:8c and 13:10b). Paul did not say the Law is love, nor did he say love is the Law. Rather, he said that love fulfils the Law. Several definitions have been rendered to πλήρου

90. Arndt and Danker, *A Greek-English Lexicon*, 65.

91. Meyer, *Critical and Exegetical Handbook*, II:286.

92. Nicoll, *Romans*, 698.

93. Käsemann, *Romans*, 361.

94. Lenski, *Romans 8–16*, 798.

95. Räisänen, *Paul and the Law*, 64.

(πεπλήρωκεν/πλήρωμα (13:8c and 13:10b). Nicoll provides four definitions for πλήροω: (1) to make full, fill (full): Matt 13:48, 23:32; Acts 2:2, Acts 5:28; John 12:3; Phil 4:19; Eph 4:10; (2) to complete a period of time, fill up, complete; (3) to bring to completion that which was already begun, complete, finish; (4) to bring to a designed end, fulfil. Under this definition, a subsection defines: the fulfilment of divine predictions or a promise (it is always in passive), a duty, or office (Col 4:17) and perform, to carry out or to bring to full expression such as in Matt 5:17.[96] Rom 13:8c is also grouped in this last section of meaning.[97]

Commentators also have attempted to define πλήροω in 13:8c: ". . . fill up by action . . . ,"[98] "to do all that the law requires . . .,"[99] attending to a specific commandment,[100] "perform properly" or "do what the law really asks for,"[101] "doing the law,"[102] and accomplish duties or complete a required task, discharge.[103] Hence, πλήροω carries *the idea of action, doing, or performing.* Without theological meaning, πεπλήρωκεν, therefore, means "has done, has performed, has carried out."

The word πλήρωμα (13:10) also has a wider semantic field: that which fills up (1 Cor 10:26), that which makes something full, complete, supplement or complement (Matt 9:10, Mark 2:12), that which is full of something, that which is brought to fullness and completion such as a full number (Rom 15:25), sum total, fullness (Rom 15:29; Col 2:9; Eph 3:19), act of fulfilling specification.[104] Commentators define it as "filling a void,"[105] "result,"[106] "content,"[107] "fulfilling,"[108] "culminate."[109] Based on the

96. Arndt and Danker, *A Greek-English Lexicon*, 828–29.

97. Arndt and Danker, *A Greek-English Lexicon*, 829.

98. Beet, *Romans*, 345.

99. Brown, *Romans*, 495.

100. Hodge, *Romans*, 407.

101. Dunn, *Romans 9–16*, 777.

102. Schreiner, *Romans*, 692.

103. Jewett, *Romans*, 809.

104. Arndt and Danker, *A Greek-English Lexicon*, 830.

105. Godet and Chambers, *Romans*, 317.

106. Byrne, *Romans*, 396; Lenski, *Romans 8–16*, 800.

107. Murray, *Romans*, 164.

108. Cranfield and Sanday, *Romans*, 2:678; Barrett, *Romans*, 231; Käsemann, *Romans*, 361; Sanday and Headlam, *Romans*, 374; Moo, *Romans*, 817.

109. Achtemeier, *Romans*, 208; Ziesler, *Romans*, 318.

definition of πλήροω (13:8c) which is a cognate of πλήρωμα, Paul is most probably using it in the active sense, meaning fulfilling, repeating 13:8c.

However, Westerholm distinguishes between "doing," for the non-believing Jews, and "fulfilling,ġ for believing Jews and Gentiles, arguing that "fulfil" in 13:8–10 is to satisfy completely what the Law requires.[110] Such definition is untenable, because in his own definition, "fulfils" means "obedience offered" that completely satisfies the requirement of the Law.[111] The difference between "doing" and "offering obedience" is superficial, for "obedience offered" is the same as doing. Further, Westerholm has already taken a position that 2:13–14 as Gentiles whereas others read it as believing Gentiles, and in Col 4:17 the word πλήροω means "performing" or "doing." Räisänen thinks it means "the Torah participates in the love command in all its individual commands."[112] Such definition also blurs the meaning of whether the love command involves keeping the Law or not, is unclear. Veronica Koperski, on the other hand, thinks that it is just a metaphorical expression of the sufficiency of love.[113] Nowhere in the letter has Paul used the Law metaphorically and neither does the literary context of the letter substantiate what Koperski claims. The most probable definition is the one that entails the action aspect of the word. Therefore, Dunn, Schreiner, and Jewett and Kotansky interpretations of πλήροω as "properly perform" or "do what the law really asks for," "doing the law," and accomplish duties or completing required task, discharge respectively maintain the action aspect of the word.[114]

The application of love fulfilling the Law, however, is ascribed to a varied degree of the Law. Räisänen argues that it refers to the moral content of the Law.[115] Others hold that it is about: one's neighbor,[116] the spirit of the Law—faith and love,[117] the commandments related to social relationships,[118] God's will apart from the Law,[119]and the requirements of

110. Westerholm, *Israel's Law and the Church's Faith*, 203–4.

111. Westerholm, *Israel's Law and the Church's Faith*, 204.

112. Räisänen, *Paul and the Law*, 1983, 26.

113. Koperski, *What Are They Saying*, 71.

114. Dunn, *Romans 9–16*, 777; Schreiner, *Romans*, 692; Jewett, *Romans*, 809.

115. Räisänen, *Paul and the Law*, 1983, 114.

116. Brown, *Romans*, 495; Calvin, *Romans 1–16*, 483.

117. Parry, *Romans*; Boyarin, *A Radical Jew*, 132.

118. Hodge, *Romans*, 407.

119. Käsemann, *Romans*, 218; Nygren, *Romans*, 433.

the Law.[120] But there is no restriction in Paul's usage as ἑτέρα ἐντολή (13:9) is a comprehensive reference to the Law particularly referring to the first table of the Decalogue. Neither can direct reference to the first table of the Decalogue be adduced. Yet, the concept is discernible in 1:22 that the commandment of no other gods and no graving image being broken. For instance, 3:30 claims monotheistic faith insinuating to the *Shema,* Deut 6:4–5, which in turn is reminiscent of the first two commandments of the first table of the Decalogue in the context of loving God. Even though the language of sacrifice (3:25) is transferred to the death of Jesus, the role of the Law is emphasized as a witness to the revelation of the righteousness of God (1:2; 3:21), and the nature of circumcision is internalized (2:28–29), no hard-core evidence can be adduced from the letter to conclude that the Law is abrogated. Nor does Paul claim exemption for Gentiles from practicing the Law despite his severe analysis of the Law with regard to sin (Rom 7:8, 9, 10, 11, and 12). Neither can Paul's prescription of keeping the whole Law be attested.

Nonetheless, granting the existence of minority Jews, God-fearing Gentiles, and the Gentiles and allowing freedom of expressing one's faith and keeping the Law in Christ before God (14:22–23), Paul's insistence seems to be that they should exercise the Law within their situation. For instance, Paul did not deny the value of circumcision, rather, he argued that it should be accompanied by obeying the Law (2:25–29; 15:8) and neither did he recommend the uncircumcised to be circumcised. Paul's argument, instead, is that all have a common problem, that is, both Jews and Gentiles have sinned and fall short of the glory of God (3:22–33 and 7). But those who are in Christ are delivered from the tyranny of sin (6:6, 7, 18, 22) therefore they should not allow sin to reign in their mortal body (6:12) because they are now slaves of righteousness (6:22). It is also argued above that the Law provides knowledge about sin, God's will and God's truth, *while love has no such role*. Granting this, Paul provides a common ground for the Jews and Gentiles, who live in the realm of the Spirit (8:4, 6), without violating their ethnic identity. All the commandments pertain to sin, God's will and God's truth, which must be understood in light of the death and resurrection of Christ and must be obeyed.

Notwithstanding the aforementioned functional differences, love and the Law are compatible and work together. The Law has abiding relevance to behavior which entails love as one of its commandments. Murray

120. Murray, *Romans*, 161.

insists that "the commandments are the norms in accordance with which love operates."[121] Further, love and the Law are both in the sphere of the Spirit. Love is poured out in the heart through the Spirit from God (5:5) whereas the Law is spiritual (7:12, 13, 14) and the goal of walking in the Spirit is pleasing God by fulfilling the requirement of the Law (8:4–8). The summary of the Law in 13:8–10, therefore, is a submission to the Law mainly to the obligation with regard to behavior under the sphere of the Spirit heading love as a prominent command among other commandments which delineate the feature and standard of genuine love.

CHAPTER SUMMARY AND CONCLUSION

The discussion on the argumentative texture of Rom 13:8–14 has evinced that the structure of Rom 13:8–14 is closely connected to chapters 12, 14, and 15 both thematically as well as in constructing the letter's argument. It is also argued that ὀφείλετε (13:8a), εἰ μὴ (13:8b), ἕτερον (13:8c), and ἡ ἀγάπη (13:10) must be translated as "love" as imperative, "except," "the other," and "love" respectively. It is also concluded that ἀλλήλους means "one another" and refers to inter-dependence within the believing community; therefore, it is about love within the community. The concept τὸν ἕτερον has a contrasting function, highlighting differences. The differences, however, would either be within the same category or in different categories, whereas πλησίον and ἀλλήλους emphasize the similarities within the same category, despite obvious differences. Thus, Gentile Jesus followers, being in the majority, the audience of the summary of the Law entails Jews and God-fearing Gentile Jesus followers. Love and the Law, seemgly dissimilar, are neither antithetical nor does one replace the other. Love, being prominent among the commandments of the Law, *provides the language to summarize the Law* and to *express the feature of its praxis*. Love means *obeying* the commandments of the Law pertaining to sin against God and fellow persons. The Law, on the other hand, delineates the *nature, content and standard* of genuine love. Romans 13:8–10 is therefore *a succinct and memorable expression* of the result and meaning of obeying the commandments of the Law—especially its prohibition against evil (sin) and its prescription of doing good towards fellow persons.

121. Murray, *Romans*, 162.

4

Matthew 22:34–40

Inner Texture Analysis

34 But when the Pharisees heard that he had silenced the Sadducees, they came together. 35 And one of them, a lawyer, asked him a question, to test him. 36 "Tacher, which is the great commandment in the law?" 37 And he said to him, "You shall love the Lord your God with all your heart, and with all your soul, and with all your mind. 38 This is the great and first commandment. 39 and a second is like it, You shall love your neighbor as yourself. 40 On these two commandments depend all the law and the prophets." Nestle–Aland Greek-English New Testament.	34 Οἱ δὲ Φαρισαῖοι ἀκούσαντες ὅτι ἐφίμωσεν τοὺς Σαδδουκαίους συνήχθησαν ἐπὶ τὸ αὐτό. 35 καὶ ἐπηρώτησεν εἷς ἐξ αὐτῶν νομικὸς πειράζων αὐτόν. 36 διδάσκαλε ποία ἐντολὴ μεγάλη ἐν τῷ νόμῳ; 37 ὁ δὲ ἔφη αὐτῷ. ἀγαπήσεις κύριον τὸν θεόν σου ἐν ὅλῃ τῇ καρδίᾳ σου καὶ ἐν ὅλῃ τῇ ψυχῇ σου καὶ ἐν ὅλῃ τῇ διανοίᾳ σου. 38 αὕτη ἐστὶν ἡ μεγάλη καὶ πρώτη ἐντολή. 39 δευτέρα δὲ ὁμοία αὐτῇ. ἀγαπήσεις τὸν πλησίον σου ὡς σεαυτόν. 40 ἐν ταύταις ταῖς δυσὶν ἐντολαῖς ὅλος ὁ νόμος κρέμαται καὶ οἱ προφῆται.

INTRODUCTION

The undertaking in this chapter is to interpret Matt 22:34–40 in light of the entire Gospel using repetitive texture, progressive texture, narrational texture and pattern; opening, middle and closing of the unit, and finally the argumentative texture. The investigation and interpretation will focus on *νόμος* and *ἀγάπη* following the progression of the Matthean storyline. Finally, a cumulative data summary and conclusion will be provided as the finding of the investigation.

MATTHEW 22:34–40: REPETITIVE TEXTURE

In this section, the repetitive texture of Matt 22:36–40 will be examined as an initial stage in the process of the interpretation of the pericope. Repeated words will be listed in the table below and the pattern, topic, and movement of the unit will be discussed.

Verses	Repeated Words in Textual Unit							
Matt 22:36	μεγάλη	ἐντολὴ	ἐν	νόμῳ				
Matt 22:37			ἐν *3		Ἀγαπήσεις	σου *3	ὅλῃ*3	καὶ*2
Matt 22:38	μεγάλη	ἐντολή						καὶ
Matt 22:39					Ἀγαπήσεις			[δὲ]
Matt 22:40		ἐντολὴ		νόμος			ὅλος	καὶ

Table 2: Repetitive Texture in Matthew 22:36–40

1. The term *μεγάλη* is an adjective which conveys the major issue in the unit.
2. The term ἐντολή is repeated three times at the beginning, middle, and conclusion. It connects the whole unit and serves as a dividing line between the first and the second part of the unit which concludes both the first part (22:36–37) and the second part (22:39–40).
3. The preposition ἐν is repeated in the middle of the first part of the unit denoting a location both in the Law and in the person. While its comparative use defines the parameter of the comparison (within the Law) in its first appearance, in the second occurrences it locates where love should be exercised.
4. The noun *νόμος* is one of three important words but it occurs only twice—once at the beginning and again at the end.
5. The second person singular is indicated by *ἀγαπήσεις*, which occurs in the middle of the first and second parts.
6. Another second person singular is *σου* which denotes an indefinite individual or an indefinite corporate community.

7. The adjective ὅλῃ is repeated three times in the first half of the unit and at the end of the second half of the unit, denoting completeness in the person and the Law.
8. The conjunction καί is repeated both in the first and the second half of the unit marking addition and progression of thought.

From the discussion above, the following can be concluded:

1. the first line (22:36) introduces the theme and the topic μεγάλη, ἐντολή, and νόμῳ.
2. The terms ἐντολή and νόμῳ serve as an *inclusio* as they are repeated at the beginning and the end of the unit enclosing the theme of the unit.
3. The middle of the first and second halves discusses the theme focusing on ἀγαπήσεις.
4. New ideas and lists are progressively added throughout the unit with the additive καί completing the unit with the addition of a new word: from commandment to Law then finally to prophets.
5. The repeated words create the context and topics for the major theme ἐντολή, νόμος, and ἀγάπη within the unit under discussion.

In sum, the repetitive texture reveals that the textual unit is progressive. It starts with a single idea and develops it within its body before concluding with an additional claim. Next, the major topics will be discussed further: namely, νόμος and ἀγάπη.

MATTHEW 22:34–40: ANALYSIS OF TOPICAL PROGRESSION

Before undertaking an analysis of any biblical text its *Sitz im Leben* needs to be determined. In regard to the Gospel of Matthew, it has been no mean feat to pin down a convincing and conclusive life setting despite scholars' rigorous historical reconstructions. Donald A. Hagner confesses the circularity of the method and its conjectural conclusions saying, "It should be obvious, however, that the reconstruction of the life–situation of an evangelist is necessarily a speculative enterprise. It is a kind of educated guesswork, and the result of such an understanding can, in the nature of the matter, seldom be considered as final."[1]

Such "educated guesswork" has resulted in divergent conclusions. They can be broadly grouped into two categories:

1. a Jewish Christian community, and
2. a mostly Gentile Christian community.

The first group entails three different positions:

a. the traditional view which maintains that Matthew was the first Gospel written to Jewish Christians (e.g., Origin, Eusebius, A. Schlatter);
b. *intra-muros*: an after 70 CE Jewish Christian community not separated from Judaism (with variations, Bornkamm, Barth, R. Hummel, Davies, Goulder, Brown, Sigal, and Saldarinii, White, Balch); and
c. *extra-muros*: an after 70 CE Jewish Christian community which had made a definite break with Judaism and was debating with it (Standahl,Moul, Schewezer, Kummel, Stanton, Przybylski).[2]

The second group argues that a complete separation from Judaism had taken place, and no debate was happening between Judaism and the Matthean community; and that the author is a Gentile and so is its audience (with variations Luz, Strecker, Trilling, Meier,Tilborg, Gaston).[3] Given the various positions on the matter, it is impossible to choose one with certainty. Nonetheless, it is possible to be certain about three things with regard to Matthew. First, although the Gospel of Matthew under question has an un–retrievable life setting, one can be certain that most studies of the Gospel assume a wider audience which includes both Jews and Gentile Jesus followers whatever their respective sizes may be. Secondly, these Jewish and Gentile Jesus followers lived in a milieu in which Judaism was alive and well. Third, the Gospel in question was written after 70 CE. This study will focus on the final text of Matthew though attention will be given to the history of the composition of the text deemed relevant to the study.

1. Hagner, "The Sitz im Leben of the Gospel of Matthew," 27–28.
2. Hagner, "The Sitz im Leben of the Gospel of Matthew," 35–37.
3. Hagner, "The Sitz im Leben of the Gospel of Matthew," 33–34.

Topical Progression of νόμος in the Gospel of Matthew

As the repetitive texture has evinced, the discussion on νόμος explicitly starts within the Sermon on the Mount (SM) (5:17–20) before being developed further in Matthew's narration.[4] The Sermon on the Mount, (a name given by Augustine), has remained popular up to the present. Harvey McArthur delineated various approaches under seven headings while Warren Kissinger attempted to sketch various treatments of the Sermon on the Mount up until the works of W. D. Davies.[5] Reviewing the published literature on the subject, however, is not easy because of its vastness. Hans Dieter Betz describes the situation well, "The multitude of books on the Sermon on the Mount appearing every year in all languages and lands, not to mention articles in journals, magazines, and newspapers, exceeds what even computerized bibliography can handle."[6] This study will therefore only mention a few of the most influential approaches to the New Testament.

In a broader classification, the first position would be that it is an ethical code which must be practised. The early church fathers (Irenaeus, Tertullian, Origen, and Chrysostom, Didache, and the Anabaptist, Tolstoy and Bonhoeffer) all insisted that the SM is a foundational ethical code that must be obeyed by all Jesus followers.[7] While these interpreters might differ in their interpretive methods and milieux, they all opine that the SM is meant to be obeyed by Jesus followers. The second position holds that following the ethic of the SM is optional; therefore, its instructions are just for some. Augustine believed that the SM forms and measures Christian life, but he did not actually believe in the fulfilment of its demands in the present life.[8] However, Thomas Aquinas explicitly declared that not all Jesus followers are expected to obey the SM. He distinguished between the concepts of "precepts" and "evangelical counsels" a distinction first introduced by Ambrose.[9] Whereas the precepts are important commands for salvation and must be obeyed, the "counsels" are advisory directives of Christ, which are to be pursued for perfection

4. Stanton, *A Gospel for a New People*, 319.

5. McArthur, *Understanding the Sermon on the Mount*; Kissinger, *The Sermon on the Mount*.

6. Betz, *The Sermon on the Mount*, 3.

7. Kissinger, *The Sermon on the Mount*.

8. Augustine, *The Lord's Sermon on the Mount*.

9. Quarles, *Sermon on the Mount*, 6.

in order to get favour from God; therefore, they are optional. The third approach argues that the demands of the SM are impracticable and thus only has a penitential purpose. According to Kissinger, Carl Strange and Gerhard Kittle the SM is the will of God but that it cannot be literally fulfilled because it is way beyond human ability to do so.[10] As the will of God, the SM exposes the sin and failure of human beings leading to them seeking repentance.[11]

The fourth reading proclaims that the SM is an ethic of attitude, that is, a right disposition or a new consciousness, rather than specific and concrete action; therefore, it is just about an attitude of love. Wilhelm Herrmann and Heinrich Julius Holtzmann espouse the view that the SM is not meant to be obeyed, but it is an ethic of attitude.[12] Therefore, the kernel must be extracted from the husk of Jesus' instruction, which is love for God as father, and all men as brothers, and that the rest must be discarded. The fifth position claims that the SM is an interim ethic and that it is thus just intended to be obeyed for a specific time.[13]Kissinger identifies Johannes Wiess and Albert Schweitzer as two prominent proponents of this interpretation.[14] They argued that the SM is not a subjective, inward or spiritual ethic. It is rather a radical rule for a short time that should be obeyed before the end arrived because Jesus was an eschatological enthusiast. According to protestant Liberation interpretations, Jesus (as eschatological enthusiast) was mistaken in believing the end is at hand and in pronouncing a radical demand for a specific short time. Its demands are therefore no longer applicable today.[15] The sixth position declares that although the principle of the SM is applicable to the Jesus followers, its purpose is not for the present age but for the age to come; therefore, it is just for the future kingdom.

The introductory survey of various exegetical outcomes above evidence that no consensus has been achieved. McArthur, however, identifies two major areas of agreement among the scholars of the nineteenth and the twentieth centuries: (1) that the SM is not a Messianic prediction; and (2) that while Christ established a community where a new possibility for fulfilment of the Law existed this was not the topic

10. Kissinger, *The Sermon on the Mount*, 66–69.
11. Guelich, *The Sermon on the Mount*, 20–21.
12. Strecker, *The Sermon on the Mount*, 18.
13. Schweizer, *The Good News According to Matthew*, 1975.
14. Kissinger, *The Sermon on the Mount*, 40–42.
15. Kissinger, *The Sermon on the Mount*, 40–42.

under consideration in the SM.[16] While the first so-called consensus is probably right, the second is dubious as the question of the fulfilling of the Law and the obedience of the Law is one of the key topics in the SM even though there is still no fruitful consensus about its understanding of the Law.

The key text in the debate over the Matthean understanding of the Law is 5:17–20 in which Matthew outlines the place of the Law within the teaching of Jesus. Investigating the topical progression of the Law in Matthew commences here, because it entails important issues raised regarding the Law in the Gospel, such as abolishment, fulfilment, scope, duration, teaching and practicing the Law. Therefore, it can serve as an outline for the whole discussion of the topical progression of *νόμος* in the entire Gospel. Under each subtopic, related texts that unravel the progression will be subsumed without violating their specific contexts within the Gospel. The breadth and depth of the discussion on each text will vary in relation to its contribution to the discussion on the Law in Matthew.

No Abolition but Rather Fulfilling the Law (οὐκ καταλῦσαι ἀλλὰ πληρῶσαι)

Matt 5:17a *Μὴ νομίσητε,*

Matt 5:17b *οὐκ καταλῦσαι [τὸν νόμον ἢ τοὺς προφήτας],*

Matt 5:17c *ἀλλὰ πληρῶσαιτὸν νόμον ἢ τοὺς προφήτας*

These will be discussed in detail in the ensuing section.

ΜΗ ΝΟΜΙΣΗΤΕ (5:17A)

The phrase *μὴ νομίσητε* (5:17a) has elicited a lot of speculation concerning the addressees of Jesus' speech. It is argued:

1. that it is against a Hellenistic libertine congregation;[17]
2. that it is against antinomians and false prophets: namely, Paul and his Gospel;[18]

16. McArthur, *Understanding the Sermon on the Mount*, 41.
17. Barth, "Matthew's Understanding of The Law," 65.
18. Betz, *Essays on the Sermon on the Mount*, 20.

3. that it is a debate between Jesus and his disciples on one side, and Jewish opponents on the other;[19]
4. that it is against lawlessness and is thus a defence against the Jews' accusation of Jesus followers, hence, it addressees the disciples and the crowds;[20] and
5. that it is against assumptions and misunderstandings of Jesus' mission or his coming.[21]

Stanton, however, argues that there is no specific way to know whether the text is addressing antinomians, Hellenistic libertines or false prophets because Matthew contains harsh criticism against each of these different groups.[22] Since historical-criticism and redaction-criticism have yielded such divergent conclusions and have thus failed to bring about a consensus, one is compelled to focus on the final redactor's text itself rather than to look behind the text for more conjectures about its meaning.

According to perspective criticism, an "evaluative speech act contains at least three elements: a *sender* who offers an evaluation of something; a *subject* that is evaluative; and a *recipient* who hears or receives this evaluation" (italics his).[23]The speech itself is divided into direct and indirect phraseology. In the former case, the subject and the recipient are the same whereas in the latter case there is a "distinction between subject and recipient." In Matt 5:3—7:29, Jesus makes a long speech as the sender of the message. The narrator informs the audience that the receivers are the disciples and the crowds (5:1 and 7:28–29) at the beginning and at the end of the speech. In 5:17–20, Jesus' relationship with the Law is the subject. The question is, however, whether the receivers of this specific subject are the disciples, or even the whole crowd or post-resurrection opponents of Matthew's reader.

The relationship of the crowd to Jesus, although at a distance, is portrayed positively until they were persuaded by the religious leaders to stand against Jesus (27:20–25). Most of the time they followed Jesus for healing (4:25; 8:1, 18; 12:15; 19:2; 20:29), were amazed by his teaching and miracles (7:28; 22:33; 9:8; 12:23; 15:32–39), warmly welcomed Jesus

19. Bornkamm, "End-Expectation and Church in Matthew," 24–25.

20. Stanton, *A Gospel for a New People*, 3, 320.

21. Guelich, *The Sermon on the Mount*, 136; Strecker, *The Sermon on the Mount*, 53.

22. Stanton, *A Gospel for a New People*, 48.

23. Powell, "Characterization on the Phraseological Plane in the Gosple of Matthew," 164.

in Jerusalem (21:8–9), and saw Jesus as a prophet (21:46). Likewise, Jesus had a positive attitude towards the crowd: he addresses them directly in his teaching (11:7; 12:46; 13:2; 13:34–35; 15:10; 23:1), had compassion towards them and therefore healed and fed them (9:36; 14:14; 15:32–39). The only time Jesus addresses the crowd negatively is in the passion story (26:55). Conversely, the only time the crowd expressed a negative comment before the passion story is in his comment about the dead girl (9:23). Notwithstanding the positive relationship between the crowd and Jesus, Matthew portrays the crowd as not being in a close relationship with Jesus and that they just want their needs to be met. They express their feelings and amazement about Jesus but are not sure whether he is the Messiah or not (12:13). They have their own scribes (7:28–29) and in the end they are not persuaded by Jesus' teaching but are dissuaded by their religious leaders and united with them to crucify him (Matt 27:20–25). In light of such a denouement, it is most probable that Jesus is warning the crowd from the very beginning that *they should not think of him as a false prophet.*

On the other hand, the disciples are portrayed as those who are following Jesus closely (8:21; 9:10, 19) and as fellow workers of Jesus (9:37; 10:1–42). They have received special teaching and revelations (13:10–12, 36; 14:26–33; 16:17–20; 17:1) and always have access to Jesus with the right to ask questions (e.g., 7:19–20; 18:1). Jesus identifies himself with them and calls them his disciples (10:40–42; 26:35), and they are his close family because they do the will of God (12:49; 12:50). They claim that they have forsaken everything to follow Jesus (19:27–28), and Jesus defends them publicly (Matt 12:1–7; 15:2), but also warned them against the teachings of the Pharisees (15:14). They know of the death and suffering of Jesus before anyone (26:1–2). But the story depicts them also as those who abandoned Jesus during his passion, denied him as their Master (26:35–56) and yet they are restored by the news of his resurrection, worshipping him (although not all) (although still some were skeptical) and were commissioned to teach what they were taught to produce disciples (28:7–20).

In light of the portrayal of the crowds and the disciples in Matthew, *μὴ νομίσητε* is directed to both of them as they run the risk of regarding Jesus as a false prophet. Grammatically, the discourse is not speaking of something which has already happened but rather forbids in advance the initiation of negative thinking or suspicion about the ministry of Jesus.[24] It functions as a warning that they must not start thinking of Jesus as someone who came to destroy the Law.

It is quite important to note the placement of the SM in the story. *Pace* Betz, Stanton has argued that the placement of the SM in the whole structure of the Gospel emphasizes the importance of the message for the ensuing narration.[25] Garland rightly noted that 5:17 is a warning to the audience in the story that they are not to think that following the teaching of Jesus on the Law is an abrogation of it.[26] Jack Dean Kingsbury has also observed that no conflict occurred in the great discourses of Jesus (Matt 5–7; 10; 13; 18; 24–25) as none of the recipients of the teachings are religious leaders.[27]

Hence, no indication of the opponents of Jesus can be deducted from *μὴ νομίσητε*, as redaction criticism attempts to do. It might be argued that except for the reference to "the law and the prophets," all 5:17 is unique to Matthew not least *μὴ νομίσητε* and therefore, it does not refer to post-resurrection debates over the place of the Law. The reason for this is that a debate with antinomians or the Pauline Gospel cannot be verified because as the text reads in its final form, its audience in the story does not support such a speculation. If it does, the burden of proof lies upon those who hold such a view. Therefore, it seems that Matthew intertwined the tradition he received with his narration for a heuristic purpose without thereby responding to specific post-resurrection opponents.

ΟΥΚ ΚΑΤΑΛΥΣΑΙ [ΤΟΝ ΝΟΜΟΝ Η ΤΟΥΣ ΠΡΟΦΗΤΑΣ] (5:17B)

The phrase the *τὸν νόμον ἢ τοὺς προφήτας* can be translated as "the Law and the prophets," or "the Law or the prophets." The two terms also appear as pairs in Matthew (7:12; 11:13; 22:40). However, some argue that *ἢ τοὺς προφήτας* is a later addition either by redaction or interpolation because while *καταλῦσαι τὸν νόμον* makes sense, for various reasons

24. *μὴ νομίσητε* is a subjunctive aorist second person plural which forbids "the occurrence of an action"; Wallace, *Greek Grammar Beyond the Basics*, 496.

25. Betz, *Essays on the Sermon on the Mount*, 20; Stanton, *A Gospel for a New People*, 318–25.

26. Garland, *Reading Matthew*, 62.

27. Kingsbury, *Matthew as Story*, 63.

καταλῦσαι τοὺς προφήτας does not make sense.[28]However, the question is whether it is a deliberate[29] or an unconscious association of ideas, or a simple expression.[30] Others take the ἤ and translate it as "or" rather than "and" arguing that Jesus might be accused of destroying the Law and therefore used ἤ to express his denial of destroying any part of the scriptures.[31] Contrary to Guelich's argument,[32] there is, however, no significant difference whether "and" or "or" is maintained.[33] Rather, the phrase refers not to particulars but to the scriptures in their entirety.[34]

However, the emphasis is on the Law for three reasons: firstly, Matthew repeats the Law in 5:18 and provides a rationale for not abolishing the Law and mentions its commandments in 5:19. Secondly, Jesus deals with specific commandments in the next section of the discourse (5:21–48). Thirdly, the repetition of the phrase in 7:12 brackets Jesus' teaching on the subject of the Law.[35] It should be noted that the term "antithesis" is a misnomer[36] because Jesus already declared that his coming is not to abolish the Law and the prophets. Further, δέ can be translated as "in contrast to," or "in addition to," or "in agreement with"[37] and even as "and" and thus mitigates the notion of opposition.

If Jesus is insisting on no abrogation of the Law and the prophets, the question arises: what is he doing with it in the ensuing discourse (5:21–48)? The term οὐκ καταλῦσαι is a purpose infinitive meaning "not to annul" in classical and Hellenistic Greek, when the Law is the object.[38] Despite his skepticism regarding the authenticity of the discourse, Sanders thinks that the antitheses are "not only . . . but also saying," and hence they affirm the Law and go beyond it.[39] For Sanders, stringency more than what is required of the Law is neither illegal nor abolishing the Law.

28. Davies and Allison, *Matthew*, 1:484; Guelich, *The Sermon on the Mount*, 138.

29. Guelich, The Sermon on the Mount, 138.

30. Banks, *Jesus and the Law in the Synoptic Tradition*, 207.

31. Quarles, *Sermon on the Mount*, 89.

32. Guelich, *The Sermon on the Mount*, 138.

33. Newman and Stine, *A Handbook on the Gospel of Matthew*, 123.

34. Sigal, *The Halakhah of Jesus of Nazareth*, 25; Snodgrass, "Matthew and the Law," 114.

35. Gundry, *Matthew*, 38–39.

36. Stanton, *A Gospel for a New People*, 301.

37. Moo, "Jesus and the Authority of the Mosaic Law,"121.

38. Guelich, *The Sermon on the Mount*, 137.

39. Sanders, *Jesus and Judaism*, 256, 260.

Abrogation of a specific percept in the time of Jesus, argues Sigal, was not unusual.[40] Snodgrass also argues that the Jews' Law is not a "monolithic entity in which all of its statement points in one direction," because there are incidents in the OT where opposite actions are commanded for the same purpose. Furthermore, he rejects the assumption that no one abrogated the Law other than Jesus since the *lex talion* was, for example, substituted by a financial penalty in the OT.[41] For Barth, the "antitheses" are not against the Law *per se* but against a rabbinate interpretation of it since the Matthean Jesus introduces them in 5:20.[42] Therefore the "antitheses" are concerned with the correct interpretation of the Law and not its abrogation. Moo, after analyzing each "antithesis,ġ contends that Jesus is not expounding, radicalizing or deepening the Law; rather, it is his independent authoritative teaching, as attested by the audience at the end of the SM (7:29).[43]

The "antitheses" are neither samples of how the Law should be interpreted nor an exhaustive discussion on the Law not least because the Decalogue is not fully presented, and the prophets are entirely neglected. Instead, they seem to be selected topics over the issue of divine judgment according to the Law that might have currency within the Jesus milieu (e.g. 5:23). The topic of judgment is also neglected in the scholarly discussion of the "antitheses." Judgment is based on the extent of the teaching and practicing of the Law (5:19), while being inside or outside of the kingdom of heaven is also based on practicing Law (5:20). Note that Jesus did not say your righteousness must exceed that of the Law but that he said that of the scribes and Pharisees. He thus compared the practice of the Law by different groups and not the content of the Law.

Each "antithesis" substantiates this argument that Jesus is declaring the basis of divine judgment in one way or another. In the first thesis, not just killing but not seeking reconciliation (which is an attitude toward the other) results in judgment (5:21–26). Similarly, judgment through retaliation based on a judicial procedure as Moo[44] noted in 5:38–42 focuses on practical judgment. Jesus did not declare the abrogation of such judicial measures against the one who wronged the other. Rather, it is about the toleration of an offence which is an extension of the first "antithesis." The

40. Snodgrass, "Matthew and the Law," 119.

41. Snodgrass, "Matthew and the Law,"118.

42. Barth, "Matthew's Understanding of The Law," 94–95.

43. Moo, "Jesus and the Authority of the Mosaic Law."

44. Moo, "Jesus and the Authority of the Mosaic Law," 22.

first "antithesis" (5:21–26) deals with the one who wronged the other whereas the fifth "antithesis" (5:38–42) deals with the one who is wronged and has the right to receive restitution according to the Law. Judgment is already incurred on the one who wronged another on the basis of the first "antithesis," therefore, Jesus does not need to repeat himself, but the one who is wronged by the other should not take revenge. Likewise, the sixth (love for enemies) "antithesis" (5:43–48) deals with the relationship with enemies similar to that of the fifth "antithesis" (5:43–48) by focusing on the reward (5:45). The topic of reward continues in 6:1–6, 16 and judgment in 7:1–2, 13–14, 19 and 27.

The second and the third "antitheses" (5:27–32) deal with the same core issue: adultery. While the second deals with adultery in general, the latter makes it specific to within marriage. Divorce not due to adultery causes one to commit adultery (5:35). Not only the act of adultery, but also the thought of adultery is condemned. Jesus insists that the cause of adultery must be removed whether it is the body itself or the act of divorce, for it leads to judgment (5:29–30). Regarding the fourth "antithesis" (5:33–37), Moo argues that the OT does not list it as one of the commandments and that Jesus might there be thinking of the scribal tradition.[45] An oath is related to truthfulness in settling issues between persons, according to Leviticus 19:12. However, although the judgment topic is not explicit, the reason for the prohibition of making an oath evokes the judgment of God as a king (5:33–36) and the limited power of human beings (5:36). Barth correctly noted that judgment and the will of God are closely tied together.[46] It is the role of the Law as a measure of judgment of sin or wrongdoing, not its prohibition or permission, which is taken over by the antithesis of Jesus as the basis of divine judgment (7:21–27). Partially granting Moo's conclusion, i.e.the "antitheses" are Jesus' independent authoritative teaching, it must be added, however, that the "antitheses" are discourses on selected topics about divine judgment. Therefore, in the antitheses Jesus is not deepening, radicalizing, expanding, explaining or abrogating the Law, but declaring what precludes one from entering the kingdom of God and the ground for God's judgment on specific topics. Therefore, Jesus claims that judgment is based on one's inner thought pattern and life and he is calling for a change of thought patterns as a way of living in accordance with his teaching.

45. Moo, "Jesus and the Authority of the Mosaic Law," 21.

46. Barth, "Matthew's Understanding of The Law," 58–62.

ΑΛΛΑ ΠΛΗΡΩΣΑΙ ΤῸΝ ΝΌΜΟΝ Ἢ ΤΟῪΣ ΠΡΟΦΉΤΑΣ (5:17C)

Determining the meaning of πληρῶσαι to understand Jesus'teaching of the Law is of vital importance. The various interpretations of πληρῶσαι can be summarised based on four positions. (1) Jesus came to accomplish or to obey the Law.[47] Although Moo refutes this reading, he nonetheless reaches a similar conclusion. In this interpretation, πληρόω seems to take a similar meaning to which it has in 3:15. The strength of this interpretation is that it takes πληρόω as a natural contrast to καταλύω. The downside of it is that it does not make sense to ascribe πληρόω as obedience to the prophets. However, Snodgrass suggests a prophetic reading of the Law as Matthew sees the Law function with a prophetic role in 11:13. (2) Jesus came to confirm the moral law and particularly the Decalogue.[48] This interpretation can be discarded for four reasons: first, it is based on the incorrect assumption that the Law is divided among moral and civil and ceremonial laws.[49] Second, Jesus explicitly stated that even the smallest letter or the least stroke will not pass away. Third, Jesus came to "fill up" or "complete" the Law by explaining what the Law really meant.[50] Matthew uses πληρόω with this meaning in 13:48 and 23:32. But applying such a reading to 5:17 changes the meaning of πληρόω to "demonstrate" or "explain" which is unusual in Matthean usage. Similar reading is espoused by Filson and Allen.[51] They read its meaning as "fill up" or "complete" by extending the demand of the Law. This reading fails when applied to the prophets. The object of πληρῶσαι is not just τὸν νόμον but also τοὺς προφήτας. Hence, any meaning ascribed to πληρόω must fit both nouns. Fourth, Jesus came as a Messiah whose life and teaching actualised what was anticipated by the Law and the prophets (with some variations).[52]

47. Luz, *Matthew 1–7*, 260–65; Snodgrass, "Matthew and the Law," 111–15; Moo, "Jesus and the Authority of the Mosaic Law," 5.

48. Wenham, "Jesus and the Law," 92–96.

49. Traditionally the Law is divided into three types: moral Law refers to the moral elements of the Law focusing on the Decalogue which has a permanent application for the Jesus followers; civil Law is the legal arrangement for Israel and could be used as a model for civil legal arrangement for any society, although an exact replica of them is not demanded; ceremonial Law (such as rituals and holidays) is a shadow of Christ that has been made obsolete because of his coming (see Calvin, *Institutes of the Christian Religion*, vol. 2, bk. 4, chap. 20, sec. 14, p. 663.

50. Lenski, *Romans 8–16*, 206–7.

51. Allen, *Matthew*, 45

52. Banks, *Jesus and the Law*, 207–10; Meier, *Law and History in Matthew's Gospel*,

It is important first to examine how Matthew used the word πληρόω before ascribing any meaning to it in this specific context. The topical progression of πληρόω, νόμος and προφήτης will therefore be analyzed. However, in regard to νόμος not only the occurrence of the word but also words and phrases that show the concept or its topic will be shown in brackets. No attempt will be made to engage in a deeper analysis of the term as the purpose here is to demonstrate how it progressed in the entire narration.

Divisions	**Texts**	νόμος	**Texts**	προφήτης	**Texts**	πληρόω
1:1–4:16			1:22	προφήτου	1:22	γέγονεν / πληρωθῇ
			2:15	προφήτου	2:15	πληρωθῇ
			2:17	προφήτου	2:17	ἐπληρώθη
			2:23	προφητῶν	2:23	πληρωθῇ
			3:3	προφήτου	(3:3)	[οὗτοςἐστιν ὁ ῥηθεὶς]
					3:15	πληρῶσαι
			4:14	προφήτου	4:14	πληρωθῇ
4:17–11:1			5:12	προφήτας τοὺς		
	5:17	τὸν νόμον(ἤ)	5:17	τοὺς προφήτας	5:17	πληρῶσαι
	5:18	νόμου				
	7:12	ὁ νόμος(καὶ)	7:12	οἱ προφῆται.		
	8:4	[δῶρον ὃ προσέταξεν Μωϋσῆς]				
			8:17	Ἠσαΐου τοῦ προφήτου	8:17	πληρωθῇ
			10:41	ὁ προφήτην ὅ προφήτου		
11:2–16:20			11:9	προφήτην προφήτου		[οὗτός ἐστιν περὶ οὗ γέγραπται]

75–85; Moo, "Jesus and the Authority of the Mosaic Law," 24–30; France, *Matthew*, 113–14. Davies and Allison *Matthew*, 1:485–87; Guelich, *The Sermon on the Mount*, 164.

	11:13	ὁ νόμος	11:13	(πάντες) οἱ προφῆται (καὶ) ἐπροφήτευσαν		
	12:1–14	[σάββασιν (8 times)]				
		[ἐν τῷ νόμῳ οἶκον τοῦθεοῦ]				
		[ἱερῷ (2 times)]				
		[οὐ θυσίαν]				
		(ἐν τῷ) νόμῳ				
11:2–16:20			12:17	Ἠσαΐου τοῦ προφήτου	12:17	(ἵνα) πληρωθ
			12:39	Ἰωνᾶ τοῦ προφήτου +v. 40		
			13:17	(πολλοὶ) προφῆται	13:17	ἀναπληροῦτ
			13:35	(διὰ)τοῦ προφήτου	13:35	(ὅπως) πληρωθῇ
					13:48	
			13:57	προφήτης (Jesus)		
			14:5	προφήτην (John)		
	15:1–20	[τὴν ἐντολὴν τοῦθεοῦ]	15:7	[περὶ ὑμῶν Ἠσαΐας λέγων]		
		[ὁ γὰρ θεὸς εἶπεν]				
		[ἠκυρώσατε τὸν λόγον τοῦ θεοῦ]				
		[κοινοῖ (4 times)]				
			16:14	Ἰωνᾶ τοῦ προφήτου		

16:21–20:34	19:3–9	Μωϋσῆς ἐνετείλατο				
	19:16–22	[τήρησον τὰς ἐντολάς] [the Decalogue vs 18–19]				
21:1—27:66			21:4	(διὰ) τοῦ προφήτου	21:4	(ἵνα) πληρωθῇ
21:1—27:66			21:11	ὁ προφήτης Ἰησοῦς		
			21:26	προφήτηντὸν Ἰωάννην		
			21:46	προφήτην		
	22:36	[ἐντολὴ] ἐν τῷ νόμῳ				
	22:38	[ἐντολή]				
	22:39	[δευτέρα δὲ ὁμοία αὐτῇ]				
	22:40	[(δυσὶν) ἐντολαῖς] (ὅλος) ὁ νόμος (καὶ)	22:40	(ὅλος) οἱ προφῆται		
	23:23	βαρύτερα τοῦ νόμου				
			23:29	τῶν προφητῶν		
			23:30	τῶν προφητῶν		
			23:31	τοὺς προφήτας		
					23:32	πληρώσατε
			23:34	προφήτας		
			23:37	τοὺς προφήτας		
			24:15	διὰ Δανιὴλ τοῦ προφήτου	24:15	[ἴδητε]
	24:20	[σαββάτῳ]				

	26:54	[αἱ γραφαὶ] *	26:54	[αἱ γραφαὶ] *	26:54	πληρωθῶσιν [ὅτι οὕτως δεῖ γενέσθαι]
21:1–27:66			26:56	[αἱγραφαὶ] τῶν προφητῶν	26:56	(ἵνα) πληρωθῶσιν το[ῦτο δὲ ὅλον γέγονεν]
			27:9	(διὰ) Ἰερεμίου τοῦ προφήτου	27:9	ἐπληρώθη
28:1–20	28:1	[σαββάτων]				

Table 3: Topical Progression of νόμος, προφήτης **and** πληρόω

The term *πληρόω* is used seventeen times in the entire Gospel but three of them (3:15; 13:48; 23:32) are not related to prophecy. Several observations can be made from the data regarding the meaning of *πληρόω*. First, *γίνομαι* is used three times along with *πληρόω*, once at the beginning by the narrator and twice by Jesus' direct speech at the beginning of his betrayal or the final section of the story (26:54 and 26:56). Particularly, it is employed in the summary of events and not with specific prophetic utterances made by a prophet in the OT. The last appearance of *γίνομαι* is in 28:11 where the guards report to the chief priest all that took place (*ἅπαντα τὰ γενόμενα*) which seems to be the way in which the narrator is reporting fulfilment of the prediction about Jesus.The term *γίνομαι* seems to be bracketing all the events happening since the conception of Jesus to his resurrection.

Second, the narrator uses *πληρόω* eleven times and all of them are used to interpret and to link specific prophetic utterances made by the OT prophets to events which happened in and around the life and ministry of Jesus. For the narrator, even a very small act of Jesus is connected to a specific prophetic prediction made by a prophet in the OT (12:16–17). The narrator never said that all the prophetic books are fulfilled but he pin-pointed which prophecy is happening or coming to pass in a specific context of Jesus' life. In no place in the data has the narrator used the Law as the source for the prediction of Jesus' life and ministry; only prophetic books are used as sources of fulfilment. While there is a high concentration of the narrator's work on interpreting and linking events to the OT prophecies at the conception and birth of Jesus, there is a low concentration on his teachings and actions. Rather there is an abstention from interpreting and direct linking of OT texts to events surrounding the betrayal, death, and resurrection (except in 27:9).

Third, the Law and the prophets as an explicit pair appear only in the direct speech of Jesus (5:17; 7:12; 11:13; 22:40), they are never paired in the narrator's report. The term πληρόω is used only once in these pairs (5:17) and γίνομα only in 5:18b. Matthew's report of Jesus words is as follows: Jesus used αἱ γραφαὶ (26:54) and αἱ γραφαὶ τῶν προφητῶν (26:56) along with πληρόω and γίνομα. Jesus used δεῖ with the former and ὅλον with the latter. Given the immediate context, αἱγραφαὶ in 26:54 is qualified with ὅλον αἱ γραφαὶτῶν προφητῶν in 26:56. Hence, it refers to the books of the prophets. It is hard to be certain here whether Jesus is including the Law in his use of αἱ γραφαὶ insofar as he does so specifically in the next verse and in his phraseology of the Law and prophets in the pairs. However, it is argued that in 11:13 the Law and the prophets represent the whole scriptures' prophesying. Considering the subject of Jesus' discussion in the context, the phrase "prophesied until John" does not necessarily indicate the prophetic function of the Law. Rather, putting the prophets first in the pair naturally forces the verb to indicate the action of the prophets as the emphasis is on the prophecy not on the Law. It is also not conjugated with πληρόω. Further, the narrator never linked or indicated to the reader that the Law and the prophets are co-predictive. Instead, he used prophets about thirty-eight times, and, in most cases, he is very specific in mentioning the names of the prophets. Therefore, there is no strong evidence that compels one to think the Law functioned as a prophetic utterance in the Gospel.

Fourth, as the data evidence says, whenever the Law is mentioned, it is a subject of *teaching, defence, debate, test, interpretation, and recommendation.* Particularly, the Decalogue takes the lion's share of the discussion. As already argued, nowhere is the Law used along with πληρόω except in 5:17 (in a pair) in the data. However, if 13:14 ἀναπληροῦται is taken as the context and 13:17 is taken as the opposite of it, then the desire to see what you see (ἐπεθύμησαν ἰδεῖν ἃβλέπετε) and to hear what you hear (καὶ ἀκοῦσαι ἃ ἀκούετε) would suggest fulfilment. Particularly, in this context, ἰδεῖν (to see Jesus and his action) and ἀκοῦσαι (to hear his teaching) would be tantamount to the fulfilment of OT prophecies. For instance, Jesus used ἴδητε when he speaks of the fulfilment of Daniel's prophecy (24:15). If this is granted, then *hearing Jesus' teachings is a form of experiencing the fulfilment of prophecy.*

In conclusion, given the discussion above on the data, πληρόω refers to things that are seen to be taking place (γέγονεν, γίνομαι) or which happened in the life and ministry of Jesus according to specific predictions made by different OT prophets. If this definition is granted, then πληρόω does not apply directly to the Law. If 5:17 and γίνομα in 5:18b (which refers to beyond the time of Jesus) are taken into consideration along with 13:17, then fulfilling the Law for Jesus means *to interpret and to defend the Law.* This can be corroborated within the context of 5:17–20. Jesus did not mention anything about prophecy but instead spoke about relaxing (5:19a), teaching (5:19b and 5:19c) and practising (5:19c) the Law as major topics. Therefore, Jesus' claim that he came not to abolish but to fulfil the Law, is *related to his teaching, defending, and practising the Law and such fulfilment is demonstrated in the teaching of Jesus in the progression of the story.*

Thus, Jesus's fulfilment of the Law in the SM is not the deepening, drawing its intent, interpretation of it, nor going beyond it, but instead, as Jesus was teaching in their synagougues (4:23) and especially as 5:2 states "and he opened his mouth and tought them," it *is about teaching* on *selected topics* of the Law which focus on human relationships. The Law prohibits killing, adultery, false witness (in this case an oath) and promotes holiness, justice, and love for the neighbor. Further, the Law functions as a source of knowledge, and guidance. But *its role as a measure of judgment is replaced by Jesus' teaching.* Jesus proclaims that judgment does not only depend on one's action but also on one's thought and attitude toward a fellow person. Therefore, Jesus calls for change in one's thought-life, demanding reconciliation with a neighbor, remaining in marriage, and avoiding the temptation of adultery by dealing with its cause from its inception. He made the commandments very stringent on these specific topics by stipulating judgment as the dire consequence of neglecting them. However, Jesus's fulfilment of the Law in the rest of the story might be understood in terms of defending the law's authority against the tradition of the fathers, and in insisting that going back to the original, the Mosaic Law, demands uncompromised obedience. This will be analyzed in the following section.

No reduction but effectuating all (Matt 5:18–19)

Matt 5:18a ἕως ἂν παρέλθῃ ὁ οὐρανὸς καὶ ἡ γῆ

Matt 5:18d ἕως ἂν πάντα γένηται

In this section, the Law will continue to be examined in light of its topical progression in the entire Gospel under two subheadings: the duration and scope of the Law.

The enduring duration of the Law: Matt 5:18b–d

Matt 5:18a is marked by *γάρ* which is a rationale for Jesus' claim in 5:17. The following two temporal clauses are of paramount importance in order to understand Jesus' claim regarding the duration of the Law: a) *ἕως ἂν π αρέλθῃ ὁ οὐρανὸς καὶ ἡ γῆ*, and b) *ἕως ἂν πάντα γένηται*. Varying interpretations have been given in regard to the relationship between these two clauses. They can be subsumed in the following manner: (1) An apocalyptic view:[53]in this reading, the two clauses are parallel and 5:18b repeats the second to emphasise that the Law is valid until the end. Thus, "until heaven and earth pass away" refers to until the redemptive purpose of God is completed. (2) The salvation–historical view:[54] this reading holds that the Law is valid now, but as it is fulfilled by Jesus. It argues that the two clauses are not parallel. Instead, the second qualifies or explains the first for *πάντα* refers to the demand of God in its particularity and entirety looking forward to the teaching of Jesus which is now to come to pass and achieve fulfilment (5:17). (3) Passion view:[55] it is similar to the second view in regard to the function of the second clause. However, it contends that the Law is valid only until the death and resurrection of Jesus.

The weakness of the second and the third readings is that they suppress the natural reading of "until heaven and earth pass away" as the clause suggests that the Law would be valid even beyond the death and resurrection of Jesus. David Sim has rightly stated that, "If the Matthean Jesus claims in 5:18 that the law does become invalid with his death or resurrection then he obviously did come to abolish the law, and this is a patent contradiction of what he says in the preceding verse."[56] The clauses also do not convey the connotation of 'never' because of "until" which limits its duration, but 5:18b is a rationale for Jesus' insistence that his

53. Moo, "Jesus and the Authority of the Mosaic Law," 26–27; Davies and Allison, *Matthew*, 1:494–95.

54. Banks, *Jesus and the Law in the Synoptic Tradition*, 215–20.

55. Meier, *Law and History in Matthew's Gospel*, 62–65.

56. Sim, *The Gospel of Matthew and Christian Judaism*, 125.

coming is not to abolish the Law because the Law continues until the end of the world (5:18d).[57]

SCOPE OF THE LAW: MATTHEW 5:18C AND D

The statements that "not an iota, not a dot will pass from the Law," "all is accomplished" and "one of the least of these commandments," raise the question ofthe scope of the Law. The reference to "not an iota, not a dot" implies that Jesus is speaking of the written Law.[58] Since it is a metaphorical expression, it refers to both detail and particular commandments of the Law.[59] In the words of Betz, "what is true of the smallest letter by implication, be true of the rest."[60] Likewise, "all is accomplished" conveys the same meaning. Therefore, both refer to the validity of the Law in its quantitative wholeness extending to its particularities.

The third expression, "one of the least of these commandments," however, created a plethora of interpretations. "the least" may imply that there is a greater commandment.[61] What are these commandments? Answers vary: (1) the apostolic decree which Gentile Christians are expected to obey;[62](2) the Jewish cult;[63] (3) a word play on Paul's self-designation; (4) the shortest of the ten commandments; (5) Jesus' teaching that follows; (6) the Judean debate over heavier and lighter commandments; (7) it refers back to the iota and one hook and until all is accomplished;[64] and (8) the commandments that have little importance and are easy to fulfil.[65] There is no need of engaging with all the arguments given for each position; it suffices to focus on the context and grammatical indications. The conjunction οὖν connects 5:19 to the preceding sentences and to the context, and as Carson (1984:146) argued τοῦτος is never a forward-referring pronoun in the Gospel of Matthew.[66] Therefore, it refers to the OT Law and demands obedience to it in its entirety until the end of the world.

57. Strecker, *The Sermon on the Mount*, 55–56.
58. Betz, *The Sermon on the Mount*, 182.
59. Snodgrass, "Matthew and the Law."
60. Betz, *Essays on the Sermon on the Mount*, 182.
61. Strecker, *The Sermon on the Mount*, 57.
62. Strecker, *The Sermon on the Mount*, 57.
63. Strecker, *The Sermon on the Mount*, 57.
64. Guelich, *The Sermon on the Mount*, 152.
65. Betz, *The Sermon on the Mount*, 187–88.
66. Carson, "Matthew,"146.

Nevertheless, Jesus seems to be forbidding oaths (5:33–37) and an eye for an eye (5:38–42), while debating the keeping of the Sabbath (12:1–14) and not being concerned about purity regulations (15:1–20). Since the first two have already been examined, the focus here will be on the last two issues, namely: Jesus' position on the Sabbath and the purity debate.

KEEPING THE SABBATH: MATT 12:1–14, 24:20 & 28:1

Keeping the Sabbath is one of the most important commandments of the Law (Exodus 31:12–17). It is an everlasting covenant sign between God and Israel, which sanctifies Israel, therefore observance is mandatory and not complying results in capital punishment (Exod 31:14; 35:2; and Num 15:32–36). However, the Sabbath controversies in 12:1–14 created a number of differing conclusions on the authenticity of the story, Jesus' attitude on the Sabbath commandment, and his interpretation thereof. On the historicity of the story: it is considered authentic (with variation),[67]and inauthentic (with variation).[68] On Jesus' attitude on the Sabbath commandment scholars have proposed that Jesus is against: the Pharisaic halakah/ oral tradition,[69] the Sabbath command itself, the universalisation and the inflexible application of the Sabbath, but obeyed the Sabbath, and is indifferent to the Sabbath command.[70] On the type of Jesus' argument, it is argued that Jesus utilised: rabbinic argumentation, that is, haggadic (David's example/ analogical) and halakic (priest's action in the temple/ legal stipulation),[71] rabbinic argument,[72]or that it is not a rabbinic argument,[73]but Hellenistic judicial rhetoric instead.[74] On Jesus' interpretation scholars have arrived at varied conclusions: Jesus reinterpreted the Sabbath commandment insisting that mercy supersedes

67. Rordorf, *Sunday*, 60–67; Borg, *Conflict, Holiness, and Politics*; Hultgren and Fuller, *Jesus and His Adversaries*.

68. Sanders, *Jesus and Judaism*.

69. Hicks, "The Sabbath Controversy in Matthew," 79–91.

70. Hagner, "Jesus and the Synoptic Sabbath Controversies."

71. Hagner, "Jesus and the Synoptic Sabbath Controversies;" Hicks, "The Sabbath Controversy in Matthew."

72. Cohn-Sherbok, "An Analysis of Jesus' Arguments Concerning the Plucking of Grain on the Sabbath," 31–41.

73. Moo, "Jesus and the Authority of the Mosaic Law."

74. Robbins, "Plucking Grain on the Sabbath."

holiness[75], human needs override the Sabbath[76], or that Christology and mission override the Sabbath (i.e. David is a type of Jesus).[77] On whether a transgression of Sabbath commandments happened or not, it is argued that Jesus did not breach them.[78] Insofar as there is no consensual conclusion, the story still needs to be understood as it stands now. However, it is too formidable a task to undertake an evaluation of each of these positions. As a result, the discussion will be limited to whether Jesus' response on the Sabbath debate is against his own insistence that "not an iota, not a dot, will pass away from the Law, and whoever then relaxes one of the least of these commandments and teaches men so, shall be called least in the kingdom of heaven. . ." (5:18–19).

Sanders argues that although it cannot be proven, the issue of the Sabbath is not that important and does not define Jesus' relationship to his contemporaries therefore there is no substantial opposition between Jesus and the Pharisees on the matter.[79] However, as the text reads in Matthew it does appear to refer to this opposition because it is situated within the context of the rejection and opposition to Jesus and his message. It follows the discourse on the rejection of the message of John and Jesus (11:16–19) and is followed by another opposition by the Pharisees on blaspheming the Spirit (12:22–12). Sanders' downplaying of the importance of this opposition and the debate over the Sabbath does not square with what the story portrays; not least because Matthew indicates that it is the cause for the Pharisees to plot, for the first time, to kill Jesus (12:14).

In the immediate context of Matt 12, Matthew introduces the opponents of Jesus as "wise and learned" (the Pharisees and the scribes)[80] while Jesus claimed that revelation is through him and that his yoke (teaching) is easy and his burden is light, and the disciples should learn from him (11:25–30). The story begins with "at that time," repeating 11:25. While the first accusation is directed against Jesus' disciples (12:1–8) holding Jesus responsible to answer for the accusation, the latter (12:9–14) is explicitly targeted against Jesus himself. Matthew also formulates his narration of the story with a complex redaction in order

75. Borg, *Conflict, Holiness, and Politics in the Teachings of Jesus.*

76. Hicks, "The Sabbath Controversy in Matthew," 84.

77. Banks, *Jesus and the Law in the Synoptic Tradition*; Hagner, "Jesus and the Synoptic Sabbath Controversies."

78. Sigal, *The Halakhah of Jesus of Nazareth*; Sanders, *Jesus and Judaism*;

79. Sanders, *Jesus and Judaism*, 264–67.

80. Viljoen, "Sabbath Controversy in Matthew," 3.

to make his point about the debates. He added to Mark (it is not in Luke): "at that time" (12:1), "πεινάω" (12:1), "your" (12:2), the whole of 12:5–6, "their" synagogue (12:9), and "lawful" in 12:12. He changed the question in Mark 2:24 into an accusation. He omitted: "at the time of the high priest Abiathar," "Sabbath came on account of man" (12:8/Mark 2:27), telling the man to stand in the middle (Mark 3:3), the detailed alternative given by Mark (Mark 3:4), and reference to Herodian (Mark 3:6). He also substituted "they asked" for "they were watching closely (12:9/ Mark 3:2), ἀγαθόν for καλῶς (12:12/Mark 3:4). His redaction of this story has provided some insight for the interpretation process, but only those elements related to the immediate interest of this investigation will be considered in the following analysis.

Jesus' responses to the accusation against his disciples both come from scripture. The first is from 1 Sam 21:1–6 and the second from Num 28:9–10. Jesus' rhetorical question, "have you not read. . . ?," particularly in his second reasoning 12:5 ἐν τῷ νόμῳ, is reminiscent of 5:17–20 which claims his coming is not to abolish the Law. The story assumes that both Jesus and the Pharisees accepted plucking heads of grain and eating them as a form of work insofar as the debate is not on reasoning whether the action is actual work or not. Instead, it is whether their actions are a violation of the Sabbath. Yong–Eu Yang thinks that Jesus' argument is not to demonstrate whether they violated the Sabbath Law or not.[81] It is rather to show that their action is the fulfilment of the OT. Sigal, however, argues that a Christological interpretation does not do justice to the debate.[82] For Sigal, Jesus' argument is based on his own halakic interpretation.[83] If Jesus' claim in 5:17–20 is kept in view here, the existence of the fulfilling concept in this story is questionable. First, the question is about a specific topic that marks out Israel from the other nations. Second, it is hardly clear how the disciples' actions would be the fulfilment of OT Scripture as they are being accused of breaching it. Further, how the act of the disciples and the response of Jesus to the accusation would be a fulfilment, is totally unclear. Third, in both Jesus' arguments the evidence adduced serves as examples of breaking a given commandment; therefore, these examples cannot convey Jesus fulfilling the Law insofar as they imply abolishing it.

81. Yang, *Jesus and the Sabbath*, 171.

82. Sigal, *The Halakhah of Jesus of Nazareth*, 151.

83. Sigal, *The Halakhah of Jesus of Nazareth*, 125–28.

The question is whether the debate is over the Sabbath commandment as it stands in the Decalogue or over a particular interpretation of it. It can be argued that the debate is not over the Sabbath commandment, but over the oral tradition or Pharisaic interpretation thereof, because among the rabbis there were diverse interpretations with regard to what is permissible on the Sabbath and what is not.[84] Sigal, who views Jesus as one of the proto-rabbis, argued that whenever Jesus is accused of violating a given commandment, it must be asked whose halakha is violated as there was an ubiquity of halakha in proto-rabbis.[85] In particular, in regard to the Sabbath, there is no precise definition of work in the OT except for forbidding the use of fire and the collection of wood (Exodus 35:2–3; Num 15:32–36).[86] Further, he contended that Jesus never questioned the system although he differs over particulars thereof.[87] Hence, for Sigal, it is most probable that the debate is over the oral tradition or interpretation of work during the Sabbath.

Jesus adduced his case by citing scripture which are examples of violating commandments of the Law in the first debate (12:1–8), albeit David's unlawful act is not directly associated with the Sabbath commandment (although there was a tradition that David's act was on the Sabbath).[88] Moo also argues in a similar way that Jesus did consider that David's action was illegal.[89] Yet, Moo interprets typologically that the story of David expresses a typological relationship between David and Jesus. Although Moo understands the weakness of this reading, he prefers it because it has fewer weaknesses than other interpretations. But the typological reading of David fails to account for the fact that Jesus himself was not accused, nor did he do unlawful deeds on the Sabbath, because it was his disciples who performed the action.

Robbins' rhetorical reading of the story might provide some insight into how to deal with the conundrum of understanding the debate. Robbins argues that the story of plucking grain on the Sabbath is judicial rhetoric for two reasons: 1) judicial rhetoric is employed to uphold truth

84. Hicks, "The Sabbath Controversy in Matthew," 81–82; Hagner, "Jesus and the Synoptic Sabbath Controversies," 235.

85. Sigal, *The Halakhah of Jesus of Nazareth*, 152.

86. Sigal, *The Halakhah of Jesus of Nazareth*, 145.

87. Sigal, *The Halakhah of Jesus of Nazareth*, 153.

88. Hicks, "The Sabbath Controversy in Matthew," 82; Moo, "Jesus and the Authority of the Mosaic Law," 8.

89. Moo, "Jesus and the Authority of the Mosaic Law," 8.

and justice; 2) judicial rhetoric entails the involvement of a third party.[90] According to Robbins, Jesus is held responsible by the Pharisees for the act of his disciples. It is the responsibility of the master to correct the behavior of his disciples but in this story, the Pharisees are intruders involving themselves with the internal affairs of Jesus and his disciples. Therefore, such an intrusion, argues Robbins, shifts the situation into judicial rhetoric which is a serious accusation based on Jewish tradition.[91] Robbins notes that the Pharisees did not present their accusation with any explicit proof from the scripture, therefore the argument is not on any legal code or Law, but on logic.[92] But Jesus responded with a form of stasis by citing scripture which exposed the unwarranted assumption of the Pharisees that holds that the Law maintains an unambiguous position in all its commandments.[93] Jesus admitted that the act of David is an unlawful act but that it was permitted by the priest, as he is the envoy of the king on a mission, thus the disciples are also permitted to do what is unlawful, in this case eating. Robbins contends that Jesus' argument is an argument from comparison, that is, from the lesser to the greater or from David to the Son of man.[94]

However, it could be argued here that in 12:1–8, Jesus claims that the disciples are not guilty because the Sabbath commandment does not prohibit their action. In so doing, he is exonerating the disciples from the Pharisees' accusation. The comparison is neither between David and Jesus nor between the priests and Jesus. Instead, it is between the disciples and David, and between the disciples and the priests in the temple. Firstly, the example of David and the religious service of the priests in the temple should not be understood as a confirmation that the acts of the disciples were a breach of the Sabbath Law. First because both examples, according to Cohn–Sherbok, do not fit either the haggadic or the halakic argument of the rabbi.[95] Secondly, while plucking grain of a neighbor's land with one's hand and eating to satisfy one's hunger is permitted in the Law, using sickles is prohibited (Deut 23:25). In this case, the disciples thus breached no command, but whether this is permitted on the Sabbath for the same

90. Robbins, "Plucking Grain on the Sabbath," 18.

91. Robbins, "Plucking Grain on the Sabbath," 112.

92. Robbins, "Plucking Grain on the Sabbath," 116.

93. Robbins, "Plucking Grain on the Sabbath," 113.

94. Robbins, "Plucking Grain on the Sabbath," 133.

95. Cohn-Sherbok, "An Analysis of Jesus' Arguments Concerning the Plucking of Grain on the Sabbath," 34–40; Robbins, "Plucking Grain on the Sabbath," 120..

reason (hunger) is not clear. Ploughing and harvesting is forbidden on the Sabbath day (Exod 34:21), but plucking grain to satisfy one's hunger is not mentioned or clearly prohibited. The Mosaic Law also has no explicit prohibition against plucking grain on the Sabbath to satisfy one's hunger therefore the debate between the Pharisees and Jesus must be about the interpretation of the command of the Sabbath on the act of the disciples on the Sabbath day[96] as the second story evinces (12:10).

Thirdly, the examples Jesus adduced to his case are a real breach of a specific command with respect to the priestly ministry in the temple, while the disciples did not breach any specific Sabbath command. David, because of hunger, ate the showbread permitted only to the priest; hence, he is guilty of transgressing an explicit commandment. But he is not condemned! David's act of transgression is justified because of his hunger. If this is correct, David cannot be the example of Jesus here because, according to the story, Jesus was neither hungry nor plucked the grain, nor did the Pharisees accuse him of breaching the Sabbath.

Fourthly, the Sabbath command is not absolute because it is already transgressed in the presence of God in the temple for the sake of carrying out perpetual sacrifice in the temple (Num 28:9–10). The act of the disciples, however, cannot be compared to the service of the priest in the temple, for the disciples are not doing religious service neither are they serving Jesus. Contrary to Banks' and Moo's claim[97] they plucked the grain because they were hungry. But one may argue that they were on a divine mission with Jesus. Yet, Jesus did not mention his divine mission as a reason for the disciples' act being permissible and neither does Matthew. Instead, Jesus argues on the basis of what God desires. God desires mercy, not sacrifice (12:7).

It is also argued that sacrifice takes precedence over the Sabbath commandment[98] but this does not seem to be the case. Jesus claimed that "something greater than the temple is here" (12:6). "Something" is neuter. Unlike Stanton, Luz argues that it does not refer to Jesus.[99] Nor does it refer to the kingdom of God through Jesus,[100] nor to the

96. Weiss, "The Sabbath in the Synoptic Gospels," 22.

97. Banks, *Jesus and the Law in the Synoptic Tradition*, 117; Moo, "Jesus and the Authority of the Mosaic Law," 16–17.

98. Sigal, *The Halakhah of Jesus of Nazareth*, 62–63.

99. Stanton, *A Gospel for a New People*, 204; Ulrich Luz, *Matthew: 8–20*, 181

100. Schweizer, *Matthew*, 279.

community of the disciples.[101] It refers to what Jesus is about to say in 12:7 about mercy. Jesus did not say that he is greater than the temple, nor that mercy is greater than the Law. Rather, what emerges from the debate in the story is that Jesus is arguing that the sacrifices *per se* are not the basis for the priest breaching the Sabbath in the temple (Numbers 28:9, 10) but *the purpose of the sacrifices,* because the sacrifices are to be continuously offered to convey the worship of the people to God and the mercy of God to Israel (Hosea 6:6). For mercy's sake, the Sabbath is breached in God's presence and the priests are not guilty as they are doing what God has ordained. Therefore, in the presence of God, the Sabbath is not the ultimate desire of God, but mercy is, and so *mercy overrides the Sabbath*, and because of their merit as mediums of mercy, the sacrifices take precedence over the Sabbath.

Therefore, according to the Matthean narration, the examples of David and the priests are not intended to show that the disciples breached the Sabbath following their examples and thus are guilty. Nor is Jesus requesting the Pharisees to have mercy on his disciples. Rather, Jesus wanted to demonstrate that both David's and the priest's acts happened in the temple where the presence of God is revered. Jesus did not say David was guiltless; he implied rather that no condemnation was incurred. In the latter case, however, the priests had to bring an offering on the Sabbath and in so doing they breached the Sabbath in the presence of God for the sake of mercy and therefore they are guiltless. The disciples are guiltless not because they are with Jesus,[102] but it is because there is no explicit prohibition of what they did in the Law.

As Robbins has argued, the debate is not based on the Law but on logic as none of the Pharisees cited any legal code.[103] Jesus is challenging, by citing an example of irregularities in the Law (12:3–5), the assumption of the Pharisees that the Law maintains an ambiguous position on a given commandment. If this is granted, then in the next section (12:6–8) Jesus is arguing that not only is the Law irregular but also that it does not give equal weight to all commandments in that it gives prominence to some commandments such as mercy. Therefore, Jesus concludes that the accusation against the disciples is the result of ignorance on the part of the Pharisees. In doing so, Jesus not only exonerates his disciples from

101. David Hill, *The Gospel of Matthew*, 211.

102. Yang, *Jesus and the Sabbath*, 182.

103. Robbins, "Plucking Grain on the Sabbath," 116.

the accusation against them but also declares his identity as the lord of the sacred day.

In the next story (12:9–14), Matthew continues to explain what it means by the statement that God desires ἔλεος. Jesus already announced that the purpose of his coming is to call sinners which he describes as ἔλεος (9:13). Jesus accused the Pharisees of not exercising ἔλεος while keeping the commandments on tithing (23:23). The term ἔλεος is a relational term which conveys God's act of love. Hicks understands ἔλεος in the OT as covenant loyalty and as an expression of one's relationship to God or one's love for God.[104] But in Matthew, the emphasis lies on the relationship of among human beings (5:7, 23:23) and yet, it is not defined in light of the love commandment here[105] because mercy is here defined in terms of Jesus' sayings and acts in the narration. In 12:9–14 Jesus, for example, demonstrates what it means to show mercy without neglecting the other commandments (23:23–24). ἔλεος is to value ἄνθρωπος (12:12a). Here Jesus' conclusion reflects his judgment on any commandments of God. The commandments are not meant to devalue humanity. Instead, the commandments place a higher value upon humanity and dignity than on anything else. By implication, *God gave the commandments because he values ἄνθρωπος higher*. If a commandment contradicts this principle in a given context, *valuing ἄνθρωπος should take priority.* Secondly, ἔλεος is to do good towards humanity (12:12b). Some scholars argue that Jesus did not do any work here.[106] But Jesus considers the healing as an example of good work (καλῶς ποιεῖν). Whether the Matthean change of ἀγαθόν for καλῶς (12:12/Mark 3:4) signals a significant change of meaning is questionable and therefore Thayer defines the phrase as "simply, *to do good*" (italics his).[107] What is good, in this story, is the restoring of the man to a healthy state and bringing back his dignity within the community. Therefore, ἔλεος is one of the weightier matters of the Law whereby the Law demonstrates how God values humanity. However, Jesus did not say that ἔλεος obliterates the other commandments but rather that the other commandments should be practised in light of its importance.

Matthew briefly mentions the Sabbath in 24:20 and 28:1 in his ensuing narration. Historical criticism and redaction criticisms have investigated 24:20 to describe the nature of the community of Matthew.

104. Hicks, "The Sabbath Controversy in Matthew," 88.

105. Banks, *Jesus and the Law in the Synoptic Tradition*, 117.

106. Sigal, *The Halakhah of Jesus of Nazareth*, 168–73.

107. Thayer, *A Greek-English Lexicon of the New Testament*, 323.

Matthew adds "your flight" and "nor on Sabbath" to his Markan source which resulted in diverse speculations about the community of Matthew. It reflects that Jesus followers fear the Jews' authority because flight on Sabbath was dangerous, for a fleeing person would be recognized easily; and it also reflects the early Jewish apocalyptic tradition.[108] In light of the discussion on the Sabbath so far, both 24:20 and 28:1 most probably indicate that the real readers of the Gospel of Matthew kept the Sabbath.

In sum, Jesus did not abrogate the Sabbath Law, and the real readers of the Gospel seem to be keeping the Sabbath. Instead, Jesus pointed out that *in the Law, there is an irregularity, and a ranking*. In such cases, *valuing human beings, doing good to them and meeting their needs* take precedence since they are expressions of the ultimate desire of God, namely: mercy.

Purity, vows and tithes (Matt 15:1–20; 23:23)

Purity, vows and tithes are part of the topical progression of the Law in Matthew particularly in regard to the scope of the Law. Matthew 15 is the climax of the debate in Galilee in which the narration of the Gospel reaches its climax in Jerusalem with the death of Jesus. Talbert observes the following triad in the chapter: provocation, withdrawal, and continuing ministry.[109] Matt 15:1–20 relates the controversy or conflict over the tradition of the fathers which begins with a question and ends with an answer. Jesus addresses his speech to three different groups: first to the scribes and Pharisees (15:1–9), then the crowds (15:10–11) and finally to his disciples (15:12–20). The question of the scribes and the Pharisees is the result of their concern with the tradition of the fathers, in this case, hand washing. However, Jesus' answer goes beyond the question of hand washing and deals with dietary Laws and the authority of the commandment of God against the tradition of the fathers. Saldarini presumes that Jesus' answer has a potential of attacking the whole biblical code on purity.[110] While Mark evades the question of hand washing and concludes with dietary laws, Matthew comes back to the question of the scribes and Pharisees and concludes with the issue of hand washing. However, Jesus, in Matthew, shifts the argument for a while to deal with the fundamental

108. Stanton, *A Gospel for a New People*, 192–97.

109. Talbert, *Matthew*, 186.

110. Saldarini, *Matthew's Christian-Jewish Community*, 134.

problem: the difference between tradition (constructed by human beings) and the commandment of God. Scholars are divided on whether Matthew is against ritual Laws or not. Schweizer argues that Matthew rejects ritual law and makes the moral Law obligatory,[111] but Bacon contends that Matthew does not reject ritual Law but subordinates it to the love commandments.[112] Barth maintains that Jesus' interpretation of the Law in the love commandment breaks the rabbinic tradition.[113] Regarding the tradition of the elders, then, there are two positions: Matthew rejects the tradition of the elders; and Matthew maintains the tradition of the elders but subordinates it to the love commandments of God. In the Gospel of Matthew, Jesus is always defending the Law in its original form and usually opposes the Pharisaic interpretation thereof. Likewise, in the controversy of hand washing, Jesus is not against the hand washing *per se* but against scribes and the Pharisees for valuing it until the point of nullifying the commandment of God. Unlike Bacon and Barth, in chapter 15, there is no hint of the love commandment except that Jesus' argument is from the Decalogue that one must honor one's mother and father. In fact, honoring one's father and mother could be an act of love, yet insofar as Jesus' response to the issue of purity is concerned, he does not mention the love commandments neither explicitly nor implicitly. Furthermore, the issue in 15:1–20 is not about purity ritual codes but about the tradition of the elders (15:3). Jesus is not interpreting the commandment of honoring one's father and mother but castigating the scribes and the Pharisees for nullifying the commandment of God because of their tradition.

The tradition of hand washing is important as it serves as a boundary marker between the Jews and outsiders and as a means of exercising holiness towards God.[114] But there are only three places where "washing" is mentioned in Scripture and none of them relates to washing hands before a meal: Exod 30:19–21 (regarding priests), Lev 15 (people's bodily emissions) and Deut 21:6 (elders wash their hands as a sign of their innocence). According to Luz, Montefiore, Neusner, and Booth maintain that hand washing before a meal was not a general rule but that it was a common practice of the Pharisees. Lay people did, however, not observe it.[115] There seems to be a hand washing practice before prayer in the Diaspora

111. Schweizer, *The Good News According to Matthew*, 327.

112. Bacon, *Studies in Matthew*, 352–53.

113. Barth, "Matthew's Understanding of The Law," 88–89.

114. Saldarini, *Matthew's Christian-Jewish Community*, 135.

115. Luz, *Matthew 8–20*, 330.

and later in the Mishna it was a debate.[116]It seems that Jesus is here taking a position against the Scribes and Pharisees for violating the written Law for the sake of the Oral laws as the rabbinic tradition values the oral law over the written Law.[117]

Jesus' contention is based on citing a concrete example of the violation of explicit commandments because of the tradition. Because of the teaching of the Scribes and Pharisees on vows, a child can dedicate a specified property to God and thereby free himself from supporting his parents. In so doing, the child violates the explicit commandment pertaining to honoring his or her father and mother (Exod 20:12; Lev 20:9; Deut 5:16). Jesus' argument is that their tradition served as an excuse and that it has become an instrument to nullify τὸν λόγον τοῦ θεοῦ. Such a tradition is a fabricated doctrine and lip service rather than a true worship of God (15:7–9). Jesus gets back to the purity question and pronounces that it is not what comes into the mouth which defiles a person but what comes out of his mouth (15:11). Later he explains to his disciples that whatever food goes into the mouth goes down to the stomach and passes on from there and that therefore there is no connection between defilement and food. But what comes out of the heart is what defiles a person: evil thoughts, murder, adultery, fornication, theft, false witness, and slander. Nevertheless, Jesus made his point explicit by stating, "to eat with unwashed hands does not defile a man." The discussion harks back to his claim that anyone who relaxes the smallest part of the Law and teaches accordingly will be last in the kingdom of God seems to echo in this debate (5:17–20). Jesus is vehemently protective of the commandments of God as he accuses the Scribes and the Pharisees of relaxing the commandments of God because of their tradition. Importantly, Jesus maintains that all evil is brought forth from the heart or thought pattern of a person.

Other purity issues are also alluded to in the act of Jesus' healing of the leper (8:1–4), entering into a Gentile territory (8:28), eating with sinners (9:10–13), being touched by a woman with a hemorrhage (9:20), and the touching of a dead girl (9:25) are considered as breaching some of the purity codes in the Law. Craig Evans has pointed out that in a culture coded with purity and impurity rules identification and association with the impure ones would disqualify one from the community.[118] In

116. Saldarini, *Matthew's Christian-Jewish Community*, 130.

117. Talbert, *Matthew*, 187–88.

118. Evan, "'Who Touched Me?' Jesus and the Ritually Impure," 355.

particular, purity is important to the Jews because it distinguishes them from other nations as the people of the covenant. Scholars such as Marcus Borg, John Dominic Crossan and N.T Wright have argued that Jesus acted against the purity codes of the Law by eating with sinners, healing the sick, lepers, the hemorrhaging woman, the demonic and by approaching a woman and Gentiles.[119] In particular, the annulling of the purity Law has reached its pinnacle when Jesus denounces the temple and overturns the tables of the moneychangers. Borg and Crossan associate purity Law with the marginalized, however, Fredriksen rejects this reading, arguing that the purity Law is associated neither with class dominion nor with sinfulness.[120] Jesus did not repudiate the purity Law because he himself kept it: he, for example, ate the Paschal lamb which requires purification according to the Law (Num 9:6–12; 19:11–12) and he was able to move around the temple, which means that he met the purity requirements.[121] Sanders argues that the purity of the body and purity of the soul and mind are not separated in Jewish thinking.[122]Purity is intertwined with the day-to-day life of the Jews, and since some unclean things cannot be avoided provision was made to be able to purify oneself from it. Therefore, purity is not a matter of ethics but of being outwardly and ritually fit, hence the so-called impure people are not necessarily morally impure as well. Jesus healing the leper and the woman with a hemorrhage as well as touching the dead body of the girl in Matthew might have made Jesus ritually impure. But instead, the healing and the touch of Jesus removed all the impurities from the sick which implied that Jesus cannot have become impure from touching them. However, Matthew also narrates that Jesus commanded the person who was cleansed of his leprosy to go to the temple, show himself to the priest, and offer the sacrifices Moses commanded so that it would be a witness to them (8:1–4). The case of the leper and Jesus commanding him to fulfil the requirements for cleansing as Moses prescribed (Lev 14:10–32) reveals that Jesus was not against the purity Law, he rather complied with its authority. This is in line with his his claim in 5:17–20 not to demolish the Law.

119. Borg, *Meeting Jesus Again for the First Time*, 49; Crossan, *The Historical Jesus*, 323; Wright, *The New Testament and the People of God*.

120. Borg, *Meeting Jesus Again for the First Time*; Crossan, *The Historical Jesus*; Fredriksen, "Did Jesus Oppose the Purity Laws?"

121. Fredriksen, "Did Jesus Oppose the Purity Laws?," 43.

122. Sanders, *Jewish Law from Jesus to the Mishnah*, 271.

The issue of purity is also evident in chapter 23 in which Jesus vehemently castigates the Pharisees. The argument over the status of the Law also reaches its climax therein; therefore, the discourse is significant because of its setting:

1. it is in Jerusalem where most key religious leaders live;
2. it is where the center of worship (the temple) is; and
3. it is the final teaching place of Jesus. In 23:25–26, Jesus' injunction of cleaning the inside of the cup and that the outside would then also be clean is understood in two ways—one literally and the other metaphorically.[123]

Maccoby contends that since there is no ritual washing of a cup only on the outside, Jesus is not speaking of ritual purity. Rather, he is speaking of hygiene. While Saldarini and Nolland understand the text in terms of the purity rules for utensils in the Mishna, Hagner prefer Maccoby's reading. The topics (scribes, prayer, tithe, vow, altar and temple) of Jesus' discourse inform that Jesus is not just using the cup as a metaphor but that it is the basis of his argument on the literal performance of purification.[124] Whether it is understood literally, or in in a metaphorical sense, in both cases Jesus' statement does not stand against the purity Laws. Rather, he affirms that both the outside and the inside must be cleansed while emphasizing the inside. Nevertheless, Jesus' concern is still for the thought pattern of the religious leaders in that they are hypocrites in their religious lives (23:28).

In this chapter, Jesus also raises the issue of vows and tithes. He is overtly resistant to vows in 5:33–48 and 23:16–22 even though it is an integral part of the social and legal system of the OT (Deut 6:13; 10:20) not least because it is ultimately invoking God (23:21–22).He does not oppose tithing but relativizes it by recommending that, while "these you ought to have done, without neglecting the others" (23:23), the weightier matters of the Law must be given ultimate priority, namely: justice, mercy, and faith.

As in the case of the Sabbath controversy in 12:1–14, Jesus still upholds the Law as he had stated that his coming was not to abolish it but instead to fulfil it. Although at times Jesus corrects the interpretation of

123. Maccoby, "The Washing of Cups," 3–14.

124. Saldarini, *Matthew's Christian-Jewish Community*, 139–40; Nolland, *The Gospel of Matthew*, 938–39; ; Gundry, *Matthew*, 466.

his contemporaries, his major emphasis is not on the right interpretation thereof, but rather on the right thought pattern guided by the Law (particularly the Decalogue). Most importantly, although he upholds the Law as it was originally given to Moses, he does not give equal weight to each commandment. Justice, mercy, and faith are made to stand out at the top of the ranking of the commandments.

Divorce (19:3–9)

The question here is whether Jesus is abrogating the commandment on divorce given in Deuteronomy 24:1–4. The Pharisees questioned Jesus whether it is lawful to divorce one's wife for any cause. Matthew adds "for any cause" to Mark's version (19:2). Jesus did not reply directly but argued from creation that God created male and female so that they can be joined in marriage. The interrogators insisted that Moses commanded divorce in the Law in Deut 24:1–4. But Jesus corrects their claim that it was "commanded" by describing it as "allowed."[125] Sigal argues that Jesus did not abrogate Deut 24:1–4 but rather took a position against the interpretation of Shemmai and Hillel.[126] While Shemmai restricts the condition of divorce to sexual immorality, Hillel allowed divorce for any reason.[127] Sigal is correct in insisting that Jesus' teaching on divorce comes from Malachi 2:14–16, which also connects marriage to creation (see Malachi 2:20).[128]Jesus had already claimed that his coming was not to abolish the Law or the prophets (5:17–20) and here he brings both the Law and the prophetic proclamation together to defend the Law by making it even stricter. There is thus no intention on his side of abrogating the Law.

Section summary and conclusion

In 5:17–20, Jesus declares his stance on the Law, and the consistency of his declaration has been demonstrated in the analysis of the topical progression νομός. In 5:17–20 the fulfilment, the duration, the scope, the teaching and practicing of the Law are introduced as issues to be explored through the narrative. The discussion has revealed that while fulfilling

125. Sigal, *The Halakhah of Jesus of Nazareth*, 114.

126. Sigal, *The Halakhah of Jesus of Nazareth*, 116.

127. Saldarini, *Matthew's Christian-Jewish Community*, 150.

128. Sigal, *The Halakhah of Jesus of Nazareth*, 116.

the prophets,' means that the life and ministry of Jesus fulfilled specific prophecies as uttered by specific prophets, fulfilling the Law means that Jesus defended it from tradition by arguing for its original state, while recommending to his followers to comply with it. He also revealed its ambiguity and the order among its commandments. Therefore, the following conclusions can be made: (1) Jesus never contradicted or violated the Law in either his teaching or practice. (2) The role of the Law as a measure of judgment is superseded by Jesus and his teaching because the Law as a standard, for judgment of sin is inadequate as it only deals with its results while sin is also a matter of one's thought–life and Jesus' teachings aimed at addressing it. Hence, insofar as judgment is based on one's thought–life, it will be based on whether one complies with the teaching of Jesus or not. (3) There is ambiguity and gradation within the Law; therefore, mercy, justice, and faith are prioritized over other commandments. (4) Since the Law is not abrogated, it still plays the role of setting behavioral boundaries detailing what is evil and good for Jesus followers and providing guidance for discerning what must be given priority.

Topical Progression of *ἀγάπη*

Like the topical progression of the Law, the topical progression of *ἀγάπη* also begins in the SM (5:43–48). Although the concept of *ἀγάπη* is not lacking in 5:38–40, it is beyond the purview of this investigation to include it in the discussion. The focus of this study will instead be on the explicit occurrence of *ἀγάπη* in Matthew in order to show its topical progression in the Gospel before its formulation in the greater commandment. Matt 5:43–48 is taken by most scholars as the climax of Jesus' discussion on the Law (which started in 5:17), in that it calls for perfection. This might be partially true, but as the discussion of the progression of the topic of the Law has demonstrated, Jesus has just begun introducing the major topics of the Law that he later expounds in his teachings and debates with his contemporary religious leaders until the whole story reaches its climax. Similarly, the topical progression of *ἀγάπη*, which begins in the SM, continues and develops in the teaching and action of Jesus until the narrative reaches its end.

The first part of the quotation, "You shall love your neighbor and hate your enemy" (5:43b) is probably taken from Lev 19:18. The second part is however not found in the OT sources. Even Lev 19:18 is not fully quoted, since "as yourself" is omitted and whether the omission is accidental or intentional is debated by scholars. Betz (1995) speculates that the omission might be due to theological reasoning making God the paradigm of love; and it might also be that it is creating an *isocolon* to formulate parallelism[129]. Differing suggestions have been given regarding the source of "hate your enemy": (1) it states an improper interpretation of Lev 19:18;[130](2) it repudiates the Qumran sect's explicit instruction of hating enemies 1QS 1.4; (3) it is a rhetorical counter formulation of Lev 19:18 aiming at confronting the reader;[131] and (4) it is an expansion of Lev 19:18.[132] The phrase'Η κούσατε ὅτι ἐρρέθη /you have heard/ implies the idea or the saying was familiar to the audience in one way or another. Considering this, readings (1) and (2) provide a better explanation, however readings (3) and (4) might be possible although they do not account for 'Η κούσατε ὅτι ἐρρέθη. John Piper undertook to investigate the source of "love your enemy."[133] His search entailed studying literature from classical philosophy, the Old Testament, the second temple period, and the New Testament books before he concludes that the early church paraphrased, interpreted and applied the saying of Jesus from the center of the paraenetic teaching on enemy love.[134] Nonetheless, there is no way in which to verify whether the church formulated the phrase or not.

Who are the neighbor and the enemy in the SM? In 5:43, Jesus reiterates what has been the norm in this regard before commenting on it later in the following verses. Hence, τὸν πλησίον σου (your neighbor) must be understood in light of what the implied audiences might have envisioned, namely the concept of neighbor in the OT. In the OT the neighbor is specifically a fellow covenant member as is described in Lev 19:1–34. It refers to a parent (v. 3), the poor (vv. 13), the hired (v. 13), the handicapped (v. 14), the slave (v. 20), the aged (v. 32) and the stranger (vv. 33–34). Betz (1995) thinks that the neighbor can also be a friend.[135] However, Guelich is right in arguing that whether the neighbor meant Israelite, fellow sectarian, fellow student of the Law, one's friend or one's

129. Betz, *The Sermon on the Mount*, 303.

130. Guelich, *The Sermon on the Mount*, 225–27; Strecker, *The Sermon on the Mount*, 88–89.

131. Betz, *The Sermon on the Mount*, 303–6.

132. Allison, *The Sermon on the Mount*, 100.

133. Piper, *Love Your Enemies*.

134. Piper, *Love Your Enemies*, 20–49.

135. Betz, *The Sermon on the Mount*, 306.

own kind has no relevancy in Jesus' injunction, because the focus lies on the contrasting element that is loving one's enemy.[136] Of course, in order to understand the enemy, clarity on the neighbor is important. However, Jesus gives no concrete identity either for the neighbor or for the enemies (plural) by putting them in general terms. The saying "as your neighbor" (5:43a) is tantamount to saying "those who love you" (5:46a), and "your brethren" (5:47a) providing examples such as tax collectors (5:46b), and Gentiles (5:47c). The examples are used for calling the audience to do more (περισσὸν ποιεῖτε). Jesus' injunction to pray for those who persecute you (5:44) implies that there are persecutors, but their identity is not revealed in the SM.

Differing candidates for the reference to enemies have been proposed which include private or personal enemies, and an inner sentiment (i.e. one can kill a person but without hate in the heart).[137] Sticking to the narration as it stands and assuming the narration is progressive, a better insight can be gained regarding the identity of the enemies. Judy Yate Siker's (2005) application of sociological identity construction theory has thrown some insight onto this. The conclusion at which Siker arrived is that the identity of the enemies in the Gospel is the amorphous "Other," however, as the narrative unfolds the enemies are revealed to be the collective Jewish leaders.[138] However, Siker's analysis did not include the force of 10:22a "you will be hated by all for my name's sake" which might include Gentiles and Gentile leaders as well. Although the identity of the enemies in the Gospel is primarily that of the religious leaders, it also includes any person, institution, community or group which stands against the disciples because of the name of Jesus (5:10, 11, and 12).

Loving one's enemy is more an action than an emotion, according to Jesus.[139] In Matthew, loving one's enemies is to pray for those who persecute you, but Mohrlang[140] thinks that it also entails doing good to "those at whose hands they suffer." Although praying for the persecutors is an act of love, the Matthean Jesus emphasises the model of love. In 5:45–48,

136. Guelich, *The Sermon on the Mount*, 225.

137. Allison, *The Sermon on the Mount*, 103; Guelich, *The Sermon on the Mount*.

138. Siker, "Unmasking the Enemy," 122–23.

139. Jesus' injunction of love of the enemy is also elaborated more in Luke than in Matthew: to do good to those who hate, to bless those who curse, and to pray for those who abuse you (Luke 6:27–28). Luke not only delineates the meaning of loving an enemy but specified different kinds of enemies Carter, "Love Your Enemies," 16.

140. Mohrlang, *Matthew and Paul*, 94.

three paradigms of love are used as an object of comparison: the model of tax collectors, the model of the Gentile, and the model of God—the father. Tax collectors are grouped among the sinners (9:20–11; 11:19; 18:17; 21:31) but Jesus called a disciple from them (10:3) while other tax collectors believed the message (21:32). Jesus also ate with them resulting in people identifying with him. Carter points out that the tax collectors' profit worsened the oppressive tax burden of Israel and as a result they were marginalised by the society.[141] They thus had to support each other. Jesus is not against this form of love of tax collectors as such because he is not against love among those who love one another on the ground of having the same interest. Instead, he is arguing that such love has no reward before the father because it is based on reciprocity and is confined to the same interest group.

The second model is love within family or the same race—i.e. between brethren. Such love occurs even among the Gentiles. Gentiles are the object of Jesus' mission, and he also commanded the disciples to focus on them as well (12:18; 21:43; 24:14; 28:16) but they are not a good model of life in the kingdom of God. Specifically, their manner of praying as well as their leadership model is rejected by Jesus (6:7; 20:25). They are also among the persecutors of the disciples and Jesus himself (10:18; 20:19; 24:9). Nonetheless, Jesus is not against the Gentiles' kind of love. Instead, the disciples are called to do more than the Gentiles do. These types of love, that is, love within the same interest group and love within family and the same social group are discriminatory and therefore are not an acceptable model for the Jesus followers.

The third model of love, the love of God the father, illustrates the meaning of loving enemies. God indiscriminately provides the most important elements to sustain life (5:44–48). God sustains the life of the evil and the good (πονηροὺς καὶ ἀγαθοὺς) and the righteous and the unrighteous (δικαίους καὶ ἀδίκους) without discrimination. God does not eradicate those who are evil or the unrighteous but allows them to live and even provides them with the necessities of life to continue to function until the judgment day (7:23; 13:28–29; 18:17). God is portrayed as πατρὸς ὑμῶν (your father) (5:45, 48). This portrayal of God elucidates that the speech assumes that the audiences, in this case the disciples, are already the children of God. Secondly, it is relational and familial language that depicts God as the model of fatherhood and the head of the

141. Carter, *Matthew and the Margins*, 156.

family to be emulated by his children. The designation of God as a father is used twelve times (excluding 6:9) and all occurrences have the phrase "your father." God stands as a paragon of love within the family. Loving one's enemies without discrimination is not just a sentimental, mental assent or emotion; it is doing good towards fellow persons without value judgment and expectation of reciprocity as modelled by God the father. Doing good works can be seen by the public and brings glory to God the father (5:16).

Loving one's enemies has a purpose and a reason for the disciples; it is acting and becoming like their father, and it leads to perfection (5:48). The purpose clause in 5:45a is not about becoming sons in terms of status but about exercising the nature of their father because Jesus' saying assumes that the disciples are already children of God as is evident in the phrase "your father." In 19:2, Jesus lists the Decalogue and "love your neighbor as yourself" as a response to the young rich man's query, but the young man responded to Jesus with confidence and a sense of perfection by asking Jesus to tell him what he is still lacking. Jesus called him to perfection. In this case, perfection is to amass treasure in heaven by giving out earthly treasure to the needy and following Jesus. But loving one's neighbor is not included as a means of perfection, nor is it among those things that one is expected to do more (περισσὸν ποιεῖτε). Perfection is doing more than the usual list of commandments. However, τέλειος in 5:48 is understood variously: as imperative, as prediction or as eschatological promise.[142] Betz classifies perfect in three important fields of meaning: cult, education and ethics[143] and opts for educational and ethical uses in the SM. Others interpret it as the total observance of the Law.[144] However, Guelich counters this position by arguing that "perfect" here misses a legal function and that such a reading does not account for 19:20–21.[145] But he interprets it as a new relationship or wholeness in one's relationship with God and with others and that the moral ingredient is secondary. Such reading is, however, not evident in the SM. Instead, perfection is not about new relationships but about doing more imitating God. Guelich's definition of perfection is abstract while Jesus concretized what perfection means in both 5:48 and 19:21. It is to do something

142. Betz, *The Sermon on the Mount*, 321.

143. Betz, *The Sermon on the Mount*, 322–23.

144. Barth, "Matthew's Understanding of The Law," 96–103; Bornkamm, "End-Expectation and Church in Matthew," 29.

145. Guelich, *The Sermon on the Mount*, 236–37.

more in line with the OT commandments but what is to be done is not explicitly stated. In other words, it is to emulate God and Jesus in doing good to others without expecting anything in return.

In conclusion, the topical progression of *ἀγάπη* reveals that love must be indiscriminate. The usual axiom of love, that is, "love your neighbor as yourself" is downplayed but "love your enemies" is set as a standard. This is not an abrogation of the Law because loving one's enemy does also include loving one's neighbor as loving one's enemy does more towards one's perfection. If this is granted, then the following conclusions can be drawn: (1) Loving a neighbor is not a means to perfection. (2) Loving a neighbor is not the teaching of Jesus that calls for doing more. (3) Loving an enemy is not only abstaining from hurting the enemy but actively doing good without expecting reciprocity from them.

SUMMARY AND CONCLUSION

The analysis in this chapter has revealed that Jesus never contradicted or abrogated the Law but that his person and teaching supplanted the role of the Law as a measuring rod for judgment. There was irregularity, ambiguity, and gradation within the commandments of the Law and therefore justice, mercy and faith must take priority over some commandments, for the commandments were meant to give a high value to human beings and to meet their needs. However, all the commandments of the Law play an important role in detailing behavioral boundary markers and in providing knowledge and guidance for discerning what is evil and what is good.

Loving one's neighbor is neither the teaching of Jesus nor the standard of love. Instead, loving enemies is set as the standard of love. Importantly, it presupposes loving the neighbor. Loving enemies is doing good, avoiding evil without discrimination and without expecting reciprocity since it is the Godkind of love which leads to perfection.

5

Matthew 22:34–40

Narrational, Opening–Middle–Closing, and Argumentative Texture

INTRODUCTION

One of the differences between the Gospel of Matthew and the letter to the Romans is their genre. Unlike Romans, Matthew is a narration which states its argument through speeches attributed to characters and narrational commentary. The three textures namely: narrational, opening–middle–closing and argumentative texture will be discussed in this chapter to closely analyze the argument of Matt 22:34–40. Accordingly, first the narrational texture and pattern will be analyzed, then opening–middle–closing and finally the argumentative texture will be investigated based on the narrational and opening–middle–closing textures.

MATTHEW 22:34–40: NARRATIONAL TEXTURE AND PATTERN ANALYSIS

The analysis of the topical progression of *νόμος* and *ἀγάπη* demonstrated that these topics are progressively developed throughout the narration up until Matt 22:34–40 and beyond it (Matt 23). The study provided a cumulative context and concept of *νόμος* and *ἀγάπη* and resulted in important conclusions that have a bearing on understanding Matt 22:34–40. In the next section, Matt 22:34–40 will be studied based on the outcomes of the previous discussions. First, the narrative texture, then the opening, middle and closing of the textual unit and finally the argumentative texture will be analyzed.

Different scholars have structured the Gospel of Matthew differently. In this investigation, Warren Carter's narrative blocks are generally followed for two reasons.[1] First, Carter amended the weakness of the five discourses structure, which ignores the first part of Jesus' life (Matt 1–4), and secondly, the divisions follow the storyline and put several episodes in one block, which allows one to see the bigger picture of the narrative. Matthew 22:34–40 is found within the fifth narration block (21:1–27:66) where Jesus gets into a heated conflict with religious leaders and eventually dies. The block begins with the triumphal entry of Jesus into Jerusalem and ends with his death.

In this particular block, the conflict begins in the temple with a question-and-answer dialogue. According to Robbins, "narrational texture reveals some kind of pattern that moves the discourse programmatically forward. Sometimes a pattern emerges when narration and attributed speech alternate with each other. Sometimes a particular type of speech, like a question or a command, occurs so frequently that it establishes a narrational pattern in the discourse."[2] In the next table, the narrational pattern is displayed.

1. Carter, *Matthew and the Margins.*

2. Robbins, *Exploring the Texture of Texts*, 15.

Text	Interrogators		Response		
			Respon-dent	Response with question	Response with statement
21:10	All the city	"Who is this?"	The crowd		Jesus the prophet from Nazareth of Galilee
21:16	Chief priests and the scribes	Indignant: "Do you hear what these [children] are saying?	Jesus	"Yes, have you never read, 'out of the mouth of babes and suck-lings thou hast brought perfect praise?'" (21:16)	
22:23	Chief priests and the scribes	"By what authority are you doing these things, and who gave you this authority?"	Jesus	"The baptism of John, whence was it? From heaven or from men?"	Refused to give direct answer
22:15	Pharisees' dis-ciples, and Herodian	Testing: "Is it lawful to pay tax to Caesar, or not?"	Jesus	"Why put me to the test, you hypocrites? Whose likeness and inscription is this [the coin]?"	Yes. Give what belongs to each kingdom
22:27	Sadducees	"in the resurrection, . . . to which of the seven[husband] will she [the woman] be wife?"	Jesus	"Have you not read . . .?" (22:31–32)	No marriage in resurrec-tion! This is ignorance
22:34–40	Pharisees & Lawyer	Testing: "Which is the great command-ment in the law?"	Jesus		Loving God, and loving neighbor as yourself
22:42–46	Jesus	"What do you think of the Christ?"	Pharisees		The Son of David
		"How is then David, inspired by the Spirit, call him Lord . . . ? If David calls him Lord, how is he his son?"	Pharisees		No answer

Table 4: Narrational Texture and Pattern of Matthew 22:34–40

The table reveals that there are several questions asked by different groups of people: the entire city, the crowd, the chief priest and scribes, Pharisees, Sadducees, the lawyer and Jesus. Every character in the section has a question. The questions, directly or indirectly, are answered except Jesus' last question. Firstly, the questions are the result of different motivations in that they could be understood as being inquisitive, indignant, mocking, testing, and challenging. While the city's question arises from the desire to know about the identity of Jesus, that of the chief priests and the scribes is out of indignation. Furthermore, whereas the Sadducees were motivated to mock the doctrine of resurrection and by implication Jesus, the Pharisees' question arises out of an attempt to test Jesus and trap him in public. However, Jesus' questions challenge and expose the intent of his opponents and their understanding of scripture.

Secondly, 21:1—22:46 seems to be framed by two questions asked by two different persons. At the triumphal entry of Jesus to Jerusalem the city in 21:10 the crowd asked, "Who is this [Jesus]" and in 22:42–46 Jesus asks, "What do you think of Christ?" In the first question, the crowd answered that Jesus is a prophet whereas in 22:42–46 Jesus' rhetorical questions reveals the identity of Jesus as Messiah in that he is the Lord of David. In the middle, the parables of Jesus and the debates over the Law programmatically develop the movement of the narration to evince the victory of Jesus over the religious leaders' traps and tests, before finally revealing the identity of the Messiah as the Lord.

Thirdly, the questions reveal that the religious leaders are the chief antagonists of the protagonist. In particular, the Pharisees and their agents' motivation connected to πειράζω (tempting/testing). The word occurs five times and it is used for describing Satan encountering Jesus in the desert in 4:1–3 and the Pharisees' testing/tempting of Jesus regarding the Law (19:3; 22:18, 35).

Fourthly, the debate over the Law is framed by the narrator as a question and answer. Such narrative texture and patterns can also be discerned in the entire Gospel of Matthew where the issue of the Law is discussed after the first declaration of Jesus in 5:17–20. Since the table above contains interrogations after 21:1, the rest will be demonstrated in the next table. Questions therein trigger a discussion or a conflict to move the story forward.

Texts	Interrogation		Response		
	Interrogator	Question	Respondent	The response	Actual response
11:3	John the Baptist disciples	"Are you he who is to come, or shall we look for another?"	Jesus		
12:1–14	Pharisees	[Accusation: "Look, your disciples are doing what is not lawful to do on the Sabbath"] Not question	Jesus	Have you not read what David did, when he was hungry . . . ? (12:3–4) Have you not read in the Law how on the Sabbath the priests in the temple profane the Sabbath and are guiltless?	They are guiltless before God
	Pharisees	Is it lawful to heal on the Sabbath? (12:10	Jesus	What man of you, if he has one sheep and it falls into a pit on the Sabbath, will not lay hold of it and lift it out?	Yes, it is. It is lawful to do good on the Sabbath
15:1–20	Pharisees	"Why do your disciples transgress the tradition of the elders? (15:2)	Jesus	"Why do you transgress the commandment of God for the sake of your tradition?	Your tradition is human fabrication
	Disciple of Jesus	"Do you know that the Pharisees were offended when they heard this saying?" (15:12)	Jesus	"Every plant which my heavenly Father has not planted will be rooted up. Let them alone; they are blind guides. And if a blind man leads a blind man, both will fall into a pit" (15:14)	The Pharisees are not of God and are ignorant leaders
	Disciples	Request: "Explain the parable to us"	Jesus	"Are you also still without understanding? Do you not see that whatever goes into the mouth passes into the stomach, and so pass on?"	It is the evil that comes out of the heart that defiles.
19:3–12	Pharisees	Testing: "Is it lawful to divorce one's wife for any cause?" (19:3)	Jesus	"Have you not read . . . ?" (19:4–6)	No. God made them one

	Pharisees	Testing: "Why then did Moses command one to give a certificate of divorce, and to put her away?" (19:7)	Jesus		It is because of hardness of your heart

Table 5: Narrational Texture and Pattern of Matthew 22:34–40 (continued)

Based on Carter's structure, 11:3 (the discourse on John the Baptist, Jesus, the Law and the prophets), and 12:1–4 (debate over the Sabbath) are within the second narrative block. Matt15:1–20 (debate over purity or washing hands) stands within the third narrative block and 19:3 (debate over the Law of marriage) in the fourth narrative block. The table shows that the discussion of the Law is narrated in the interrogative narrational texture. Putting together the entire occurrence of the narrational questions on the discussion of the Law, a distinct pattern emerges. Firstly, the debates are designed either to accuse Jesus or to test Jesus. Secondly, the act of the disciples, and the act and the speech of Jesus trigger questions in the mind of the debaters. Thirdly, the debate is based on Scripture. Fourthly, in many cases Jesus first replies with counter–questions on the understanding of his opponents, but most of the time he does not wait to receive answers from them, instead, he continues to make his point. His questions focus mostly on how they read the Scripture or interpret a particular text in Scripture. Fifthly, Jesus' answers depict that Jesus knows and understands the Law better than his opponents, but his opponents are either ill–informed or ignorant.

Jack Dean Kingsbury observed that the character groups that influenced the plot of Matthew next to Jesus, the protagonist, are the Jewish leaders.[3] The leaders of the Jews comprise Pharisees, the Sadducees, the Scribes, the chief priests, and the elders. The chief priests and the elders are related to Jerusalem and the temple while the Scribes and the Pharisees are linked mainly to the synagogue.[4]

Characters in a story are either "flat" or "round." While the former are easily recognizable and built around a single idea the latter are

3. Kingsbury, "The Developing Conflict between Jesus and the Jewish Leaders in Matthew's Gospel," 194.

4. Kingsbury, "The Developing Conflict between Jesus and the Jewish Leaders in Matthew's Gospel," 180.

not.[5] The Pharisees, Sadducees and Scribes are flat characters in the story as their characters are overtly portrayed. The Gospel of Matthew begins drawing the Pharisees and Sadducees with the appearance of John the Baptist (3:7) and continues with this progressively until the last chapter. Here only the summary of the depiction of the Pharisees' and the Scribes' interaction with Jesus is provided: they are evil, think evil, and speak evil (2:4–6; 9:3–4; 12:34; 22:18); they are an adulterous generation (12:39; 16:4) and deceptive (22:15). They test Jesus (4:1, 3; 16:1; 19:3; 22:18, 35), blaspheme the Spirit (9:32–34; 12:22–24), and mock Jesus and call him an imposter (27:41–43; 27:63). Although they claim to be experts in the Scripture, they are ignorant (9:13). They are hypocrites being inwardly full of lawlessness (23:28).

Hence, the narrational texture reveals a pattern that the topic of the Law is discussed within a conflict atmosphere and in the form of questions and answers. The topic of the Law is the basis for the enmity between Jesus and the religious leaders. Religious leaders are practical examples of enemies and persecutors. The context of the Law is conflict; Matt 22:34–40 seems to be at the peak of the progression of the conflict on the topic in that it concludes the whole debate in the entire Gospel although Jesus again mentions the Law in 23:23 which is almost a recapitulation of what he debated in the previous sections.

MATTHEW 22:34–40: OPENING, MIDDLE AND CLOSING

Robbins states that repetition, progression and narration create the opening, middle and closing of a textual unit.[6] The narrational texture revealed that 22:34–40 is within a conflict and debate narrative block. It can stand as a unit within the bigger block because it has a clear beginning, middle and end; 22:34–36 is the opening and introduces both the interrogators and the topic of the argument; 22:37–39 is the middle and discusses the topic; 22:40 is the closing and concludes the topic.

The movement in the unit can also be seen from the repetition. In the opening, the thesis question is stated, which introduces three important words, namely: "great," "commandment" and "Law." In the middle, the three words are repeated but a new word is added, "love," which is used twice. Such an introduction of a new word depicts the progression

5. Forster, *Aspects of The Novel*, 103–5, 103–18.

6. Robbins, *Exploring the Texture of Texts*, 19.

of ideas and movement within the unit. The closing serves as a resolution of the main idea repeating the key terms "commandments," and "Law" but it also adds new words and changes the first formulation in the thesis: instead of "in the Law" is changed to "the whole Law" to which is added "the prophets." Hence, the unit's movement develops the thesis raised at the beginning and concluding with a new insight.

MATTHEW 22:34–40: ARGUMENTATIVE TEXTURE ANALYSIS

Except 5:17–20 which can serve as a declaration of the thesis on the topic of the Law, wherever the topic appears again it appears as a debate between Jesus and the religious leaders in the form of an interrogation as the narrational texture and pattern have revealed. But in the final analysis, Jesus is vindicated as the one who knows the Law and understands it better than his opponents. One of the conclusions in the discussion on the topical progression of the Law is that there is ambiguity and gradation within the Law. The topical progression of Love has evinced that love for the neighbor is relativized by love for enemies.

In this section, the investigation will focus on the argumentative texture of Matt 22:34–30 and its parts. Robbins has argued that logical reasoning in narration "occurs in context where narrators attribute speech or action to specific people."[7] Robbins, in fact, discusses rhetorical chreia along this line. But searching for the chreia of the unit is beyond the interest of this study. However, it applies the general principle that Robbins formulated for the investigation of the argument.[8] The nature of logical argument is the role of the unstated premises, the enthymeme.

There are unstated premises with regard to the commandments of the Law in the opening of 22:34–40. The Pharisees raise the topic regarding the nature of the Law and Jesus. The question itself embodies an unstated assumption because it asks, "Which is the great commandment in the Law?" (Nestle–Aland RSV). This question assumes that there is one great commandment in the Law for the question is formulated in the singular. Furthermore, there is an unstated premise behind this conclusion, that is, all commandments do not have equal weight in the Law. From the intent of the question, which is to test Jesus, there is a third assumption that

7. Robbins, *The Tapestry of Early Christian Discourse*, 59.

8. Robbins, *The Tapestry of Early Christian Discourse*, 59.

Jesus does not know this great commandment. Although it is difficult to demonstrate the assumption in an Aristotelian syllogism, it is quite clear that there is basic reasoning working behind the question of the Pharisees and the response of Jesus that can be demonstrated in the following way.

Unstated reasoning of the Pharisees:

- All commandments do not have equal weight in the Law
- There is one great commandment in the Law known by educated elite within the Pharisaic circle
- If Jesus does not know it, he is disqualified as a teacher
- Stated and unstated reasoning of Jesus:
- All commandments do not have equal weight in the Law (unstated)
- There are two great commandments in the Law known by him (stated)
- Therefore, on these commandments the entire Law and the prophets hang (stated)

Comparing the two reasonings in regard to the Law, both Jesus and the Pharisees concede that all commandments do not have equal weight in the Law, but they disagree on the number of the commandments that are great. The Pharisees seem to be thinking there is one great commandment but there is no way to know which commandment they have in mind. However, Jesus explicitly states that there are two great commandments, not just one. Jesus not only states two great commandments but also concludes that these commandments are critically important with respect to the whole Law and the prophets. In so arguing, it seems that Jesus silenced the Pharisees as he did the Sadducees insofar as the conversation abruptly ceased.

Grading the Commandments: No Equal Weight

Matthew has made a number of significant redactions of Mark. Omission: Mark 12:32–34—no friendly discussion between Jesus and scribe, the *Shema* (Mark 12; 29), and the whole of your strength (Mark 12:30). He delays Mark 12:34 until 22:46. Additions: "lawyer" (v. 35), "testing him" (v. 35/Luke 10:25), "teacher" (v. 36), "in the Law" and "this is the great and first commandment," "similar to it" (v. 39), and "on these two commandments hang the whole of the Law and the prophets" (v. 40). Replaced: "first" in Mark is replaced by "great and first." All of his redactions are indications of how the Matthew narration is carefully situated into the context of conflict between Jesus and his opponents, Jesus' understanding of the Scripture and the progression of the Gospel's perspective on the Law, prophets, and love (5:17–20; 7:12; 22:34–40 and 23:23).

The first step in order to proceed with the discussion of the unit is to understand what νομικός (Lawyer), which is tantamount to say scribe, means by μεγάλη ἐν τῷ νόμῳ (great in the Law) and Jesus means by ἡ μεγάλη καὶ πρώτη (the great and first). Commentators agree that μεγάλη is a Semitic superlative[9] but Luz thinks that it is not necessarily a superlative as the text lacks a comparative and article.[10] But ἐν τῷ νόμῳ indicates that it is comparative so long as ἐντολή is a singular commandment to be selected out of other unspecified number of commandments. But should μεγάλη be understood as: summarising the Law,[11] ranking the Law[12] or reducing the Law or as a Hermeneutical key?[13] The concept of summarising seems to be imported from Paul in Rom 13:8–10. The language of summarising is, however, lacking in the question of the lawyer since he did not ask which one of the Law summarise the whole Law. Reducing the Law into a single commandment or a hermeneutical key cannot be detected from the question. Rather the question is, "What sort of commandment?" or "Which commandment?" but not "Which commandment is the hermeneutical key for the entire Law?" Viljoen also argued that "It is not valid to assume that Matthew subsumes the detail of *Torah* by the double love command as sum total of the *Torah* and the Prophets in (Matthew 22:34–40)" (italics his).[14] If this is granted, then the question is about grading commandments within the entire Law. Such a notion of ranking is evident in the Gospel: one of the least of these commandments (5:19), the weightier matters of the Law (23:23), and the greatest commandment in the Law (22:36).

Although Jesus does not state the smallest commandment, he has mentioned the weightier matters of the Law (mercy, justice and

9. Davies and Allison, *Matthew* 19–28; Hagner, *Matthew 14–28*, 646.

10. Luz, *Matthew 21–28*, 81.

11. Davies and Allison, *Matthew*, 3:236; France, *Matthew*, 842–43.

12. Nolland, *The Gospel of Matthew*, 910.

13. Talbert, *Matthew*, 255.

14. Viljoen, "Jesus' Teaching on the 'Torah' In the Sermon on The Mount," 152.

faithfulness), and the great commandments (loving God and loving neighbor). The smallest might refer to commandments related to tithing as the tithing regulations are minutiae whereas the weightier matters of the Law are those commandments which are "important"[15]. The three weightier matters of the Law (τὰ βαρύτερα τοῦ νόμου) are κρίσις (5:22; 10:15; 11:22, 24; 12:41, 42), ἔλεος (9:13; 12:7; 23; 23), and πίστις. The term κρίσις is related to eschatological judgment in 5:22; 10:15; 11:22, 24; 12:18, 41, 42 but in 12:18 and 20 it is the ministry of the Messiah to the Gentiles that bring hope. However, in 23:23 it is probably to bring deliverance to the oppressed (12:18). The concept ἔλεος (9:13; 12:7; 23:23) is doing good to those who need help and valuing human beings as argued earlier in chapter of this study. The term πίστις is not faith in Jesus or prayer or act of love, but faithfulness.[16] Faithfulness is a relational term denoting humbly walking with God and to remain to be true to his will. They are not supplanting the Law, but they should be practiced along with other commandments. In one way or another, all of them value humanity and relationship more than any other activities in the Law. Therefore, although all the commandments are meant to be obeyed, they do not carry equal weight in terms of emphasis and priority.

Loving God (Matt 22:37–38)

The history of interpretation of loving God revolves around the question of how one loves an unseen God. Therefore, it is interpreted in terms of knowledge and ethics. Love involves cognitive experience; and ethically, it is obedience to God's commandment therefore it is a matter of will not emotion.[17] In Matthew, God is portrayed as a father in relation to the disciples.[18] This is particularly emphasised in Matthew 6. It is also in 6:24 that love is mentioned in relation to God. Jesus used five important words to express love for God: δουλεύειν (δουλεύω) refers to serving in a humble manner responding to a demand or a command (LN 35.27); μισήσει (μισέω) means to hate with aversion and hostility (LN 88.198); ἀγαπήσει (ἀγαπάω) means to love; ἀνθέξεται (ἀντέχομαι) is to be devoted

15. Luz, *Matthew 21–28*, 122–23.

16. Luz, *Matthew 21–28*, 124.

17. Luz, *Matthew 21–28*, 77.

18. Matt 5:16, 44, 45, 48; 6:1, 3, 4, 6, 8, 14, 15, 17, 18, 26, 32; 7:11; 10:20, 29; 15:4; 18:14; and 23:9.

or to be loyal (LN 34.24), and καταφρονήσε (καταφρονέω) is to despise. While to serve, to be devoted or loyal and to love are in one group, to hate and to despise are in the opposite group. From these words, the following definition can be deduced about the nature of a loving God.

1. It is to serve God with absolute devotion and loyalty. Such devotion is the result of having high regard and value for God's kingdom (6:33) or for the things of God as the word ἀντέχομαι is contrasted to "despise" (καταφρονέω) implying value judgment (LN 88.192). Serving and devotion entail not only obedience to the commandments but also espousing the causes of the kingdom of God.
2. Love is a choice to be made on the ground of value. It is impossible both to love God and to devalue the things of God (6:24).
3. Love involves emotion, for ἀγαπήσει/ἀγαπάω is contrasted against μισήσει/μισέω which is a strong dislike. It is hard to separate love and hatred from emotion.

In sum, loving God is to serve God in absolute loyalty and devotion with one's whole being.

If this definition is granted, loving God in the great and first commandment (22:38) entails the whole (ὅλος) of one's καρδία, ψυχή, and διάνοια. Carter posits that heart, soul and mind denote the whole of human existence. According to Carter, the heart (καρδία) is the centre of a person's willing, thinking, knowing, deciding, and doing,[19] the soul (ψυχή) is one's life or daily existence given either to God's service or to something else,[20] and the mind (διάνοια) denotes the whole self in daily living oriented to God.[21] A closer look at the word καρδία in the entire Gospel reveals that it is used by Jesus and its first occurrence is related to purity (5:8). It is mainly thought of as a hidden storehouse within a person where either good or evil is stored and contemplated as a ground for one's speech and actions. Therefore, the heart is more fundamental than the other two because all fundamental thought patterns and ideology that govern one's speech, action, and relationships arise from it. The soul and the mind as defined by Carter depend on what is stored in the heart. Hence, love of God claims one's entire being and life.

19. Matt 5:8, 28; 6:21; 9:4; 11:29; 12:34, 40; 13:15, 19; 15:8, 18, 19; 18:35; 24:48.

20. Matt 2:20; 6:25; 10:28, 39; 11:29; 12:18; 16:25–26; 20:28; 26:38.

21. Carter, *Matthew and the Margins*, 445.

The Jewish understanding of loving God based on Deut 6:5 is an act of obedience, piety and faithfulness to the Law.[22] Luz argues that loving God is not a feeling but a knowing of God and obeying God in this world.[23] Likewise, Davies and Allison think that it does not involve emotion because loving God is a commandment.[24] But as argued above, it is impossible to separate love from emotion as the love of God demands the entire being of a person. Loving God is a way of life that emanates from one's disposition shaped by the words of Jesus (13:19) and his exemplary life (11:29), and it is being loyal and devoted to God to serve God in obedience to God's will. It is a decision and a choice one makes; that is why it is the greatest and first commandment which is foundational to all other commandments.

Loving One's Neighbor (Matt 22:39)

Loving one's neighbor has already been studied in the progressive texture of love and it will therefore be discussed only briefly here. Varied readings of δευτέρα δὲ ὁμοία αὐτῇ (the second like it) have been proposed: it refers to a numerical value or something second in order and not to something second in importance and therefore it has equal footing with the commandment of loving God.[25] Nolland, however, reads it as second in importance compared to the great commandment.[26] LN (60.49) defines it as "second in series" or that it means "secondly"; it is thus its numerical value and not its importance but its temporal order which is important. Both loving God and loving the neighbor are important, but they are not exactly the same. The term Ὁμοία does not necessarily mean exactly the same but it could mean something similar. LN (64.1) defines it as "being similar to something else in some respect." Both commandments are similar in that they focus on love, but they emphasize that loving God stands first in order as a foundation for loving the neighbor. Firstly, loving the neighbor is the result of loving God and loving God goes beyond loving the neighbor for it claims the whole being of a person is to be devoted to God which includes suffering for the cause of God's

22. Luz, *Matthew 21–28*, 82.

23. Luz, *Matthew 21–28*, 83.

24. Davies and Allison, *Matthew*, 2:241.

25. Davies and Allison, *Matthew*, 3:243; Schweizer, *Matthew*, 425; Luz, *Matthew 21–28*, 84.

26. Nolland, *Matthew*, 912.

will. Secondly, loving one's neighbor has the boundary "as yourself" while there is no boundary set in loving God.

Loving the neighbor should be interpreted in light of Lev 19:18 as Jesus has quoted it from Lev 19 which context entails doing good and avoiding evil. Doing good consists of respecting one's parents and providing food for the poor and strangers (9:3, 11–10) and avoiding evil includes such acts as stealing, lying, false dealings, falsely swearing by God's name, defrauding, robbing, cursing, slandering, being biased in judgment or a talebearer, murder, hatred, avenging, and grudging (19:11–18). Jesus castigated the religious leaders for nullifying the word of God due to their tradition because they allowed parents to be devoid of support and their misunderstanding of the Sabbath denied them access to food.[27] Unlike the religious leaders, Jesus showed mercy by healing the sick and upholding the law by teaching that they should honor their parents, avoid stealing, and bearing false witness or swearing and taking revenge (5:33–42; 19:18–19). Love is, therefore, a practical form of behavior[28] or obedience to those commandments related to relationships.

A neighbor in Lev 19 is not limited to the members of the covenant as a stranger must also be seen as a neighbor (Lev 19:11). Perkins points out that although loving one's neighbor in Lev 19:18 is used to reinforce the boundaries of the Jewish community, there is an openness in Jewish tradition in referring to anyone with whom one has dealings.[29] But it should be noted that Jesus' answer is motivated by the question of the lawyer therefore it is a discussion on the ranking of the commandments within the Law (ἐν τῷ νόμῳ). As discussed earlier, Jesus' teaching on love goes beyond loving a neighbor as oneself; it is loving one's enemies which is an emulation of God's own love (5:43–48). Therefore, loving a neighbor is included in a Godly kind of love which does not make any discrimination. The standard for love is God, not self love.

Hanging the Law and the Prophets (Matt 22:40)

Hanging the Law and the prophets on the love commandment has generated different interpretations:

27. Carter, *Matthew and the Margins*, 445.
28. Luz, *Matthew 21–28*, 83.
29. Perkins, *Love Commands in the New Testament*, 12, 90.

1. The love commandments are a hermeneutical key for interpretation and determining the validity and importance of the other commandments.[30]
2. The other commandments can be derived from these two commandments.[31]
3. They underline the unity, coherency and centrality of God's will.[32]
4. They are simply important and basic commandments. They do not replace the Law but state its true goal.[33]

Reading (3) and (4) can be combined as all commentators agree that hanging is a figurative expression meaning "depend." As Carter has rightly noted, it shows interconnectedness among the commandments of God without one supplanting the other. The Law and the prophets refer back to 5:17 and 7:12 where Jesus declared that the intent of his coming is not to abolish the Law but to fulfil it. Such fulfilment can only be actualized through loyalty and devotedness to God and his will with a concern for the neighbor. But, as argued above, loving a neighbor is no more the standard for Love. Instead, loving enemies has become the standard for doing good and avoiding evil without discrimination. If this is the case, although the two commandments are fundamentally important, Jesus has amended the second love commandment (love your neighbor as yourself) by removing its restriction and changing its standard.

SUMMARY AND CONCLUSION

The narrational texture has revealed that the topic of the Law is invariably a point of contention between Jesus and the religious leaders and is the basis of enmity. Hence the opening, middle and closing texture of Matt 22:34–40 is arranged in such a way that Jesus progressively adds insight into his response to the test to challenge the confrontation from the lawyer.

The analysis of the argumentative texture of Matt 22:34–34 has demonstrated that both Jesus and the religious leaders of the Jews agreed

30. Barth, "Matthew's Understanding of The Law;" Bornkamm, "End-Expectation and Church in Matthew;" Hagner, *Matthew 14–28*.

31. Schweizer, *Matthew*, 425.

32. Carter, *Matthew and the Margins*, 446.

33. Davies and Allison, *Matthew*, 246; France, *Matthew*, 844.

that there is a ranking within the Law and that all commandments do not carry equal weight. Although loving God and loving a neighbor are the two great commandments, loving God is the first in the rank and is fundamental for the other commandments. Loving God is serving and obeying God with absolute devotion with one's whole being while loving one's neighbor is avoiding evil and doing good to fellow persons. The latter is not the standard of love anymore, as it is qualified by the teaching of Jesus in 5:43–48, which states that the standard of love is God's kind of love—loving one's enemies. That the whole Law and the prophets "hang on it" does not mean the great commandment summarizes the whole Law, neither is it an interpretive key. Instead, it means that they are foundational and give reasons for obeying other commandments. Therefore, they rank higher among the commandments.

6

Comparing Romans 13:8–14 and Matthew 22:34–40

Intertexture, Concepts, and Texts

INTRODUCTION

THIS CHAPTER IS COMPRISED of two parts. In the first part the intertexture of Rom 13:8–14 and Matt 22:34–40 will be investigated in terms of their relevant literary worlds. To this end, Jewish and Greco-Roman literature as well as the undisputed Pauline letters will be explored, analyzed and compared. In the second part, a direct comparison of Romans and the Gospel of Matthew will be made. The comparison will be made on their respective concepts of judgment, sin, Jewish and Gentile relations, love and the Law in Rom 3:31, 7:4–5, 8:3–5, 10:4a vs Matt 5:17–19 and Rom 13:8–10 vs. Matt 22:34–40. Finally, an appraisal of the interpretation of the Gospel of Matthew as an anti-Pauline text will be undertaken.

THE INTERTEXTURE OF ROMANS 13:8–14 AND MATTHEW 22:34–40

The search for intertexture to form the basis for comparing Rom 13:8–14 and Matt 22:34–40 will only focus on selected earlier Jewish literature (the OT, the Apocryphal and Pseudepigrapha books, the Dead Sea

Scrolls, Philo of Alexandria); and contemporary Greco–Roman and Pauline literatures relevant to the topic of *ἀγάπη* and *νόμος*. This section will explore the conceptual (cultural intertexture) as well as the oral–scribal intertexture of the units under investigation.

Jewish Literature

The analysis in this section focuses only on those books that have textual and conceptual affinities with Rom 13:8–10 and Matt 22:34–40. Accordingly, OT books such as Deut 6:5 and Lev 19:18 and some texts from Apocryphal and Pseudepigrapha, the Dead Sea Scrolls and Philo of Alexandria will be compared and analyzed.

The Hebrew Bible and the LXX

From the OT, Deut 6:5 and Lev 19:18 are directly relevant to this study. These two texts, as they occur in both the Masoretic and LXX text will be compared with their occurrences in the Synoptic Gospels and Romans.

Deuteronomy 6:5

The authorship, literary structure, and the theology of Deuteronomy is complex.[1] However, there is a general consensus that Deut 5–26 came from the same hand.[2] Insofar as the interest of this section is on the oral–scribal intertexture[3] of Rom 13:8–10 and Matt 22:30–44, there will be no detailed discussion of all possible exegetical approaches to these texts. The occurrences of the texts on loving God and loving one's neighbor in Deuteronomy will, however, be considered in order to evaluate how Paul and Matthew used their respective sources. In the ensuing section, the occurrence of the text will be analyzed and evaluated against Romans and the Gospel of Matthew.

Loving God is one of the themes in the book of Deuteronomy (cf. 6:5; 10:12; 11:1; 13:22; 19:9; 30:6, 19–20). In addition to Deuteronomy,

1. Robson, "The Literary Composition of Deuteronomy," 57–59.
2. Robson, "The Literary Composition of Deuteronomy," 31.
3. Robbins, *Exploring the Texture of Texts*, 40. has shown that the oral-scribal texture appears in the form of recitation, reconfiguration, re-contextualization, narrative amplification and thematic elaboration.

love of God is mentioned thirteen times in the Old Testament (Exod 20:6; Josh 22:5; 23:11; Judg 5:31; 1 Kgs 3:3; Neh 1:5; Pss 18:2; 31:24; 91:14; 97:10; 116:1; 145:20; Dan 9:4). This indicates that the love of Israel of God is the emphasis of the book.[4] Moran has also noted that אָהַב summarizes "the book's central occupation, namely, observance of the law" which cements the relationship between God and Israel.[5] His studies on the near eastern background love for God asserted that אָהַב refers to covenantal love, a relationship similar to that between king and subject, which is expressed in loyalty, service and unqualified obedience to the demands of the Law of God.[6] McKay, however, finds a parallel in wisdom literature and argues that Deuteronomy's אָהַב refers to the "filial obedience, reverential love" of Israel as the son of God in a father/teacher—son/student relationship combines both insights, that is, God is depicted as a father, a king and a teacher whereas Israel is described as a son, a vassal and a student respectively; therefore, the injunction of אָהַב is a heartfelt obedience to God.[7]

God's injunction of love is on the basis of God's love for Israel, which he demonstrated through his deliverance of them from slavery and the gift of land. Israel's response of love should spring from her whole being, which is expressed as "with all your heart, with all your mind, with all your might" through obedience to the commandments. Such obedience is expressed in terms of being loyal to God (Deut 11:1, 12; 30:20), walking in God's ways (Deut 10:12; 11:1, 22; 19:9; 30:16), keeping God's commandments (Deut 10:12; 11:1, 22) or carrying them out (Deut 11:22; 19:9), heeding God's voice (Deut 11:13; 30:16), and serving God (Deut 10:12; 11:1–13). In general, loving God is expressed by obedience to the Law. However, the Law must first be in the heart which is the "seat of motivation for personal commitment"[8] and the faculty of "intellectual assimilation"[9] before it is practiced (Deut 6:6). Therefore, the commandments are elements of love shaping the reason, value and worldview of the people of Israel.

4. Willoughby, "A Heartfelt Love: An Exegesis of Deuteronomy 6:4–19," 80.

5. Moran, "Ancient Near Eastern Background of the Love of God in Deuteronomy," 77.

6. Moran, "Ancient Near Eastern Background of the Love of God in Deuteronomy," 81.

7. McKay, "Man's Love for God in Deuteronomy," 435; Willoughby, "A Heartfelt Love," 76.

8. Willoughby, "A Heartfelt Love," 82.

9. McKay, "Man's Love for God in Deuteronomy," 428–29.

The scholarly consensus on the definition of love in Deuteronomy as obedience to the commandment of God and loyalty to God has, however, been challenged by Jacqueline E. Lapsley.[10]She has argued that the consensus is based on William Moran's influential article in which she faults his methodology.[11] Firstly, because it is wholly dependent on the comparative study of the ancient near east. Such an approach to the text imposed an extra biblical concept on the biblical understanding of love. Moran, furthermore, made an atomistic study of the text without allowing for a broader consideration of Deuteronomy. In so doing, he ignored peculiarities and emphasized common elements in the text. Secondly, his reading is anachronistic in that it depends on modern concepts of love and emotion. A modern concept of love believes that love is socially constructed and subject to change ascribing emotion to private life in the category of feeling.[12] Lapsley also rejected the view that God's love for Israel is emotional while Israel's love is not, in that it is rather rational and based on obedience and loyalty to God. She instead makes a case for the contention that love in Deuteronomy entails emotion on the side of both God and Israel in that,

1. God is portrayed as a father (Deut 1; 31; 8:5; 14:1; 32:5; 19), even though the language of love is not employed.
2. The call for Israel to love God is followed by God's love for Israel and love of God for Israel is irrational (i.e. there is no prior cause for loving) (Deut 7:7–8).
3. God's love of the stranger is not only rational; it is also emotional which Israel must imitate (Deut 10:18–19).
4. Israel is reminded that she once was a stranger and should thus identify herself with the strangers within her land.
5. The circumcision of the heart is an inner experience of transformation which involves emotion, will and intention.[13]

Considering Lapsley's contention, love as obedience to the commandment and loyalty to God as covenantal faithfulness does not negate emotion. But Lapsley's caveat that action and emotion are inseparable is

10. Lapsley, "Feeling Our Way," 350–69.
11. Moran, "Ancient Near Eastern Background of the Love of God in Deuteronomy."
12. Lapsley, "Feeling Our Way," 354.
13. Lapsley, "Feeling Our Way," 361, 363.

based on the study of Nussbaum in which she reasoned that emotions are necessary for a moral life as they constitute values.[14] The relationship between God and Israel is not just based on legislative rules and commandments but also on the experience of deliverance from slavery which left a fundamental mark on their entire understanding of God. God's act of deliverance comes before his command in that his commands are given to Israel on the basis of God's deliverance. The deliverance of Israel from their abject condition created an experience that involved both their minds and emotions (Exod 15); a sense of being unique as well as a new identity as a free people. It is God's love for Israel (whether emotional or not) expressed through his act of deliverance that formed the basis of his relationship with Israel. God in turn required, and commanded, a love that demonstrates itself (with or without affection) through actions directed by God's will and desire as expressed in the Law.

In the next section, Deut 6:5 in the LXX and Masoretic Text will be compared to that of Matt 22:37; Mark 12:29–31; and Luke 10:27 and will also be analyzed in light of their similarity and differences.

The table shows the differences and analogies of the four texts, namely, the LXX, Mark, Matthew, and Luke. Focusing on the relation between the LXX and the Synoptic analogies and differences are clearly discernible.

Firstly, the analogies: (1) the command ἀγαπήσεις Κύριον τὸν Θεόν σου is an exact rendition of the LXX by Mark that is followed by the other two Synoptic Gospels. (2) The construction ἐξὅλης τῆς + genitive only occurs in Mark and once as ἐξ ὅλης [τῆς] καρδίας σου in the construction of Luke. (3) All of them use καρδίᾳ and ψυχῄ as it is used by the LXX.

Secondly, the differences: (1) Only Mark keeps ἐξὅλης τῆς + genitive construction of LXX all the way through the quotation. He, however, changes the δυνάμεώς of the LXX to διανοίας in which he is followed by Matthew and Luke. (2) Mark adds ἰσχύς, which Luke also retains. (3) Matthew reduces Mark's list of four to three, thereby making it closer to the list of Deut 6:5, while Mark and Luke extend it to four (which differs in their order). (4) Matthew diverges from the LXX in using ἐν ὅλῃ τῇ + dative construction all the way through the quotation and Luke follows him in this from the second list. (5) Mark retains the introductory phrase as an opening whereas Matthew and Luke omit it completely. (6) Mark's and Matthew's context for the quotation is a question about the most

14. Lapsley, "Feeling Our Way," 369.

important commandment in the Law (Mark ends with the scribe's answer and Jesus' praise while Matthew does not). (7) Luke uses the quotation for an entirely different question, i.e. concerning inheriting eternal life and puts the words in the mouth of the lawyer. Having done a thorough analysis, Gundry concludes that Matthew is closer to the Hebrew text whereas Mark stands closer to the LXX, although Luke conflates his source.[15]

LXX Deut 6:5	Mark 12:29–31	Matt 22:37	Luke 10:27
	29 ἀπεκρίθη ὁ Ἰησοῦς ὅτι Πρώτη ἐστίν, Ἄκουε, Ἰσραήλ, κύριος ὁ θεὸς ἡμῶν κύριοςεἷς ἐστιν,		27 ὁ δὲ ἀποκριθεὶς εἶπεν,
καὶ ἀγαπήσεις Κύριον τὸν Θεόν σου	καὶ ἀγαπήσεις κύριον τὸν θεόν σου	Ἀγαπήσεις κύριον τὸνθεόν σου	Ἀγαπήσεις κύριον τὸν θεόν σου
ἐξ ὅλης τῆς καρδίας σου καὶ	ἐξ ὅλης τῆς καρδίας σου καὶ	ἐνὅλῃ τῇ καρδίᾳ σου καὶ	ἐξ ὅλης [τῆς] καρδίας σου καὶ
ἐξ ὅλης τῆς ψυχῆς σου καὶ	ἐξ ὅλης τῆς ψυχῆς σου καὶ	ἐν ὅλῃ τῇ ψυχῇ σου καὶ	ἐν ὅλῃ τῇ ψυχῇ σου καὶ
ἐξ ὅλης τῆς δυνάμεώς σου. (LXX)	ἐξ ὅλης τῆς διανοίας σου καὶ	ἐν ὅλῃ τῇ διανοίᾳ σου (NT)	ἐν ὅλῃ τῇ ἰσχύϊ σου καὶ
	ἐξ ὅλης τῆς ἰσχύος σου.		ἐν ὅλῃ τῇ διανοίᾳ σου,
Heb Deut 6:5 וְאָהַבְתָּ אֵת יְהוָה אֱלֹהֶיךָ בְּכָל־לְבָבְךָ וּבְכָל־נַפְשְׁךָ וּבְכָל־מְאֹדֶךָ׃	καὶ τὸ ἀγαπᾶν αὐτὸν ἐξ ὅλης τῆς καρδίας καὶ ἐξ ὅλης τῆς συνέσεως καὶ ἐξ ὅλης τῆς ἰσχύος (Mark 12:33)		

Table 6: Comparison of Deuteronomy 6:5 with Matthew 22:34–40 (LXX, MT, and the Gospels)

15. Gundry, *The Use of the Old Testament*, 22–24.

The differences and analogies reveal that the authors of the Gospels employed their available sources in their own formulation to fit a specific context. Matthew replicates neither the LXX nor MT as it is but recites Deut 6:5 replacing δύναμις with διάνοια. The rendering of מאד with διάνοια is unique as it changes the concept of physical might to mental power. Recalling the discussion above on the context of Deut 6:5, Deut 6:5 is probably the gist of the Decalogue on the basis of monotheism (Deut 6:4) in a memorable fashion.[16] Matthew, in the context of testing Jesus, is probably insinuating the context of Deut 6:4 and Deut 13:3 where a false prophet should be tested. In sum, conceptually and textually Matt 22:37 is very much closer to Deut 6:5. Conceptually, loving God is to be wholly committed to monotheism and to the faithful obedience to the commandments of God. Paul, in Romans, does not make any direct quotation of Deut 6:5, rather, it is most probable that it is cultural intertexture for Rom 3:29–30 as an allusion to monotheism stated in Deut 6:5.

LEVITICUS 19:18: "LOVE YOUR NEIGHBOR AS YOURSELF"

The immediate context of Lev 19:18 is Lev 19:11–18 where the author discusses a number of prohibitions concerning relationship with countrymen. The chapter begins with a call for holiness and differs from other chapters by dealing with different laws.[17] Structurally, Lev 19:18 is the middle of Leviticus 19. It is the culmination of the holiness code, the pinnacle of Leviticus, the central book of the Torah. It is also the climax within its own pericope which prohibits deceit, oppression of the weak, injustice, hatred, and revenge. It is "*doing good* (love)" (italics his).[18] "Your neighbor" refers to fellow Israelites because the pericope uses terms such as "your kin/brother" and "your people" (19:17–18) whereas the concern for aliens is expressed by 19:34. The object of אָהַב (*ʾahab*) "love" is normally in the accusative but in 19:18 it is preceded by the preposition "to" probably indicating a nuanced difference with the preposition centring a helpful action.[19] In short, אָהַב (*ʾahab*) in the context of Lev 19:1–18 is to act in a manner diametrically opposite to the prohibited evil things and to do good proactively to a fellow countryman. In the table below,

16. Beale and Carson, *Use of the Old Testament*, 80–82.

17. Milgrom, *Leviticus 17–22*, 1596.

18. Milgrom, *Leviticus 17–22*, 1656.

19. Hartley, *Leviticus*, 318.

texts that used Lev 19:18 are presented for the purpose of analyzing the intertexture of Matt 22:39 and Rom 13:9 in light of the context which will be briefly discussed.

MT	LXX	Matthew	Mark	Luke 10:27b	Rom 13:9
		Ἀγαπήσεις τὸν πλησίον σου (Matt 5:43)			
		Ἀγαπήσεις τὸν πλησίον σου ὡς σεαυτόν. (Matt 19:19)			
וְאָהַבְתָּ לְרֵעֲךָ כָּמוֹךָ (Lev 19:18)	ἀγαπήσεις τὸν πλησίον σου ὡς σεαυτόν (Lev 19:18)	Ἀγαπήσεις τὸν πλησίον σου ὡς σεαυτόν (Matt 22:39)	Ἀγαπήσεις τὸν πλησίον σου ὡς σεαυτόν. (Mark 12:31) τὸ ἀγαπᾶν τὸν πλησίον ὡς ἑαυτὸν (12:33)	καὶ τὸν πλησίον σου ὡς σεαυτόν.	Ἀγαπήσεις τὸν πλησίον σου ὡς σεαυτόν.

Table 7: Comparison of Romans 13:8–10 and Matthew 22:34–40 (LXX, MT, and the Gospels)

Leviticus 19:18 is cited in the NT more than any other texts from the Pentateuch.[20] In the table above, with the exception of Matt 5:43, which leaves out "as yourself" all the citations above are a replica of the MT and LXX. But the context of each citation differs in that Matt 5:43 appears in the SM and is contrasted against loving one's enemy (Matt 5:44–45). In Matt 19:19, it occurs as part of an answer given by the quester himself along with the Decalogue. This citation of Lev 19:18 in combination with the Decalogue, is peculiar to Matthew, although it is combined with the *Shema* in Matt 22:39 and Mark 12:31 and 33.[21] In Matt 22:39 and Mark 12:31 and 33, it occurs as one of the great commandments of the Law. In Luke 10:27b it occurs as an answer to a lawyer testing Jesus. In Rom 13:9, Lev 19:18 occurs as a succinct representation of the Law within the context of Paul's discussion concerning the relationship within and outside the community of Jesus followers. Romans 13:9 and Matt 19:19

20. Davies and Allison, *Matthew*, 3:44.

21. Stendahl, *The School of St. Matthew*, 63.

juxtapose it with the Decalogue although there is a variation listing it. In Matthew, Jesus lists: you shall not kill, you shall not commit adultery, you shall not steal, you shall not bear false witness and honor your father and your mother. In Romans Paul lists: you shall not commit adultery, you shall not kill, you shall not steal, you shall not covet and any other commandment. Paul's list is open-ended but both Jesus and Paul conclude their lists with a quotation of Lev 19:18. Hence, Lev 19:18 is recited in the Synoptics and Romans in different contexts not least as an important commandment both as an answer to getting eternal life (Synoptics) and as a succinct representation of the Law (Romans) pertaining to one's relationship with one's fellow man.

In conclusion, Deut 6:5 is recited in Matt 22:37. However, Matthew's purpose in quoting Deut 6:5 is to argue that all commandments do not carry equal weight. Conceptually, loving God, although it entrails an emotional aspect, is to be wholly dedicated to God and it is a faithful obedience to the commandments. Similarly, Lev 19:18 is quoted to show ranking within the commandments conceptually carrying the concept of doing good and avoiding evil as described and prescribed in the commandments of the Law. Paul alludes to monotheism in his argument for the inclusion of the Gentiles, and he maintains that those who love God are those who endure suffering (Rom 8:28). Both Paul (Rom 13:8–13) and Matthew (Matt 19:19) connect Lev 19:18 to the Decalogue which relates to the prohibition that Lev 19:18 makes against the neighbor. Hence, not only the text but the context of Lev 19:18 has been taken into consideration in both authors' application of the text.

Second Temple Literature

According to Robbins, one of the ways in which intertexture occurs is through cultural intertexture which is "insider" knowledge or "knowledge known only by people inside a particular culture or by people who have learned about that culture through some kind of interaction with it . . . [appearing] in words and concept patterns . . ."[22] There is not a word for word replica of the two texts (Deut 6:5 and Lev 19:18) in the Second Temple literature. It comprises mainly phrases and concepts that are used for differing purposes. The interest in this section is not to deal with the texts as such but to demonstrate how the concept of loving God

22. Robbins, *Exploring the Texture of Texts*, 58.

and loving one's neighbor continued in the second temple period before its formulation in the New Testament. It is hardly possible to discuss all the second temple period literature due to space limitations; only representative texts will be analyzed to assess the cultural intertexture of Matt 22:34–40 and Rom 13:8–10.

Apocryphal and Pseudepigraphal Books

The cultural intertexture of Deut 6:5 appears in both Pseudepigrapha and apocryphal books. They state that a person who loves God keeps his commandments or ways, love for wisdom and avoids idol worship (Jub. 17:15–16; Jub. 20:7; Sir 2:15; 10:19; T. Benj. 3:1). It can also be commanded (Eccl 13:14; Jub. 20:2, 7). In Jubilee in particular, loving God is to be faithful by enduring trials and tests. Abraham is called a lover of God which is demonstrated through his faithfulness in enduring tests. He was tried through famine, through separation from his wife, through circumcision, through separation from Ishmael and Hagar but was found to be faithful (Jub 17:15–16). Deuteronomy 6:5 is probably the background for presenting Abraham as an example of what it means to love God with one's whole heart, mind, and strength. In the fragment of Noah 108:8–10, those who love God are those who love neither gold, nor silver, nor anything of this world, but rather to endure physical suffering for his cause. A similar concept is reflected in 1 Enoch 105:23–25 which states that those who love God are those who suffer for righteousness' sake and renounce silver, gold and good things of this world.

A broad cultural intertexture of Lev 19:18 can also be discerned, but it is mainly found in the Testament of the Twelve Patriarchs. The Patriarchs give directions to their sons to love one another as brothers and their neighbor (Eccl 27:18; Jub. 7:20; 20:2; 36:4–5; T. Reub. 6:9; T. Sim 4:7; T. Gad 6:1, 3; 5:2; T. Zeb. 8:5–6). Jubilee 7:20 states Noah's commandment which includes part of the Decalogue such as honoring your father and mother, abstaining from fornication and Leviticus 19:18 (loving one's neighbor). He commands that "each one love his neighbor" but "as yourself" is omitted. Likewise, Abraham commands his children to love their neighbor: "each might love his neighbor" (Jub. 20:2). This echoes Lev 19:18b but omits the key phrase "as yourself." Isaac's commands to Esau and Jacob focus on loving one's brother (Jub. 36:4, 7, 8). However, the three persons' (Noah, Abraham, and Isaac) love commands in Jubilee are mainly of filial love and the sphere of neighborhood is limited to Israelites. Romans 13:9; Matt 5:43; 19:19; 22:39; Mark 12:31, 33; and Luke 10:27b are thus in line with the cultural intertexture of a wider tradition of using Deut 6:5 and Lev 19:18. Romans 13:9 re-contextualizes Lev 19:18, and the Apocryphal and Pseudepigrapha's tradition, which limits neighborliness to ethnic Israelites in that it limits neighborliness to Jews and Gentiles who follow Jesus. In doing so, Paul insists that all Jesus followers are the people of God and are family in faith even though they may be ethnically different therefore they are to obey the commandments that are given to Israel.

The first conjoined appearance of Deut 6:5 and Lev 19:18 is found in the Testament of the Twelve Patriarchs. The date of origin of these Testaments is, however, uncertain. Meier[23] contends that they are from the medieval or modern periods since there is evidence of Christian influence in them, and the moral exhortations are of a Stoic type which was familiar in Jewish and Christian circles in late Antiquity. Even if this is granted, it is noteworthy that a close recitation of Deut 6:5 and Lev 19:18b occurs in T. Issachar and T. Dan. They are formulated in the following manner:

T. Dan 5:3: "Love the Lord through all your life, and one another with a true heart"

T. Iss. 5:2: "Love the Lord and your neighbor."

T. Iss. 7:6: "I loved the Lord, likewise also every man with all my heart."

Deut 6:5 and Lev 29:28 appear without being fully recited. From Deut 6:5 "with all your heart, with all your mind, and with all your might" is cut off and from Lev 19:18 "as yourself" is omitted. The omission of words in recitation are usually done to make the statement as brief as possible[24] or to make it memorable. The juxtaposition of these two commandments is clear but due to its late date, it is not possible to be certain in regard to whether Jesus is dependent on these texts for his laconic formulation of Deut 6:5 and Lev 19:18b in Matt 22:37.

In sum, loving God and loving one's neighbor is conceptually used in both Apocryphal and Pseudepigrapha based on Deut 6:5 and Lev 19:18 and serve as the cultural intertexture for Rom 13:8–10 and Matt

23. Meier, *A Marginal Jew*, 4:507.

24. Robbins, *Exploring the Texture of Texts*, 41.

22:34–40. However, it cannot be established with any degree of certainty that Paul or Matthew is dependent on them.

The Dead Sea Scrolls

In the Dead Sea Scrolls the exhortation pertaining to love is ubiquitous but all its occurrence refers to the "brothers." Some specific commands from the context of Lev 19:17–18 are replicated verbatim while an allusion is made to Lev 19:18b. For instance, CD 9:2 repeats Lev 19:18a and omits Lev 19:18b i.e. "and you shall love your neighbor as yourself." Similarly, Lev 19:17b is cited as "you shall firmly rebuke your neighbor and shall not incur sin because of him" in CD 9:7–8 but Lev 19:18b is not included. A closer recitation appears in CD 6:20–21 "each man to love his brother as himself." The "brother" refers to an insider—a fellow Essene. Lev 19:18b is absent in non-biblical Qumran documents.[25]

Likewise, the recitation of Deut 6:5 is absent in non-biblical Qumran documents. But part of it is echoed in the introduction of the community rule in column 1 of the Rule (1QS 1:1–2, 3–4, 9) "to seek God with all one's heart and with all one's soul. . . and to love everything that he has chosen . . . and to love the sons of light" "with all one's heart and with all one's soul" echoes Deut 6:5.[26]And "to love the sons of light" might be an echo of "and love your neighbor as yourself" (Lev 19:18b). However, "the sons of light" refers to the members of the community. At any rate, no explicit conjoining has been made between Deut 6:5 and Lev 19:18b in the Dead Sea Scrolls, however, alluding to them and partially reciting them to apply to a specific community and perceiving them as important commandments was clearly already underway before the writing of the NT. Jesus' explicit connection and ranking of the two texts in Matt 22:34–40, however, seems to be original to him. Paul's identification of "love your neighbor as yourself" as one of the most important commandments among other commandments does not appear in the Dead Sea Scrolls. But the cultural intertexture of Lev 19:18 has probably influenced Paul to give the commandments a prominent place among the other commandments.

25. Meier, *A Marginal Jew*, 4:505.

26. Meier, *A Marginal Jew*, 4:505.

Philo of Alexandria

Philo, the first extant Jewish thinker who reflected on the Decalogue, for heuristic purposes, divides the Decalogue into two parts: duties to God and duties to fellow Israelites (love of humanity). In his work "*On the Special Law*" Philo thinks that all individual Laws of the Jews can be subsumed in two headings: (1) duty to God as shown by piety and holiness, i.e. reverence and holiness (τό τεπρὸς θεὸν δῖ εὐσεβείας καὶ ὁσιότητος) and (2) duty to men, i.e. love of humanity and justice (τὸ πρὸς ἀν θροώπους διὰ φιλανθρωπίας).[27] Philo's headings of the commandments under these two categories are not a complete summary of the Law and the prophets and two types of Love but of reverence and philanthropy. However, in *The Decalogue*, Philo presumes that there are two kinds of Jews, those who attend to serving God and thus they are lovers of God (*Philotheoi*) whereas those who spend their time and heart to companionship with men are lovers of humans (*philanthroi*).[28] But Philo argues that keeping the balance between loving God and loving neighbor is not easy. For instance, Moses' experience on Mount Sinai reiterated how one could be caught in the dilemma of choosing between love for God and love for a human.[29] Despite the challenge of keeping the balance between these two objects of love, Philo insists that both sides of love must be maintained to achieve honor in both departments.

Meier argues that Jesus' formulation of the summary of the Law is closer to Qumran and Jubilee than Philo or *Aristeas*. The latter two reflect Greek influence because both use abstract nouns to express human obligation to God and fellow humans rather than verbs, which was a Jewish way of conveying obligations and imperatives that Jesus also uses.[30] Philo, however, never mentions Lev 19:18b in his discussion of the individual commandments in Lev 19. But the restriction of the neighbor is also evident in Philo's system, because according to him love should be exercised towards those who reciprocate love, while contact with sinners and laypersons should be avoided.[31]Although no word-for-word recitation occurs in Philo, the concepts of love for God and love for human beings are both highlighted as important aspects of the Law. The Jewish tradition

27. Philo, *Philo VII*, 347.
28. Philo, *Philo* VII, 63.
29. Philo, *Philo VI*, 529.
30. Meier, *A Marginal Jew*, 4:511.
31. Meier, *A Marginal Jew*, 4:512.

is, however, re-contextualized in Philo to fit into the Greek philosophical system.

Section Summary and Conclusion

The following conclusions can be derived from the foregoing analysis:

1. the concepts of loving God and loving one's neighbor had been understood as key commandments in the second temple literature, although no formulation proved it textually (Deut 6:5 and Lev 19:18) and conceptually tied them together as Jesus did in Matt 22:34–40.
2. The concept of loving one's neighbor is limited to the nation of Israel, or to a sectarian community which might be the case in Matt 19:19, but Paul seems to be more inclusive in Rom 13:8–10 as he is addressing both Jews and Gentiles who are Jesus followers. Rom 13:8–10 seems to be a Pauline re-contextualizing of the concept and formulation of the text of Lev 19:18.
3. The concept of loving God, as expressed in obedience to his commandment and loving one's neighbor as an act of doing good and avoiding evil as described and prescribed in the commandments continued in the second temple period.

Greco–Roman Literature

With regard to Greco–Roman literature, the older distinction made between ἔρως and ἀγαπή by Anders Nygren is now rejected by many scholars.[32] The semantic range of ἀγαπάω (ἀγαπή) and φιλέω (φίλος) is broad and the two concepts are difficult to distinguish from each other.[33] Having made a thorough analysis of the word ἀγαπάν, Stauffer concludes that its meaning is imprecise when it is conjoined with ἐρᾶν or φιλεῖν.[34] However, in pre-biblical Greek, according to Stauffer, ἐρᾶν "is a passionate love which desires the other for itself."[35] Religiously such ἔρως was a god, which played an important role in the cult and who was considered

32. Nygren, *Agape and Eros.*
33. Kloppenborg, "Love in the NT," 704.
34. Stauffer, "Ἀγαπάω," 37.
35. Stauffer, "Ἀγαπάω,"35.

to be an irresistible power that compels one, but who is never compelled by anyone in return.

Later ἔρως infiltrated the philosophical discourse since the time of Plato when it was considered as the uttermost fulfilment of life and elevation. However, in Platonic philosophy ἔρως was purged from its sensual traits and re-conceptualized as the ideal of humanity.[36] For Plato, ἔρως is "the desire of the lover united with his beloved to produce, to "bring forth in beauty"—a desire which is no longer acquisitive but creative."[37] Kloppernborg argues that ἀγαπάω "to love" is not the exclusive domain of Judean or Christian literature since it was a common word from the time of Homer with a range of meanings which include "to welcome warmly," "to be content," "to set one's heart on," and generally "to love."[38] The concept φιλῖν (φιλία) refers to the "love of gods for men or friends for friends."[39]The term ἀγαπάν, however, has neither the power of ἔρως nor the war of φιλεῖν, rather it has an imprecise meaning in that it "makes distinctions, choosing and keeping to its object" and therefore its meaning is determined by the presence of its subject. Nonetheless, the "substantive ἀγαπή is almost completely absent in pre-biblical Greek."[40]

It is hardly possible to discuss all Greco-Roman literature on love, and therefore the focus of this study will be on representative authors from this period. The term φιλέω, in a literal sense means to be a friend but philosophically it has a deeper meaning. For Aristotle, there are levels of love: (1) utility i.e. loving the other for the sake of utility (advantage); (2) pleasure i.e. loving the other for the sake of what is pleasant (Eth. nic. 1156a15–18); and (3) character friendship i.e. loving the other for the sake of virtue and it exists between persons who are good and have similar virtues. The first two kinds of relationships are based on self-advancement but the third one is concerned for the other just because of herself/himself and for her/his own sake. Both wish the other well, but they do not love for self-centred advantage (*Eth. nic.* 1156b8–10). Such love only occurs where there is equality between people otherwise it is imperfect. Therefore, it is infrequent (*Eth. nic.* 1156b23–32) and impossible to have many such lovers or friends (*Eth. nic.* 1170b29–1171a21). In fact, for Aristotle, love begins from self-love as the "other" is the second self

36. Stauffer, "Ἀγαπάω," 36.
37. Kloppenborg, "Love in the NT," 703.
38. Kloppenborg, "Love in the NT," 703.
39. Stauffer, "Ἀγαπάω," 36.
40. Stauffer, "Love in the NT," 37.

(*Eth. nic.* 1166a1–b29). However, he argues that a human being is a social being and designed (by nature) to share his life (*Eth. nic.*1169b18–19). Hence, he insists that for the good of oneself one requires concern for the good of another.

Although a human being is a social being, self-sufficiency is the ultimate happiness but self-sufficiency does not presuppose living a life of isolation; rather it presupposes a limited friendship (*Eth. nic.* 1097a28–b21). This social nature of a human being is the basis of justice which is good in itself (*Eth. nic.* 1129b11–1130a5). Justice embraces all the virtues because it is practiced towards others. Virtuous people value the good of others for the sake of other people. In doing so, they seek virtuous action for their own sake.

According to the Stoics, such as Seneca, a wise person can reconcile ἔρως as divine gift and ἔρως as uncontrollable power and destructive madness by suppressing its negative traits (*Eph* 116.5; Cicero, *Fin* 3.68). For Plutarch, φιλαδελφία (brotherly love) is "a model for most loving relationships."[41] But Epictetus expressed a similar idea of loving one's enemy when he speaks of the true Cynic who "while he is being flogged . . . loves (φλέω) the men who flog him, as though he were the father or brother of them all" (*Disc* 3.22.54–55). Love (as φιλαντροπος) and suffering are also connected in Epictetus who mentions an earlier Cynic philosopher Diogenes who purportedly "gladly took upon himself all those troubles and physical hardships for the sake of the common weal [humankind]" (*Disc* 3.24.64). Epictetus believes that loving one's own interest is part of human nature (*Disc* 2.22.15). Gaius Musonius Rufus, the teacher of Epicetus (ca 30–101 CE), thinks that human beings are not created as being self-centered but they investigate others' interest as well and come together like bees "and toil and work together with the neighbor (πλησίον)."[42] But the connection between the Law and love in the Greco–Roman world is not attested.

Therefore, it can be concluded from the analysis above that love in the Greco–Roman world is not basically different from the biblical concept of love regarding human relationships. It is doing good to another although there is a subjective preference. If Rufus' understanding of the neighbor is taken as representative of the Greco-Roman world, it might refer to any person one encounters in a given community. Particularly

41. Kloppenborg, "Love in the NT," 705.

42. Lutz, *Yale Classical Studies*, 93.

Rufus argues that the concept of living together and helping one another is what makes man different from animals. No direct connection between love and the Law is made but there seems to be a connection between love and justice. In light of this, although some similar concepts could be connected to the Greco-Roman concept of love, it is hard to think Matt in 22:30–44 or Paul in Rom 13:8–10 draw their understanding of the Law–love relationship from it. However, it might be plausible that the audiences of Romans might be able to connect to Paul's injunction of love and the Law to their context in Romans.

Pauline Literature

In this section only the extant letters of Paul that were written before Romans will be discussed. The earliest use of the concept of love in a Pauline letter is in 1 Thessalonians (1:3, 4; 3:6, 12; 4:9; 5:8, 13). Although Paul did not formulate the concept in a very memorable manner, he closely ties the love of God for believers and believers' love for fellow Jesus followers to each other. Particularly the word φιλαδελφία is used the first time in this letter to express fraternal love. In Thessalonians it is a fictitious kinship relationship taking divine love as a model (1 Thess 4:9). The pinnacle of Pauline ἀγαπή comes in 1 Cor 13:1–8. Although Paul is not against knowledge, he elevates ἀγαπή among other virtues that Jesus followers must exercise among themselves. Paul does not define ἀγαπή but personifies it and describes its character. Beginning with two positive descriptions of ἀγαπή which are patience and gentleness, he continues to describe it with a negation, i.e. what love is not: envious, boastful, arrogant, rude, selfish, irritable, or resentful. Then with negating active verbs, i.e. love does not: rejoice at wrongdoing, but rejoices in the truth and finally concludes with "all": it bears with all things, believes all things, hopes all things, and endures all things (1 Cor 13:1–12). Such a description of love is concerned within the believing community.

The closest text to Rom 13:8–10 that connects love and the Law is Gal 5:14. It reads, "for the whole Law is fulfilled in one word, You shall love your neighbor as yourself." The context elucidates what it means loving one's neighbor in Pauline terms in Gal 5:14. It means avoiding works of the flesh: fornication, impurity, licentiousness, idolatry, sorcery, enmity, strife, jealousy, anger, selfishness, dissension, party spirit, envy, drunkenness, carousing, and the like. Those who do such things do not inherit the kingdom of God. Such characteristics are contrasted with love, peace, kindness, goodness, faithfulness, gentleness and self-control. Against such things there is no Law (Gal 5:19–25). Paul argues that the Law confirms the fruit of the Spirit but stands against the works of the flesh. In other words, both the Law and love are against the works of the flesh therefore they are inseparably connected not least because "you shall love your neighbor as yourself" itself is the commandment of the Law that succinctly represents and gives the language to summarize the weighty matter of the Law. Therefore, in the Pauline literature, the Law and love are positively intertwined without one replacing or negating the other, instead they demonstrate the impossibility of the existence of the one without the other.

Section Summary and Conclusion

The analysis of the intertexture of Rom 13:8–10 and Matt 22:34–40 has demonstrated that in Jewish literature Deut 6:5 and Lev 19:11–18 are foundational texts that all other Jewish literature used to formulate their concept of love for God and love for one's neighbor. Although textual intertexture can be detected in other Jewish literature analyzed in this study, no explicit evidence can be ascertained for the conjoining and ranking of the two texts like Jesus did in Matt 22:34–40. Lev 19:18 is used, however, albeit not in an exact formulation, to enhance love within the Jewish community, whereas Paul's formulation is a re-contextualization of the Lev 19:18 to the context of Jesus' followers in Romans. Pauline literature evinces that the relationship of the Law and love are inseparably intertwined. The Greco-Roman literature discussed here does not show any textual affinity but might serve as cultural context for Matthew and Paul. Nonetheless, no direct and explicit evidence can be adduced with certainty from the literature analyzed in this study that Paul and Matthew depended on them either to conceptualize the relationship of love and the Law or for the formulation of their texts.

COMPARISON OF ROMANS 13:8–14 AND MATTHEW 22:34–44

In this section, Rom 13:8–14 and Matt 22:34–44 will be compared. But before comparing these two specific textual units, attempts will be made to find a specific possible textual, conceptual and thematic link between Romans and the Gospel of Matthew at various levels. Then a comparison of the summary of the Law will follow. No attempt will be made to harmonize the two texts; nonetheless, every possible convergence and divergence will be assessed to arrive at a synthesized conclusion.

The comparison is based on the following assumptions, as was argued in the introduction of this study:

1. chronologically, the Epistle to the Romans was written before the Gospel of Matthew between 55 and 58 CE whereas Matthew was written around 80 CE.
2. There might be a possibility for Matthew to have access to the Epistle to the Romans.[43]
3. Each book is written to address a specific purpose and context which differs in time, location and need.
4. Both books differ in their genre and rhetorical concern.
5. Both stand in Jewish tradition and scripture in interpreting the Christ event.[44]

The goal of the comparison is to ferret out how the role of the summary of the Law is described, understood, and how they relate to one another in both books. The previous chapters of this study have already undertaken a detailed analysis of Rom 13:8–14 and Matt 22:34–40 and the topic of the Law and love separately, therefore there is no need for extensive discussions thereof. However, specific texts and concepts will be compared based on the analysis and findings of the previous chapters.

Conceptual and Thematic Comparison

Only the concepts and themes raised in chapters two, three and four on the themes of judgment, sin, Jews and Gentiles, love, and the Law will be compared in this section. These particular topics are selected because they are deemed to be important for understanding the overall perspective of both authors on the Law and love as they stand connected in their texts.

43. Sim, "Matthew and the Pauline Corpus," 8.

44. Mohrlang, *Matthew and Paul*, 42.

Perspective on Judgment

Romans	Matthew	
1:18–32;	3:7–10 (7:19)–21:34, 41, 43; 13:35	11:20–24
2:2, 5, 9, 12, 16;	5:13, 22, 25, 28, 29, 30, 31, 34	12:41–42
3:6, 9–20, 23	6:12, 14	13:30, 37–42, 50
6:16, 21, 23	7:1, 13, 21 (21:28–32), 24–27	18:3, 10
8:1, 6, 13	8:12, 29	22:13
9:22–23	10:15, 26–28	24:51
14:10–12 (2:6–16)		25:30–46

Table 8: Comparison of Verses Referring to Judgment in Romans and Matthew

As the table shows, "judgment" is one of the key themes that both Romans and Matthew address. Paul speaks that judgment of God as an expression of the wrath of God due to suppressing the truth (Rom 1:18b), for they did not honor and glorify God (Rom 1:21b), but worshipped idols (Rom 1:23) which resulted in the moral desolation of human society as a direct result of God's wrath and judgment (Rom 1:18–32). The judgment in Rom 1:18 is revealed (ἀποκαλύπτεται); it is in the present tense and so is the tense of the revelation of God's righteousness.[45] Judging others is presumed to be the same as judging oneself if the person judging the other is doing the same thing (Rom 2:1–5). Judgment is based on one's action; and a hard and unrepentant heart hoards the wrath of God (Rom 2:5). In Rom 2:6–11, Paul argues that eschatological judgment is based on one's good work. Persistence in good work leads to eternal life and rewards honor, peace and glory. Such persistence in good work is possible through the works of the Spirit (Rom 2:25–29). Eschatological judgment is not only based on one's works but also on the secrets of men (their inner thoughts) (Rom 2:16). Jesus is the person through whom eschatological judgment will take place.

However, God's judgment is without partiality since both Jews and Gentiles will be judged according to the same standard. In Rom 3:6 Paul argues that if the Jews who sinned against God escape the judgment of God, then the impartiality of God compels God to have the Gentile go free from judgment. Had this been the case, there would not have been any judgment at all. But Paul argues that God judges sin and evil doers impartially in his sovereignty (Rom 9:22–24). Those who are in

45. Schreiner, *Romans*, 85.

Christ are now without condemnation (Rom 8:1). Thus, Paul insists that Jesus followers should not pass judgment on one another on the basis of different practices of faith because all believers will stand before God's judgment seat during the eschatological judgment (Rom 5:9; 14:10–12). Therefore, for Paul both the believers and the unbelievers will be judged by the impartial judgment of God according to the Gospel he preached.

There is a prolific discussion of judgment in the Gospel of Matthew. Matthew introduces the theme of judgment with the entrance of John the Baptist in the story. The wrath of God is upon those who do not repent and produce fruit of repentance (Matt 3:7–10). Jesus is introduced as the inaugurator of the kingdom of God and an agent of judgment. A similar concept is conveyed in the parables in Matt 11:20–24; 12:38–42; 13:30, 37, 42, 50; 21:34, 41, 43. As argued early in Chapter four, the SM is not only stricter in its demand of a righteous life but also stricter in its judgment (Matt 5:22, 25, 28–30): anger, lustfulness, unforgiving heart (so also Matt 6:15), and judging others without dealing with one's own problem (Matt 7:1) deserves the judgment of God. Judgment is based on the individual's choice of their way of life (Matt 7:13) and obedience to the teaching of Jesus and the will of God (Matt 7:21–27). Unbelief in Jesus and rejecting the signs and miracles performed through him is to reject the kingdom of God and therefore results in judgment (Matt 8:12; 10:15). Such judgment is the casting of both soul and body into hell (Matt 10:26–28). Unfaithfulness to the kingdom results in judgment (Matt 24:51). The coming of the Son of Man on the judgment day brings both salvation and judgment (Matt 24). The story depicts the nature of judgment as eternal: eternal punishment on one hand and eternal life on the other, depending on one's attitude and action towards the neighbor with whom Jesus identifies himself (Matt 25:30–46). However, the theme of judgment in Matthew ends with the Son of Man being judged by religious leaders (Matt 26:57–66) but promising the coming of the Son of Man on the clouds of heaven (Matt 26:64) to repay every person for what he has done (Matt 16:27). Thus, Jesus judges the whole world as reiterated in the story of Noah (Matt 24:36–34).

Comparing the two books on the theme of judgment yields the following conclusions. Both converge on the following concepts: (1) the wrath of God results in eschatological judgment. (2) The judgment of God is because of the rejection of the message of the Gospel, and an unrepentant heart. (3) Repentance, faith in Jesus Christ and obedience to the message of the Gospel are the basis for entering eternal life. (4) In one way or another good works have a role in God's system of judgment and therefore believers will be held accountable for their actions on earth. (5) Both denounce judging one another and specifically criticise those who denounce others while they themselves are guilty of doing the things they denounce in others. (6) Jesus is the agent of executing God's judgment.

But the two authors also differ in the following: (1) Paul believes that all human beings are under the wrath of God, Jews and Gentiles, while Matthew confines the judgment of God to those (especially the Jews) who heard the message of the kingdom of God, the teaching of Jesus but refuse to repent. (2) Paul believes that a Christ-believing community are in Christ and therefore have no condemnation at present but stand at the judgment throne of God whereas in Matthew one's faith in Christ and way of life determines one's eternal destiny.

Perspective on ἁμαρτία

	Romans	Matthew
ἁμαρτία	5:8, 12, 13, 20, 21; 6:1, 2, 6, 7, 10, 11, 12, 13, 14, 16, 17, 18, 20, 22, 23; 7:7, 8, 9, 11, 13, 14, 17, 20, 23, 25; 8:2, 3, 10; 11:27, 23	1:21; 3:6; 5:29–30; 6:12; 9:2–6, 10–13; 11:19; 18:15, 21; 26:28 (Rom 11:26–27)
ἁμαρτωλός /λοι/	3:7, 9, 20; 4:7–8; 5:8, 12, 19; 7:13	11:16–19; 26:45
Πονηρός		5:11, 37, 39, 45; 6:13, 23; 7:11, 17, 18; 12:34, 35, 39; 13:19, 38, 49; 16:4; 20:15; 22:10, 18
Πονηρία	1:29	18:32; 24:48; 25:26
ἀνομία	4:7; 6:19	7:23; 13:41; 23:28; 24:12
ἀδικία	1:18, 29; 2:8; 3:5; 6:13; 9:14	

Table 9: Comparison of Verses on Sin in Romans and Matthew

The table above shows that *ἁμρτία*, *πονηρός* (*πονηρία*), *ἀνομία*, *ἀδικία* are concerns for both Romans and Matthew. There is no need to repeat the discussion on *ἁμρτία* in Chapter two. In Chapter two it is argued that *ἁμρτία* existed before the coming of the Law and got its power because of the dominion of death extending to all of humanity through the transgression of one man—Adam (Rom 5). As a result, those who are under the Law cannot fulfil the righteous requirement of the Law because of sin's power in their life. But both the Jews and the Gentiles are all under the power of sin, hence they are sinners, and are under the judgment of God unless they believe in Jesus who died for the justification of sinners. However, those who are in union with Christ through faith and baptism are under the realm of the Spirit and thus they are free from the power of sin (old person) and can resist the temptation of sin to live a righteous life (Rom 6:1–23). But persistent sinning reverts the sin-freed person into the dominion of death (Rom 6:16).

For Paul, πονηρία is not his main term with which to express wickedness. It is only used as one of many general moral descriptions of those who are under the wrath of God (Rom 1:29). Likewise, he used ἀνομία only in two places in Rom 4:7–8 and Rom 6:19. In the quotation the word could be used interchangeably with ἁμαρτία since both vv. 7 and 8 repeat ἁμρτία twice. But it could be possible that ἀνομία serves as an introduction to the theme of transgressing the Law (Rom 4:15b). However, in Rom 6:19, Paul uses ἀνομία with ἀκαθαρσία (which usually refers to sexual sin in the Pauline writings) with ἀνομία referring to "a life characterized by sin and transgression of God's moral norms."[46] Hence, ἀνομία in Romans is used to convey the transgression of the Law (Rom 4:7) as well as a general sinful disposition.

Paul introduced ἀδικία in Rom 1:18 in which he describes what it means in Rom 1:19–32. In Romans, the wrath of God is revealed because of the ἀδικία of human beings. The term does not convey only one sin but is rather a comprehensive presentation of human sin which is mainly the rejection of the one true God and worshipping idols. Stated differently: the breaking of the first commandants of the Decalogue (Rom 1:23; Exod 20:4–6; Deut 4:15–18) and his moral principles. Particularly, it is related to life opposite to the truth (Rom 2:8). The truth is most probably referring to knowledge embodied in the Law (Rom 2:20). Not least the word ἀδικία is used in Rom 3:5 to refer to the Jews' unfaithfulness or disobedience to the oracle they were entrusted with. In Rom 6:13, it refers to wickedness or sin as a dominating power as well as to practices which oppose righteousness as a dominating power and behavior in the realm of the Spirit. In sum, in Romans πονηρός (πονηρία), ἀνομία, and ἀδικία are

46. Schreiner, *Romans*, 337.

in the same category; namely ἁμαρτία. They have an interrelated meaning and seeking a specific meaning, for each leads to a false distinction among them.

Matthew uses ἁμαρτία, πονηρός (πονηρία), and ἀνομία, but ἄδικιος. ῾Αμαρτία is introduced in the first chapter (Matt 1:21) by an angel. The coming or the mission of the Messiah is to save "his people" from ἁμρτία. Sin is perceived as an enemy from whom "his people" need to be delivered although problems such as sickness, evil spirits, and death are also part of the delivering ministry of the Messiah. But ἁμαρτία must be avoided at any cost (Matt 5:19–30) as it is a cause for the destruction of the soul. Jesus has the authority to forgive sin on earth even before the cross (Matt 9:2–6) and his death on the cross is for the forgiveness of sin in the new covenant (Matt 26:28). Every ἁμαρτία is forgivable except two kinds of sins: (1) ἁμαρτία against the Holy Spirit can never be forgiven (Matt 13:31) and (2) ἁμαρτία against a fellow Jesus follower which requires reciprocal forgiveness (i.e. unless one forgives a fellow believer, God the father does not grant forgiveness to the offended believer) (Matt 6:12; 18:15–34).

Not only ἁμαρτία, but also ἁμαρτωλος is used in Matthew. Sanders argues that ἁμαρτωλος does not refer to the common people but to those "who sinned wilfully and heinously and do not repent" they are "professional sinners" who renounce the covenant and commandment of God.[47] Sanders further contends that Jesus was not accused of loving ἁμαρτωλος but of claiming that following him and his message allowed them into the kingdom of God without repenting in accordance with the normal procedures set out by the Jewish tradition.[48] If Sanders' description of ἁμαρτωλος is accepted, then Matt 9:9–13 and 11:16–19 refer to those who are wicked and transgressors of the Law and the covenant of God. The religious leaders call them sinners while Jesus sees them as sick and in need of healing. But Matthew seems to dichotomise the righteous and sinners (Matt 9:13). Ironically the story of Matthew designates the Jewish religious leaders as ἁμαρτωλος (Matt 26:45). In fact, some argue that it refers to the Romans but the statement Jesus made that "the Son of man is betrayed into the hands of sinners" fits well in the immediate context (cf. the statement "Now the betrayer had given them a sign" (Matt 26:47).

Matthew employs the word πονηρός (πονηρία) which is translated as "evil" by the RSV. It could refer to an evil utterance (Matt 5:11), spirit

47. Sanders, *Jesus and Judaism*, 177.

48. Sanders, *Jesus and Judaism*, 210.

being (Matt 5:37; 6:13; 13:19; 38, 49),[49] a person who does evil (Matt 5:39, 45), or metaphorically refer to greed (Matt 6:23; 7:11; 20:15),or a character not in line with the teaching of Jesus and those who had rejected the message of Jesus (Matt 7:17–18; 12:39; 18:32; 16:4). It is an inner disposition (Matt 15:19). But such people are invited to the kingdom of God (Matt 22:10). Those who are in the kingdom could also be wicked or evil or be guilty of such as transgressions as un-forgiveness, unfaithfulness and laziness and unproductivity (Matt 18:32, 24:48; 25:26). According to the data, when the word refers to humans it refers to any person's character and actions that deviate from the teaching of Jesus Christ.Such a person still has the potential to be saved (Matt 20:10). However, it also refers to a spirit being or Satan and his followers.

The term *ἀνομία* in Matthew is used in reference to those who are disobedient to the will of God despite their claims to have charismatic experience (false prophets) (Matt 7:23), those who are sons of Satan (Matt 13:41), the religious leaders (the Pharisees and the Scribes) who teach but do not practice the Law (the hypocrites) (Matt 23:28) and such people will increase in the end-time (Matt 24:12).

Comparing the concept and use of the terms regarding *ἁμαρτία*, the following convergence and divergence of the concept of sin emerges:

1. Convergence: (a) both agree that *ἁμαρτία* is the cause of divine judgment. (b) Both perceive that *πονηρός* (*πονηρία*), and *ἀνομία* are *ἁμαρτία*. (c) Both understand that sin is a transgression of the Law and the truth of God.
2. Divergence: (a) while Paul thinks *ἁμαρτία* is a domineering power and character, Matthew does not view sin as a power but instead argues that one can remove the cause of sinning from one's own life (Matt 5:30). (b) While Paul believes that all human beings are sinners, Matthew distinguishes the righteous from sinners. For Matthew *ἁμαρτωλος* are a special group of people who deviated from the covenant of God who can be restored. But the religious leaders remain unrepentant *ἁμαρτωλος*.

49. Turner, *Matthew*, 173.

Perspective on Jews and Gentiles

Paul has a positive view of the Gentiles. He is called to reach them with the Gospel of the Son of God (Rom 1:13, 16); they will be rewarded for their obedience (Rom 2:10); the God of the Jews is also the God of the Gentiles (Rom 3:29; 10:12); they are the children of Abraham by faith (Rom 4) and are called by God just as Jews are called (Rom 9:24); the fall of the Jews' opened the door for their salvation (Rom 11:11, 12) and their full incoming will be a means for Israel's salvation (Rom 11:15); they glorify God for his mercy (Rom 15:9, 11) and participate in the joy of the people (Rom 15:10); the Messiah rules them (Rom 15:16); miracles are performed to bring them to obedience (Rom 15:18); they shared the spiritual blessing of the Jews' church (Rom 15:27); and they are called the Gentile church (Rom 16:4).

However, Paul also says a few negative things about the Gentiles: they do not have the Law (Rom 2:14); their disobedience results in judgment (Rom 2:9); they blaspheme God because of the Jews' disobedience (Rom 2:24); they did not pursue righteousness (Rom 9:30) and Paul warns them not to be proud of their position in God (Rom 11:13). Gentiles are wild olive trees (Rom 11:17). Although Paul did not use the term Gentile in Rom 1:18–32, Gentiles are also involved in the description that the whole world is under the judgment of God with which he concludes in Chapter three.

For Paul, the Jews are the first recipients of the Gospel (Rom 1:15; 2:9). They receive a reward for their obedience (Rom 2:10), rely on the Law (Rom 2:17), but true Jewishness is an inward disposition not due to an outward circumcision (Rom 2:28–29). They are entrusted with the oracle of God and have an advantage (Rom 3:1–2) in having Abraham as their father (Rom 4). Paul has a great concern for their salvation (Rom 9:1–2) because they are his kinsmen by race. The sonship, the glory, the covenants, the giving of the Law, the worship and the promise given to the patriarchs are to them and their race according to the flesh (Rom 9:1–5). But all are not children of Israel nor children of Abraham (Rom 9:6–7) and thus only remnants of them will be saved (Rom 9:27). They pursue the righteousness of the Law (Rom 9:33) and have un–enlightened zeal for God (Rom 10:1) but did not submit to God's righteousness (Rom 10:3). They are disobedient and contrary people (Rom 10:21). But God did not reject them (Rom 11:1); they are a cultivated olive tree by nature, but they are broken so that Gentiles may be engrafted (Rom 11:20). They can be grafted in again by the power of God (Rom 11:23) but they are hardened until the fullness of the Gentiles coming in (Rom 11:25). They are enemies of God regarding the Gospel but beloved of God because of their forefathers. The calling of God upon them is irrevocable (Rom 11:29).

Matthew includes Gentiles from the very beginning in the genealogy of Jesus: Tamar (Matt 1:3), the widow of Jacob's eldest son could be a Canaanite, Rahab (Gen 28; Matt 1:5), a Canaanite prostitute (Josh 2:6), Ruth (Matt 1:5), a Moabite (Ruth 1:4), and Bathsheba (Matt 1:6), possibly a Hittite (2 Sam 11:3).[50] Nothing is said about each of these women in the story but Matthew assumes that the reader grasps that Jesus' lineage is a mixture of Gentile women and Jewish men. The magi are also people from the East, most probably Gentiles, who lead by divine portents (Matt 2). They are contrasted against the Jews' leaders Herod, the chief priest and elders as they proclaimed the kingship of Jesus and worshipped him. Matthew 4:12–17 introduces the beginning of Jesus' ministry in Galilee which is called "Galilee of the Gentiles." It is possibly an indirect reference to the inclusion of Gentiles. Jesus' fame spread throughout Syria where a diverse population and Jewish minority lived (Matt 4:24). A Roman centurion's faith is admired and contrasted against Israel's faith in Jesus (Matt 8:5–13). Gentiles will have access to the kingdom of heaven (Matt 8:11). Disciples will witness to them (Matt 10:17–18). The Queen of Sheba (a Gentile) who admired the Wisdom of Solomon is contrasted against those who did not respond to the miracles and teachings of Jesus (Matt 12:38–42). Jesus' ministry is not limited to Israel (Matt 12:1–14) as he proclaims justice to the nations. The Canaanite women's faith is also admired by Jesus (Matt 15:26). Jesus' innocence is revealed to a Gentile woman in a dream (Matt 27:18, 19) and it is a Gentile centurion and those with him who confess that Jesus is the Son of God (Matt 27:54). The Gospel will furthermore be preached to the whole world and nations (Matt 24:14).

However, Gentiles are also negatively portrayed as they do not love their enemies (Matt 5:47), pray correctly (Matt 6:7), are worried about material goods (Matt 6:32), associated with tax collectors (Matt 6:46–47; 18:15–17), their leadership style is rejected (Matt 20:25; 22:7) and they wage war against one another (Matt 24:6–7). Conjoined with the Jewish religious leaders, they collude to crucify Jesus (Matt 27).

50. Saldarini, *Matthew's Christian-Jewish Community*, 69.

Matthew uses 'Ἰουδαίοις in Matt 2:2; 27:11, 29, 37; 28:15. Except Matt 28:15 which is used by the narrator, all of them are spoken by Gentiles, first as a declaration of Jesus as the king of the Jews by the wise men but then at the passion it is used to mock Jesus. Other terms such as ὄχλος, and λαός are important in this regard. According to Cousland[51] ὄχλος[52] can be defined as a "crowd, throng, multitude of people" and also "the common people," "populace." The crowd is distinct from the leaders. They follow Jesus (Matt 4:25; 8:1; 12:15; 14:13; 19:2 and 20:19), marvel (Matt 9:33; 15:31), astonish (Matt 7:28; 22:33), are besides themselves (Matt 12:23), afraid (Matt 9:8), glorify God (9:8; 15:31), consider John the Baptist (Matt 14:5; 21:26) and Jesus as prophets (Matt 21:11, 21:46) and also consider Jesus to be the Son of David (Matt 12:23; 21:91) and are feared by the religious leaders (Matt 14:5; 21:26, 46).

Nonetheless, it is hard to identify the composition of the crowd to determine whether they are purely Jews or a mixture of Jews and Gentiles. Yet they are portrayed positively.[53] But Matt 7:28 and 29 (their scribes), 9:33 (the crowds comment that never such a thing happened in Israel), 10:6 (the lost sheep of Israel), 15:24, 31 (glorified the God of Israel), 27:9 (sons of Israel) probably show that most of the crowds are composed of Jews. Likewise, λαός[54] are also identified as Jews in Matt 28:15. Most probably both terms refer mainly to the Jews but there are also Gentiles even though they disappear in the story as characters but become targets ofa universal mission that is proclaimed by the resurrected Jesus.[55]

The leaders are also Jews and they are not portrayed positively in the story. Pharisees and Scribes are children of hell (23:15), blind fools (23:17), blind guides (23:24), snakes and brood of vipers (Matt 3:7; 23:33), full of hypocrisy and lawlessness (23:28), willingly take the curse upon themselves (which includes the crowd) (Matt 27:25), deceptive and liars (Matt 27:62–66; 28:11–15). The people and the leaders joined together in killing Jesus. They are addressed as a distanced group: cf. their synagogue (Matt 4:23; 9:35; 10:17; 12:9; 13:54) and your synagogues (Matt 23:34; 7:29; 28:15).

51. Cousland, *The Crowds in the Gospel of Matthew*, 35.

52. Matt 4:25; 5:1; 7:28; 8:1, 18; 9:8, 25, 33, 36; 11:7; 12:23, 46; 13:2, 26, 34, 36; 14:5, 13, 14, 15, 19, 22, 23; 15:10, 31, 32, 33, 35, 36, 39; 17:14; 20:31; 21:19, 11, 26, 33, 46; 23:1; 26:55; 27:20, 24.

53. Konradt, *Israel, Church, and the Gentiles*, 101.

54. Matt 1:21; 2:4, 6; 4:16, 23; 13:15; 15:8; 21:23; 26:3, 47; 27:1, 25.

55. Konradt, *Israel, Church, and the Gentiles*, 101.

Jesus has made a seemingly positive remark about the religious leaders (Matt 23:2). All twelve disciples are Jews and are portrayed positively. For Matthew 'Ιουδαίοις is comprised of the disciples, virtually all the crowds, the people and their leaders (Matt 2:2). But he makes a distinction between the three. The crowds and the people are to be healed, taught, served and searched and the disciples extend the mission of Jesus whereas the leaders deceived and lied to 'Ιουδαίοις and remain the enemies of Jesus. Therefore, Matthew perceives the Jews as being deceived by the teaching of the Pharisees and the story they made up about Jesus (Matt 28:15) while they had rejected their king (Matt 2:2).

Comparing the two authors' perspectives, the following conclusions can be reached:

1. Convergence: (a) both believe that Gentiles are to be saved by believing the Gospel through preaching. (b) The Jews rejected the Gospel but it is first preached to them. Yet a remnant believed, such as the disciples and the apostles who are Jews themselves, and they are sent to preach the Gospel beyond the nation of Israel.
2. Divergence: (a) while Paul believes that there is no difference between the Jews and Gentiles because there is only one God, Matthew does not reflect such a position. (b) While Paul believes that Jews and Gentiles have a redemptive relationship i.e. the fall of the Jews leads to the salvation of the Gentiles and the salvation of the Gentiles leads to the salvation of the Jews, Matthew does not see anything of such a relationship. (c) For Paul, both the Jews and the Gentiles are sinners before God, but Matthew does not make any differentiation within the Jews between sinners and the righteous. (d) While Paul sees the Jews as enemies of the Gospel, they seek the righteousness of the Law but there is hope for their salvation, Matthew perceives them as persuaded and deceived by their religious leaders to kill Jesus and willingly declared their responsibility for his death by self-cursing. They remained deceived by the fabricated story of their leaders about the resurrection of Jesus although they might be one of the nations to be reached.

Perspective on ἀγάπη

A detailed study on ἀγάπη has been done in Chapters two, three and four of this study and therefore need not be repeated here. Therefore, suffice it to compare the two authors' understanding of love based on the conclusion arrived at in those chapters.

1. Convergence: (a) Both use God the father as the model of genuine love: namely, loving one's enemy. (b) Both conceptualise love as an intellectual, conscious and deliberate choice and an act of Jesus' followers whether it is to love God or to love another fellow person. (c) Both understand love as doing good and abstaining from doing evil, as defined and explicated by the Law. (d) Both think that love is one of the fundamental commandments of the Law.
2. Divergence: (a) while Paul explicitly states that the source of love for believers is God through the Spirit, Matthew does not say anything about the source of love. (b) Although Paul presents God the father as an example of the love of enemies, he does not explicitly draw imperative conclusions such as "love your enemies" but Matthew explicitly states that Jesus followers must love their enemies after the example of God. (c) While Paul focuses on loving one's neighbor (which includes the outsider), Matthew argues that loving one's neighbor is not sufficient and does not lead to perfection (God's kind of love) therefore one must love one's enemy (which is the standard) as a child of God. (d) Whereas Paul understands that love could be pretended unless it is restricted with content, Matthew does not discuss such an aspect of love. (e) For Paul loving one's neighbor fulfils the Law, but for Matthew it is just one of the most important commandments within the ranking of the Law and it does not lead to perfection.

Perspective on νόμος

Similarly, a detailed analysis and discussion is given on νόμος in Chapters two, three and four. Here only the comparison of both authors will be done based on the conclusion arrived at in the chapters.

1. Convergence: (a) both claim that the Law is not the standard of judgment but that the Gospel is the standard of Judgment (Rom

2:16; Matt 7:23, 16:27–28; 24:30; 25:11; 25:31–46). (b) Both ascertain that the Law is given to the Jews and have authority over their lives (Rom 2:17–24; 3:1–3, 19; 5:14; 9:4–5; Matt 5:17–43; 19:16–20; 23:2). (c) Both confirm the continuity of the Law. (d) Both affirm that the commandments of the Law function as a way of life for Jesus followers. It still fulfils the role of setting behavioral boundaries detailing what is evil and good for Jesus followers and providing guidance for discerning what is pleasing to God (Rom 8:4, 7; 2:25–29; 3:31; 13:8–10; Matt 5:19). (e) Both do not make the Law a requirement for membership of God's people. Both affirm that faith in Jesus Christ as a Messiah makes one a member of the Jesus followers. (f) Both focus on the Decalogue.

2. Divergence: (a) While Paul argues that the Law aggravated iniquity and disobedience in the life of the Jews, Matthew does not see it as such. (b) For Paul, the Law and the prophets are witnesses to the righteousness of God, Matthew uses the prophets' prediction as a testimony for the identity of Jesus and his ministry but does not speak of the righteousness of God. (c) While Paul affirms the continuity of the Law, he does not discuss specifically its span and duration (except an ambiguous claim in Rom 4:10a). Yet, he does not deny the validity of circumcision to the Jews if accompanied with obedience to the other commandments (Rom 2:25). Neither does he condemn those who glorify God by keeping specific days as special and abstaining from eating some food or discriminate between clean and unclean (Rom 14). But Matthew clearly claims that the scope and validity of the Law continues until heaven and the earth pass away. (d) Paul claims that disobedience to the Law brings blasphemy against the name of God and disobedience to the Law puts one at enmity with God and by implication obedience to the Law pleases God (Rom 2:24; 8:7). Matthew states that disobedience to the Law makes one the least in the kingdom of God. (e) For Paul the Law is *good, holy, and just, but* Matthew, although he indirectly affirms this, argues that the commandments in the Law do not carry equal weight and that there is an irregularity in the Law (Matt12:1–14; 23:23–24). (f) While Paul contends that one needs to be in the sphere of the Spirit to fulfil the righteous requirements of the Law, Matthew does not discuss the role of the Spirit in relation to obedience to the Law. (g) Although Paul never

talks about perfection, he speaks of confirming the image of Christ (God's Son) as the destiny of Jesus followers; Matthew does not deal with such ideas. But Matthew does argue that the Law does not lead to perfection but that absolute allegiance to Jesus and God's kind of love leads to perfection, i.e. being like God the Father (Matt 5:43–48; 19:21–22). (h) Paul consents that the Law embodies knowledge of God's truth and will, and reveals sin and thereby providing the ability to discern good and bad (Rom 2:17–23). Matthew, although agreeing with Paul on this, contends that the embodiment of God's knowledge and truth is in Jesus and no one knows God without the revealing ministry of Jesus; and his teaching has a final authority (Matt 7:28–29; 11:25–30).

Specific Texts

In this section, texts that reflect a possible agreement and disagreement will be compared based on the conclusions arrived at regarding these texts in the earlier chapters of this study. The texts are Rom 3:31, Rom 8:3–4, Matt 5:17, and Rom 10:4a; and Rom 13:8–10 and Matt 22:34–40. Since each text has been thoroughly discussed in the previous chapters, the discussion will not be repeated. Instead a comparison will be made between the two authors.

Romans 3:31; 7:4–5; 8:3–4; and 10:4a seen against Matthew 5:17–19

The view taken in this research with regard to Rom 3:31 is that Jesus followers continued obeying the Law through faith in Christ although Paul did not specify which commandments they continued to keep. Death to the Law (Rom 7:4–5) is understood as freedom from the condemnation that the Law of Moses levelled against sinners particularly the Jews (not abrogation of the Law) through union with the death of Jesus Christ which is the due penalty of sin. Through the death of Jesus Christ, God is able to punish the old person (sin in the flesh, Rom 8:3) and to create a union between Jesus and believers and to place them in the sphere of the Spirit. In light of this reading, Rom 8:3–4 is interpreted as those who walk in the Spirit and who do not walk according to the flesh, fulfilling the righteous requirement of the Law (as demanded by the Law) by virtue of their union with Christ and their status in the sphere of the Spirit.

Living in the flesh is hostility to God which is tantamount to saying no to submitting to God's Law is hostility to God and not to please God (Rom 8:7–8). Hence, for Paul the Jesus followers are those who united with Christ and live in the sphere of the Spirit and submit to God's Law. In other words, they continue to obey all the righteous acts that the Law demands.

Matthew 5:19 claims that a person who keeps and teaches the Law will be called great in the kingdom of heaven and that the disciples' righteousness must exceed that of the Scribes and the Pharisees in order for them to enter the kingdom of heaven. The righteous that excel will be the ones that obey the teachings of Jesus Christ. He who[56] does relax the commandments of the Law and teach men will be least in the kingdom of heaven.

Paul and Matthew converge on the concept that Jesus' followers should obey the Law. But they diverge in that Matthew insists that every minute commandment must be obeyed and must be taught in order to be called great in the kingdom of heaven whereas Paul does not say anything about to what extent the Jesus followers should obey the Law and for what purpose they should do it. Paul is general in his statement whereas Matthew is specific in the extent and purpose of obedience to the Law and yet he demands perfection which goes beyond the demands of the Law.

Paul in Rom 10:4 claims that Christ is the τέλος of the Law. It is argued in this study that the word is ambiguous and can be interpreted either as "end" or "goal" but the context supports the interpretation that Paul is arguing that because of the ignorance of the righteousness of God and the desire to establish their own, the Jews did not submit to the righteousness of God that is witnessed by the Law and the prophets (3:21), furthermore, they refused to accept the Gospel (Rom 10:21). But Paul contends that the role of the Law as a special mark of God's people for the Jews has ended, it is through faith in Jesus Christ that Jews will be re-engrafted as people of God.

If the two texts are contrasted in an atomistic way, they seem to be contradictory but since Paul is ambiguous in his usage of the term τέλος it is hard to say for certain that they are contradictory as Paul already confirms that the Law must be kept and not destroyed (Rom 3:31).

56. Matthew used the Greek indefinite pronoun ὅς and has never defined the identity of the person who possibly relaxes the commandments of the Law. Therefore, it refers to any person who encounters the Law.

Romans 13:8–14 Seen Against Matthew 22:34–40

The two textual units have been discussed thoroughly in Chapters three and four respectively. Only the result of these discussions will be compared here.

(1) Convergence: (a) the source of the tradition of "love your neighbor as yourself" for both is Lev 19:18. (b) Both highlight the importance of love. (2) Divergence: (a) While Paul deals with only love for the neighbor, Matthew deals with love for God and love for one's neighbor. (b) For Paul, the purpose is to present the commandments related to person-to-person relationship in a succinct form with the language of love with the content of the Law, Matthew's concern is to show the existence of important commandments among the commandments of the Law. (c) Paul recommends loving one's neighbor as the focus of the Law, but Matthew argues that loving one's neighbor is inadequate and restrictive and therefore must be amended by "love your enemies." Furthermore, loving your neighbor is not the teaching of Jesus and does not lead to perfection. (d) For Paul loving one's neighbor fulfils the Law, but Matthew argues that not only loving one's neighbor but also loving God are the two important reasons for obeying all the Laws and the prophets. (e) For Paul, love leads the Decalogue and other commandments in fulfilling the Law. But Matthew contends that the Decalogue and the love commandments can be obeyed by the Jews without being the disciple of Jesus (Matt 19:16–20) but perfection is following Jesus Christ (Matt 19:21). Therefore, for entering the kingdom of heaven and attaining perfection one has to renounce everything and follow Jesus.

Section Summary and Conclusion

The comparison above on specific concepts and texts has shown that Paul in Romans and the Gospel of Matthew have some overlaps and differences in their understanding of the Law but that these differences are not contradictory. Rather, there are tensions arising due to differing emphases and issues that the books address.

APPRAISAL OF THE INTERPRETATION OF THE GOSPEL OF MATTHEW AS ANTI-PAULINE TEXT

The question of whether Matthew is opposing Paul or not has been an ongoing debate. The argument against and for has been adduced based on comparing and contrasting specific texts collected from Matthew and Pauline letters. It is not based on a specific book and a specific topic. Here the discussion will focus only on the letter to the Romans and the Gospel of Matthew based on the analysis in the foregoing sections of this chapter. The appraisal will focus mainly on David Sim's thesis that "the evangelist [Matthew] was motivated, at least to some extent, to write his Gospel in order to discredit Paul and to falsify the Pauline version of the Gospel.[57]

In Chapter one of this study a preliminary argument against Sim's (2002; 2007; 2008; 2009) thesis is given; therefore, there is no need to repeat it here. But as Sim's arguments hinge on texts from Matt 5:17–19; 7:13–23; 13:36–33; 16:27 along with the concept of the elevation of Peter and Jesus' rejection of those who call him "Lord," suffice it to focus on these texts and concepts. Sim's assumption is that Matt 5:17 speaks about the full obedience of the Law and Matt 7:21–27 is the redaction of Matthew of the pre-existing Q. It speaks of judgment on those who are charismatic, but lawless. Paul speaks of the end of the Law in Rom 10:4a, uses the epithet "Lord" in Rom 10:9–13 and 1 Cor 12:3. Paul and the Pauline churches are also known for their charismatic gifts. Therefore, it follows that Matthew is opposing Paul's claim.[58] The basic assumption of Sim is that contradicting verses are opposition of claims.

The comparison made between Romans and the Gospel of Matthew does not support Sim's position. There is no need to engage in a text–for–text response as such an approach is to repeat Sim's weakness in handling the text in an atomistic manner. The comparison has also been made in the analysis undertaken in each chapter at the appropriate place. Here only those findings that mitigate Sim's conclusion will be stated.

In Romans, (1) the Law embodies God's truth, provides knowledge of God's will, the ability to discern what's good and what is evil, guides the blind by being light to those in darkness, corrects foolishness, and specifies sin. (2) For Paul, true Jewishness is keeping the Law (Rom 2:25–29). Paul never denied the value of circumcision (Rom 2:25) but he also demanded obedience to the Law in full along with circumcision

57. Sim, "Matthew's Anti-Paulinism," 769.

58. Sim, "Matthew 7.21–23," 324–43.

from them (Rom 2:25). (3) Paul accuses the Jews of breaking the Law and of not keeping the Law (Rom 2:17–24; 3:1–19). (4) Breaking the Law results in blaspheming the name of God among the Gentiles (Rom 2:24). (5) The Jesus followers do not abolish (καταργέω which is closer to Matthew's 5:17–καταλύω) but establish its authority and function (ἵστημι). (6) The Law is holy, just and good but the Jews who were entrusted with the Law are under the dominion of death and sin and therefore could not perform the demands of the Law even though they are pleased with it (Rom 5:20; 7:12). However, with the coming of the Law, condemnation (punishment) came to Israel because of their breaking of the Law; therefore, the coming of the Law aggravated the power of sin to bring judgment upon Israel. They need deliverance not from the Law but from its condemning authority. (7) The Jesus followers (Jews and Gentiles) can fulfil the righteous requirement of the Law (Rom 8:4) because of their union with Christ and by virtue of their existence in the sphere of the Spirit. They are under the dominion of life and grace and not under the dominion of the Law (as instruments of judgment). (8) Those who do not submit to God's Law are enemies of God because they choose to walk in the flesh (Rom 8:7). (9) The problem with the Jews is not their pursuit of the Law but their not pursuing it through faith (Rom 9:32), establishing righteousness without faith in Christ (Rom 10:3) and refusing the message of the Gospel (Rom 10:21). (10) The assertion that Christ is the τέλος of the Law (Rom 10:4) is ambiguous in that it can be interpreted as either "end" or "goal" and therefore cannot be taken as evidence for a negative connotation of Paul's perspective on the Law. The context, the Jews' status before the Law, and other texts such as Rom 2:17–29; 3:21, 31; 7:12; 8:4, 7; 13:8–10; and 15:8–9 mitigate against a negative connotation of Rom 10:4. (11) Calling the name of the Lord (Rom 10:13) is not a magical spell but obedience to the teachings of the Gospel (Rom 6:17) or obedience of faith to bring glory to the name of God (Rom 1:5 and 15:18) which requires offering the whole being of the Jesus followers as a living sacrifice to the will of God (Rom 12:1–2) and submitting to the rule of righteousness (Rom 6:18–19); and finally, judgment is given according to work (Rom 2:6–11; Rom 14:10–12). (12). The Law is meant to be fulfilled (Rom 13:8–10) not to be abolished. It is the Law that love fulfils, i.e. the intention of love is to fulfil the Law. (13) The authority of the Law as a standard of judgment is compromised but not dismissed, although the ultimate judgment is based on the Gospel (Rom 2:12–16). (13) Paul used ἀνομία (Rom 1:29) as moral transgression and transgression of the Law

(Rom 4:7). The word does not necessarily indicate conceptually opposing the Law, *pace* Sim.[59] It generally means disobedience to the will of God which Paul affirms. (14) Paul and the Pauline churches had a peaceful relationship with the Jerusalem church (Rom 15:25–33). Receiving the support of Gentiles means receiving their faith. His request for prayer is to be delivered from unbelievers and not from the believers in Jerusalem (Rom 15:31). The other prayer request is that his service might be pleasing to the believers in Jerusalem not because they are at odds with his ministry but because he wants his service to bring joy among the saints.

Therefore, on the face of all this evidence from Romans, Matthew cannot be an anti-Pauline Gospel. For Matthew, the Law is irregular, and the commandments do not carry equal weight, the Law does not lead to perfection, the Law is not a source of knowledge, but Jesus is a source of revelation, and the Law is not the final standard of judgment, but Jesus and his teaching is the basis of judgment.

Sim's argument that Matthew elevates Peter does not square with the progression of Matthew's portrayal of Peter in his story.[60] Peter, is a fisherman (Matt 4:18); is counted among the twelve apostles (Matt 10:2); started performing miracles but failed because of fear (Matt 14:29); has difficulty in understanding parables (Matt 15:15); received a revelation but misunderstood it (Matt 16:16); was rebuked by Jesus and equated with Satan and declared as an obstacle to the ministry of Jesus (Matt 16:23); misunderstands and confuses the revelation of Jesus and wants to make Jesus equal with Moses and Elijah (Matt 17:14); does not understand his status as a child of the kingdom (Matt 17:24–25); understands that forgiveness has to be done for a limited number of times (Matt 19:21); requests a reward for following Jesus (Matt 19:27), although the response from Jesus is positive here; Peter presumptuously claims that he is better than others and vows to stand the persecution even to death but later denies Jesus three times, but repents later (Matt 26:3, 58–75); could not even pray for an hour with Jesus (Matt 26:40) and he is not the first one to see the resurrected Jesus. His name is not mentioned after the resurrection. All of the above data show that although Peter is mentioned several times and actively converses with Jesus, Matthew has no intention of elevating him above the other disciples. Instead, he revealed his weakness and inconsistency and equated him with other disciples after

59. Sim, "Matthew 7.21–23."

60. Gathercole, "A Law unto Themselves," 778.

the resurrection (Matt 28:16). Peter is a good starter but never endures. Sim fails to account for the portrayal of Peter in the Gospel of Matthew. In sum, Sim's thesis that Matthew is anti-Pauline text has a flimsy basis and imposes unwarranted speculation and conclusions.

CHAPTER SUMMARY AND CONCLUSION

The aim of this chapter is to analyze the intertexture of Rom 13:8–14 and Matt 22:34–44 and to compare the concepts of the two units. The analysis has demonstrated that while for Matthew Deuteronomy 6:5 and Lev 19:18 are the intertexture for Matt 22:34–44, the intertexture for Rom 13:9 is Lev 19:18 with its context of the prohibition of evil acts against one's neighbor. Rom 3:30 alludes to Deut 6:5. The explicit juxtaposition and ranking of Deut 6:5 and Lev 19:18 in Matt 22:34–44 is not found in any of the literature that was investigated. The concept of love as obedience to the commandment of the Law had been a well-established concept throughout Jewish literature but "neighbor" refers to a restricted community within which the injunction of love is addressed. The Greco-Roman literature that has been investigated here does not show any textual affinity to Rom 13:9 or Matt 22:34–44. Conceptually, with regard to love, they have maintained a similar notion. No strong connection was found between love and Law in the Greco-Roman literature which was undertaken in this research.

Since a detailed summary and conclusions have been provided under each subtopic only key conclusions need to be stated here.

Convergence:

1. Rom 13:8–10 and Matt 34–44 relied on the common text (Deut 6:5 and Lev 19:18).
2. The Law is the content for love, and it is the Law that love fulfils; it is not the Law that fulfils love.
3. Both Romans and Matthew affirm the continuity of the Law and obedience to the Law.
4. Both understand that sin is against the revealed truth of God as revealed through the Law and the Gospel.
5. Both claim that Jews and Gentiles are sinners and following Jesus is the only way to have a right relationship with God.

Divergence:

1. For Paul sin is a domineering power but Matthew does not perceive sin as such.
2. While Matthew is consistent and clear on judgment, Paul in Romans is unclear particularly about the judgment of Jesus followers.
3. While Paul sees Jews as stubbornly having zeal without proper knowledge, their current spiritual condition has a reciprocal redemptive purpose for the Gentiles, Matthew perceives the Jews as deluded and that they believed the false story about Jesus which was told by their religious leaders. Matthew also conceives that the Jewish religious leaders are incorrigible sinners.
4. For Matthew loving one's neighbor can be obeyed without being the follower of Jesus. It does not make one perfect but following Jesus and loving one's enemies is the standard for Jesus followers. He, therefore, downplays the injunction "love your neighbor as yourself," whereas for Paul "loving your neighbor" is the pinnacle of the Law.
5. While Paul thinks that the Law plays the role of providing knowledge, truth, and the ability to discern the will of God and guidance, Matthew perceives that the commandments of the Law must be obeyed. They do not carry equal weight and are not the source of knowledge—instead, Jesus is the source of knowledge of God's will and his teachings are authoritative for Jesus followers.
6. While Matthew clearly states the duration and the scope of the Law, Paul is not interested and therefore leaves it ambiguous.

Hence, it can be safely concluded that the letter to the Romans and the Gospel of Matthew are not opposing texts but that due to differences in the genre they employed and the issues they are dealing with, there is some divergence of concepts in them, but that they overlap even though a number of concepts cannot be harmonized. Romans and Matthew seriously differ with regard to their positions on "loving your neighbor" but not on the Law.

7

The Role of Romans 13:8–14 and Matthew 22:34–40 as an Identity-Shaping Text for the Community of Jesus Followers

INTRODUCTION

THIS CHAPTER EXPLORES THE role of Rom 13:8–14 and Matt 22:34–40 in the identity formation of Jesus followers in the respective books. It argues that Rom 13:8–14 and Matt 22:34–40 are of paramount importance in shaping the perceptible identity of Jesus followers. To this effect, first the topical concept of identity theories is discussed, then characters in Romans and in Matthew are analyzed in search of identity descriptors. Finally, the role of Rom 13:8–14 and Matt 22:34–40 in identity-shaping of Jesus followers is discussed, followed by a summary and conclusion to the chapter.

IDENTITY THEORY: RELEVANT KEY CONCEPTS AND INSIGHTS

Explaining the concept of identity is no easy task because of the complexity involved regarding what identity means and how it is used across a wide range of disciplines and contexts.[1] However, two widely discussed theories are identity theory and social identity theory and are introduced here simply to provide a platform for the discussion and not as methodological framework as such. Identity theory perceives that the social nature of the self stems from role positions and the self is multifaceted, which is defined by diverse role identities.[2] Social identity theory, on the other hand, is concerned with social, cultural, belief, social–self, group process and intergroup relationship; and it is integrated with social-categorization theory (in–group and out-group categorization) through which a person's self-definition is shaped.[3] Although Stets and Burke argue for the overlap between social identity theory and identity theory,[4] positing that both theories can be usefully combined for the study of identity, in this study there is no need to combine both studies. This study perceives that Jesus followers function as a group and individual members sharing the same identity, consider one another members of the group, have a shared belief, practice and individual behavior (subsumed under the concept of group). This is an outcome of the normative expectations of group membership.[5] As long as the interest of this section is to investigate the role of Rom 13:8–14 and Matt 22:34–40 in the identity formation of Jesus followers group, social identity theory is taken as the most suitable theory. The concept of identity has also been employed in two different understandings: (1) identity as primordial, naturally given and therefore static and (2) identity as "negotiated and renegotiated, expressed and re-expressed," therefore not static.[6] It is argued early in the introductory chapter of this research that identity is not static and therefore it is subject

1. See discussion on identity.

2. Stryker, "Identity Theory," 89–104; Stets and Burke, "Identity Theory," 88–110.

3. Tajfel, "Social and Cultural Factors in Perception," 315–94; Abrams and Hogg, "Introduction to the Social Identity Approach," 1–9; Hogg and McGarty, "Self-Categorization and Social Identity," 10–27.

4. Stets and Burke, "Identity Theory and Social Identity Theory," 2000.

5. Stets and Burke "Identity Theory and Social Identity Theory."

6. Harland, *Dynamics of Identity*, 9; Bengt Holmberg, "Understanding the First Hundred Years of Christian Identity," 29; Lieu, *Christian Identity*, 14.

to change and can be transformed into an agreed ideal model aspired to by the group.

Basically, identity refers to "where one (a person or a group) belongs, and what is expressed as "self–image" or/and "common–image," what integrates them inside self or a group existence, what differentiates them *vis–a–vis* the 'others.'"[7] In particular, the concepts of "internal definitions" within the group and "external definition" (or "external categorizations") by contemporary outsiders" are important for the present work.[8] Insiders are categorized and labelled by outsiders in ways which might as well concur with or be in conflict with the insiders' self-definition and *vice versa*. Such conflicting or concurring identity labelling plays a significant role in formation and maintenance of individual or group identity, in this case, Jesus followers. Internal labelling, being an expression of identity, formulates the basis for a group's sense of belonging and constructs boundaries between insiders and outsiders. According to anthropologists, identity is "embodied in corporative action of a deeply formative nature, such as common prayer, worship, and ritual praxis, as well as in shared behavior patterns, customs, and ethos."[9]

Hence, the theoretical framework of social identity theory is briefly expounded, since it serves as useful point of reference for identity formation as discussed in this research. The concept includes, but is not limited to, the theory that identity is shaped through belief, normative behavioral expectation by ingroup members and outsiders, labelling (by insiders and outsiders); and, importantly, that identity is not static but negotiable.

Accordingly, in the next section, identity (particularly patterns and ethos) descriptors and defining or labelling terms, actions and phrases in Romans and Matthew will be traced and analyzed. Although the ideological point of view and many other elements contribute to the identity–shaping process, the discussion of identity in this study will be undertaken mainly with regard to labelling terms, actions and phrases as identity forming, defining and shaping tools, because the major interest of this research is to focus on the text as it stands and to do in–depth analysis of the text itself. Hence, particularly groups and individual persons (as characters) will be analyzed based on the ways in which each book portrays and presents them to their respective readers, followed by

7. Golubović, "An Anthropological Conceptualisation of Identity," 25.

8. Harland, *Dynamics of Identity*, 9.

9. Holmberg, "Understanding the First Hundred Years of Christian Identity," 29.

a discussion of the role of Rom 13:8–14 and Matt 22:34–44 in identity formation of the community of Jesus-followers.

CHARACTERS IN ROMANS 13:8–14[10]

Romans 13:8–14 addresses implied characters, employing pronouns. Such characters in the rhetorical unit are not self-evident from this passage insofar as Paul already wrote twelve chapters addressing different groups of audiences, mainly believing Jews, believing Gentiles and possibly believing Gentile God-fearers.

The use of pronouns within Romans serves as identity descriptors or labelling for the characters submitted in the letter. However, it is hardly possible to present an analysis of all the pronouns; hence, a summary of some of important pronouns such as: "we" "you," "they," "those who . . ." and "He who . . ." will be analyzed. The purpose is not so much about establishing the identity of the audience as it is identifying the audiences' disposition and self-definition as it stands within the text; not least on Rom 13:8a and b.

We, You, and They

Romans 13:8a and 13:8b employ two different subjects, namely, the second person plural and third person singular respectively. While in 13:8a ὀφείλετε implies a plural object or receiver of the message, the sentence in 13:8b *ὁ γὰρ ἀγαπῶν τὸν ἕτερον νόμον πελήρωκεν* involves a singular subject. It is hardly possible to identify the identity of the receiver of this particular command without a thorough investigation of its development within the rhetorical movement of the letter. For example, in the citation section of Rom 13:8–10, Paul uses second person singular, which might as well be understood as collective individuals. Nevertheless, the texts in the citation originally targeted the Jews and not Jesus followers. Thus, it raises the question of how the identity of the addressees of ὀφείλετε and

10. Employing the term "characters" might be considered an anomaly in so far as Romans is not a narration but a letter. Although Romans as letter does not have an explicit setting and plot, Paul depicts persons in his arguments in terms of their actions, behaviors and status, which distinguishes them categorically from one another. In this research the term "characters" in Romans, therefore, speaks of different groups and persons depicted in the letters in different ways, in terms of their behavior, action and status.

ὁ γὰρ ἀγαπῶν, if one can clearly identify it, relates to the identity of the person originally addressed in the text of the citation.

The identity of the object of ὀφείλετε and ὁ γὰρ ἀγαπῶν is further complicated as Paul employs several characters in the letter: Pronouns such as "I," "we," "you" (both singular and plural) and "they." Others such as God, Jesus, Son, Saints, Gentiles, Roman, Greek, Barbarian, Jew, Abraham, Adam, a woman, Israel, Beloved, brothers, the strong, the weak, and lists of names are important characters in the letter. Detailed study and analysis of these characters and verses is beyond the scope of this study, but an overall summary of the survey of persona based on the pronoun (we, you and they) will be provided as per Lun–Kowng's proposal of persona analysis as a mirror reading to identify the characters in the epistle to the Romans.[11]

We/Our/Us: Commonality of Jesus Followers

The "we/our/us" section of the Romans evinces that Paul inclusively addresses the audience[12] and that he stresses the *commonality of Jesus followers*. By commonality, it means common features and shared identity. Those who are designated as "we" are not only Gentile believers[13] but also Jewish believers as argued in Chapter four of this study. The data[14] shows the following features: before their faith in Christ, Jesus followers had the same experience and status: sinners, enemies of God and weak, as qualities that they held in common with the outsiders. But by virtue of their faith in Christ and all being under the lordship of Jesus Christ, they share common benefits, experiences and values despite their ethnic differences. Such benefits entail deliverance from sin; guidance of the Spirit; the fatherhood of God; suffering, hope and a glorious future; the approval of God; and victory over evil.[15] The "we" therefore, represents the insiders—mainly the Jews and the Gentile Jesus followers.

11. Lo, *Paul's Purpose in Writing Romans*, 14.

12. McDonald, "Romans 5:1-11 as a Rhetorical Bridge," 86; Minear, *The Obedience of Faith*, 58.

13. Stowers, *A Rereading of Romans*, 248.

14. Rom 1:4, 5, 7; 5:1–11; 8:12, 15, 16, 17, 18, 22, 23, 26, 31, 32, 34, 35, 36, 36, 37, 39, 39.

15. Dunn, *Romans 1–8*, 308; Jewett, *Romans*, 394; Minear, *The Obedience of Faith*, 58.

"You": Status, Behavior, and Obligation

The result of the analysis of the "you" section based on the data shown in the footnote[16] depicts how status, behavior and obligation of both the insiders and outsiders are encapsulated by these pronouns. "You" in Rom 2:1–5 expounds the behavior of a person who is pretentious and stubborn and Rom 2:17–27 describes the behavior of a hypocritical Jew who boasts about the Law, God and teaches the Law but does not practice it. Such a Jew is committing blasphemy. The behavior of both people is described through their action and attitude. In this case, the "you" section describes the characters of outsiders who failed in carrying out their obligation and who are hypocritical and pretentious.

However, Jesus followers are saints, belong to Christ and have one Father and Lord, and geographically live in Rome, but they are connected to a wider community of faith through Jesus Christ. They are welcomed by Christ and should welcome one another (15:7). They are full of goodness, knowledge and are able to instruct one another (15:14); are freed from the power of sin and are united with Christ through baptism. They are not under the Law but under grace, in Christ and in the Spirit, and are obedient to the teaching of the apostles and have become slaves of righteousness and slaves of God and armies of righteousness against sin.

Obligations are also addressed: they are to resist sin and put to death the deeds of the body (8:10). The "you" in Rom 10:9–10 is also about responsibility that has positive results, namely, believing and confessing the Word. The "you" in Rom 12, 13, and 14 is all about obligation and character of the community within and outside the community. Therefore, in the "you" section Paul clearly states the status given to Jesus followers, i.e. freedom from sin but slavery to righteousness and God. This results in being a warrior against sin, which is the responsibility and obligation of the community of Jesus followers.

"They": Failure in Status, Behavior, and Obligation

The third person plural "they" occurs in Rom 1:18–32; 3:12–24; 9:27, 32; and 10:1–3, 14, 18; 11:1–3, 9–12, 14–15, 20–31 and depicts failure

16. Rom 1:7, 8, 9, 10, 11, 12, 13, 15; 2:1, 3, 4, 5, 17, 18, 19, 20, 21, 22, 23, 24, 25, 27; 6:11, 12, 13, 14, 16, 17, 18, 19, 20, 21, 22; 8:2, 9, 10, 11, 13, 15; 10:8, 9; 12:1, 2, 14, 18, 19, 20; 13:3, 4, 6, 9, 11; 14:4, 10, 15, 16, 21; 15:5, 6, 7, 8, 13, 14, 15, 22, 23, 24; 16:6, 16, 17, 19, 20, 21–25.

in status, behavior and obligations of the outsiders. In Rom 1:18–32, the description of the characters is negative. They are the object of God's wrath because of what they did. However, scholars debate the identity of these characters. Sanday and Headlam, Godet and chamber, Bruce, Hultgren, and Fitzmyer and others contend that the people described in this pericope must be from the Gentiles or the pagan world.[17] However, others like and argued that Paul is describing the fall of all humanity, that includes both Jews and Gentiles.[18]

Likewise, there is no agreement as to the identity of the persons described in 3:10–18. Although there is consensus among the scholars that the text in one way or another, includes Jews, there is no agreement as to whom Paul is specifically referring to by quoting from Scripture. For instance, while Sanday and Headlam and Wright argue for a group consisting entirely of Jews,[19] Dunn, Fitzmyer, Bruce, Godet and Chamber, Hultgren, and Jewett see it referring to all humanity.[20] However, both groups of scholars consent that eventually it is about the impartiality of God's judgment on all humanity upon their disobedience to the truth. This is revealed to humanity either through nature (1:18–32) or through the Scripture according to 2:17–3:10–18.

It is obvious that 1:18–32 portrays the characters by their attitudes and actions against the respective revelation available to them: they know God (1:21). Their actions are stated as related to "all ungodliness and wickedness of men" (1:18). Paul is not exhaustive in his list of vices because the wrath of God is revealed on "all" which is "all-embracing" . The word ἀσέβεια appears only here and in 4:5, 5:6 and 11:26, but ἀδικία is frequently used in the letter. Those mentioned are accused of idolatry (1:22) and many other immoralities but ἀσέβεια and ἀδικία summarize all the evil things that deserve the wrath and judgment of God. Owing to their action and attitudes such people are handed over by God because of the desire of their hearts to uncleanness (1:24), to dishonoring passions (1:26), and to a debased mind of improper conduct or what is not fitting (1:28). The term to "hand over" (παραδίδωμι) has a sense of control or

17. Sanday and Headlam, *Romans*, 39; Godet and Chambers, *Romans*, 99; Bruce, *Romans*, 77; Hultgren, *Romans*, 88; Fitzmyer, *Romans*, 270.

18. Dunn, *Romans 1–8*, 50; Jewett, *Romans*, 152; Cranfield, *Romans*, 1:105–6.

19. Sanday and Headlam, *Romans*, 63; Wright, Romans, 456.

20. Fitzmyer, *Romans*, 333; Bruce, *Romans*, 92; Godet and Chambers, *Romans*, 139; Hultgren, *Romans*, 140; Jewett, *Romans*, 256–80.

responsibility for[21] but according to Stowers the word "very frequently" refers to "handing someone over to be tortured or to be sent to prison, to the police, or to the courts of law."[22] In other words, they are handed over to be slaves of their own unclean desires, dishonoring passions and of improper conducts. Paul has never described these characters based on ethnic identity but based on their knowledge of God, attitudes towards God's expectations and their actions. A similar portrayal is given within the discussion of the place of Jews in light of disobedience to the revelation they received in 3:10–18. Paul concludes that all are under the judgment of God.

In Rom 9:27, 32 and 10:1–3, 14, 18; 11:1–3, 9–12, 14–15, 20–31, where Paul describes the status of Israel in detail, although he did not describe them in the same way as the characters in 1:18–32, he still sees them as under the judgment of God. They trespassed (11:11–12) and practiced ungodliness (11:26); they are disobedient and contrary people (10:21), enemies of God as regards the Gospel (11:28), but the believing remnant is compared to those who did not worship Baal and by implication those who rejected the Gospel seem to be compared to people worshipping Baal (11:4). Therefore, God judged them by hardening their hearts by giving them spirit of stupor (11:7–9), which may be compared to Pharaoh in 9:18 and Chapter 1:18–32.

By using "they" to describe such characters in his letter, Paul distinguishes them from the community of Jesus followers. They are the "other" contrasted against the "we," the "us," and the "you" of the insiders, the Jesus followers. They are also a pool of potential members to be reached by the preaching of the Gospel; until then they are the "them" against the "us." Owing to failure in their status, behavior, obligation and responsibility to their creator and neighbors, they are enslaved under the power of sin despite their ethnic identity. The unbelieving Jews and the unbelieving Gentiles are, therefore, the "others" or the outsiders.

However, Paul envisions another group of characters in the letter, which will be surveyed and about whom it will be argued in the ensuing section that these characters are the paradigmatic characters towards which Paul is calling all other characters portrayed under "we, you, and they" in his letter.

21. Dunn, *Romans 1–8*, 62.

22. Stowers, *A Rereading of Romans*, 91–92.

"Those who . . ." and "He who . . .": The Paradigmatic Characters

The "we" section describes shared status, benefits, values, hope and destiny of the Jesus followers. While the "you" section delineates to Jesus followers their new status, expected behavior and obligations towards God and neighbors, and the "they" section portrays the "others" or outsiders who have failed in their responsibilities and obligations, although they may be potential members in the future. This section argues that "those who . . ." and "he who . . ." are paradigmatic characters who conformed to the image of the Son that the contemporary Jesus followers either emulate or reject in the course towards their destiny.

Almost all the verses that contain the expressions "those who . . ." and "he who . . ." are in participle and occur at strategic places in the overall rhetorical structure of Romans:[23] 1:16; 2:7–10; 3:22; 8:5; 8:28; and 13:8. All the participles are articular and independent therefore unlike the infinitive, semantically, they denote concrete concepts and speak about the person or the thing they describe.[24] Although a participle functions as an adjective or substantive, it does not lose its verbal aspect. If this is so, the participles in the texts above qualify the subjects of their sentences through their verbal aspect or through the actions described by the verb. They therefore delineate the characters by their actions that define, identify, restrict, and distinguish them from other groups.

The loci of the verses also have significance: 1:16 comes after Paul has greeted his addressee where he sets his agenda for the whole letter. In particular, *παντὶ τῷ πιστεύοντι* is one of the key concepts that Paul expounds upon further in the letter. Romans 2:7–10 comes after Paul's panoramic description of the lifestyle of all wickedness and unrighteousness of man (1:18) and before the conclusion of God's impartial justice in 2:16. So, 2:7–10 is a pivotal point for 2:1–6, because the 2:1–6 is explained

23. Rom 1:16 τῷ πιστεύπντι (he who believes); 2:7 ζητοῦσιν (those who seek); 2:8 ἀπειθοῦσιτῇ ἀληθείᾳ (those who disobey the truth), πειθομένοιςδὲ τῇ ἀδικίᾳ (those who obeyed unrighteousness); 2:9 ψυχὴνἀνθρώπουτοῦ κατεργαζομένουτὸ κακόν (every human being who does evil); 2:10 παντὶ τῷ ἐργαζουμένῳ τὸ ἀγαθόν (all who do good); 3:22 πάνταςτοὺςπιστεύοντας (all who believe); 6:7 ἀποθανὼν δεδικάω ται ἀπὸ τῆς ἁμαρτίας (He who has died freed from sin); 8:5 οἱ γὰρκατὰ σάρκαὄντεςτὰ τῆςσαρκὸςφρονοῆσιν, οἱ δὲ κατὰ πνεῦματὰ τοῦ πνεύματος (those who are (living) according to the flesh . . . and those who are (living) according to the spirit); 8:28 ἀγαπῶσιντὸνθεὸν/those who love God; 13:8 ὁ γὰρἀγαπῶντὸνἕτερον (he who loves the other).

24. Wallace, *Greek Grammar Beyond the Basics*, 620.

in 2:7–10; and 2:8–16 amplifies 2:7–10[25] because it lays the criteria for God's impartial judgment.

Romans 3:22 takes a very significant locus because it comes at a place where Paul is concluding his lengthy argument regarding sin and the judgment of God. Romans 8:5 and 8:28 are situated in the second major block of Paul's rhetorical argument regarding sin and the law. Significantly, 8:5 comes within the conclusive and contrastive elaboration of life under the spirit of Christ and life under sin (8:1–17). However, 8:5 is located within the pericope 8:18–30 where Paul elucidates the result of the righteousness of God and its climax. Finally, 13:8 exists within the imperatives for Jesus followers' way of life that started in 12:1 and at the verge of its conclusion. Therefore, the locus of each verse in its specific context as well as in the overall rhetorical discourse of the letter adduces that the characters described by the participles have a unique role in describing Paul's envisioned disposition of the paradigmatic characters for the Jesus community.

The characters in 1:16 παντὶ τῷ πιστεύοντι and 3:22 πάντας τοὺς πιστεύοντας have the same identity—they are the ones who believe. While in 1:16 they are receivers of the power of God, in 3:22 they are beneficiaries of the righteousness of God through Jesus Christ. The text 1:16 speaks of individuals; "everyone who believes" as the participle is singular. Hence, this feature first marks off at the individual level in order to be manifested as the corporate identity. Minear has also observed that 1:16 "sets forth a theme applicable equally to all participants in the dialogue."[26] Yet, Minear's reading is confined within the five groups of the Jesus followers he reconstructed from Rom 14 and hence he does not see it as referring to indefinite characters.[27] Many commentators have discerned the universality of 1:16 and 3:22.[28]

Jewett observes that παντὶ τῷ πιστεύοντι (1:16) refers to respondents of the Gospel "by participating in faith community."[29] Reading it in the Roman context, he argues that it takes a particular emphasis because the Jesus followers are rejecting one another. Moo observes that τῷ παντὶ πιστεύοντι occurs four times where the tension between the Jews

25. Louw, *A Semantic Discourse Analysis of Romans*, 48.

26. Minear, *The Obedience of Faith*, 44.

27. Minear, *The Obedience of Faith*, 8–14.

28. Käsemann, *Romans*, 22; Cranfield, *Romans*, 1:90; Murray, *Romans*, 1959, 28.

29. Jewett, *Romans*, 139.

and the Gentiles is discussed.[30] But Jewett and Moo have not perceived "the one who has faith" as the model character for the community.[31] It can be argued that παντὶ τῷ πιστεύοντι serves as a point of reflection for the Christ-believing community in Rome as it is indefinite and does not specify any group; instead, it declares a specific hallmark that distinguishes a definitive Jesus follower.

Paul refers to a wider "other" in 1:16c, first the Jew and then the Greek but in 3:22–23 "all have sinned." Both texts mark off the ones who have faith from the ones who do not have. In so doing, the feature of the characters divides the nations into two despite their ethnicity. It also embodies all the Jesus followers in all contexts who have faith despite their specific location and ethnicity. Therefore, the identity of the character described as "to all who believe" goes beyond the letter of Romans and the community of Jesus followers in Rome. Paul adduces that such a feature is evident in the community: ". . . but for us also. It will be reckoned to us who believe in him that raised from the dead Jesus our Lord" (4:23–24).

Scholars have observed that in Rom 2:7–10, Paul is characterizing two classes of people. According to Wright, vv. 7–8 contrasts the underlining attitude of two classes and vv. 9–10 their final state.[32] The first group is delineated in terms of what they seek and the means they use to achieve what they seek and the second group is defined in terms of obedience and disobedience; therefore, the former obey the truth while the latter do not patiently seek for glory.[33]For Wright, those who seek the glory, honor and immortality are Jesus followers.[34] Godet argues that the section divides the world based on moral goals such as glory, honor and eternal life. He writes, "The Jews divided men into circumcised, and consequently saved, and uncircumcised, and consequently damned. Here is a new classification . . . which is found solely on the moral aim."[35] Fitzmyer reads it as a description of Jesus' followers because Paul "formulates the destiny of Christian existence, which he will further specify in time as a share in the "glory" of God (3:23; 5:2) in the life of the risen Christ (6:4) . . . the quality of the destiny of Christians . . . glory . . . honor . . . and . . . immortality."[36]

30. Moo, *Romans*, 68.

31. Jewett, *Romans*; Moo, *Romans*.

32. Wright, Romans.

33. Wright, *Romans*, 439–40.

34. Wright, *Romans*, 580.

35. Godet, *Romans*, 118.

36. Fitzmyer, *Romans*, 1993, 302.

For Hultgren, it is about two ways of living.[37] Dunn says, "Paul here seems deliberately to choose language of broad appeal, particularly in describing the goal sought after."[38] Esler also thinks that Paul speaks of "two broad groups of people within his purview."[39] Cranfield observes that the verses "indicate two categories of men."[40] However, Jewett insists that Paul also has the readers of the letter in mind.[41]

Therefore, there is consensus that 2:7–10 speaks of two groups of people contrasted against the other. There is no agreement as to the identity of the groups, particularly v. 7. Cranfield offers a few possible, different interpretations: (1) Paul is inconsistent; (2) it is hypothetical; (3) it is about the good work of faith of Christians (Christian–faith); (4) Christian conduct as expression of their faith, (5) it refers to Old Testament believers and Christians; (6) it refers to Christians, Old Testament believers, and some Gentiles, and (7) it refers to only Old Testament believers. Cranfield rejects all and concludes that reading (4) namely: Christian conduct as an expression of their faith should be taken as the most probable interpretation.[42] Davies rejects Cranfield's conclusion arguing that the name of Christ is not mentioned as an object of faith and that the text has to be understood in light of God's patience leading to repentance.[43] The principle of impartiality of God is not new in the Old Testament and Paul speaks in general terms; therefore, it embraces all who exercise faith before or after Christ.

The scholarly attempt to establish the identity of groups described in the text defines reading the text as delineating paradigmatic characters, if not hypothetical, this portrays both accepted and rejected ways of life before God. As Louw has shown, v. 7 has three semantic features: reward, deed and attitude; but v. 10 speaks of reward, deed and the person.[44] Verse 8 has three parts: attitude, deed and reward; but v. 9 lists reward, deed and the person. Both sides of rewards are the result of deeds and attitude. If this is so, then the two important features of the characters are attitude and deeds. The attitude of the first group is steadfastness in doing

37. Hultgren, *Romans*, 116.

38. Dunn, *Romans 1–8*, 85.

39. Esler, *Conflict and Identity in Romans*, 151.

40. Cranfield, *Romans*, 1:147.

41. Jewett, *Romans*, 204.

42. Cranfield, *Romans*, 1:151–52.

43. Davies, *Faith and Obedience in Romans*, 57.

44. Louw, *A Semantic Discourse Analysis of Romans*, 2:49–52.

good works (v. 7); therefore, their attitude is persistent in continuing to do the good deeds. This is not a wish nor "a passive waiting for divine intervention," rather it is "a vigorous form of moral endeavour; conducive to the performance of 'good work.'"[45]

Persistence implies continuity even in the face of challenges. Paul stresses endurance (ὑπομονή) in four Romans (2:7; 5:3, 4; 8:25 and 15:4, 5) in the letter and all of them are employed in contexts of challenges and suffering. In 5:3–4 suffering produces endurance and endurance tests character. In 8:25, the word is used within the context of sharing the glory and suffering of Christ, which begins in v. 17 and ends in v. 39. It might be read as "But if we hope for what we do not see, we await it eagerly with patient endurance" (YLT). In Rom 15:4 Paul addresses the strong to "bear the failings of the weak" and not to please themselves. He offers the following evidence: the life of Christ who did not focus on himself, the Scripture, and God. While Jesus becomes the ideal person to be emulated, the Scripture gives instruction in the ways in which one attains the hope through endurance. In 15:5, God endures and gives the ability of steadfastness to the strong. Therefore, Jesus and God are the quintessential paragon of the character of endurance to be emulated.

In 2:7, the attitude is not just steadfastness in whatever sense but in doing good works and seeking glory, honor, and eternal life. Both the goal of persistence and doing good works is lucidly stated. However, v. 9 and v. 10 explicitly state the core mark of the two groups: *τοῦ κατεργαζουένου τὸ κακόν* (a person who does evil) versus *παντὶ τῷ ἐπγαζομένῳ* (everyone who does good). Paul's emphasis is not on the work as it were but on the kind of work, one does. "Good" and "evil" are the two hallmarks that mark off one group from the other as identity markers.

Paul portrays these characters in light of the final impartial judgment of God (2:11, 16). The wrath of God is already revealed in 1:18–32 which resulted in handing over those who practice ungodliness and unrighteousness although that is not the end of it. Rather, there will be a final judgment coming when the secrets of men will be judged according to the Gospel of Paul (2:16). In fact, the Jesus followers will also be judged (14:12). Granting this, Paul is not speaking about Israel in the Old Testament so long as the Gospel is not considered to be the standard for judgment for Israel in the Old Testament. Nor is he describing Christians living only in Rome as Wright claims, Christians "seek for glory,

45. Jewett, *Romans*, 204.

honor, and immortality."[46] Rather, Paul is setting forth the kind of people of whom God approves in the end. If this is granted, they would be the paragon of the desired believing community that Paul is envisioning. He is making it the goal of his ministry (1:5) to produce such a community and is now summoning the Jesus followers at Rome towards this goal.

Romans 6:7 comes as a thick discussion on sin, death and the Law, on the one hand, and Jesus, grace and righteousness on the other. The context of 2:7–10 and 6:7 might correlate because Paul in 1:18–2:6 lists and describes wickedness and unrighteousness that bring about judgment and death. In 1:32, he insists, "though they know God's decree that those who do such things deserve to die, they not only do them but approve of those who practice them." Dunn (1988a:271) points out that 5:12–21 serves as a conclusion for the opening section (1:18–5:21). Yet, 5:12–21 not only concludes but also sets the next theme that needs further exposition, not least: sin, the law, obedience to righteousness. Therefore, the immediate context of 6:7 begins at 5:12 where three characters are at the forefront—Adam, Moses, and Jesus. These three characters are agents of elements that affect humankind: Adam brought sin, condemnation, judgment, and death. Moses brought the Law that exposed sin and explicitly stated its reward while through Jesus grace, righteousness, and life came into the world. However, it can be summarized in two kinds of life: in Adam disobedient people (unrighteousness, wickedness, judgment, condemnation, death) and in Christ obedient people (righteousness, grace, life), and both resonate with Rom 2:7–10, which divides people into two groups based on their work.

Romans 6 picks up on the "disobedience and obedience" theme and expounds it in light of the rhetorical question rendered in 6:1 whether one continues living in a disobedient life because life is just a gift. However, Paul insists that obedience is the goal. But regarding how the desired obedience comes, he claims baptism as a way of co-crucifixion, burial and resurrection of Jesus Christ (6:4).

Therefore, 6:7 states generically that a baptized person (he who has died) is free from sin. The ongoing, larger debate can be summarized as follows: Almost all the commentators interpret ὁ γαρ ἀποθανὼν δεδικαίωται ἀπὸ τῆς ἁμαρτίας either as justified or freed from sin but never consider the indefinite person that the verse portrays in the mind of a reader. Granted that this theological reading is legitimate, nonetheless,

46. Wright, *Romans*, 580.

the investigation here is based on the kind of character Paul is depicting in the image of the reader. The theological meaning states that baptism is a co-death and co-resurrection with Jesus Christ which brings freedom from sin, according to v. 6. However, "he who has died" projects the desired community of faith that is freed from the power and the bondage of sin and lives for God (6:10–11).

The paradigmatic character is compared with Jesus; even scholars like Conleth Kearns argued that the "he" is Jesus.[47]Jewett is right in rejecting this reading as it decontextualizes v. 7.[48] Nonetheless, Kearns' observation, albeit wrong, points out that the unidentified character in the participle could be mistaken for Christ. Paul also separates the readers and himself from this person by employing "we/our" (6:6). Further, "he who" is between the "if we" (6:8–10) that describes the death of the readers and Jesus. Paul then shifts to the second person plural imperative λογίζομαι (6:11) insisting that the readers must emulate the "he who has died" character who is closely similar to Christ. A further reading within Rom 6 evinces that Paul is calling the readers to be servants of righteousness or servants of God, with complete obedience to God (6:13, 18, 19, and 22). It is also worth noting that 6:23 speaks of reward which is reminiscent of 1:32; 2:8–9 (death as reward) and of 2:7 and 10 (eternal life as reward). Therefore, Paul portrays a paradigmatic character in 6:7 who is closely similar to that of Jesus.

In Rom 8:5, Paul further develops the paradigmatic characters' identity. The text is situated within the pericope of 8:1–17 which comes right after Paul's analysis of the struggle that takes place between sin, law and flesh. The key text is 8:2 while the rest is an elaboration and extension. In 8:5 κατὰ σάρκα ὄντες is translated by the RSV as "those who live . . ." but others translate it as "those who exist . . ." emphasizing rather their being than their behavior.[49] However, existence and behavior are intertwined phenomena and cannot be separated as the existence reflected in action as περιπατοῦσιν (v. 4) denotes behavior. Jewett observes that Paul is "describing two classes of people, believers and non-believers, whose very being is determined by the realm to which they belong."[50] However, Dunn understands it as an idealized model: "In modern terms, the sociological category 'type' comes closer to Paul's meaning—the type

47. Jewett, *Romans*, 404.

48. Jewett, *Romans*, 404.

49. Dunn, *Romans 1–8*, 424; Jewett, *Romans*, 486; Wright, *Romans*.

50. Jewett, *Romans*, 486.

as an abstracted, even idealized model to which individuals conform to a greater or lesser degree, but rarely (if at all) completely."[51] Dunn's observation is commendable because the characters are separated from the audience and Paul himself and are described as an envisioned prototype to which the community is called forth to conform (to that particular character).

From 8:5–8, the following image emerges. There are those who are in the Spirit who have peace and life, and they are the ones who can fulfil the righteous requirement of the Law and they are the ones who are the friends of God because they please God. This image emerges because Paul contrasts them against those who are in the flesh and set their mind on the things of the flesh. They are the enemies of God, they do not submit to God's Law, they cannot please God, and their end is death.

Paul is not dividing the Jesus followers in the Roman congregation, but he is portraying the kind of community of Jesus followers that God desires. The congregation in Rome is in the category of those who are of the Spirit. Paul says that: if the Spirit of God dwells in them (8:9), if Christ is in them (8:10), if the Spirit who raised Christ dwells in them (8:11), if they put the deeds of the flesh by the Spirit (8:13), they will continue to belong to this community of Jesus followers because they have already received the spirit of sonship (8:15). Note that Paul uses an "if" clause to express the condition of the community in Rome while he makes a strong claim for the model characters or community of Jesus followers.

The next portrayal of the paradigmatic characters picks up on the opposite of hostility or enmity expressed in 8:7 and develops the picture of love (8:28)—τοῖς ἀγαπῶσιν τὸν θεὸν. Those "who love God" are not limited to the congregation of Rome but goes beyond it and encompasses others. Such lovers of God are called according to the purpose of God. Here Paul draws from the common knowledge of the Jesus followers that those who love God will have a positive destiny, which is conformity to the image of God's Son.

The above analysis shows that the characters depicted in participial form carry the image of characters through their noun and verbal roles. The image that emerges from the analysis is that Paul is scripting desired paradigmatic characters as a blueprint for the construction of the identity of the community of Jesus followers. The characters are neither locally nor ethnically limited but they stand as identity-shaping paragons with

51. Dunn, *Romans 1–8*, 425.

the Messiah and God as the source of their identity. The hallmarks of the ultimate identity of the believing are dying to sin (6:7), living in the realm of the Spirit (8:5), doing good persistently (2:7–10, seeking peace, honor, glory and life), loving God and their neighbor (13:8–10), submitting to God's Law, and conforming to the image of the risen Messiah.

Section Summary and Conclusion

The "we/our/us" mainly refers to the commonality of the Jesus followers such as shared values and destiny. Some of the "you" refers to the status, behavior, and obligation of the Jesus followers in Romans. "They" refers to the "other" or the outsiders who failed in their status, behavior, and obligation. "Those who . . ." and "he who . . ." portrays the desired paradigmatic community envisioned to be constructed through the Gospel.

The Jesus followers in Rome can mainly be described in the category of "we" and "you" while Paul was writing the letter, but he is insisting that they be transformed and embrace the model character in their day-to-day life (Rom 12:1–2). They are, as argued in Chapter four, believing Jews, Gentiles and God-fearers. In contrast, the ones described in the indefinite form function as a paradigmatic community for all Jesus followers (the "we" and "you") despite their geographical locations and ethnicity. Hence, the identity of ὀφείλετε and ὁ ἀγαπῶν can be categorised accordingly. The term ὀφείλετε is a second person plural imperative and is in the category of "you" referring to the obligation laid upon the Jesus followers in Rome whereas ὁ ἀγαπῶν is in the category of desired paradigmatic characters that Paul is envisioning as the goal of the Gospel in the construction of the community of Jesus followers.

The following table shows the identity descriptors of the community that Paul is envisioning to build. Some of the data that overlaps in the "we/our/us" and "you" and the paradigmatic characters are conflated under the category of "we/our/us" and you." The table shows those that uniquely characterise the paragon community which serves as blueprint in shaping the identity of the Jesus followers at any place and time.

Outsiders	Entry requirement: Faith in the Messiah	**Insiders: in Christ, in the Spirit, under Grace**			
They/them: Current state of Identity		We/our/us/you: (Attribution)	By identity-shaping agents: The Spirit and the Scriptures	Paradigmatic (Perceptible)	Proto-type
Slaves of Sin		Baptised Saints		Persistent, doers of good	The image of the son of God, the first-born and God the Father
Under the wrath of God		Delivered from Sin		Lovers of God and their neighbors	
Enemies of God		Sons of God		Doers of God's Law	
Evildoers / disobedient		Slaves of God		Bearers of the Son's image	
In Adam		Slaves of Righteousness		Emulate Jesus and the Father	
		Armies of Righteousness			
		Conquerors of all evils			

Table 10: Identity Descriptors of Jesus' Followers in Romans

CHARACTERS IN MATTHEW 22:34–40

Due to differing genres, it is impossible to apply the same method used for Romans to the Gospel of Matthew to investigate the paradigmatic community of Jesus followers that Jesus envisioned to build. However, an attempt will be made to trace the descriptions of a few of the characters in the story as portrayed by Matthew. In the context of Matt 22:34–40, the characters are Jesus, the Pharisees and *νομικός*, the disciples and the crowd (implicit in 23:1) and God and the neighbor (see discussion in sections 4.3.2 and 4.6.3). The analysis of the characters in the rhetorical unit under question is discussed at two levels. Firstly, within the literary context of Matt 22:34–40: the literary context of Matt 22:34–40 is conflict as argued in this study in Chapter four section 4:4. However, the wider literary context is the entire story of Matthew particularly because the characters in the rhetorical unit are the most important flat characters from the beginning of the story to the end. Similarly, the topic (the Law and love) raised in the rhetorical unit are crucial for Matthew beginning from Matt 5:17 onwards as shown in Chapter four of this study. Hence, the second level of analysis looks at the description of the character in the entire Gospel in order to come up with collective conclusions on the identity of the characters.

Matthew also employs several characters in his story in addition to the above: in the genealogy, Joseph and Mary, angels, the Magi, Herod, the chief Priests and Scribes, John the Baptist and his disciples, Caesar, the leaders of the Jews, a Gentile woman, the Roman soldiers, and the women who announced the resurrection of Jesus, among others. The description of Jesus, his disciples, the crowds, Pharisees, the Scribes and the Lawyer are discussed here.

The Pharisees and the Lawyer (*νομικός*)

Φαρισαῖοι (Matt 22:34, 41) and *νομικός* are the two important characters in the rhetorical unit. However, according to Carter[52] *νομικός* is a scribe who belongs to the Pharisees and is a professional and an expert at teaching, interpreting and administering the Law. The *νομικός* is one of the members of the Pharisaic group (Matt 22:34), hence, he might be one of the learned Pharisees who is an expert in the Law.[53] If this is accepted, then the Pharisees and the Scribes, from the very beginning, are portrayed negatively as an evil and destructive group and are therefore warned of the wrath of God (Matt 3:7–10). They are characterized as a "brood of poisonous snakes" and as a united opposition group against John the Baptist (Matt 3:7). Carter argues that "coming for baptism" could be translated as "coming against the baptism," because the Greek *ἐπί* can be translated as "against" indicating that they are opponents of God's will and purposes.[54] Characterizing them as offspring of poisonous snakes is a stark contrast against the origin of Jesus who is the Son of Abraham, the Son of David conceived by the Spirit, the promised leader of Israel and greater than John the Baptist (Matt 1:1–2:6; 3:11–12). In so doing, Matthew denies the origin of their identity as covenant people of God, arguing that the fruits of repentance (obedience to the will of God) are marks of the Abrahamic family and that God can raise such fruit-producing children to Abraham (Matt 3:8–9).

52. Carter, *Matthew and the Margins*, 444.

53. Davies and Allison, *Matthew*, 3:239.

54. Carter, *Matthew and the Margins*, 96.

Lucidly, Matt 12:34 states that the Pharisees are evil (πονηρός) as opposed to good (ἀγαθός) persons (Matt 12:35) and that they think evil (Matt 9:4; 22:18; 23:33). The metaphor of poisonous snakes gets its interpretation and application here by singling out the Pharisees as not only opponents of John the Baptist but also the opponents of Jesus' identity and actions. But Jesus turns their claim against him back to them by calling them evil, namely "the devil" in Matt 5:37; 6:13.[55] Matt 12 also applies the metaphor of the tree and fruit as Matt 3:7–10 emphasizes the type of fruit (bad or good) as the mark to identify the origin of words, actions and persons whether they are of God (good) or of the devil (bad). But the Pharisees are producing bad fruit, they are bad persons and filled with evil treasure in their heart and an adulterous generation who will be possessed by the evilest demons (Matt 12:43–45; 16:1–4); and will be judged by Gentiles (who repented) on the day of judgment (Matt 12:41–42).

Furthermore, the Pharisees and the Scribes are transgressors of God's commandments, hypocrites; their hearts are far from God, they are false teachers, they counsel to kill Jesus, they are disobedient, murderous, they refuse to give fruit to the owner of the vineyard, attempt to trap and tempt Jesus, they are blind guides, they do not practice what they teach, they are excluded from the kingdom of God, foolish, and full of iniquity and uncleanness (Matt 15:7–9, 16; 16:6–12; 21:15–45; 22:18; 23). They distance themselves from Jesus and his disciples in their dialogue: "your disciples," and "your teacher" (Matt 9:11; 15:2). Their sacred space, the synagogue, is distanced from the Jesus followers and described as a place where the disciples will suffer (Matt 4:23; 9:35; 10:17; 12:9; 13:54; 23:34). Their title is rejected as a model for the Jesus followers (Matt 23:7–12).

The Disciples and the Crowds

The disciples and the crowds are not explicitly mentioned in the rhetorical unit under investigation. However, Matthew takes for granted that the readers know their presence around the debate between Jesus and the religious leaders as he narrates Jesus directly addressing the disciples and the crowd in Matt 23:1. Hence, the disciples and the crowds are part of the literary context of the rhetorical unit under question and can be taken as one of the characters. The characterization of the crowd and the disciples has been discussed in Chapter four; thus, there is no need to repeat it

55. Carter, *Matthew and the Margins*, 275.

here, except for a few things regarding the disciples. The disciples belong to Jesus. They are designated as the disciples of Jesus by the Pharisees and Scribes (outsiders) as "your disciples" (Matt 12:2; 15:2) and by the father of the sick daughter (Matt 17:16), but by Matthew, the angels and the leaders of the Jews they are called "his disciples" (Matt 9:10, 18, 37; 10:1; 11:1; 12:1, 49; 19:22; 28:13). They belong to the family and household of God the father, therefore, they are Jesus' brothers, sisters, and mothers who do the will of the father of Jesus Christ who is in heaven (5:45, 48; 6:1, 4, 8, 9, 14, 15, 18, 26, 32; 7:11, 21; 12:46–50; 23:8–9). They are the assembly (ἐκκλησίας) of Jesus with the authority of binding and loosing (Matt 16:19; 18:17–20) and commissioned to make the whole nations disciples of Jesus (Matt 28:16–20). But they have little faith (Matt 6:30; 8:26; 14:31; 16:8) and share the evilness of human beings (Matt 7:11).

But the disciples are taught to be a community characterized by the SM which marks the paradigmatic community that Jesus aspires to build (Matt 5–7; 16:19). The beatitudes "constitute, affirm, and challenge a community's distinctive identity and practices."[56]They are poor in the spirit but they will be comforted; they are meek, but they will inherit the earth; they are hungry and thirst for righteousness and they will be filled. They are merciful, pure in heart, peacemakers, and persecuted for righteousness (Matt 5:3–1). They have a mission of being salt and light to the world to bring glory to their heavenly father by their good works (Matt 5:13–16), i.e. exceeding in righteousness that of the scribes and Pharisees: no anger against brother, no lust and adultery in the heart, no divorce, no retaliation, no oath, no hypocrisy, no judging the other, no love for money (mammoth), but reconciliation, love and prayer for enemies, trust in God, priority for the kingdom of God and his righteousness, performing the will of God and the words of Jesus which lead to perfection just as their heavenly father is perfect (Matt 5:20—7:27).

Jesus—Διδάσκαλος

In Matt 22:36, Jesus is addressed by νομικός as a teacher. In fact, Jesus affirms this position to himself (Matt 23:8 if 23:10 is taken together with it). It is not only in this place that Jesus is called "Teacher" but in many other places in the Gospel: by "Scribe": Matt 8:19; by Pharisees "your teacher": Matt 9:11; by scribes and Pharisees: Matt 12:38; a tax collector

56. Carter, *Matthew and the Margins*, 130.

Matt 17:24; and by the rich young man: Matt 19:16. Matthew presents Jesus, the protagonist of the story, in several descriptions which define his identity from both the inside and outside, as presented in the table below.

As the data shows, the positive labels (definition) come from the insiders i.e. the narrator (Matthew), angels, God the father, Jesus himself, the disciples, individuals who got healed or who seek healing. The positive labels that come from the religious leaders: Pharisees, Scribes, Sadducees, High Priest at the cross, Pilate and Roman soldiers are mocking the internal definition of the Jesus' identity. In particular, the religious leaders' true labelling of Jesus is negative, such as Beelzebul (Matt 10:25; 12:24), blasphemer (Matt 26:65), and imposter (Matt 27:63). However, the Magi, Satan or Demons, Pilate's wife and the Roman centurion and others with him seem to be subscribing to the internal labelling of Jesus' identity not least the voice from heaven, "this is my beloved Son" (Matt 3:17). The crowds are not sure of the identity of Jesus but seem to be ascribing to some extent the positive insiders' definition of Jesus' identity at times but another time they label Jesus as a glutton and a drunkard and friends of tax collectors and end up consenting that he is an imposter (Matt 27:24–26).

However, Jesus set God the father and himself as the ultimate model and standard to his community: "It is enough for the disciple to be like his teacher [διδάσκαλον̀] and the servant [δῦλος] like his master [κύριος]" (Matt 10:25). Jesus denies the labelling of Rabbi (Ραββί), teacher (διδάσκαλος), master (καθηγηταί), and father (πατέρα) to any of his community or disciples. Rather, the teaching and master position is given to the Christ presumably himself and the fatherhood position is only ascribed to God—their heavenly father. Jesus uses the possessive pronoun: "one is your teacher" and "one is your heavenly father" (YLT). His community—the disciples—are all brothers (ὑμεῖς ἐστε πάντες ἀδελφοί) (Matt 23:8). They are of one family and have only one father and one teacher to whom they must listen (Matt 17:5) and learn from and follow his example (Matt 11:25–30). Jesus' definition of himself and his community is of paramount importance for the identity-shaping of the Jesus followers. Jesus defines himself as teacher and master; and he defines God as the father to be emulated as a perfect model (Matt 5:48; 10:25; 11:25–30) and his disciples are children of God, his brothers, his sisters and his mother (Matt12:50), and μου τήν ἐκκλησίαν (Matt 18:18; 18:18). But the mark of Jesus' community is doing the will of his father who is in heaven (Matt 12:50).

Jesus' Identity-Defining Epithets[57]		
Insiders: By Matthew (narrator), the disciples, Jesus himself, angels, God the Father, and individuals	**Outsiders**	
	By religious leaders and demons	By the crowds / the people
Jesus Christ[58]		
The Christ[59]	(The) Christ[60]	
Son of David[61]		Son of David[62]
Son of Abraham[63]		
Savior and Emmanuel[64]		
My beloved Son[65]		
Son of the living God[66]	Son of God[67]	
Lord[68]		
Son of Man[69]		
Master/καθηγηταί[70]		
Sender of prophets[71]	Prophet[72]	Prophet[73]

57. Malina and Neyrey, *Calling Jesus Names*, 155–57.

58. By Matthew, the narrator: 1:1.

59. By Matthew, 1:17, 18; 2:4; 11:2 by Peter: 16:16; by Jesus himself: 22:41–46; 23:10

60. By the High Priest: 26:63; by Pilate: 27:37; by the Sanhedrin: 26:28

61. By Matthew: 1:1; by the two blind men: 9:27; by Canaanite woman: 15:22; by two blind men at Jericho 20:30, 31, 33.

62. By the people: 12:23; by the crowd: 21:9; by children at the temple: 21:15

63. By Matthew: 1:1

64. By angel of the Lord and Matthew: 1:21, 23

65. By God the Father: 3:17; 17:5

66. By Peter: 16:16

67. By Demons (tempter): 4:3, 6; 8:29; the High Priest: 26:63; by passers-by at the cross: 27:40; by centurion and others: 27:54.

68. By anonymous disciple: 7:21; by leper: 8:2; by centurion: 8:6, 8; by the disciple: 8:19; blind men :9:27; by Peter 14:28, 30; 16:22; 17:4; 18:21; by Canaanite woman: 15:22, 25, 27; by the father of epileptic son: 17:22; by Jesus: 21:3; (your Lord) 24:42.

69. By Jesus: 9:6; 16:13; 17:12, 22; 19:28; 20:18, 28; 24:30, 39; 25:31; 26:2, 24, 64.

70. By Jesus "on Master": 23:10.

71. By Jesus: 23:34.

72. By Herod the tetrarch: 14:5.

73. By the people 16:14; 21:46.

Teacher[74]	Teacher and Rabbi[75]	
King[76]	King of the Jews/Israel[77]	
Has authority over heaven and earth[78]	Righteous man (Matt 27:19)	Authorized by God[79]

Table 11: Jesus' Identity Descriptors in Matthew

Although the crowd seems to be seeking to be part of the community, they finally rejected Jesus and his message. However, they are the lost sheep of Israel (Matt 10:5). But if some of the towns that condemned him are taken as samples of the unrepentant crowd (Matt 11:18–22), then they are worse than Sodom and Gomorrah, portrayed as goats and cursed (Matt 25:32–41). Gentiles are undeserving of the blessing of God (Matt15:26) and they sit in the darkness (Matt 4:16) but demonstrated extraordinary faith in Jesus and therefore must be made disciples (Matt 28:19–20). Both the crowd and the Gentiles are pools of potential members who will be made disciples by the insiders.

Section Summary and Conclusion

The Pharisees and a scribe (νομικός) in the literary context of Matt 22:34–40 are portrayed negatively and as opponents of Jesus and his community. Their identity is defined mainly by external categorization; namely by Jesus (e.g Matt 23). Similarly, the identity of Jesus is also defined by external categorization; namely by νομικός (the scribe) in 22:36. Characters in Matt 22:34–40 are active flat characters from the very beginning of the story, and their debate and attitude towards Jesus and his teaching in the entire narration connect the literary context of Matt 22:34–40. Following the data adduced in the table it could be concluded that the identity of Jesus is defined externally by the religious leaders, the crowd

74. By Jesus: 10:24, 25; "one teacher, your teacher" 23:8; 26:18.

75. By scribe: 8:19; by Pharisees "your teacher" 9:11; by scribes and Pharisees: 12:38; tax collector 17:24; by (rich young man) one who came up to Jesus: 19:16; by Pharisees disciples, Herodians, Sadducees: 22:16, 24, 36; by Judas 26:25:49.

76. By Jesus himself: 25:34

77. By Wise men: 2:2; 27:19; Pilate, Roman soldiers, Chief Priests, scribes, elders: 27:11, 29, 37, and 42.

78. By Jesus himself: Matt 28:16–20.

79. By the crowd: Matt 9:8.

and Romans (Pilate and his wife, and the Roman soldiers). However, the internal definition of the identity of Jesus is mainly from God, the angels, Jesus himself, the disciples and those who benefited from Jesus. The majority of the outsiders are potential members for whom Jesus has compassion and to whom he reaches out to make them disciples. The community Matthew aspires to construct is fundamentally defined by Jesus himself. The key identity—the defining markers of the outsiders, insiders and paradigmatic (perceptible) insiders' identity and prototype of the community are presented in the table below.

Outsiders	Entry requirement: Faith in theMessiah	**Insiders**			
Current state of Identity		Current state of Identity (attribution)	Identity-shaping agents:Jesus and his teaching	Paradimatic Identity: (perceptible)	Prototype
Sinners (need repentance)		Disciples		Demonstrate exceeding righteousness	Jesus and the perfect God the Father
Under the wrath of God		Have little faith		Lovers of their enemies, God, and neighbor	
Opponents		Children of God:(meek, pure in heart, hunger and thirst for righteousness)		Doers of God's Law	
Evildoers / disobedient		Brothers, sisters, mothers of Jesus		Doers of the will of God	
Lost sheep Those who live in darkness		Sent to the world Conquerors (Matt 16:18)		Peacemakers	

Table 12: Identity Descriptors of Jesus' Followers in Matthew

THE ROLE OF ROMANS 13:8–14 AND MATTHEW 22:34–40

In the above analysis, the identity descriptors both in Romans and in Matthew show some convergence. But the analysis is not exhaustive, as it rather represents the key identity markers of the insiders (Jesus followers) and the outsiders as depicted in both texts as they stand. The query here is what the role of Rom 13:8–14 and Matt 22:34–40 is in identity construction and how these identity markers are in the process of achieving the aspired identity of Jesus followers. This question already assumes that identity is not static but changes through processes aiming at reaching a desired and agreed identity set as standard by the community, which is argued above, as the paradigmatic identity. Among other identity markers or definers, characters or "moral" ways of life (ethos) have significant roles. Meeks argues that "character signifies identity, and it implies specifically moral identity. Character takes shape, moreover, within a social process."[80]

The identity that the members of the community of Jesus followers should strive to emulates and parallels that of the social identity concept of the prototype. In social identity theory, speaking of groups is speaking of categories of people. Social categorization is the cognitive basis for social identity processes by which people cognitively represent a group.[81] Such categories are the basis for accentuating the similarity between in–group members and the difference between the insiders and outsiders. Categories "center around a prototype i.e. an ideal or typical picture of the attributes of the members of the category."[82] Roitto, borrowing from social cognitive theory, employs the concept of perceptible and attributed sides of the role category of prototype.[83] The perceptible side refers to those marks of identity that can be observed such as "behavior, utterance, bodily and facial expression, smell, clothes, symbols and property, etc." On the other hand, the attributed side refers to "character traits and goals" which can be inferred from the perceptible side. Attribution is purported to be a cause for the behavior or acts that are perceptible. Roitto also argues that such attribution is found in first century milieu of Jesus followers in the form of virtues and vices, spiritual agents (e.g., gods) and role (e.g., gender roles).[84] Therefore, he helpfully outlines eight functions of the prototype: describes what the group is like; contrasts the group with out–group stereotype and ideally makes the group distinct, better and increases self–esteem; functions as standard for evaluation of the group; serves as a standard to be emulated by members of the group,

80. Meeks, *The Moral World of the First Christians*, 12.

81. Hogg, "Social Identity Theory," 116.

82. Roitto, "Behaving Like a Christ-Believer," 102.

83. Roitto, "Behaving Like a Christ-Believer," 103.

84. Roitto, "Behaving Like a Christ-Believer," 105.

evaluates other members of the group; and serves for in-group status differentiations.[85]

Accordingly, the social identity concept of prototype better explains the data in the above two tables. Roitto's lists of the function of prototype rather fits the role of Jesus in the community of Jesus followers, whereas the attributive and perceptible traits are markers of his followers. Combining data in both Romans and Matthew shows that the Jesus followers were once outsiders, namely: they were sinners, enemies of God, under the wrath of God, lived in darkness, they were lost sheep, and they were in Adam. But through faith in Jesus, they gained a new status identity in both books: they have become saints, sons/children of God, slaves of God, slaves of righteousness, disciples, brothers, sisters, and mothers of Jesus and conquerors of evil. Such epithets are attributions of the community of Jesus followers that ascribe to the identity of their status and cause them to behave in a certain manner and emulate the prototype.

The epithets mean nothing without corresponding actions (perceptible side) that demonstrate and concretize ontologically declared or claimed identity as argued by Holmberg.[86]Such actions involve ethos (behavior, habit or specific actions that correspond to conviction of self-image) which functionally display identity.[87] Essentially, ethos is comprised of habits or practicing virtues until they become second nature.[88] Geertz also points out that ethos is character, quality of life, and "the underlying attitude toward themselves, and their world that life reflects."[89]Moreover, identity is an answer to "who are you?" which is also intertwined with the answer to the question "how do you behave or what do you do?" Hence, identity presupposes action (perceptible side).

Attribution, Perceptible Identity and the Ultimate Prototype in Romans 13:8–14

In Paul's letter to the Romans, the attributive side of Jesus followers' identity has a causal effect on their perceptible identity. The attributed identity of Jesus followers presupposes sameness. Lieu contends that identity

85. Roitto, "Behaving Like a Christ-Believer," 109.

86. Holmberg, "Understanding the First Hundred Years of Christian Identity," 29.

87. Watt and Malan, *Identity, Ethics, and Ethos in the New Testament*, vii.

88. Meeks, *The Moral World of the First Christians*, 15.

89. Meeks, *The Moral World of the First Christians*, 15.

involves sameness which presupposes difference, that is, "us" demands "them" and the positive demands the negative.[90] The Jesus followers are united with Christ, in the realm of the Spirit and Christ, God's friends and family, and united in one body functioning with a particular role. Such granted status shows the sameness of the community of Jesus followers which is in contrast to the attribution of the outsiders who live in the flesh or in the realm of Adam, death, and sin hence they are enemies of God (Rom 5:10–21; 8:7). Therefore, they cannot please God, cannot submit to God's Law (Rom 8:5–8), and do not honor God (Rom 1:21). The attribution shows that the contrast is between the enemies of God which is the whole world or all humanity who are outside of the realm of Christ (Rom 3:23; 8:38–39; 12:3 13:11–14) and the community of Jesus followers, who are in Christ, are friends and lovers of God (Rom 5:1; 8:28).

Roitto states that perceptible traits involve behaviors that can be perceived by others i.e. by insiders and outsiders.[91] Within the letter of Romans, the perceptible traits of the Jesus followers are the ones that mark them off from those described as outsiders in Rom 1:18–32. Sin (Rom 1:18–32) (also ἀδικία) characterizes outsiders while obedience and righteousness (δικαιοσύνη) characterize the Jesus followers (Rom 6:16). Not least, Rom 6:17 reminds us that the Jesus followers were once slaves of sin i.e. they were among those described in Rom 1:18–32 and now have become slaves of righteousness (Rom 6:18) or slaves of God (Rom 6:22). In their old identity, they were serving wickedness (ἀδικία) (Rom 6:13), impurity (ἀκαθαρσία) and lawlessness (ἀνομία) and hence they were deprived of righteousness (δικαιοσύνη). Therefore, while ἀδικία is an identity marker for outsiders and Jesus followers before their union with Christ, δικαιοσύνη are identity markers of the Jesus followers in Christ.

However, ἁμαρτία and ἀδικία remain a threat to the identity of Jesus followers in their new identity. Paul used ἀκαθαρσία in Rom 1:24 to describe the behavior of those who worship idols and the word ἀνομία to differentiate between Jews and Gentiles. Esler argues that since Paul switches from first person plural (Rom 6:1–11) to second person plural (Rom 6:12–23) excepting in v. 23, he is referring to Gentiles rather than Jews.[92]Although Esler's observation is plausible, it is not conclusive for the following reasons: first, in Rom 6:16–17 Paul uses a general principle i.e. obedience (to any one) makes one a slave; and the Jesus followers

90. Lieu, *Christian Identity in the Jewish and Graeco-Roman World*, 15.

91. Roitto, "Behaving Like a Christ-Believer," 103.

92. Esler, *Conflict and Identity in Romans*, 219–21.

(Jews and Gentiles) were slaves of sin (Rom 6:17); and most of the statements in the context are imperatives where Paul mostly uses the second person plural. Nonetheless, it might be possible that ἀκαθαρσία, ἀδικία and ἀνομία are mainly speaking to the Gentile Jesus followers but the opposite of these behaviors, δικαιοσύνη, must be practiced by all Jesus followers despite their ethnic identity.

But what is δικαιοσύνη? Is it power, moral or forensic in nature? Like ἁμαρτία, δικαιοσύνη could be associated with power to which one is enslaved (Rom 6:18) and parallels with being slave to God (Rom 6:22). Although such reading is possible as righteousness is the realm under which one submits, it cannot be separated from activities not least because it is contrasted with ἀκαθαρσία, ἀδικία and ἀνομία which refer to specific activities. Paul also stated that slavery to sin means freedom from righteousness (Rom 6:20) which is a shameful life (Rom 6:21). Freedom from sin produces fruits (concrete action) of sanctification. Similarly, it is impossible to maintain one consistent forensic meaning for its entire usage in the letter, particularly because the righteousness in Rom 6:16 is the result of obedience[93] in contrast to obedience to sin which is death. The concept Δικαιοσύνη refers to the right conduct in the presence of God which results in ἁγιασμός–holiness (Rom 6:19) "a product of a life living in service of righteousness . . ." which "result in living that is increasingly God-centered and world–renouncing."[94]

Paul used ἅγιος in several places in Romans with reference to scriptures (Rom 1:4), Spirit (Rom 1:4; 5:5; 15:13, 16), Jesus followers (Rom 1:7; 12:1; 16:16), the Law and the commandments (Rom 7:12), and the Jews (Rom 11:16). The term ἅγιος describes how God is; and it refers to distinction and distinctive behavior.[95] It is used as attribution to describe the state of the Jesus followers which is expected to be perceptible in their day-to-day life (Rom 12:1). Paul urges them to present their whole person (bodies) as a living sacrifice, holy, and acceptable to God. The word παραίστημι (Rom 12:1) connects the chapter to the theme of being a slave to δικαιοσύνη in chapter 6 where it is repeatedly used in Rom 6:13, 16, and 19.

Romans 12:1–2 summarizes how the Jesus followers should respond to the attribution side of their identity in Christ. Sacrifices were common in the Greek and Roman religious worlds and were easy for

93. Moo, *The Epistle to the Romans*, 386.

94. Moo, *The Epistle to the Romans*, 405.

95. Ehrensperger, "'Called to Be Saints,' 102.

the audiences to understand in their own respective backgrounds. Paul neither abrogated nor spiritualized the sacrificial aspect of the Law; rather he transferred its concept from literal animal blood sacrifices to the bodies (the entire life) of Jesus followers. In fact, Jesus' death replaced animal blood sacrifices (Rom 3:25). But the bodies that the Jesus followers are requested to present as sacrifice, speak of their whole being. The concept ζῶσαν/ "living" might refer to the new life (Rom 6:11, 19) but fittingly would be referring to the sacrifices itself as opposed to OT sacrifice which requires the literal death of the sacrifice. Such a living sacrifice must be holy (ἅγιος), which still carries the concept of the Law speaking of separation. Hence, ἅγιος also marks off true worship (λατρεύω) from lies (Rom 1:25) and thus it is a perceptible identity marker of Jesus followers that distinguishes them from outsiders, as described in Rom 1:18–32. But such holiness (avoiding conformity to this age) is appropriated through transformation of one's thought pattern to one that discerns and conforms to God-pleasing (εὐάρεστος), good (ἀγαθός) and perfect (τέλειος) will (θέλημα) of God.

The Law	The will of God
It is good (Rom 7:12; 7:16)—ἀγαθός	It is good (12:2)—ἀγαθός
It is holy (Rom 7:12)—ἅγιος	Demands holiness (12:1)—ἅγιος
It is righteous (Rom 7:12)—δίκαιος	
It is spiritual (Rom 7:14)—πνευματικός	
Provides knowledge of God's will (2:18)—γνῶσις, θέλημα	The (knowledge) will of God (12:2c) —θέλημα
Provides the ability to discern (2:18) —δοκιμάζω	Should be discerned (12:2c) —δοκιμάζω
Embodies knowledge and truth (2:20)—γνῶσις, ἀλήθεια	
so also Scriptures are holy (Rom 1:2)	

Table 13: Comparison of the Law and the Will of God

However, identifying the source of knowledge of the will of God is important. Moo thinks that the source of knowledge is left to the renewed mind and the law of Christ, and therefore Jesus followers can decide the will of God at any given situation.[96] However, Paul never mentions the Law of Christ in Romans but Moo imported it from Gal 6:2 and furthermore, Paul elaborates on the perfect will of God in the rest of the chapters. Moo also entirely ascribes the commandments of the Law to "external commands"[97] but for Paul the Law is πνευματικός (Rom 7:14) and can be written in the inner part of a person (Rom 2:14) and even circumcision can be spiritual (Rom 2:29). In particular, Paul's description of the Law is closely similar to the description of the will of God in Rom 12:1–2 and Rom 7:12, 14, and 16.

The Law is the source of God's γνῶσις, ἀλήθεια, and θέλημα which corresponds to the knowledge and truth outsiders gain through creation (Rom 1:20, 25). But Rom 12:1–2 employs the two important functions of the Law: δοκιμάζω and θέλημα. Paul never denied the role of the Law as source of knowledge of the truth and will of God even though he disparages the Jew who claims knowledge but does not practise it. Rather, Paul denies its power of effectiveness in producing the intended life (Rom 8:3). The Law is weak because of the state of Jews in the realm of the flesh therefore they cannot overcome sin under its leadership (Rom 6:15). The Law had authority to judge and condemn those under it (Rom 2:12) but Paul denies such authority (Rom 8:1) and transfers the authority to the Gospel he preached and God and Jesus Christ (Rom 2:16; 8:33–35) who are the ultimate prototypes to be emulated as an ultimate standard for the identity of the community of Jesus.

Ehrensperger has convincingly shown that even in Rom 14:14 (κοινός) Paul is not speaking of abrogating the Law of clean and unclean food; rather the word is about a category that applies to people, namely Gentiles in the sight of the Jews could be perceived as profane but not impure.[98] Therefore, the Law serves in the community of Jesus followers as revealing sin (Rom 7:7; 3:19), providing God's truth and knowledge (Rom 2:20) and witnessing to God's promise and plan (Rom 1:2; 3:21). Scriptures (whatever written in the past which includes the Law) provide encouragement and teaching of the will of God (Rom 15:4). Those who are now under the authority and power of the Spirit and walk according to their claims will fulfil the righteous requirements of the Law (Rom 8:4). Therefore, the Law still functions in providing knowledge and the will of God in creating identity boundaries between sin and God, and

96. Moo, *The Epistle to the Romans*, 757–58.

97. Moo, *The Epistle to the Romans*, 758.

98. Ehrensperger, "Called to Be Saints," 100.

between those who are slaves of sin and slaves of righteousness. The Law defines righteousness, holiness, good, love, acceptable will of God, and what is spiritual. Such a defining role categorizes the Law in the realm of Jesus and God where the source of the perceptible identity traits of the Jesus followers emanate whether they are Jews, Jesus followers or Gentile Jesus followers.

If the above analysis is granted, Rom 13:8–10 fulfils a similar function. Paul cites Rom 13:9, "you shall love your neighbor as yourself" from the context of holiness in Leviticus 18 and 19. Israelites are called to be holy as God is holy (Lev 18:2) and holiness is extended to a day-to-day life (Lev 19:9–10, 13–14, 15–18, 33–34) which is similar to that of Rom 12:1–2.[99] By implication, loving one's neighbor is a mark of holiness. As argued earlier in this study in Chapter four, Rom 13:8–10 succinctly summarizes the Law but neither replaces nor abrogates it, *Pace* Esler.[100] It is also concluded that the Law defines love; and it restricts and provides content to it. Esler claims that the right place to start the interpretation of 13:8–10 is Gal 5:14,[101] but he has never considered the context and what Paul means by Gal 5:14 and his conclusion. Paul concludes that the Law confirms the fruit of the Spirit and stands against the works of the flesh (Gal 5:19–25) and therefore it is still the standard to authenticate the right character.

One important thing must be stressed: the commandment of "love your neighbor as yourself" is one of the commandments of the Law in the OT and Paul is not being innovative here. He simply emphasized that the Law can be stated in such a manner as to stress love as a means to fulfil the Law. Paul's argument is that the ten commandments (adultery, killing, stealing, coveting, abhorring idols (Rom 1:18–32; 2:22) as well as those commandments that keep the community holy in terms of behavior, knowledge and truth, continue to mark off the boundary between sin and God, between idols and a true God, and between slaves to sin and slaves to righteousness within the community of Jesus followers. That is, according to Watson, "a law without circumcision, dietary restrictions, cultus, or sacred days" remains operative in the community of Jesus followers.[102] Therefore, Rom 13:8–10 serves as a perceptible identity-shaping text for the paradigmatic community of Jesus followers by emphasizing the

99. Ehrensperger, "Called to Be Saints," 102.

100. Esler, *Conflict and Identity in Romans*, 334.

101. Esler, *Conflict and Identity in Romans*.

102. Watson, *Paul, Judaism, and the Gentiles*, 214.

commandments of the Law that construct a shared identity within the diverse ways in which faith in Jesus is exercised by Jews and Gentile Jesus followers. Furthermore, by succinctly presenting the Law that focuses on the ethos of the community of Jesus followers, it marks them off as a holy and God honoring community distinct from the world of darkness, flesh and sin as defined by the Law in Rom 1:32–32; 5:12–21; 7 and 13:11–14.

Attribution, Perceptible Identity, and the Ultimate Prototype in Matthew 22:34–44

The key markers of the attribution side of identity in the data above namely, disciples, children of God, brothers, sisters, and mother of Jesus and conquerors of evil have the basis for the perceptible identity of Jesus followers. Such attributions must be manifested in the day–to–day life of the disciples that mark off the disciples from outsiders. God the father and Jesus being the prototype for identity formation of the Jesus community—the perceptible side of the identity of the community to be shaped—are given in the teaching of Jesus Christ.[103]

The perceptible side of the identity of the community is stated in the beatitudes, which "mark out features of a faithful and favored or blessed and honorable group, constitute, affirm, and challenge a community's distinctive identity and practices."[104] and in the SM where the commandments are radicalized and applied to disposition.[105] Matthew's Jesus has already criticized the old teaching of the Law in the SM and demanded a higher righteousness which is contrasted against the righteousness of the Pharisees. Such righteousness entails loving one's enemies and obeying the Law, but giving priority to its weightier matters: mercy, justice and forgiveness.

But Meeks argues that the only valid standard is "the will of the Father in heaven."[106] However, it is not knowing the will of the father in heaven but doing the will of the father that marks off the identity of the disciples from the inauthentic ones (Matt 7:21–27). The will of the father entails the teachings of Jesus in the SM[107] where Jesus comments on the

103. Meeks, *The Moral World of the First Christians*, 138.

104. Carter, *Matthew and the Margins*, 130.

105. Meeks, *The Moral World of the First Christians*, 139.

106. Meeks, *The Moral World of the First Christians*, 139.

107. Davies and Allison, *Matthew*, 1:712.

OT Law and authoritatively insists on his own demands. Particularly, the exceeding δικαιοσύνη is one of the salient marks that distinguishes the disciples from the outsiders. The concept of Δικαιοσύνη, with the exception of Matt 3:15, refers to the behavior or conduct of the Jesus followers in 5:10, 20; 6:1.[108] Such righteousness is, however, expressed as "the will of the Father in the heaven," in which Riches finds that Matthew's mode of language in the SM indicates what style of life and identity is expected from the Jesus followers; for instance, loving enemies closes the section on the Law (Matt 5:48).[109] The parables in Matt 13 depict the identity of the Jesus followers as a community which takes risks for the kingdom of heaven and also forgives without keeping score.

Given the above, what is the role of Matt 22:34–40 in the identity formation of the Jesus followers according to Matthew? The Gospel of Matthew argues that the Law must be obeyed (Matt 5:17–20) but Matt 22:34–40 makes differentiations within the commandments through ranking. Such ranking gives priority to loving God which is a summary of all the first five commandments of the Decalogue. The concept of loving God is demonstrated by the ultimate prototype—Jesus in Matt 4:1–11 where he refused to worship Satan and the benefit of wealth and glory of the world and chose to go hungry. In fact, Jesus also warned his followers to set their priorities right by choosing between God and money (Matt 6:24). Jesus argued in Matt 5:18 that not an iota, not a dot will pass from the Law until all is accomplished, but he never argued that all commandments of the Law carry equal weight. The immediate context of 5:18 which is 5:21–48 shows Jesus is demanding more than the commandments of the Law are demanding. By the same token, loving one's neighbor does not par with loving God because loving God is the greatest and first commandment (αὕτη ἐστὶν ἡμεγάλη καὶ πρώτη ἐντολή) of all the commandments (Matt 22:38). Loving one's neighbor is similar (ὅμοιος) not equal so long as Jesus already said loving God is greater and is the first commandment. Therefore, although loving one's neighbor is an important commandment, in light of Matt 5:48, Matthew goes beyond loving one's neighbor and sets the perceptible identity of the Jesus followers as those who love their enemies like their heavenly father by showing mercy, justice and forgiveness. Therefore, the role of Matt 22:34–40 as identity-shaping text is to set the foundational commandments of the Law

108. Riches, *Conflicting Mythologies*, 194.

109. Riches, *Conflicting Mythologies*, 36–40.

of Moses and to function as an evaluative standard for the community of Jesus followers when applying other commandments. However, it is not the final identity marker in terms of a relationship with one's neighbor. Rather, the teachings of Jesus, namely: loving one's enemies,[110] justice, mercy and forgiveness are the hallmarks of the perceptible identity of the Jesus followers in the Gospel of Matthew. This sets God the father and Jesus as ultimate prototype and standard for the shaping of the identity of the community of Jesus followers despite their ethnic differences.

SUMMARY AND CONCLUSION

This chapter has demonstrated that identity formation of Jesus followers is one of the goals of Paul in Romans and Matthew in his Gospel. Both have clearly marked the difference between the insiders and outsiders by means of labelling an epithet to both groups. It is argued that such labelling can be divided into attributable and perceptible sides of the identity of the community of Jesus followers. Attribution is the status the Jesus followers have by virtue of their relationship with Jesus and serves as the basis for the perceptible side of their identity. The perceptible side is their behavior in action which is easily identifiable, marking the insiders off from the outsiders. Such behavior is paradigmatically portrayed in both books serving as a model to be put into practice. However, the perceptible side models itself after the ultimate prototype—God the father and Jesus Christ.

In light of such a frame of understanding, Rom 13:8–14 serves as an identity-shaping text by recontextualizing and laconically presenting the commandments of the Law that serve as boundaries, as well as the content of the observable identity of the Jesus followers. Matthew 22:34–40, however, presents an example of weighing important aspects of the Law among its commandments, not summarizing, within the Law for the Jesus followers to choose the weightier matter of the Law whenever they attempt to apply the Law. Its role in identity formation is of paramount importance as it outlines the content and priority required for the perceptible identity of the Jesus followers. But the second commandment, loving your neighbor as yourself, is explicitly mitigated by loving your enemies which has become the paradigmatic perceptible character traits to be practiced by the Jesus followers.

110. See Chapter four for the discussion on the identity of "enemies" in the Gospel of Matthew.

8

Conclusion

INTRODUCTION

This chapter brings the earlier analysis of the dissertation to a conclusion. The conclusion begins by drawing out the contribution of each chapter in the search for an answer to the original research question and by testing the hypothesis of the research based on the findings of the study. Then cumulative conclusions are provided. Finally, the contribution and implications of the study follow.

CONTRIBUTION OF EACH CHAPTER

This research addressed the following question: *What is the role of the summary of the Law in Rom 13:8–14 and Matt 22:34–40 in the identity formation of the Jesus followers?* It set itself to test the hypothesis that *neither Matthew nor Paul claims the nullification or the irrelevance of the Law for Jesus followers, but they interpreted it anew in light of the summary of the Law in order to construct the identity of Jesus followers as a holy community*. In addition, it attempted to investigate a subsidiary question: *What are Paul's and Matthew's positions with regard to the place of the Law according to the letter to the Romans and the Gospel of Matthew?* As stated in the introductory chapter of the research, a methodological decision was taken to follow the socio-rhetorical method as provided by Vernon Robbins. Since it is impossible to employ all the methodological aspects proposed in the socio-rhetorical method, only selected principles of interpretation within the socio-rhetorical method were used, namely, the intertexture: repetitive texture, topical progression texture, and argumentative texture. As for aspects of intertexture, oral scribal texture was applied. The topical progression method of investigation in particular was applied to understand love and the Law in the entire books of Romans and Matthew as they stand. The study focused on the texts without giving much attention to their historical background. This does not mean, however, that historical information about the books are unimportant, but due to the vastness of the range of books and the complexity of the issues the research raises, the study was narrowed down and focused on the texts without becoming unduly entangled in the complex historical issues that other scholars have undertaken.

Accordingly, each chapter has contributed specific results that build towards the search for the answer to the research question. After dealing with introductory matters in Chapter one, Chapter two identified the repetitive texture of Rom 13:8–14 and *clarified important concepts* to unpack Rom 13:8–14 by analyzing the progression of the concept of love and the Law in the entire letter. Consequently, the chapter yielded important conclusions:

1. Paul uses the Mosaic Law in the letter to the Romans consistently.
2. The phrase "without the Law (ἀνόμως and χωρὶς νόμου)" refers to the absence of the Law of Moses in the form of knowledge (for Jews and Gentiles) or basis of operation (for God). The living ἐγὼ (Rom 7:8b–9b) refers to Israel's relations to God between the time of Abraham and the giving of the Law through Moses; it was also concluded that there is no intrinsic cause and effect relationship between the Law, and sin and death.
3. The phrase "under the Law (ἐν νόμῳ and ὑπὸ νόμον)" refers to the unbelieving Jews, not to the Jesus followers. The struggle Paul referred to in Rom 7 is the life of the Jews under the Law or life under the flesh without Christ. Likewise, "works of the Law" refers to both boundary markers and behavioral commandments of the Law with regard to the unbelieving Jews.

4. The phrase "doers of the Law (οἱ ποιηταὶ νόμου)" refers to the Jesus followers who, under the sphere of the Spirit and union with Christ, can keep the Law. Keeping the Law is encouraged, for it pleases and honors God.

5. The source of ἀγάπη for the Jesus followers is God, but it is carried out by a conscious, intellectual and deliberate act of choice towards God and fellow believers and the "other," in accordance with the content delineated in the letter to the Romans, despite an opposing and adversary condition.

Based on the conclusion of Chapter two, Chapter three analyzed the argumentative texture of Rom 13:8–14 and followed up with a focused analysis on the central concepts of the rhetorical unit namely, love and the Law, and reached the following conclusions:

1. the summary of the Law in Rom 13:8–14 is based on the assumption that the Jesus followers should fulfil the Law;
2. the audience of the summary of the Law are Jesus followers that are comprised of Jews, God–fearing Gentiles and Gentiles;
3. the summary is not a replacement of the Law with love, rather, it is Paul using love as a language to present the commandments of the Law to the Jesus followers;
4. although love has an emotional and intimate dimension, it is ultimately obeying the commandments of the Law; and
5. the commandments of the Law provide the content and standard for genuine love by delineating what is good and what is evil.

Chapter Four and Five dealt with repetitive texture, the topical progression of ἀγάπη and νόμος, and the narrative pattern, opening–middle–closing and argumentative texture of Matt 22:34–40 and reached the following conclusions:

1. Although Jesus argued for the full function of the Law, he qualified it
    a. by giving priority to his own teaching in Sermon on the Mount,
    b. by disclosing the existence of irregularity, ambiguity, and gradation within the commandments of the Law in his teaching and performances;

c. by insisting that justice, mercy and faith must take priority over other commandments although he adds a comment that other commandments should not be neglected.

2. Matthew 22:34–40 is not the summary of the Law, but it stands as foundation for other commandments giving the reason for exercising other commandments and it also demonstrates that all commandments do not carry equal weight in the Law.
3. Loving one's neighbor in Matthew reflects exercising love within the community of Jesus followers, but it is not a standard of love because for Jesus loving one's enemy (which is doing good and avoiding evil like God the father) is the quintessential standard for his followers.

Chapter Six undertook an intertextual investigation of Rom 13:8–14 and Matt 22:34–40, compared the convergence and divergence between Rom 13:8–14 and Matt 22:34–40, and concluded:

1. that Greco-Roman literature, and Second Temple Jewish literature reflect similar concepts of the love that is expressed in Romans and Matthew. Matthew used Lev 19:18 and Deut 6:5 to formulate Matt 22:34–40 while Paul employed only Lev 19:18 for connecting love and the Law. Hence, Paul and Matthew used the text and concept of Lev 19:18 in addressing the issue of loving one's neighbor, that is, they employed a common source;
2. Romans and the Gospel of Matthew do not contradict each other nor is Matthew an anti-Pauline text, but instead both converge at several points, while their divergence is the result of the genre and purpose of writing.

Hence, they are symphonic in relation to each other, but without either of them losing their distinct voice.

Finally, Chapter Seven used the conclusions reached in the previous chapters and investigated the role of Rom 13:8–14 and Matt 22:34–40 in shaping the identity of the Jesus followers:

1. there is a clear demarcation between the insiders (the Jesus followers) and the outsiders (unbelievers);
2. allegiance or faith in Jesus provides attributive identity which states the membership status of the community of Jesus followers. Attributive identity must, however, express itself in perceptible identity

through actions and behavior which serve as a boundary between insiders and outsiders;

3. the role of Rom 13:8–14 and Matt 22:34–40 is to present the commandments of the Law to serve as identity markers and content for shaping the perceptible identity of the Jesus followers' communities.

These conclusions can now be used to test the hypothesis set at the beginning of the research in Chapter one and a cumulative conclusion be formulated as an answer to the research questions.

TESTING THE RESEARCH HYPOTHESIS

The research hypothesis states that *neither Matthew nor Paul claims the nullification or the irrelevance of the Law for Jesus followers, but they interpreted it anew in light of the summary of the Law in order to construct the identity of Jesus followers as a holy community.* This hypothesis has three parts:

1. that *Matthew and Paul did not claim the nullification or irrelevance of the Law for Jesus followers*. The analysis in this research verified this claim to be true. The study has shown that while Matthew explicitly speaks of the continuity of the Law in his Gospel, Paul speaks of freedom from the Law which is understood in the research as addressed to the Jews who are under the Law. And the freedom is *from the condemnation of the Law* not the Law *per se* because Paul argued that those who live in the realm of the Spirit because of their union with Christ can obey the Law and fulfil the righteous requirements of the Law (Rom 8:1–9) and obeying the commandments of the Law pleases God and brings glory to his name (Rom 2:24; 8:7–9). Hence, the summary of the Law in Rom 13:8–14 which the Jesus followers are called to obey presents the continuation of the Law in the language of love but with the content of the Law.
2. The second part of the hypothesis states that *Paul and Matthew interpreted the Law anew in light of the summary of the Law*. According to the study, this claim cannot be verified and therefore must be rejected. Neither Paul nor Matthew claimed any new interpretation of the Law in light of the summary of the Law. The research has shown that both depended on the common sources to formulate their respective texts and there is no evidence that either of the two authors used it to interpret the whole Law.

3. The third part of the hypothesis speaks of purpose. But its claim depends on the two earlier claims of the hypothesis, i.e. the continuity of the Law and its interpretation on the basis that the summary of the Law is *to construct the identity of the Jesus followers as a holy community*. This claim is partially verifiable because its assumption on the continuity of the Law, according to this study, is verified but its assumption of new interpretation must be rejected. However, the research has shown that Rom 13:8–14 and Matt 22:34–40 are identity-shaping texts. However, they do not shape attributive identity although they do shape the perceptible identity, because the holiness of the community is due to faith and union with Christ (Romans) and allegiance to Jesus (Matthew); holiness does not result from keeping the commandments. Furthermore, Matthew does not make explicit statements about the holiness of the community of Jesus followers. Therefore, the hypothesis that the summary of the Law is to construct a holy community must be rejected, because holiness is a status given to the community due to their allegiance or faith in Christ. However, the hypothesis can be verified partially according to the study. Romans 13:8–14 and Matt 22:34–40 shape the perceptible identity of the Jesus followers by providing the boundary markers and specific content for the ethos of the community. Such identity could be called holiness, but holiness is mainly attributive.
4. The hypothesis assumes that Rom 13:8–14 and Matt 22:34–40 can both be called summaries of the Law.

However, the title is a misnomer for both Rom 13:8–14 Matt 22:34–40. Therefore, the title cannot be used for both.

CUMULATIVE CONCLUSIONS

The following cumulative conclusions can be drawn from the study:

The Continuity of the Law

a. Both the letter of Romans and the Gospel of Matthew affirm the continuity of the Law. While Matthew affirms this with a specific and lucid statement, Paul is assertive but general and open ended regarding the extent of its continuity. However, Rom 13:8–10 is a way of affirmation of the Law's continuity and application within the community of Jesus followers.

b. Love and the Law in Rom 13:8–14 and Matt 22:34–40 are intertwined without replacing one another in both books.

Love, being a subset of the commandments of the Law, provides the language and the atmosphere of the relationship among God, Jesus followers, and the outsiders, while the Law provides the content and specifies the practice, the nature, and boundaries of genuine love.

The Role of Romans 13:8–14 and Matthew 22:34–40 as an Identity-Shaping Text

Although Jesus and God are the ultimate prototypes to be emulated by the communities of Jesus followers as an ultimate identity, it is the commandments of the Law in formulation of Rom 13:8–14 and Matt 22:34–40 that specify and provide the content and boundary markers for the kind of perceptible identity to be shaped. The three natures of the Law (holy, righteous and good) in Rom 7 correspond to the identity markers of the Jesus followers described in both books.

The Law (Rom 7:12)	**The Jesus followers**	**Texts**	
Holy	Called holy (attributive identity)	Rom 1:1	
Good	Seek good, do good, and produce good (perceptible identity)	Rom 2:7, 10	Matt 7:17 (5:16, 44; 7:17;12:33–35; 13:23–24, 48; 19:16, 17; 20:10; 25:21–23)
Righteous	Slaves of righteousness do righteous things, seek righteousness (perceptible identity)	Rom 6:13, 18; 8:4	Matt 13:43; 25:3, 46 (3:15; 5:6, 10, 20; 6:33; and 21:32)

Table 14: Comparison: The Nature of the Law and the Identity of Jesus' Followers

The Law provides knowledge to discern between the good and the evil and the righteous and the unrighteous. Jesus followers are slaves of righteousness and doers of righteousness. Righteousness is their way of life (ethos), and *their perceptible identity therefore must be informed, guided, and marked by the commandments of the Law (i.e. genuine love) as formulated in Rom 13:8–10 and Matt 22:34–40.*

Paul and Matthew

According to the letter to the Romans and the Gospel of Matthew, Paul's and Matthew's positions on the Law do not contradict each other, nor is Matthew an anti-Pauline text but both have a common understanding of the Law at a theoretical level according to the texts investigated in this research, although there may be differences in shaping the identity of their respective communities at a practical level. Their differences at some points can be accounted for by the genre and purpose of composing their respective books. Judging their positions based on specific texts, such as Rom 7:6; 10:4 against Matt 5:17–19 is unconvincing, particularly because the interpretation of Rom 7:6 and Rom 10:4 cannot be pinned down as Paul's negative statement about the Law, as a result of the ambiguity of the texts and Paul's clear statement regarding his stance against abolishing the Law in Rom 3:31. Therefore, neither are Paul (according to the letter to the Romans) and Matthew enemies regarding their understanding of the subject of the Law, nor is Matthew correcting Paul, as such claims depend on speculation. Rather, Paul and Matthew, while agreeing on many important points regarding the Law, are polyphonic in dealing with their individual concerns at the times of their writing.

CONTRIBUTION OF THE STUDY

This study contributes to research on the letter to the Romans and the Gospel of Matthew particularly in the comparative study of the Law and Love:

1. The studies reviewed in this research did not devote a profound study to the summary of the Law. Thus, this research provided an in-depth study on the subject. In particular, a comparison between the letter of the Romans and the Gospel of Matthew about the *summary of the Law* has never been done before; this work therefore fills the knowledge gap in the subject.
2. This research has affirmed that the traditional understanding of the Law and grace as theologically and practically antithetical is an

eschewed interpretation and has no strong exegetical evidence in the letter of Romans and the Gospel of Matthew.

3. Differing interpretations on Rom 13:8–10 have contributed to an understanding of the Law, with scholars often focusing on the importance of the love but downplaying the role of the Law. Such interpretations include that the summary of the Law accentuates *the centrality of love and the continuity of the Law*[1] that it replaces the Mosaic Law[2]and also that it radically reduces but never abrogates the Law.[3] Another interpretation is that it supplements the paraenesis with information but does not validate the whole law or the Decalogue and neither does it possess relevance to the Jesus followers.[4] All these interpretations give leverage to the partial existence or continuity of the Law in some form in relation to the moral aspect of the Jesus followers. However, this research has shown that Paul in the Romans insists on the continuity of the Law and that he is against the abrogation of the Law. He has never explicitly stated which aspect of the Law should be continued to be obeyed, except for stating that the Jesus followers are expected to fulfil the righteous requirements of the Law. However, since the communities of the Jesus followers include Jews, God–fearing Gentiles and Gentiles, *the extent of the commandments to be obeyed is left open to the individual faith*, although Paul's discussion of the Law is mostly in relation to the Decalogue. It is most probable that the Jewish Jesus followers did continue to obey all the commandments of the Law while the Gentile Jesus followers obey the righteous requirements of the Law except food, holidays, the Sabbath and circumcision (identity markers of the Jews). The research has also shown that the role of the summary of the Law in Rom 13:8–14 is not primarily responding to the argument whether the Law continues or not; rather, it claims that the Law should be fulfilled by the Jesus followers and shows that love (which is an endowment in the heart of the Jesus followers through the Spirit) discloses the very nature of the Law (an act of doing good and avoiding evil). The commandments of

1. Murray, *Romans*, 160; Cranfield, *Romans*, 1:274; Käsemann, *Romans*, 361; Thielman, *Paul & the Law*, 53; Dunn, *Romans 1–8*.

2. Witherington and Hyatt, *Romans;* Moo, *Romans*, 816.

3. Watson, *Paul, Judaism, and the Gentiles;* Räisänen, *Paul and the Law*; Hübner, *Law in Paul's Thought*, 85.

4. Thurén, *Derhetorizing Paul.*

the Law are *the content, expression and hallmarks of genuine love.* The research further indicated that the role of the summary of the Law in Rom 13:8–14 is shaping the perceptible identity of the Jesus followers by the commandments of the law which delineates the boundary markers.

4. Studies on Matt 22:34–40 have concluded that it exhibits the essence of the Law and functions as interpretive principle in the process of interpreting the Law.[5] Although this study affirmed that Matt 22:34–40 shows the essence of the Law, it has demonstrated that loving one's neighbor as oneself is not the kind of love that Jesus set as a standard for the Jesus followers but loving one's enemy is the quintessential mark of the Jesus followers. The enemies that Matthew referred to are not only the Jews, or Jewish religious leaders, but any person that stands against the Jesus followers because of their allegiance to Jesus Christ. The research has also shown that there is irregularity, and gradation within the Law according to Jesus' teaching; therefore, the commandments of the Law do not carry equal weight. The role of Matt 22:34–40 as an identity-shaping text lies on providing the basis for obeying the commandments of the Law and evaluative standard in practical application of the commandments in the process of shaping the perceptible identity of the Jesus followers.

Due to the voluminous nature of the books, and the complexity of the topic, a text-focused hermeneutical approach has been taken, and therefore the study has not engaged in historical questions of the rhetorical unit of Rom 13:8–14 and Matt 22:34–40. Further study is required to understand how the role of Rom 13:8–14 and Matt 22:34–40 function as identity-shaping texts for the Jesus followers within the Greek-infused Roman imperial world, in order to understand how such texts were applied and practiced in the wider milieu of the addresses.

Nevertheless, the research has shown that the Law had an important identity-defining role to play among first-century Jesus followers (particularly in the letter to the Romans and the Gospel of Matthew). The study of the Law in Romans has shown that Paul has not distinguished which commandment of the Law ceased to function and which commandment continued in the communities of Jesus followers; he left it open to individuals to determine this, based on their faith in Christ with regard to commandments related to food, holidays and purity. Therefore,

5. Bornkamm, Barth, and Held, *Tradition and Interpretation in Matthew.*

Jewish Jesus followers were most probably fully observing the Law in Rome while the Gentile Jesus followers were not forced to observe the requirements related to food, the Sabbath, and holidays. Hence, the Law is not the antithesis of grace but functioned to shape the perceptible identity of the Jesus followers (who are in the realm of the Spirit) insofar as they gained their identity through faith in Jesus Christ, which shapes them into one family of God (both Jews and Gentile Jesus followers). This understanding challenges the traditional interpretation of the Law as antithesis of grace.

Finally, this study challenges the interpretation of Matthew's Gospel as an anti-Pauline text and insists that the joint listening to Paul (Romans) and Matthew does not lead to cacophony, but that they should rather be listened to as a symphony in which each participant plays with its own distinct cords.

Bibliography

Abrams, D., and Michael A. Hogg. "Introduction to the Social Identity Approach." In *Social Identity Theory: Constructive and Critical Ddvances*, edited by D. Abrams and Michael A. Hogg, 1–9. London: Harvester Wheatsheaf, 1990.

Achtemeier, Paul J. *Romans*. Interpretation. Louisville: Westminster John Knox, 1985.

Alford, Henry. *Alford's Greek Testament: An Exegetical and Critical Commentary, Acts-2 Corinthians*. 7th ed. Grand Rapids: Guardian, 1877.

Allison, Dale C. *The Sermon on the Mount: Inspiring the Moral Imagination*. New York: Crossroad, 1999.

Arndt, William, and Frederick W. Danker. *A Greek-English Lexicon of the New Testament and Other Early Christian Literature*. Chicago: University of Chicago Press, 2000.

Augustine. *The Lord's Sermon on the Mount*. Translated by John J. Jepson. Ancient Christian Writers 5. Westminster, MD: Newman, 1948.

Babor, Eddie. R. *Ethics' 2006 Ed. (the Philosophical Discipline of Action)*. Manila: Rex Bookstore, 2006.

Bacon, Benjamin Wisner. *Studies in Matthew*. New York: Holt, 1930.

Badenas, Robert. *Christ the End of the Law: Romans 10.4 in Pauline Perspective*. JSNTSup 10. Sheffield: JSOT Press, 1985.

Bandstra, Andrew John. *The Law and the Elements of the World: An Exegetical Study in Aspects of Paul's Teaching*. Kampen: Kok, 1964.

Banks, Robert. *Jesus and the Law in the Synoptic Tradition*. SNTSMS 28. Cambridge: Cambridge University Press, 1975.

Barclay G., John M. "Do We Undermine the Law? A Study of Romans 14.1—15.6." In *Paul and the Mosaic Law*, edited by James D. G. Dunn, 287–308. WUNT 89. Tübingen: Mohr Siebeck, 1996.

Barrett, C. K. *The Epistle to the Romans*. Peabody, MA: Hendrickson, 1991.

Barth, Gerhard. "Matthew's Understanding of the Law." In *Tradition and Interpretation in Matthew*, 58–164. Translated by Percy Scott. NTL. Philadel-phia: Westminster, 1963.

Barth, Karl. *Christ and Adam: Man and Humanity in Romans 5*. Translated by Tom Smail. Scottish Journal of Theology: Occasional Papers 5. Edinburgh: Oliver & Boyd, 1956.

———. *The Epistle to the Romans*. Translated by Edwyn C. Hoskyns. London: Oxford University Press, 1968.

Bauckham, Richard. *Gospels for All Christians: Rethinking the Gospel Audiences*. Grand Rapids: Eerdmans, 1998.

Beale, G. K., and D. A. Carson. *Commentary on the New Testament Use of the Old Testament*. Grand Rapids: Baker, 2007.

Bechtler, Steven Richard. "Christ, the Telos of the Law: The Goal of Romans 10:4." *CBQ* 56 (1994) 288–308.

Beet, Joseph Agar. *A Commentary on St. Paul's Epistle to the Romans*. London: Hodder & Stoughton, 1882.

———. *A Commentary on St. Paul's Epistle to the Romans*. London: Hodder & Stoughton, 1882.

Beker, Johan Christiaan. *Paul the Apostle: The Triumph of God in Life and Thought*. Philadelphia: Fortress, 1980.

Betz, Hans Dieter. *Essays on the Sermon on the Mount*. Translated by L. L. Welborn. Philadelphia: Fortress,1984.

———. *The Sermon on the Mount: A Commentary on the Sermon on the Mount, Including the Sermon on the Plain*. Hermeneia. Minneapolis: Fortress, 1995.

Borg, Marcus. *Conflict, Holiness, and Politics in the Teachings of Jesus*. New York: Bloomsbury, 1998.

———. *Meeting Jesus Again for the First Time: The Historical Jesus and the Heart of Contemporary Faith*. San Franscisco: Harper SanFrancisco, 1994.

Bornkamm, Günther. "End-Expectation and Church in Matthew." In *Tradition and Interpretation in Matthew*, 15–51. Translated by Percy Scott. NTL. Philadelphia: Westminster, 1963.

Bornkamm, Günther, Gerhard Barth, and Heinz Joachim Held. *Tradition and Interpretation in Matthew*. Translated by Percy Scott. NTL. Philadelphia: Westminster, 1963.

Boyarin, Daniel. *A Radical Jew: Paul and the Politics of Identity*. Berkeley: University of California, 1994.

Braet, Antoine C. "The Enthymeme in Aristotle's Rhetoric: From Argumentation Theory to Logic." *Informal Logic* 19 (1999) 101–17.

Brandon, S. G. F. *The Fall of Jerusalem and the Christian Church: A Study of the Effects of the Jewish Overthrow of AD 70 on Christianity*. 2nd ed. London: SPCK, 1957.

Bray, Gerald L., ed. *Romans*. Ancient Christian Commentary on Scripture 6. Downers Grove, IL: InterVarsity, 2005.

Brown, David. *Commentary on the Epistle to the Romans Embracing the Latest Results of Criticism*. Glasgow: Collins, 1860.

Brown, John. *Analytical Exposition of the Epistle of Paul to the Romans*. New York: Carter, 1857.

Bruce, F. F. *The Letter of Paul to the Romans: An Introduction and Commentary*. Grand Rapids: Eerdmans, 1985.

Bultmann, Rudolf. *The History of the Synoptic Tradition*. Translated by John Marsh. New York: Harper & Row, 1963.

———. *Theology of the New Testament*. Vol. 1. 1951. Reprint, Waco, TX: Baylor University Press, 2007.

Burton, Ernest De Witt. *A Critical and Exegetical Commentary on the Epistle to the Galatians*. International Critical Commentary. Edinburgh: T. & T. Clark, 1921.

Byrne, Brendan. *Romans*. Sacra Pagina 6. Collegeville, MN: Liturgical, 1996.

Calvin, John. *Calvin's Commentaries Volume XIX Acts 14–28, Romans 1–16*. 500th Anniversary Edition. Grand Rapids: Baker, 1979.

———. *Epistles of Paul to the Romans and Thessalonians*. Translated by R. MacKenzie. New ed. Grand Rapids: Eerdmans, 1960.

———. *Institutes of the Christian Religion*. Translated by Henry Beveridge. Cambridge: James Clark, 1962.

Carson, D. A. "Matthew." In *The Expositor's Bible Commentary*, edited by Ma. Grand Rapids: Zondervan, 1984.

Carter, Warren. "Love Your Enemies." *Word & World* 28 (2008) 13–21.

———. *Matthew and the Margins*. London: T. & T. Clark, 2000.

Cohn-Sherbok, Dan. "An Analysis of Jesus' Arguments Concerning the Plucking of Grain on the Sabbath." *JSNT* 2 (1979) 31–41.

Conradie, E. M. *Christian Identity: An Introduction*. Stellenbosch: Sun Press, 2005.

Conzelmann, Hans. *An Outline of the Theology of the New Testament*. NTL. London: SCM, 1969.

Cousland, J. R. C. *The Crowds in the Gospel of Matthew*. NovTSup 102. Leiden: Brill, 2002.

Cranfield, C. E. B. *A Critical and Exegetical Commentary on The Epistle to the Romans*. Vol. 1. 2 vols. International Critical Commentary. Edinburgh: T. & T. Clark, 1975.

———. "St. Paul and the Law." *Scottish Journal of Theology* 17 (1964) 43–68.

Cranfield, C. E. B., and William Sanday. *A Critical and Exegetical Commentary on the Epistle to the Romans: Commentary on Romans IX–XVI and Essays*. Vol. 2. Edinburgh: T. & T. Clark, 1979.

Crossan, John Dominic. *The Historical Jesus: The Life of a Mediterranean Jewish Peasant*. San Francisco: HarperSanFrancisco, 1993.

Danker, F. W. "Romans v. 12: Sin under Law." *NTS* 14 (1968) 424–39.

Das, A. Andrew. "The Gentile-Encoded Auduebce of Romans: The Church Outside the Synagogue." In *Reading Paul's Letter to the Romans*, edited by Jerry L. Sumney, 29–46. Resources for Biblical Study 73. Atlanta: Society of Biblical Literature, 2012. http://www.jstor.org/stable/j.ctt32bzb7.

———. *Paul, the Law, and the Covenant*. Peabody, MA: Hendrickson, 2001.

———. *Solving the Romans Debate*. Minneapolis: Fortress, 2007.

Davies, Glenn N. *Faith and Obedience in Romans: A Study in Romans 1–4*. JSNTSup 39. London: Bloomsbury, 1990.

Davies, W. D. *The Sermon on the Mount*. Cambridge University Press, 1966.

Davies, W. D., and Dale C. Allison. *A Critical and Exegetical Commentary on the Gospel According to Saint Matthew*. Vol. 1. International Critical Commentary. T. & T. Clark, 1988.

———. *A Critical and Exegetical Commentary on the Gospel According to Saint Matthew Commentary on Matthew*. Rev. ed. Vol. 2. International Critical Commentary. Edinburgh: T. & T. Clark, 1997.

Debanne, Marc. *Enthymemes in the Letters of Paul*. London: A. & C. Black, 2006.

Denney, James. "St.Paul's Epistle to the Romans." In *The Expositor's Greek Testament*. Vol. 5. Grand Rapids: Eerdmans, 1900.

Donaldson, Terence L. "The Law That Hangs (Matthew 22:40): Rabbinic Formulation and Matthean Social World." *CBQ* 57 (1995) 689–709.

Dunn, James D. G. *The New Perspective on Paul*. Grand Rapids: Eerdmans, 2008.

———. *Paul and the Mosaic Law*. Tübingen: Mohr Siebeck, 1996.

———. *Romans 1–8*. Word Biblical Commentary 38A. Nashville: Nelson, 1988.

———. "Rom 7,14–25 in the Theology of Paul." *Theologische Zeitschrift* 31 (1975) 257–73.

———. *Romans 9–16*. Word Biblical Commenatry 38B. Waco, TX: Word, 1988.

———. *The Theology of Paul the Apostle*. Grand Rapids: Eerdmans, 1998.

———. "Yet Once More—'The Works of the Law': A Response." *JSNT* (1992) 99–117.

Ehrensperger, Kathy. "'Called to Be Saints'—the Identity-Shaping Dimension of Paul's Priestly Discourse in Romans." In *Reading Paul in Context: Explorations in Identity Formation*, edited by Kathy Ehrensperger and J. Brian Tucker, 90–109. New York: T. & T. Clark, 2010.

Ellison, Henry Leopold. *The Mystery of Israel: An Exposition of Romans 9–11*. Grand Rapids: Eerdmans, 1966.

Englezakis, Benedict. "Romans 5:12–15 and the Pauline Teaching of the Lord's Death." *Biblica* 58 (1977) 231–36.

Esler, Philip F. *Conflict and Identity in Romans: The Social Setting in Paul's Letter*. Minneapolis: Fortress, 2003.

Evans, Craig A. "'Who Touched Me?' Jesus and the Ritually Impure." In *Jesus in Context: Temple, Purity, and Restoration*, edited by Bruce Chilton and Craig A. Evans, 353–76. Arbeiten zur Geschichte des antiken Judentums und des Urchristentums 39. Leiden: Brill, 1997.

Fee, Gordon D. *God's Empowering Presence: The Holy Spirit in the Letters of Paul*. Peabody, MA: Hendrickson, 1994.

Filson, Floyd Vivian. *A Commentary on the Gospel According to St. Matthew*. London: A. & C. Black, 1960.

Fitzmyer, Joseph A. *Romans*. Anchor Bible 33. New York: Doubleday, 1993.

Forster, E. M. *Aspects of the Novel*. New York, 1954.

France, R. T. *The Gospel According to Matthew: An Introduction and Commentary*. Tyndale New Testament Commentaries. Grand Rapids: Eerdmans, 1985.

———. *Matthew: Evangelist and Teacher*. Exeter: Paternsonster, 1987.

Fredriksen, Paula. "Did Jesus Oppose the Purity Laws?" The BAS Library." 1995.

———. "Paul's Letter to the Romans, the Ten Commandments, and Pagan 'Justification by Faith': For Alan Segal ז"ל." *Journal of Biblical Literature* 133 (2014) 801–8.

Fuller, Daniel P. *Gospel and Law: Contrast or Continuum—The Hermeneutics of Dispensationalism and Covenant Theology*. Grand Rapids: Eerdmans, 1980.

———. "Paul and the Works of the Law." *Westminster Theological Journal* 38 (1975) 28–42.

Fung, Ronald Y. K. "The Impotence of the Law: Toward a Fresh Understanding of Romans 7:14–25." In *Scripture, Tradition, and Interpretation: Essays Presented to Everett F. Harrison by His Students and Colleagues in Honor of His Seventy-fifth Birthday*, edited by W. Ward Gasque and William Sanford LaSor, 34–48. Grand Rapids: Eerdmans, 1978.

Furnish, Victor Paul. *The Love Command in the New Testament*. Nashville: Abingdon, 1972.

Gager, John G. *The Origins of Anti-Semitism: Attitudes toward Judaism in Pagan and Christian Antiquity*. Oxford: Oxford University Press, 1983.

Gagnon, Robert A J. "Why the 'Weak' at Rome Cannot Be Non-Christian Jews." *CBQ* 62 (2000) 64–82.

Garland, David E. *Reading Matthew: A Literary and Theological Commentary on the First Gospel.* Macon, GA: Smyth & Helwys, 2001.

Garlington, Don B. *Faith, Obedience, and Perseverance: Aspects of Paul's Letter to the Romans.* WUNT 79. Tübingen: Mohr Siebeck, 1994.

———. "Romans 7:14–25 and the Creation Theology of Paul." *Trinity Journal* 11 (1990) 197–235.

Gaston, Lloyd. *Paul and the Torah.* Vancouver: University of British Columbia Press, 1987.

———. "Reading the Text and Digging the Past: The First Audience of Romans." In *Text and Artifact in the Religions of Mediterranean Antiquity: Essays in Honour of Peter Richardson*, edited by Stephen G. Wilson and Michel Desjardins, 35–44. Studies in Christianity and Judaism 9. Waterloo, ON: Wilfrid Laurier University Press, 2000.

Gathercole, Simon J. "A Conversion of Augustine: From Natural Law to Restored Nature in Romans 2:13–16." *Society of Biblical Literature Seminar Papers* 38 (1999) 327–58.

———. "A Law unto Themselves: The Gentiles in Romans 2.14–15 Revisited." *JSNT* (2002).

———. *Where Is Boasting?: Early Jewish Soteriology and Paul's Response in Romans 1–5.* Grand Rapids: Eerdmans, 2002.

Gerhardsson, Biger. "The Hermeneutic Program in Matthew 22:37–40." In *Jews, Greeks and Christians: Religious Culture in Late Antiquity: Essays in Honor of W. D. Davies*, edited by Robert Hamerton-Kelly and Robin Scroggs. Studies in Judaism in Late Antiquity 21. Leiden: Brill, 1976.

Gieniusz, Andrzej. "Rom 7,1–6: Lack of Imagination? Function of the Passage in the Argumentation of Rom 6,1—7,6." *Biblica* 74 (1993) 389–400.

Godet, Frédéric Louis. *Commentary on the Epistle to the Romans.* Classic Commentary Library. Grand Rapids: Zondervan, 1956.

Godet, Frédéric Louis. *Commentary on Saint Paul's Epistle to the Romans.* Translated by A. Cusin. New York: Funk & Wagnalls, 1883.

Golubović, Zagorka. "An Anthropological Conceptualisation of Identity." *Synthesis Philosophica* 51 (2011) 25–43.

Goulder, Michael. D. *Midrash and Lection in Matthew.* London: SPCK, 1974.

Guelich, Robert A. *The Sermon on the Mount.* Waco, TX: Word, 1982.

Gundry, Robert H. *Commentary on the New Testament.* Grand Rapids: Baker, 2010.

———. "Grace, Works, and Staying Saved in Paul." *Biblica* 66 (1985) 1–38.

———. *Matthew: A Commentary on His Handbook for a Mixed Church Under Persecution.* Grand Rapids: Eerdmans, 1994.

———. "The Moral Frustration of Paul before His Conversion: Sexual Lust in Romans 7:7–25." In *Pauline Studies: Essays Presented to Professor F. F. Bruce on His 70th Birthday*, 228–45. Grand Rapids: Eerdmans, 1980.

———. *The Use of the Old Testament in St. Matthew's Gospel with Speacial Refernce to the Messianic Hope.* NovTSup 18. Leiden: Brill, 1975.

Hafemann, Scott J. *Paul, Moses, and the History of Israel: The Letter/Spirit Contrast and the Argument from Scripture in 2 Corinthians 3.* WUNT 81. Tübingen: Mohr Siebeck, 1995.

Hagner, Donald A. "Jesus and the Synoptic Sabbath Controversies." *Bulletin for Biblical Research* 19 (2009) 215–48.

———. *Matthew 14–28*. Word Biblical Commentary 33B. Waco, TX: Word, 1995.

———. "The Sitz im Leben of the Gospel of Matthew." In *Treasures New and Old: Recent Contributions to Matthean Studies*, edited by David R. Bauer and Mark Allan Powell, 27–68. Symposium Series 1. Atlanta: Scholars, 1996.

Harland, Philip A. *Dynamics of Identity in the World of the Early Christians*. New York: T. & T. Clark, 2009.

Harper, Nancy. "An Analytical Description of Aristotle's Enthymeme." *Central States Speech Journal* 24 (1973) 304–9.

Harrington, Daniel J. *The Gospel of Matthew*. Sacra Pagina 1. Collegeville, MN: Liturgical, 1991.

Hartley, John E. *Leviticus*. Word Biblical Commentary 3. Waco, TX: Word, 1992.

Hendriksen, William. *Romans*. Vol. 2. Grand Rapids: Baker, 1981.

Hicks, John Mark. "The Sabbath Controversy in Matthew: An Exegesis of Matthew 12:1–14." *Restoration Quarterly* 27 (1984) 79–91.

Hill, David. *The Gospel of Matthew*. New Century Bible. London: Marshall, Morgan & Scott, 1972.

Hodge, Charles. *A Commentary on the Epistle to the Romans*. Edinburgh: Elliot, 1875.

Hogg, Michael A. "Social Identity Theory." In *Contemporary Social Psychological Theories*, edited by Peter J. Burke, 111–36. Stanford: Stanford University Press, 2006.

Hogg, Michael A., Deborah J. Terry, and Katherine M. White. "A Tale of Two Theories: A Critical Comparison of Identity Theory with Social Identity Theory." *Social Psychology Quarterly* 58 (1995) 255–69.

Holmberg, Bengt. "Understanding the First Hundred Years of Christian Identity." In *Exploring Early Christain Identity*, edited by Bengt Holmberg, 1–32. Wissenschaftliche Untersuchungen zum Neuen Testament 226. Tübingen: Mohr Siebeck, 2008.

Hooker, Morna D. *From Adam to Christ: Essays on Paul*. Cambridge: Cambridge University Press, 1990.

Horrell, David G. *Solidarity and Difference: A Contemporary Reading of Paul's Ethics*. London: T. & T. Clark, 2005.

Howard, George E. "Christ the End of the Law: The Meaning of Romans 10:4 ff." *Journal of Biblical Literature* 88 (1969) 331–37.

Hübner, Hans. *Law in Paul's Thought*. Studies of the New Testament and Its World. Edinburgh: T. & T. Clark, 1986.

Hultgren, Arland J. *Paul's Letter to the Romans: A Commentary*. Grand Rapids: Eerdmans, 2011.

Jewett, Robert, with Roy D. Kotansky. *Romans: A Commentary*. Hermeneia. Minneapolis: Fortress, 2007.

Karlberg, Mark W. "Israel's History Personified: Romans 7:7–13 in Relation to Paul's Teaching on the 'Old Man.'" *Trinity Journal* 7 (1986) 65–74.

Karris, Robert J. "Romans 14:1—15:13 and the Occasion of Romans." In *The Romans Debate*, edited by Karl P. Donfried, 65–84. Peabody, MA: Hendrickson, 1991.

Käsemann, Ernst. *Commentary on Romans*. Translated by Geoffrey W. Bromiley. Grand Rapids: Eerdmans, 1980.

Kaye, Bruce Norman. *The Thought Structure of Romans With Special Reference to Chapter Six*. Fort Worth: Schola, 1979.

Keener, Craig S. *The Gospel of Matthew: A Socio-Rhetorical Commentary*. Grand Rapids: Eerdmans, 2009.

Kennedy, George A. *New Testament Interpretation Through Rhetorical Criticism*. Chapel Hill: University of North Carolina Press, 1984.

Kingsbury, Jack Dean. "The Developing Conflict between Jesus and the Jewish Leaders in Matthew's Gospel: A Literary -Critical Study (1987)." In *The Interpretation of Matthew*, edited by Graham Stanton, 179–97. Issues in Religion and Theology 3. Edinburgh: T. & T. Clark, 1995.

———. *Matthew as Story*. 2nd ed. Philadelphia: Fortress, 1988.

Kissinger, Warren S. *The Sermon on the Mount: A History of Interpretation and Bibliography*. Metuchen, NJ: Scarecrow, 1975.

Klassen, William, and Graydon F. Snyder, eds. *Current Issues in New Testament Interpretation: Essays in Honor of Otto A. Piper*. New York: Harper, 1962.

Kloppenborg, John S. "Love in the NT." In *The New Interpreter's Dictionary of the Bible*, edited by Katharine Doob Sakenfeld, 3:703–18. Nashville: Abingdon, 2008.

Kömig, Adrio. "Gentiles or Gentile Christians? On the Meaning of Romans 2:12–16." *Journal of Theology for Southern Africa* 15 (1976) 53–60.

Konradt, Matthias. *Israel, Church, and the Gentiles in the Gospel of Matthew*. Translated by Kathleen Ess. Baylor-Mohr Siebeck Studies in Early Christianity. Waco, TX: Baylor University Press, 2014.

Koperski, Veronica. *What Are They Saying About Paul and the Law?* 1st ed. New York: Paulist, 2001.

Kruse, Colin G. *Paul's Letter to the Romans*. Pillar New Testament Commentary. Grand Rapids: Eerdmans, 2012.

Ladd, George Eldon. *A Theology of the New Testament*. Rev. ed. Edited by Donald A. Hagner Grand Rapids: Eerdmans, 1993.

Lambrecht, Jan. *The Wretched "I" & Its Liberation: Paul in Romans 7 & 8*. Louvain Theological and Pastoral Monographs 14. Louvain: Peeters, 1992.

Lapsley, Jacqueline E. "Feeling Our Way: Love for God in Deuteronomy." *CBQ* 65 (2003) 350–69.

Leenhardt, Franz J. *Epistle to the Romans: A Commentary*. London: Lutterworth, 1961.

Lenski, R. C. H. *The Interpretation of St. Paul's Epistle to the Romans 8–16*. 1945. Reprint, Minneapolis: Augsburg Fortress, 1993.

Liddon, Henry Parry. *Explanatory Analysis of St. Paul's Epistle to the Romans by H. P. Liddon, D.D., D.C.L., LL.D. Late Canon and Chancellor of St. Paul's Ireland Professor of Exegesis in the University of Oxford* 1870–1882. New York: Longmans, Green, 1893.

Lieu, Judith. *Christian Identity in the Jewish and Graeco-Roman World*. Oxford: Oxford University, 2004.

Lo, Lung-Kwong. *Paul's Purpose in Writing Romans: The Upbuilding of a Jewish and Gentile Christian Community in Rome*. Jian Dao Dissertation Series 6. Hong Kong: Alliance Bible Seminary, 1998.

Loader, William R. G. *Jesus' Attitude Towards the Law: A Study of the Gospels*. WUNT 2/97. Tübingen: Mohr Siebeck, 1997.

Longenecker, Bruce W. *Eschatology and the Covenant: A Comparison of 4 Ezra and Romans* 1–11. JSNTSup 57. Shefield: JSOT Press, 1991.

Longenecker, Richard N. *Introducing Romans: Critical Issues in Paul's Most Famous Letter*. Grand Rapids: Eerdmans, 2011.

———. *Introducing Romans: Critical Issues in Paul's Most Famous Letter*. Grand Rapids: Eerdmans, 2011.

———. *New Dimensions in New Testament Study*. Grand Rapids: Zondervan, 1974.

———. *Paul, Apostle of Liberty*. Twin Book Series. Grand Rapids: Baker, 1964.

Louw, Johannes P. *A Semantic Discourse Analysis of Romans: Commentary*. Vol. 2. Pretoria: University of Pretoria, 1979.

Luther, Martin. *Commentary on Epistle to the Romans*. Grand Rapids: Zondervan, 1954.

———. *Luther's Works, Volume 25 (Lectures on Roman Glosses and Scholia)*. St. Louis: Concordia, 1972.

Lutz, Cora. *Musonius Rufus, "The Roman Socrates."* Yale Classical Studies 10. New Haven: Yale University Press, 1947.

Luz, Ulrich. *Matthew 1–7*. Translated by Wilhelm C. Linss. Continental Commentary. Philadelphia: Fortress, 1986.

———. *Matthew 8–20*. Translated by James E. Crouch. Hermeneia. Minneapolis: Fortress, 2001.

———. *Matthew 21–28: A Commentary*. Translated by James E. Crouch. Hermeneia. Minneapolis: Fortress, 2005.

———. *The Theology of the Gospel of Matthew*. Cambridge: Cambridge University Press, 1995.

Maccoby, Hyam. "The Washing of Cups." *JSNT* 14 (1982) 3–15.

Malina, Bruce J., and Jerome Neyrey. *Calling Jesus Names: The Social Value of Labels in Matthew*. Foundations & Facets: Social Facets. Sonoma, CA: Polebridge, 1988.

Martin, Brice L. *Christ and the Law in Paul*. NovTSup 62. Leiden: Brill, 1989.

McArthur, Harvey K. *Understanding the Sermon on the Mount*. New York: Harper, 1960.

McDonald, Patricia M. "Romans 5:1–11 as a Rhetorical Bridge." *JSNT* 40 (1990) 81–96.

McKay, J W. (John William). "Man's Love for God in Deuteronomy and the Father/Teacher—Son/Pupil Relationship." *Vetus Testamentum* 22 (1972) 426–35.

McNeile, Alan. *The Gospel According to Saint Matthew*. New York: Macmillan, 1965.

Meeks, Wayne A. *The Moral World of the First Christians*. Library of Early Christianity. Louisville: Westminster John Knox, 1986.

———. *The Origins of Christian Morality: The First Two Centuries*. New Heaven: Yale University Press, 1993.

Meier, John P. *A Marginal Jew: Rethinking the Historical Jesus*. Vol. 4. New Heaven: Yale University Press, 2009.

———. *Law and History in Matthew's Gospel: A Redactional Study of Mt. 5:17–48*. Analecta Biblica 71. Biblical Institute, 1976.

Meyer, Heinrich August Wilhelm. *Critical and Exegetical Handbook to the Epistle to the Romans*. Vol. 2. Edinburgh: T. & T. Clark, 1874.

Meyer, Henerich August Wilhelm. *The Epistle to the Romans*. Meyer's Commentary on the New Testament Series. Vol. 1. Edinburgh: T. & T. Clark, 1884.

Meyer, Paul W. "The Worm at the Core of the Apple: Exegetical Reflections on Romans 7." In *Conversation Continues: Studies in Paul & John in Honor of J. Louis Martyn*, edited by Robert T. Fortna and Beverly R. Gaventa, 62–84. Nashville: Abingdon, 1990.

Milgrom, Jacob. *Leviticus 17–22*. Anchor Bible 3A. New Haven: Yale University Press, 2000.

Milne, Douglas J W. "Romans 7:7–12, Paul's Pre-Conversion Experience." *Reformed Theological Review* 43.1 (1984) 9–17.

Minear, Paul S. *The Obedience of Faith: The Purposes of Paul in the Epistle to the Romans.* London: SCM, 1971.

Mohrlang, Roger. *Matthew and Paul: A Comparison of Ethical Perspectives.* SNTSMS 48. Cambridge: Cambridge University Press, 1984.

Moo, Douglas J. *The Epistle to the Romans.* New International Commentary on the New Testament. Grand Rapids: Eerdmans, 1996.

———. "Israel and Paul in Romans 7:7–12." *NTS* 32 (1986) 122–35.

———. "Jesus and the Authority of the Mosaic Law." Issuu, 1984. http://issuu.com/rapalculict/docs/douglas-j.-moo—-jesus-and-the-authority-of-the-mo/17.

———. *Romans 1–8.* Wycliffe Exegetical Commentary. Chicago: Moody, 1991.

Moran, William L. "Ancient Near Eastern Background of the Love of God in Deuteronomy." *CBQ* 25 (1963) 77–87.

Morris, Leon. *Epistle to the Romans.* Pillar Commentary. Grand Rapids: Eerdmans, 1988.

Morrison, Bruce, and John Woodhouse. "The Coherence of Romans 7:1—8:8." *Reformed Theological Review* 47.1 (1988) 8–16.

Moule, C. F. D. *An Idiom Book of New Testament Greek.* Cambridge: Cambridge University Press, 1959.

Moule, H. C. G. *The Epistle to the Romans.* London: Pickering & Inglis, 1879.

Mounce, Robert H. *Romans.* New American Commentary 27. Nashville: B&H, 1995.

Munck, Johannes. *Paul and the Salvation of Mankind.* Translated by Frank Clarke. London: SCM, 1959.

Murray, John. *The Epistle to the Romans.* Grand Rapids: Eerdmans, 1959.

———. *Epistle to the Romans.* Grand Rapids: Eerdmans, 1997.

Nanos, Mark D. *The Mystery of Romans: The Jewish Context of Paul's Letter.* Minneapolis: Fortress, 1996.

Napier, Daniel. "Paul's Analysis of Sin and Torah in Romans 7:7–25." *Restoration Quarterly* 44 (2002) 15–32.

Newman, Barclay Moon, and Philip C. Stine. *A Handbook on the Gospel of Matthew.* Helps for Translators Series. London: United Bible Societies, 1988.

Nicoll, William Robertson. *The Expositor's Greek Testament: Knowling, R. J. The Acts of the Apostles. Denney, J. St. Paul's Epistle to the Romans. Findlay, G. G. St. Paul's First Epistle to the Corinthians.* London: Hodder & Stoughton, 1900.

Nolland, John. *The Gospel of Matthew.* New International Greek Testament Commentary. Grand Rapids: Eerdmans, 2005.

Nygren, Anders. *Agape and Eros.* Translated by Philip S. Watson. London: SPCK, 1953.

———. *Commentary on Romans.* Translated by Carl C. Rasmussen. Philadelphia: Muhlenberg, 1949.

Parry, Reginald St John. *The Epistle to the Romans.* Cambridge Greek Testament for Schools and Colleges. Cambridge: Cambridge University Press, 1912.

Peng, Kuo-Wei. *Hate the Evil, Hold Fast to the Good: Structuring Romans 12.1—15.13.* Library of New Testament Studies 200. London: T. & T. Clark, 2006.

Perkins, Pheme. *Love Commands in the New Testament.* New York: Paulist, 1982.

Philo of Alexandria. *Philo VI.* Translated by F. H. Colson. Loeb Classical Library Cambridge: Harvard University Press, 2002.

———. *Philo VII.* Translated by F. H. Colson. Loeb Classical Library. Cambridge: Harvard University Press, 1998.

Piper, John. *"Love Your Enemies": Jesus' Love Command in the Synoptic Gospels and in the Early Christian Paraenesis: A History of the Tradition and Interpretation of Its Uses*. London: Cambridge University Press, 1979.

Porter, Stanley E., and Craig A. Evans, eds. *Pauline Writings: A Sheffield Reader*. Biblical Seminar 34. Sheffield: Sheffield Academic, 1995.

Powell, Mark Allan. "Characterization on the Phraseological Plane in the Gosple of Matthew." In *Treasures New and Old: Recent Contributions to Matthean Studies*, edited by David R. Bauer and Mark Allan Powell, 161–77. SBL Symposium Series 1. Atlanta: Scholars, 1996.

Punt, Jeremy. "Enscripturalised Identity: Scripture and Identity in Christian Communities." *Dutch Reformed Theological Journal* 43 (2002) 83–93.

Quarles, Charles. *Sermon on the Mount: Restoring Christ's Message to the Modern Church*. NAC Studies in Bible & Theology. Nashville: B&H Academic, 2011.

Räisänen, Heikki. *Jesus, Paul and Torah: Collected Essays*. JSNTSup 43. Sheffield: Sheffield Academic, 1992.

———. *Paul and the Law*. WUNT 29. 2nd ed., 1987. Reprint, Eugene, OR: Wipf & Stock, 2010.

Reasoner, Mark. *The Strong and the Weak: Romans 14.1—15.13 in Context*. SNTSMS 103. Cambridge: Cambridge University Press, 1999.

Rhyne, Clyde T. *Faith Establishes the Law: A Study on the Continuity between Judaism and Christianity Romans 3:31*. SBLDS 55. Chico, CA: Scholars, 1981.

Riches, John K. *Conflicting Mythologies: Identity Formation in the Gospel of Mark and Matthew*. Studies on the New Testament and Its World. Edinburgh: T. & T. Clark, 2000.

Robbins, Vernon K. "Dictionary of Socio-Rhetorical Terms: J–L Definitions," 1996. http://www.religion.emory.edu/faculty/robbins/SRI/defns/j_l_defns.cfm.

———. *Exploring the Texture of Texts: A Guide to Socio-Rhetorical Interpretations*. Valley Forge, PA: Trinity, 1996.

———. "Plucking Grain on the Sabbath." In *Patterns of Persuasion in the Gospels*, by Burton L. Mack and Vernon K. Robbins, 107–42. 1989. Reprint, Eugene, OR: Wipf & Stock, 2008.

———. *The Tapestry of Early Christian Discourse: Rhetoric, Society and Ideology*. New York: Routledge, 2002.

Robson, James. "The Literary Composition of Deuteronomy." In *Interpreting Deuteronomy: Issues and Approaches*, edited by David G. Firth and Philip S. Johnston. Downers Grove, IL: InterVarsity, 2012.

Roitto, Rikard. "Behaving Like a Christ-Believer." In *Exploring Early Christian Identity*, edited by Bengt Holmberg, 91–114. WUNT 226. Tübingen: Mohr Siebeck, 2008.

Rordorf, Willy. *Sunday: The History of the Day of Rest and Worship in the Earliest Centuries of the Christian Church*. Translated by A. A. K. Graham. London: SCM, 1968.

Russell, Walt. "Insights from Postmodernism's Emphasis on Interpretive Communities in the Interpretation of Romans 7." *Journal of the Evangelical Theological Society* 37 (1994) 511–27.

Saint-Thierry, William of Saint-Thierry. *The Works of William of St. Thierry: Exposition on the Epistle to the Romans*. Cistercian Father Series. Spencer, MA: Cistercian, 1980.

Saldarini, Anthony J. *Matthew's Christian-Jewish Community*. Chicago: University of Chicago Press, 1994.

Sanday, William, and Arthur Cayley Headlam. *A Critical and Exegetical Commentary on the Epistle to the Romans*. Edinburgh: T. & T. Clark, 1902.

Sanders, E. P. *Jesus and Judaism*. Philadelphia: Fortress, 1985.

———. *Jewish Law from Jesus to the Mishnah: Five Studies*. London: SCM, 1990.

———. *Judaism: Practice and Belief, 63 BCE–66 CE*. London: SCM, 1992.

———. *Paul and Palestinian Judaism: A Comparison of Patterns of Religion*. Philadelphia: Fortress, 1977.

———. *Paul, the Law, and the Jewish People*. Philadelphia: Fortress, 1983.

Schnabel, Eckhard J. *Law and Wisdom from Ben Sira to Paul: A Tradition Historical Enquiry into the Relation of Law, Wisdom, and Ethics*. WUNT 2/16. Tübingen: Mohr Siebeck, 1985.

Schoeps, Hans Joachim. *Paul: The Theology of the Apostle in the Light of Jewish Religious History*. Translated by Harold Knight. Philadelphia: Westminster, 1961.

Schottroff, Luise et al. *Essays on the Love Commandment*. Translated by Reginald H. and Ilse Fuller. Philadelphia: Fortress, 1978.

Schreiner, Thomas R. *Romans*. Grand Rapids: Baker Academic, 1998.

———. *The Law and Its Fulfillment: A Pauline Theology of Law*. Grand Rapids: Baker, 1993.

Schweitzer, Albert. *The Mysticism of Paul the Apostle*. Translated by William Montgomery. New York: Holt, 1931.

Schweizer, Eduard. *The Good News According to Matthew*. Translated by David E. Green. Philadelphia: Westminster, 1975.

Segal, Alan F. *Paul the Convert: The Apostolate and Apostasy of Saul the Pharisee*. New Haven: Yale University Press, 1990.

Seifrid, Mark A. *Justification by Faith: The Origin and Development of a Central Pauline Theme*. NovTSup 68. Leiden: Brill, 1992.

———. "Paul's Approach to the Old Testament in Rom 10:6–8." *Trinity Journal* 6 (1985) 3–37.

———. "The Subject of Rom 7:14–25." *NovT* 34 (1992) 313–33.

Sigal, Phillip. *The Halakhah of Jesus of Nazareth According to the Gospel of Matthew*. Studies in Biblical Literature 18. Atlanta: Society of Biblical Literature, 2007.

Siker, Judy Yates. "Unmasking the Enemy: Deconstructing the 'Other' in the Gospel of Matthew." *Perspectives in Religious Studies* 32.2 (2005) 109–23.

Sim, David C. *The Gospel of Matthew and Christian Judaism: The History and Social Setting of the Matthean Community*. London: Bloomsbury Academic, 1998.

———. "The Gospel of Matthew and the Gentiles." *JSNT* 57 (1995) 19–48.

———. "Matthew and the Pauline Corpus: A Preliminary Intertextual Study." *JSNT* 31 (2009) 401–22.

———. "Matthew, Paul and the Origin and Nature of the Gentile Mission: The Great Commission in Matthew 28:16–20 as an Anti-Pauline Tradition." *HTS Teologiese Studies / Theological Studies* 64.1 (2008). https://doi.org/10.4102/hts.v64i1.28.

———. "Matthew 7.21–23: Further Evidence of Its Anti-Pauline Perspective." *NTS* 53 (2007) 325–43.

———. "Matthew's Anti-Paulinism: A Neglected Feature of Matthean Studies." *HTS Teologiese Studies / Theological Studies* 58.2 (2002) 767–83. https://doi.org/10.4102/hts.v58i2.557.

Snodgrass, Klyne. "Matthew and the Law." In *Treasures New and Old: Recent Contributions to Matthean Studies*, edited by David R. Bauer and Mark Allan Powell, 99–127. SBL Symposium Series 1. Atlanta: Scholars, 1996.

Stanton, Graham. *A Gospel for a New People: Studies in Matthew*. Edinburgh: T. & T. Clark, 1992.

Stauffer, Ethelbert. *New Testament Theology*. Translated by John Marsh. London: SCM, 1955.

———. "Ἀγαπάω." In *Theological Dictionary of the New Testament*, edited by Gerhard Kittel, vol. 1. Grand Rapids: Eerdmans, 1964.

Stendahl, Krister. *The School of St. Matthew: And Its Use of the Old Testament*. Lund: Gleerup, 1954.

Stets, Jan E., and Peter J. Burke. "Identity Theory and Social Identity Theory." *Social Psychology Quarterly* 63 (2000) 224–37.

Stowers, Stanley K. *A Rereading of Romans: Justice, Jews, and Gentiles*. New Haven: Yale University Press, 1994.

Strecker, Georg. *The Sermon on the Mount: An Exegetical Commentary*. Translated by O. C. Dean Jr. Nashville: Abingdon, 1988.

Stryker, S. "Identity Theory: Developments and Extensions." In *Self and Identity: Perspectives Across the Lifespan*, edited by Terry Honess and Krysia Yardley, 89–104. International Library of Psychology. New York: Routledge & Kegan Paul, 1987.

Stuhlmacher, Peter. *Paul's Letter to the Romans: A Commentary*. Translated by Scott J. Hafemann. Westminster John Knox, 1994.

Tajfel, Henri. "Social and Cultural Factors in Perception." In *The Handbook of Scoial Psychology*, edited by Gardner Lindzey and Elliott Aronson, 315–94. Human Relations Collection. Reading, MA: Addison-Wesley, 1969.

Talbert, Charles H. *Matthew*. Grand Rapids: Baker Academic, 2010.

Thayer, Joseph Henry. *A Greek-English Lexicon of the New Testament*. Grand Rapids: Baker, 1977.

Theissen, Gerd. *Psychological Aspects of Pauline Theology*. Translated by John Galvin. Philadelphia: Fortress, 1997.

Thielman, Frank. *From Plight to Solution: A Jewish Framework for Understanding Paul's View of the Law in Galatians and Romans*. NovTSup 61. 1989. Reprint, Eugene, OR: Wipf and Stock, 2007.

———. *Paul & the Law: A Contextual Approach*. Downers Grove, IL: InterVarsity, 1994.

Thurén, Lauri. *Derhetorizing Paul: A Dynamic Perspective on Paulne Theology and the Law*. WUNT 124. Tübingen: Mohr Siebeck, 2000.

Tolmie, D. F. "Liberty-Love-the Spirit:Ethics and Ethos According to the Letter the Galatians." In *Identity, Ethics, and Ethos in the New Testament*, edited by Jan Gabriël van der Watt, 241–56. Beihefte zur Zeitschrift für die Neutestamentliche Wissenschaft und die Kunde der Älteren Kirche 141. Berlin: de Gruyter, 2006.

Tomson, Peter J. *Paul and the Jewish Law: Halakha in the Letters of the Apostle to the Gentiles*. Assen: Van Gorcum, 1990.

Trudinger, Paul. "An Autobiographical Digression? A Note on Romans 7:7–25." *Expository Times* 107.6 (1996) 173–74.

Turner, David L. *Matthew*. Grand Rapids: Baker Academic, 2008.

Vermes, Geza. *Jesus the Jew*. Philadelphia: Fortress, 1973.

Vignoles, Vivian L., Seth J. Schwartz, and Koen Luyckx. "Introduction: Toward an Integrative View of Identity." In *Handbook of Identity Theory and Research*. New York: Springer, 2011.

Viljoen, Francois P. "Jesus' Teaching on the 'Torah' in the Sermon on the Mount." *Neotestamentica* 40 (2006) 135–55.

———. "Sabbath Controversy in Matthew." *Verbum et Ecclesia* 32.1 (2011) art. #418, 8pp. https://doi.org/10.4102/ve.v32i1.418.

Wallace, Daniel B. *Greek Grammar Beyond the Basics: An Exegetical Syntax of the New Testament*. Zondervan, 1996.

Watson, Francis. *Paul, Judaism, and the Gentiles: A Sociological Approach*. Cambridge: Cambridge University Press, 1986.

———. *Paul, Judaism, and the Gentiles: Beyond the New Perspective*. Grand Rapids: Eerdmans, 2007.

———. *Paul, Judaism, and the Gentiles: Beyond the New Perspective*. Grand Rapids: Eerdmans, 2007.

Watt, Jan Gabriël Van der, and Francois Stephanus Malan, eds. *Identity, Ethics, and Ethos in the New Testament*. Beihefte zur Zeitschrift für die neutestamentliche Wissenschaft 171. Berlin: de Gruyter, 2006.

Wedderburn, A. J. M. *The Reasons for Romans*. A. & C. Black, 1988.

———. "The Theological Structure of Romans v. 12." *NTS* 19 (1973) 339–54. https://doi.org/10.1017/S0028688500008171.

Weiss, H. "The Sabbath in the Synoptic Gospels." *JSNT* 12/38 (1990) 13–27.

Wenham, David. "Jesus and the Law: An Exegesis of Matthew 5:17–20." *Themelios* 4.3 (1979) 92–95.

Westerholm, Stephen. *Israel's Law and the Church's Faith: Paul and His Recent Interpreters*. Grand Rapids: Eerdmans, 1988.

———. *Perspectives Old and New on Paul: The "Lutheran" Paul and His Critics*. Grand Rapids: Eerdmans, 2004.

Wiles, Mourice. *The Divine Apostle: The Interpretation of St. Paul's Epistles in the Early Church*. London: Cambridge University Press, 1967.

Willoughby, Bruce E. "A Heartfelt Love: An Exegesis of Deuteronomy 6: 4–19." *Restoration Quarterly* 20 (1977) 73–87.

Wilson, Walter T. *Love Without Pretense: Romans 12.9–21 and Hellenistic-Jewish Wisdom Literature*. WUNT 2/46. Tübingen: Mohr Siebeck, 1991.

Winger, Michael. *By What Law? The Meaning of Nomos in the Letters of Paul*. SBLDS 128. Atlanta: Scholars, 1992.

Witherington, Ben, III, and Darlene Hyatt. *Paul's Letter to the Romans: A Socio-Rhetorical Commentary*. Grand Rapids: Eerdmans, 2004.

Wright, N. T., and J. Paul Sampley. *The New Interpreter's Bible: Acts. Introduction to Epistolary Literature. Romans. 1 Corinthians*. Nashville: Abingdon, 2002.

Yang, Yong-Eui. *Jesus and the Sabbath in Matthew's Gospel*. Sheffield: Sheffield Academic, 1997.

Zetterholm, Magnus. *Approaches to Paul: A Student's Guide to Recent Scholarship*. Minneapolis: Fortress, 2009.

Ziesler, John. *Paul's Letter to the Romans*. TPI New Testament Commentaries. Philadelphia: Trinity, 1989.

www.ingramcontent.com/pod-product-compliance
Lightning Source LLC
LaVergne TN
LVHW020537100826
845148LV00010B/1506

* 9 7 9 8 3 8 5 2 5 9 0 0 7 *